↞ IDOLS IN THE EAST

IDOLS
IN THE
EAST

EUROPEAN REPRESENTATIONS
OF ISLAM AND THE ORIENT,
1100–1450

SUZANNE CONKLIN AKBARI

CORNELL UNIVERSITY PRESS
Ithaca and London

First published 2009 by Cornell University Press
First printing, Cornell Paperbacks, 2012

Library of Congress Cataloging-in-Publication Data

Akbari, Suzanne Conklin.
    Idols in the east : European representations of Islam and the Orient, 1100–1450 / Suzanne Conklin Akbari.
        p.   cm.
    Includes bibliographical references and index.
    ISBN 978-0-8014-4807-2 (cloth)
    ISBN 978-0-8014-7781-2 (paper)
    1. Europe—Relations—Islamic Empire.   2. Islamic Empire—Relations—Europe.   3. Europe—Relations—Latin Orient.   4. Latin Orient—Relations—Europe.   5. Christianity and other religions—Islam.   6. Islam—Relations—Christianity.   7. Orientalism—History—To 1500.   8. Islam in literature.   9. Latin Orient—In literature.   10. East and West in literature.   11. Orientalism in literature.   12. Literature, Medieval—History and criticism.   I. Title.

    DS35.74.E85A43 2009
    303.48'256040902—dc22

2009008264

Cornell University Press strives to use environmentally responsible suppliers and materials to the fullest extent possible in the publishing of its books. Such materials include vegetable-based, low-VOC inks and acid-free papers that are recycled, totally chlorine-free, or partly composed of nonwood fibers. For further information, visit our website at www.cornellpress.cornell.edu.

Cloth printing   10 9 8 7 6 5 4 3 2 1
Paperback printing   10 9 8 7 6 5 4 3 2 1

For Eddie

⚔ CONTENTS

✦ ILLUSTRATIONS

✦ ACKNOWLEDGMENTS

This book has been on my mind for almost twenty years, and I have worked on it in earnest for over a decade. Many things have changed over that time, but one thing that has not changed is the support and encouragement of my husband and children, as well as that of nurturing friends and colleagues. Among these, I would especially like to thank Ruth Harvey, Elizabeth Legge, Karla Mallette, Ruth Nissé, and Fiona Somerset. Thanks also to those who read and commented on portions of the manuscript, to whom I'm deeply grateful: Tom Burman, Isabelle Cochelin, Jeremy Cohen, Thelma Fenster, Bill Jordan, Sharon Kinoshita, Stephen Menn, Mark Meyerson, Barbara Newman, George Rigg, Jay Rubenstein, Brian Stock, Markus Stock, John Tolan, David Townsend, and Nicholas Watson. I would like to thank Keith Snedegar, for allowing me to consult his doctoral thesis, and John Williams, for his kind assistance in locating a map image. Iain Higgins and an anonymous reader for Cornell University Press provided astute commentary and improved this book very much, while Peter Potter shepherded the manuscript with insight (and patience!). It goes without saying that the defects remaining are my own.

The research for *Idols in the East* has been supported by a Standard Research Grant from the Social Sciences and Humanities Research Council of Canada. Permission to reproduce images in this book was generously granted by the Bibliothéque nationale, Paris, France; Lawrence University Library and Beloit College; the British Library, London, U.K.; the Herzog August Bibliothek, Wolfenbüttel, Germany; Vicent García Editores, S.A., Spain; and the Library of Congress. I wish to thank the following publishers for allowing me to draw upon short passages from earlier essays in preparing this book: these include Palgrave Macmillan ("Due East"), Cambridge University Press ("Alexander in the Orient"), University Press of New England ("Placing the Jews"), the Arizona Center for Medieval and Renaissance Studies ("Woman as Mediator"), and the Canadian Institute for Mediterranean Studies ("Imagining Islam"). Thanks to Elizabeth Watkins for compilation of the bibliography, and to Yasin Akbari for drawing schematics of medieval maps.

Earlier versions of material in these chapters have been presented at a range of venues, including meetings of the International Medieval Congress at Leeds (2006), the American Comparative Literature Association (2006), the International Congress for the Historical Sciences (2005), the Medieval Academy of America (1996, 1999, 2004), the Canadian Society of Medievalists (2002), the International Congress on Medieval Studies at Kalamazoo (1996, 1998, 2000, 2001, 2002), the Modern Language Association (1994, 2000, 2001), the New Chaucer Society (1998), and the Social Sciences and Humanities Council of Canada (1998). I am grateful for the warm reception and thoughtful criticisms received when I presented preliminary fruits of the research that would lead to *Idols in the East* at Fordham University (1995, 2006), Brown University (2006), the University of Michigan (2005), the University of Tennessee (2005), the University of California, Santa Cruz (2005), the University of California, Santa Barbara (2005), the University of Leicester (2004), the University of British Columbia (2004), Columbia University (2001, 2003), Harvard University (1996, 2002), Trinity College, Cambridge (2001), the University of Western Ontario (2001), Cornell University (2000), and the College of William and Mary (1997). I owe special gratitude to the Medieval Club of New York, where in 1992 I presented the first glimmerings of this project in a paper on the *Jeu de saint Nicolas,* and to the Pontifical Institute for Mediaeval Studies, where I was honored to give a Friends of the Library lecture in 2004. I hope always to be a friend of the PIMS library, *hortus conclusus,* paradise on earth.

I would like to dedicate this book to my husband, who has always believed in me, and who has given me everything I really wanted.

Introduction

Medieval Orientalism?

Representations of Muslims have never been more common in the Western imagination than they are now. Building on Orientalist stereotypes constructed over centuries, the figure of the wily Arab has given rise, at the dawn of the twenty-first century, to the "Islamist" terrorist. The feared and hated "other" is understood as being different from "us" not only in religious terms but also in ethnic, even racial terms: difference of faith and diversity of skin color appear as two sides of a single coin, each aspect reinforcing the other. This book is about the premodern background of some of the Orientalist stereotypes still pervasive today—the irascible and irrational Arab, the religiously deviant Muslim—and about how these stereotypes developed over time. The beginning and end points of this study, 1100 and 1450, are chosen to highlight moments when the language used to characterize Islam and the Orient shifted significantly: it begins at the time of the First Crusade, with the Crusaders' dramatic assault on the holy city of Jerusalem, and ends with the Ottoman conquest of the Byzantine capital of Constantinople, when Muslim "Turks" raised their banner over the last remaining stronghold of ancient Roman imperial might. *Idols in the East* explores the continuities linking medieval and modern discourses concerning Islam and the Orient in order to unearth the roots of modern Orientalism, and to examine the categories, hierarchies, and symbolic systems that were used to differentiate the Western self from its Eastern other.

Although this book may seem to some as a timely intervention in debates about Muslims and the West in the wake of the events of September 11, 2001, the book's origins actually date back much farther (almost twenty years) in the past. As a young graduate student who knew something about Islam, I was puzzled when, in a seminar on medieval drama, I read in the *Jeu de saint Nicolas* a peculiar description of Muslim worship featuring an assortment of idols, including one called "Mahom." Aware of Islam's extreme iconoclasm, I could not understand why Muslims were being depicted as idolaters, with an idol—instead of a prophet—named Muhammad. This puzzlement was later compounded when I reread Dante's description of Muhammad in the *Inferno,* paired with his companion Ali. Here was a much more accurate (if very negative) depiction of Islam as a religion closely related to Christianity, featuring a prophet and his successor in the caliphate. Did this mean that some people during the Middle Ages had a relatively full understanding of the nature of Islam, while others were simply ignorant? Or did it indicate a more complicated relationship between Western Christians' images of themselves and their understanding of what Muslims might be like?

From these uncertain, naïve beginnings, *Idols in the East* has developed into an ambitious effort to give a synoptic picture of Western Christian views of Islam and the Orient. It would be impossible to give a comprehensive account of such views; what this book tries to do instead is to describe how Western discourses concerning Islam and the Orient developed and how they mutually reinforced one another. While a set of terms predicated on religious difference must certainly be distinguished from one based on geographical diversity, the key purpose of *Idols in the East* is to demonstrate how they are interrelated, focusing particularly on the role of space and orientation as the key features of medieval efforts to categorize difference, both religious and ethnic. Unlike previous studies, such as the masterful work of Norman Daniel and John Tolan on views of Islam, and the studies of Dorothee Metlitzki and John Block Friedman on conceptions of the Orient, this book seeks to explain how medieval people in the West understood the figure of the "Saracen" who, like the figure of the Jew, was thought to be essentially different not only in terms of religious orientation, but also in terms of bodily diversity. To some extent, then, this book is as much about the nature of premodern efforts to understand difference and identity as it is about the specific figure of the Muslim in the medieval imagination. Accordingly, *Idols in the East* begins, so to speak, at the beginning, with an account of medieval representations of the shape of the world, ranging from the three known continents of Asia, Europe, and Africa as depicted on mappaemundi and in encyclopedias, to the climatic zonal maps that accompany scientific and geographical works. The dichotomy of "East" and "West," ubiquitous in modern scholarship, is rare in medieval texts, which instead divide the world into three continents, four cardinal directions, or seven climatic zones. The binary distinction of "East" and "West," as well as the teleological narrative of imperial and intellectual progress moving continually westward in the form of *translatio imperiii* and *translatio studii,* was virtually unknown to medieval readers. In the universal history written by the fifth-century historian Orosius, as in the many adaptations of his work compiled throughout the Middle Ages, the rise of the Roman Empire in the western regions was simply the fourth stage in a quadripartite progression corresponding to the four cardinal directions.

The medieval notion of the "East" or the "Orient" is very different from modern conceptions, and this distinction is the particular focus of the opening chapters of *Idols in the East,* which seek to reconstruct the system of knowledge and the category divisions intrinsic to medieval Orientalism. The Orient was a place of both geographical and temporal origins, with the earthly paradise located at once in the region furthest east and in the remotest past. Medieval maps, oriented with the east at the top rather than the north as on modern maps, depict the rivers of paradise flowing downward to water the earth in a striking image of the progress of mankind through historical time and geographical space. In the medieval imagination, the Orient was the place of origins and of mankind's beginning; it was also, however, a place of enigma and mystery, including strange marvels and monstrous chimeras, peculiarities generated by the extraordinary climate. The bodies of the inhabitants of such eastern regions were marked by the sun, not only in the color of their skin and their anatomy but also in their physiology; these corporeal differences were consequently manifested in their behaviors, emotions, and intellectual capacity. For medieval readers, the irascible Saracen was as much a product of the Oriental climate that was natural to him as of the deviant "law of Muhammad" to which he was obedient. The Orient was the place of origins, but it was also the place of the future apocalypse, the place from which the avenging armies of Prester John were expected to arise and, ultimately, the site where the events of Armageddon would unfold. It was both beginning and end, charged with potentiality and danger.

The third and fourth chapters of *Idols in the East* turn to the ways in which bodily diversity was understood to arise from the geographical and climatic divisions of the world, beginning—in a move that may surprise some readers—with the figure of the Jew. It is not surprising that Jewish identity served, in religious terms, as a template for understanding the pernicious "law of Muhammad"; more surprising, perhaps, is the extent to which Jewish

identity also served as a template for understanding the bodily nature of Saracens, molded by the Oriental climate natural to them. The diasporic body of
the Jew was seen as a microcosm of the place of Jews in the world at large.
Their forlorn wandering outward from the ruins of Jerusalem was mirrored
in the leaky, unbalanced humoral composition of the individual Jewish body
described in medieval scientific texts, as well as in the dismembered bodies of Jews portrayed in elaborate detail in literary and poetic works. This
correspondence of body and geography in medieval depictions of the Jew
served as a template for medieval conceptualizations of the "Saracen" body:
like the Jew, the Saracen was thought to differ from his Western Christian
counterpart not only in religious terms, but also in racial or ethnic terms. His
bodily diversity was shaped by climate, but it was also an outward manifestation of his inward spiritual deviancy. Accordingly, religious conversion of
the Saracen as depicted in literary texts is commonly accompanied by bodily
metamorphosis, ranging from a dramatic black-white color change to more
subtle physiological shifts in which the violent, irascible Saracen becomes
a pacific, tearful Christian. Unlike Jewish bodies, however, Saracen bodies
were thought to be open to assimilation: through conversion, the female
Saracen was especially available to the Christian community, her pollution
erased both through a change in faith and through the physical bond of marriage within the Christian community. Male Saracens, conversely, were more
strictly limited, their physical differences less likely to be erased and their
passage into the Christian community more tenuous. The case of the hybrid
offspring of the Christian and Saracen was an even more elaborate ground
on which Saracen assimilability could be staged: the category violations arising from such a union sometimes gave rise to monstrous abomination, sometimes to transcendent evidence of the omnipotence of the Christian God.

The close relationship of spiritual orientation and bodily diversity in medieval depictions of Saracens, in which religious conversion goes hand in hand
with bodily metamorphosis, highlights the key role of space in articulating
identity and difference. Saracens differ from Christians both in terms of soul
and in terms of body, their adherence to a false religion mirrored in the appearance of their flesh. The final chapters of *Idols in the East* turn, therefore,
to the depiction of religious difference, exploring how Islam was described
by medieval Westerners both as a schismatic offshoot of Christianity and as
a retrogressive return to the "old law" of the Jews. The fanciful image of
Muslims as polytheistic idolaters (which so took me aback as a young reader
of medieval drama) and the more fact-based depiction of Muhammad as the
founder of a religion closely related to Christianity (as in Dante's *Inferno*) are
neither two elements in a gradually more realistic understanding of Islam,

nor the products of a premodern world in which astonishing ignorance of a major religion could exist alongside a more nuanced understanding. Instead, these two apparently very different modes of characterizing Islam are part of a single discourse in which Islam is, one way or another, identified as idolatry: it is simply the practice of adoring the object rather than what it represents, the letter rather than the spirit. This conception of Islam as essentially idolatrous proved to be yet another way to reinforce the fundamental identity of Islam and Judaism in the medieval imagination: both rejecting the revelation of Christ, both spiritually blind to the salvation offered through the Incarnation and Crucifixion, the Saracen obedient to the "law of Muhammad" could readily be identified as simply another follower of the "law of Moses."

In spite of the extreme demonization of Saracens who were obedient to this retrogressive "law," and the energetic condemnation of Islam as a source of spiritual and bodily pollution, the Islamic world—including the Islamic notion of Paradise—remained stubbornly alluring to the medieval Western Christian. The bejeweled, sensuous paradise of the *mi'raj* account of Muhammad's ascent through the multi-layered heavens was a potent temptation to medieval writers, including Dante, who drew upon the *mi'raj* in order to describe the Christian paradise. Medieval writers and readers at once rejected Islam and the Muslim world and sought to integrate elements of it within their own milieu, ranging from its transcendent vision of the afterlife to the pure philosophical thought expressed by Avicenna and Averroës. The Islamic Orient was both beautiful and dangerous, open to assimilation and that which must be utterly rejected. This paradox shaped premodern attitudes, determining not only how medieval Westerners saw the Islamic "other" but also how they saw themselves.

This mirroring function, in which the Orient serves as a kind of negative image, being everything that the West is not, was influentially formulated in and disseminated through Edward Said's *Orientalism;* it is not too much to say that every study of representations of Islam and the Orient published since the appearance of *Orientalism* in 1978 has made reference—either affirmatively or negatively—to Said's work. The present study can be no exception, especially because the question of periodization, essential to the argument of *Idols in the East,* is built upon the foundations of Said's work, though often in opposition to its assumptions, particularly with regard to how Orientalism might be historicized and how periods in its development might be identified and delimited.

To paraphrase Jane Austen, it is a truth universally acknowledged, that a modern theoretical paradigm in possession of a wide currency must be in want of a medieval text. Too often, theories developed on the basis of shifts in nineteenth- or twentieth-century culture have come to be applied to texts of earlier periods without much consideration of what social and intellectual disjunctions might exist between modern theory and the premodern text.[1] This tendency is evident in the casual way in which many critics have referred to "medieval Orientalism," with little explanation of how a theory based on the history of eighteenth- and nineteenth-century French and British colonialism might be expressed in literature of much earlier periods.[2] This tendency is partly due to Said's own imprecision: as Aijaz Ahmad notes, *Orientalism* posits at least two points of origin for the phenomenon it defines, so that "one does not really know whether 'Orientalist Discourse' begins in the post-Enlightenment period or at the dawn of European civilization."[3] Orientalism, in Said's original formulation, is plural; it is both a general "style of thought" based on an arbitrary, polarized distinction between the Orient and the Occident and also "the corporate institution for dealing with the Orient."[4] The latter definition is clearly the product of the colonial era of European conquest, while the former is a discursive mode defined in such elastic terms as to be discernible in almost any place or time. In his 1994 afterword to *Orientalism,* Said makes this distinction more explicit, suggesting that the overall discourse of Orientalism, which dates back to Antiquity, can be distinguished from "the modern global phase" that began "with Napoleon's invasion of Egypt in 1798."[5] This double chronology allows Said to claim that Orientalism is both the necessary precondition of imperialism and its consequence.

There is clearly no point in belaboring the limitations of a theory introduced in the late 1970s in the context of a very different political and academic climate: it is often necessary to couch an argument in extreme, overly general terms in order to effect a shift in contemporary debate. It is also not my purpose to deny that Orientalism is a feature of texts, literary or otherwise, predating the rise of modern colonialisms. Instead, I would simply like to consider whether and, if so, in what terms we can speak of "medieval Orientalism." In order to do this, it is necessary to delve more deeply into

---

1. See some of the caveats found in Paul Strohm's introduction to *Theory and the Premodern Text* and the adventurous critique of Patterson, "Chaucer's Pardoner on the Couch," 638–80. On the special case of postcolonial theory, see Holsinger, "Medieval Studies," 1195–1227.

2. To cite only a few, see Campbell, *Witness and the Other World;* Delany, "Geographies of Desire"; Lynch, "East Meets West"; Schibanoff, "Worlds Apart," 59–96. A superb departure from this tendency appears in Higgins, "Shades of the East," 197–228.

3. Ahmad, *In Theory,* 181.

4. Said, *Orientalism,* 2–3.

5. Ibid., 333.

what is at stake in Said's description of Orientalism as a "discourse," a term that Said adopts from Foucault in order to identify the "style of thought" that has both shaped and been shaped by the categories, binary oppositions, and hierarchies used by Europeans to characterize the Islamic Orient. It is necessary, first, to examine more closely the historical and chronological limitations associated with the rise of discourses, which Foucault identifies as a specifically post-Enlightenment phenomenon; second, to consider the competing claims of canonical literature (used extensively by Said) and peripheral documents and texts (recommended by Foucault) in the reconstruction of the contours of Orientalism; third, to consider how power relations might have inflected the development of Orientalism, with Western colonial might surpassing Eastern military and technological superiority only comparatively late in that process. Only after considering some of these questions surrounding the nature and development of Orientalist discourse does it become possible to define the parameters of specifically *medieval* Orientalism; we can then go on to a closer examination of its relationship to postcolonial theory and of the crucial role of space—both location and orientation—in premodern modes of representing Islam and the Orient.

Said explicitly identifies Orientalism, both in the premodern and modern eras, as a discourse as defined by Foucault in *The Archeology of Knowledge* and *The Order of Things*.[6] On the face of it, this identification seems tenuous, since Foucault is quite specific in his characterization of discourse as a modern phenomenon, one made possible only by the institutional practices engendered by the *ancien regime* and ontological categories of Enlightenment thought.[7] If, however, by a discourse we mean a system of classification that establishes hierarchies, delimits one category from another, and exercises power through that system of classification, there can be no doubt that discourses existed in the premodern era; medieval maps and encyclopedias, scientific works and universal histories, all participate in the construction of an elaborate system of thought that categorizes, hierarchizes, and defines.[8] A second significant feature in Said's adaptation of Foucauldian discourse pertains to the kinds of

---

6. Foucault, *Archéologie du savoir; Les mots et les choses: Une archéologie des sciences humaines,* translated by A. M. Sheridan as *The Order of Things.*

7. The nature of Said's use of Foucault's theory of discourse has been exhaustively discussed elsewhere, beginning with James Clifford's remarkably perceptive 1980 review of the book, which appeared soon after its initial publication in 1978, and was reprinted as "On *Orientalism,*" 255–76. On Said's use of Foucault, see also Ahmad, *In Theory,* 164–67; Kennedy, *Edward Said,* 21–37; Brennan, "Illusion of a Future," 558–83, esp. 566–75.

8. This is an argument that I have made at greater length with regard to the closely related question of premodern expressions of nationalism and national identity; see Akbari, "Orientation and Nation," 102–34, esp. 102–3, 111–13, 124.

source materials used to reconstruct its contours. According to Foucault, certain types of sources are more revealing than others, with canonical literature being of particularly limited value. Said, peculiarly, inverts this practice, highlighting the role of canonical texts of the Western tradition in the evolution of Orientalism. As Said frankly acknowledges, "Unlike Michel Foucault... I do believe in the determining imprint of individual writers upon the otherwise anonymous collective body of texts constituting a discursive formation like Orientalism."[9] Consequently, Said cites a host of canonical texts in his genealogy of Orientalism: *The Persians* of Aeschylus and *The Bacchae* of Euripides, the *Chanson de Roland,* Dante's *Inferno,* and so on.[10] As James Clifford immediately noted in his 1980 review of *Orientalism,* even while Said aggressively criticizes the "Western critical tradition," he "derives most of his standards" from it.[11]

Aijaz Ahmad goes further in probing why Said might have chosen the texts he does to illustrate the general face of Orientalism as "a style of thought": "If there is an absent hero in Said's own counter-classic, it is Erich Auerbach."[12] Ahmad insightfully suggests that Said deliberately takes up the very canon of high European humanism so lovingly described by Auerbach in his own books on the Western literary tradition, which exercised a formative influence on the development of comparative literature as an academic discipline—Said's own academic discipline. To put it another way, the very texts Said himself taught as a novice professor in the core literature course at Columbia College are those marshaled by the mature scholar as evidence of the crushing hegemony of premodern Orientalism.[13] It may not be too much to suggest that, in *Orientalism,* the texts of the high humanist tradition that Said clearly venerates are shown, as it were, to betray him; perhaps this contributes to the undercurrent of anger that flows through *Orientalism.*[14] This adaptation on the part of Said, defining discourse as comprising *both* canonical authors *and* institutional or administrative texts, is key to the methodology of *Idols in the East,* which uses major writers of the European literary tradition in tandem with obscure, even marginal histories and documents in

---

9. Said, *Orientalism,* 23. On this distinction between Foucault and Said, see Clifford, "On *Orientalism,*" 269–71; Brennan, "The Illusion of a Future," 574.

10. Said, *Orientalism,* 56, 61, 68.

11. Clifford, "On *Orientalism,*" 275.

12. Ahmad, *In Theory,* 163.

13. See the representative Literature Humanities syllabi reprinted in Denby, *Great Books.*

14. As Ahmad puts it, "Said denounces with Foucauldian vitriol what he loves with Auerbachian passion" (*In Theory,* 168). On the "palpable" anger in *Orientalism* as a response to the plight of the Palestinians and the U.S. support of Zionism, see Brennan, "The Illusion of a Future," 580.

order to generate a thick description of premodern Orientalism. The interplay of canonical literature and peripheral document, so fruitfully mined by Said, is deployed in this study in the effort to produce a synoptic picture of one stage in the development of premodern Orientalism.

A third aspect that must be considered in Said's adaptation of Foucault's notion of discourse concerns the role of power relations. Like Foucault, Said emphasizes the thrust of institutional and imperial power that lay behind the development of Orientalist discourse in the West. In doing so, however, Said elides the narrative of Roman imperial power with modern expressions of European colonialism, overlooking the steep depreciation in Western military might, technology, science, philosophy, and literature experienced during the Middle Ages. For most of that period, the dominant power in the world was not the Christian West but rather the Islamic East, and European awareness of that inferiority played a crucial role in the development of Orientalism, as the following chapters of *Idols in the East* illustrate. This dramatic shift in the locus of imperial and intellectual power also inflects the way in which we must read textual examples of premodern Orientalism, particularly with attention to the local, regional centers of power that produced them. Again, to approach this problem, it is helpful to see how the relationship of discourse and power is framed by Foucault and, subsequently, by Said. For Foucault, the same discursive authority must be accorded to texts emanating from national and even imperial centers as to texts produced at the periphery.[15] This is precisely not the case for Said, who again and again reaffirms the imperial center as crucial in driving the discourse of Orientalism. This is most evident in his discussion of modern (i.e., post-1798) Orientalism, defined as "the corporate institution for managing the Orient," but is also apparent in his account of earlier periods, where the canonical status of Said's source texts within the Orientalist "system for citing works and authors"[16] places them firmly at the center of the European literary genealogy that he traces.

Based on his depiction of the hegemonic exercise of power through the discourse of Orientalism, one would fully expect Said to endorse Foucault's view of power as inescapable and overwhelming, invulnerable to resistance at the margins of empire. In his later writings, however, especially *Culture and Imperialism,* Said's reconstruction of Orientalism intersects with his emerging postcolonial sensibility, and he consequently seeks to redress what he has come to see as Foucault's inadequate attention to instances of resistance.

---

15. Ahmad, *In Theory,* 167.
16. Said, *Orientalism,* 23.

As Said puts it, "Foucault's imagination of power is largely *with* rather than *against* it."[17] The same comment is true of Said's own presentation of Orientalism, with the provision that he positions himself, in Brennan's words, as the "appalled witness of applied terror, an embodied rather than a disembodied 'power.'"[18] Linda Hutcheon accordingly distinguishes between Said's "postimperial" writing, such as *Orientalism,* and his "postcolonial" writing, including *Culture and Imperialism* and his three books on modern Palestine.[19] The former highlights the overwhelming power of the Orientalist discourse and its intimate relationship (both necessary precursor to and consequence of) imperial power, while the latter highlights the resistance to Orientalism, what Said refers to as counter-discourses.[20]

Dividing Said's work into these two phases is helpful for defining the parameters of medieval Orientalism, because it foregrounds the distinction between the discourse analysis practiced in *Orientalism* and that practiced in postcolonial studies.[21] There are certainly some medieval texts in which it is possible to identify counter-discursive moves, efforts to resist the prevailing hegemony; such texts tend to center on gender, sexual orientation, and national identity.[22] Orientalism during the Middle Ages is rather different, being far less likely to elicit counter-discourses of resistance, at least in the western European tradition under scrutiny in this study. The case is significantly different in the literature produced in border territories such as Norman Sicily or post-Reconquista Spain, where "Oriental" subjects might "write back" against the dominant discourse.[23] This story is not one told in *Idols in the East,* which is centered on European representations of what is strange and distant rather than what is familiar and close at hand, in which fantasies of the Islamic East serve as much to define the self as to define the other. There is a separate story also to be told about Europe's encounter with the Islamic world, recounted in part in Maria Rosa Menocal's seminal study of *The Arabic Role in Medieval Literary History* and continued in the abundant scholarship inspired by her work in a range of fields, including philological and literary

17. Said, "Foucault and the Imagination of Power," 149–55; quotation from 152. See also Said, *Culture and Imperialism.*

18. Brennan, "Illusion of a Future," 582.

19. Hutcheon, "*Orientalism* as Post-Imperial Witnessing," 91–106; quotation from 94.

20. Said, "Foucault," 153.

21. On discourse analysis in the postcolonial setting, see the foundational work of Partha Chatterjee, especially *Nationalist Thought and the Colonial World.*

22. For efforts of this kind, see, for example, Burger, "Cilician Armenian Métissage," 67–83; Townsend and Mehan, " 'Nation' and the Gaze at the Other."

23. In referring to the subject who "writes back," I allude to the title of the influential collection by Ashcroft, Griffiths, and Tiffin, *Empire Writes Back.*

studies, musicology, and art history.[24] Frame-tale narratives, including *Kalila wa Dimna,* the *Thousand and One Nights,* and the *Disciplina clericalis* of Petrus Alfonsi, are loquacious witnesses to the fertile interactions of the Mediterranean culture that embraced both the southern borders of Europe and the crescent of Islamic societies surrounding the Sea.[25]

The account of medieval Orientalism provided in *Idols in the East* is restricted specifically to Western views of the Islamic Orient, leaving to one side premodern European views of East Asia. This is not to discount the importance of texts such as Marco Polo's early thirteenth-century travel narrative, the *Devisement dou monde,* but simply to make clear the extent to which medieval Orientalism was shaped by a very specific discourse of religious alterity centered on the relationship of Christianity to Islam. The related yet separate study of the East Asian encounter is the focus of my recent collaborative collection on *Marco Polo and the Encounter of East and West.* That study, the scholarly twin of *Idols in the East,* explores the remarkably different ways in which discourses of alterity functioned within the mercantile romance narrative recounted by Marco Polo and his collaborator, Rustichello, and the implications of that exchange-oriented, pragmatic language for modern understandings of the binary opposition of East and West.[26] By the same logic, *Idols in the East* gives only limited attention to the role of Greek identity in the emergence of an early modern concept of Western civilization. That story, which concerns the complex interplay in the medieval European imagination of the intellectual legacy of Greek antiquity and its role in the rise of Renaissance humanism, the role of Alexander the Great in consolidating world-wide imperial might, and the continued half-life of the Roman Empire in Constantinople and its defeat at the hands of the Ottomans, has been partially recounted in recent studies by Sharon Kinoshita, Nancy Bisaha, and Margaret Meserve, and is the specific focus of Emily Reiner's work.[27]

Unlike those studies, *Idols in the East* centers on the relationship of religious and geographical alterity, and on the ways in which the discourse of Islamic religious difference both reinforced and was reinforced by the discourse of

---

24. See Menocal, *Arabic Role in Medieval Literary History.* A parallel account of Sicily inspired by Menocal's work on Spain can be found in Mallette, *Kingdom of Sicily.* The impact of Menocal's work is explicitly assessed in Akbari and Mallette, *Sea of Languages* (forthcoming).

25. On the impact of *Kalila wa Dimna* on European literature, see Amer, *Esope au féminin: Marie de France et la politique de l'interculturalité;* on the *Thousand and One Nights,* see Mallette, "Reading Backward"; on the *Disciplina clericalis,* see Akbari, "Between Diaspora and Conquest," 17–37.

26. See Akbari, "East, West, and In-between" and "Currents and Currency," 3–20, 110–30.

27. Kinoshita, *Medieval Boundaries;* Bisaha, *Creating East and West;* Meserve, *Empires of Islam in Renaissance Historical Thought;* Reiner, "Ambiguous Greek."

bodily, ethnic Oriental difference. While it is possible to distinguish these as two separate discourses, it is absolutely crucial not to lose sight of their inter-relation: this relationship, more than anything else, is what I attempt to establish in the following chapters. My effort to tease out the separate yet linked nature of religious and geographical alterity in the medieval discourse of Orientalism is, in part, a response to the casual way in which "Islam" and "the Orient" are elided in *Orientalism* and in much of the literature engendered by it. Said constantly wobbles between the basic dichotomy of Orient and Occident and a whole range of loosely related variations: "Europe" and "the Orient," "the West" and "Islam," "the Orient—that is, Islam," and so on.

This easy conflation of Islam and the Orient is particularly troubling to the medievalist, for a great number of medieval texts draw a clear distinction between cultural polarization framed in terms of religion and that framed in terms of geography; at the same time, an equally large number draw upon the conventions of one mode of alterity to strengthen the other. The distinction—and the relationship—between religious and geographical difference is the organizing principle of *Idols in the East,* which argues that the Orientalism that emerged in the late Middle Ages is constituted not only on the basis of bodily qualities associated with "Oriental" physiology, but also on the basis of religious orientation. Geographical location determines the nature of bodily diversity, including the ethnic characteristics of nations such as the oriental "Saracen." Spiritual orientation, whether expressed in terms of a fantastical devotion to pagan idols or in terms of a stubborn adherence to the letter of the law rather than the spirit that imbues it, was similarly articulated in terms of place and location. In the premodern period, Saracen identity is conceived of as an amalgam of Oriental body and Muslim soul, with the alterity of each of these being expressed in terms of location.

Location, in both a literal and a figurative sense, is key to the medieval articulation of bodily diversity and religious difference: this is especially evident in the categories and hierarchies that make up Orientalism. My exploration of these is informed not so much by Foucault's concept of a genealogy of knowledge, described most clearly in his *Discipline and Punish,* but rather by his archeological approach as presented in *The Archeology of Knowledge* and *The Order of Things.*[28] This choice is motivated by two factors: first, Foucault's definition of discursive formations and his account of how discourses arise and change are presented most fully in this stage of his work; second, the

---

28. On the distinction between Foucault's methodologies of "archeology" and "genealogy," see Davidson, "Archeology, Genealogy, Ethics," 221–34, and Elden, *Mapping the Present,* 104.

cross-generic and interdisciplinary nature of those discursive formations, together with the way in which categories and hierarchies interact in the conduct of the discourse, are displayed in a variety of medieval works. Texts as diverse as encyclopedias, maps, medical and astronomical treatises, *chansons de geste,* romances, and universal histories—both in their earliest forms and in a variety of translations and adaptations—participate in the expression of the Western discourse of Islam, on the one hand, and discourse of the Orient, on the other. Together, I argue, these two contribute to the emergence of a specifically medieval form of Orientalism. My emphasis on its dynamism and self-propelling nature is deliberate, for central to Foucault's definition of discourse is its status as process. A discourse is not the expression, in a variety of forms, of some hidden truth that is held in reserve, nor is it a common knowledge, universally accepted, that need not be openly stated but merely obliquely referred to. Rather, it is, in Rudi Visker's words, "a *practice* which cannot be reduced to a function of reference or expression. Rather than refer to pre-given objects, it brings its own objects into being." A discourse is "an active principle... [which] specif[ies] a series of relations between institutions, socio-economic processes, behavioral patterns, and systems of norms and classifications."[29] Categories, hierarchies and, especially, spatial relations are crucial constitutive elements in the discourses of Islam and the Orient and, ultimately, in the emergent discourse of Orientalism.

Stuart Elden has illustrated the extent to which Foucault's work makes use of the concept of space. Foucault's use of spatial language (terms such as limit, boundary, transgression, and threshold) has long been noted; Elden adds, however, that Foucault's use of such terminology differs from that found in contemporary Structuralist theory in that he alone couples his spatial metaphors with analyses of actual spaces. Moreover, Elden argues that "Foucault's work can perhaps be subsumed under the designation not simply of writing a history of the present, but *mapping the present.*"[30] When Foucault uses the term *repérage* in texts such as *The Archeology of Knowledge,* Elden claims, he does so with the military connotations of the term: it refers not only to the process of making a map, but of surveying territory or locating targets. Elden's analysis of Foucault's work as "spatial history" is particularly useful in bridging the gap between Foucault's definition of discourse and its adaptation by Said, for "imaginative geography" is central both to Foucault's archeology and Said's excavation of premodern Orientalism.

---

29. Visker, *Michel Foucault,* 119–20. On knowledge as practice, see also Cousins and Hussain, *Michel Foucault,* 87, 94, as well as Foucault's own *Archeology of Knowledge,* 45ff. and 115.

30. Elden, *Mapping the Present,* 94, 101, 114–15; quotation from 114.

Said himself comments on Foucault's habit of analyzing "actual spaces, territories, domains, and sites." Perhaps this sensitivity to what Said calls Foucault's "geographical bent" accounts for Said's own use of the haunting phrase "imaginative geography" in his account of the premodern discourse of Orientalism.[31] Foucault uses a similar phrase, in his *Histoire de la folie,* to describe the enforced river voyage of the madman, deported to some place of asylum: he travels across a "half-real, half-imaginary geography."[32] His liminal position is both literal (physically located between two shores) and metaphorical. In a later essay, Said returns once more to this evocative phrase, applying it now not only to premodern texts but also to contemporary debates over the history (and, hence, ownership) of territory in Israel and Palestine.[33] In a comparable shift of place and time, it may be fruitful to apply the term "imaginative geography" to medieval texts more comprehensively and more carefully than Said was able to do in his brief overview of premodern Orientalism.[34] Many medieval texts anatomize, categorize, and hierarchize space, including encyclopedias, scientific writings, pilgrimage itineraries, literary texts, and—above all—maps.[35] These can be used to reconstruct the contours of an imaginative geography whose status is not that of a universally accepted "truth," but rather a discourse that is continually in the process of being articulated and thus creating, as it were, its own truth.

This process can be best understood in the terms set by the geographer David Harvey, who insists that maps and other schemata must be understood as participating in a dialectical process in which apparently permanent entities (such as the Orient or the Occident) are constructed, taking their place in the generation of "a landscape of knowledge seemingly impermeable to change." Medieval efforts to map the world, whether in the images of the *mappaemundi* or in the words of the descriptive geographies found in literary texts and encyclopedias, reveal moments of "crystallization," as Harvey calls it, when the process of mapping brings an entity into apparent being.[36] Harvey's formulation emphasizes the crucial point, obscured in the phrase "imaginative geography," that there is no corresponding reality—not even

31. Said, "Foucault," 150, 149.

32. Michel Foucault, *Histoire de la folie* (Paris: Gallimard, 1972), 22; cf. *Madness in Culture,* 11 (noted in Elden, *Mapping the Present,* 124).

33. Said, "Invention, Memory, Place," 175–92, esp. 181 ff.

34. See Mary B. Campbell's ambitious effort to explore "imaginative geography" from late antiquity to the early modern period in *Witness and the Other World.*

35. See the range of texts, both literary and historical, examined in terms of spatial theory in Hanawalt and Kobialka, *Medieval Practices of Space,* and Crang and Thrift, *Thinking Space.*

36. Harvey, *Justice, Nature and the Geography of Difference,* 80–83; quotation at 81.

in the collective imagination—to "the Orient." Rather, the sites of "crystal-lization" described by Harvey mark identifiable, recognizable moments in the practice of the discourse. For example, on medieval maps and in encyclo-pedias, the three sons of Noah are conventionally associated with the three known continents of Asia, Africa, and Europe. Some texts, however, refer to a fourth region, east of Asia, inhabited by a fourth son of Noah who is known only from apocalyptic sources. In such moments, the geographical discourse of the Orient is not simply expanded but reoriented, with the introduction of a remote domain—the "regio solis," or "region of the sun"—that relocates the eastern horizon.

The nature of these "moments of crystallization" and the scope of medi-eval paradigm shifts are the recurring theme of *Idols in the East*. Chapter 1, "The Shape of the World," centers on the fourteenth-century emergence of the binary opposition of Orient and Occident. While earlier maps and texts identifying the climates and their properties naturally associated extreme heat and its effects with the south, and extreme cold and its effects with the north, a paradigm shift took place in the fourteenth century that transferred these properties: from the twelfth century, the East was increasingly characterized in terms of heat, and its reciprocal, the West, came to be characterized in terms of (formerly northern) cold. The result was the production of a binary opposition of East and West, the first a torrid climate populated by irascible people having weak, swarthy bodies, the second a cool climate populated by rational people having strong, fair bodies. While this chapter includes a wide range of texts and maps in its survey of medieval geography, it is anchored by a detailed reading of how the shape of the world is presented in one of the most popular works of the Middle Ages, *The Book of John Mandeville*.

Chapter 2 chronicles the shift "From Jerusalem to India" as the desirable center of the imaginative geography manifested in maps, itineraries, and en-cyclopedias of the later Middle Ages. In this chapter, the "moments of crys-tallization" described by Harvey are powerfully realized as maps increasingly focus the eye on the regions furthest east, sites ripe for colonization, while prose geographies devote more and more space to the wonders of India. In literature, nowhere is the simultaneous allure and danger of the Orient more vividly presented than in the popular romances of Alexander the Great. This chapter accordingly traces the changing contours of the Alexander legend from the twelfth to the fifteenth centuries, focusing particularly on the *Liber Floridus* of Lambert of Saint-Omer, the *Roman de toute chevalerie* of Thomas of Kent, and the anonymous *Kyng Alisaunder*. Here, the compelling attractions of oriental wealth and luxury are counterbalanced by the dangerous knowl-edge gained in those remote regions. The example of Alexander reveals that the regions furthest east are a place from which one returns profoundly changed, if one returns at all.

Chapter 3, "The Place of the Jews," turns to the striking overlap seen in premodern depictions of Muslims and Jews and locates the fundamental distinction between the two in the increasing specificity of medieval descriptions of the "Oriental" body. In the discourse of religious difference, Jews and Muslims are seen as interchangeable: for example, in the *Song of Roland,* Muslims are said to worship in "synagogues," while in medieval mystery plays, Herod swears in the name of Muhammad as he presides over the slaughter of the Innocents. The discourse of geographical difference, however, distinguishes clearly between Jewish and Muslim bodies. They are regarded as culturally similar, both Jewish and Muslim males being circumcised, but biologically different, having different humoral dispositions. Unlike the Jew, who is presented as belonging nowhere yet found everywhere, the Muslim is depicted as the product of a particular climate, possessing a range of invariable, immutable bodily and behavioral qualities.

Taken together, the paradigm shifts chronicled in the three opening chapters of *Idols in the East* outline the development of Orientalist discourse during the Middle Ages. These paradigm shifts must be understood not only in terms of Foucault's theory of rupture as articulated in *The Archeology of Knowledge,* but also in terms of Kuhn's description of scientific change in terms of "conversion experiences" in *The Structure of Scientific Revolutions.*[37] Certainly, the cyclical view central to Kuhn's theory is not fully assimilable to Foucault's archeological approach, which declares that the premodern episteme is inaccessible to the modern subject. Nonetheless, Kuhn's theory of cyclical change offers useful insights into the transformation of late medieval scientific thought concerning the relationship of climate to bodily diversity.[38]

Bodily diversity, shown to be the natural manifestation of climatic variation in the first three chapters of this study, is the focus of chapter 4, which is devoted to the literary depictions of the Oriental body. The intersection of gender categories with categories based on religious difference and geographically determined bodily diversity generates phenomena that seem to defy the laws of nature: men of monstrous stature and beautiful form; women possessing extraordinary powers of aggression overlaid with a veneer of conventionally feminine beauty; half-breed offspring whose misshapen form or variegated color reflects their liminal status, trapped in the gap separating

---

37. Kuhn, *Structure of Scientific Revolutions.*

38. On the difficulty of reconciling Kuhn and Foucault, see Kusch, *Foucault's Strata and Fields,* 96–109; Delaporte, "History of Medicine According to Foucault," 137–49, esp. 145–46.

two distinct categories. Caroline Bynum, Sarah Beckwith, and Miri Rubin have established to what extent and in what ways eucharistic symbolism was invoked to describe the nature of the Christian community, conceived as an organic whole in reflection of the body of Christ and, appropriately, united through the consumption of that body in the form of the eucharistic Host.[39] This means of defining the boundaries of the Christian community came, in the fourteenth and fifteenth centuries, to be extended to the imagined community of the nation.[40] The liminal status of "Saracen" bodies is shown in chapter 4 to be essential to the process of imagining the nation based on the framework of the imaginative geography outlined in the opening chapters.

The final chapters center on the medieval discourse of Islam. Building on the seminal work of Marie-Thérèse d'Alverny and Norman Daniel, as well as more recent studies by Thomas Burman and John Tolan, these chapters illustrate the extent to which the discourse of Islam was unified, in spite of its apparent heterogeneity.[41] It is often assumed that there were two fundamentally different ways of viewing Islam in the medieval West, one "fanciful" (in the words of Norman Daniel), one "realistic," a binary opposition that Daniel reinforced throughout his work.[42] He was far from alone in drawing this distinction; at least Daniel did not, like Richard Southern, imply that the development of Western images of Islam could be described in terms of "progress" from an "age of ignorance" to a transcendent "moment of vision."[43] Such a position could hardly be maintained in light of the sophisticated assessments of Islamic theology produced in twelfth-century Spain.[44] Chapter 5, "Empty Idols and a False Prophet," demonstrates that the distinction between "fanciful" and "realistic" depictions of Islam obscures a fundamental continuity in

---

39. See Bynum, *Holy Feast, Holy Fast,* 48–66; Rubin, "Small Groups." See also the seminal article by James, "Ritual, Drama and Social Body," 3–29.

40. Akbari, "Incorporation in the *Siege of Melayne,*" 22–44, and "Hunger for National Identity," 198–227.

41. Several of Marie-Thérèse d'Alverny's seminal articles on this subject are collected in *La connaissance de l'Islam dans l'Occident médiéval.* Of Norman Daniel's many works, see especially *Islam and the West.* See also Thomas E. Burman's work on Western medieval translations of the Qur'an, especially *"Tafsir* and Translation," 703–32, and "Cambridge University Library MS Mm.v.26," 335–63; adaptations of material in these essays also appear in *Reading the Qur'an in Latin Christendom.* See also Tolan, *Medieval Christian Perceptions of Islam* and *Saracens.*

42. Daniel, *Heroes and Saracens;* see also Daniel, *Islam and the West,* 24–26.

43. Southern, *Western Views of Islam in the Middle Ages.* Southern divides his teleological narrative into three sections: "The Age of Ignorance" (to the mid-twelfth century), "The Century of Reason and Hope" (to the late thirteenth century), and "The Moment of Vision" (to the mid-fifteenth century). For a very perceptive analysis of Daniel's approach, see Blanks, "Western Views of Islam in the Premodern Period," 11–53, esp. 24–29.

44. See the essays collected in d'Alverny, *Connaissance de l'Islam;* Burman, *"Tafsir* and Translation"; and Kritzeck, *Peter the Venerable and Islam.*

the tradition. It is significant, for example, that the "realistic" polemics against Islam centered on the life of the Prophet claim that Muhammad set himself up as an idol before the people, while "fanciful" depictions of Muslims as idolaters include "Muhammad" as the name of the one of the members of the pagan anti-Trinity. As shown in chapter 5, these apparently heterogeneous caricatures are far from being distinct traditions; rather, they form two mutually reinforcing aspects of the Western discourse of Islam.

The sixth chapter, "The Form of Heaven," surveys Western depictions of the Islamic heaven as a place of sensuous pleasures and relates them to the understanding of Islam as being (like Judaism) a religion or "law" based on the letter rather than the spirit. This insistence on Muslim literalism bears striking affinities not only to Christian assessments of Judaism, but also to late fourteenth- and early fifteenth-century condemnations of religious heterodoxy, especially Lollardy. Religious deviance, whether located at the borders of Christian culture or emanating from within it, is identified, condemned, and ultimately cut away from the community of the faithful. The discourse of Islam outlined in the final chapters of this study centers incessantly on the focus of devotion; that is, the location of the divine. The idolatrous image is identified as precisely the wrong object of worship. Far from being a mediator between humanity and the divine, it is a spiritual dead end, a barren wasteland where devotion is poured out like water on dry sand. The discourse of the Orient outlined in the first chapters of this study, on the other hand, centers on orientation; that is, locating the fixed site to be identified as the center of the world, both in a literal and a metaphorical sense. Medieval texts frequently identify this center as Jerusalem. This fixed point is the focus of salvation history, located both in the past (as the site of Christ's crucifixion and the consequent rebirth of mankind) and in the future (as the site where the apocalypse will begin).

In the late medieval convergence of these two discourses—one of Islam, one of the Orient—we can discern the emergence of Orientalism. This medieval Orientalism, however, is distinct from the modern phenomenon, produced in the context of eighteenth- and nineteenth-century French and British colonialism. One might say that the discourse of Orientalism has several phases of development. One of these phases may have begun (as Said suggests) with Napoleon's conquest of Egypt in 1798 while another, I would suggest, began in the late fifteenth century with increasing Western awareness of the power of the Ottomans following the fall of Constantinople in 1453. This early modern break in Orientalist discourse, like the eleventh-century rupture around the time of the First Crusade, was manifested in terms of religious and geographical orientation. With the conquest of Constantinople by the Ottomans, the territory disputed by Muslims and Christians shifted from Jerusalem to the eastern marches of Europe. This shift was both literal and symbolic: literal in that the effort to conquer Jerusalem through military means had largely been abandoned, while efforts to deflect Ottoman incursions into eastern Europe were intensified; symbolic in that the pilgrimage to Jerusalem had come to be supplanted by the pilgrimage of the soul, a trend in late medieval piety that became increasingly prominent with the dawn of the Reformation. The paradigm shift around 1450 is underscored by the change in the terminology applied to Muslims, as the preferred term came to be "Turk" or "Moor" instead of "Saracen."[45] This change illustrates two aspects of the early modern paradigm shift: first, the movement from a term based on both religious and bodily difference to terms based on the latter; and, second, the movement from a single term to multiple terms, reflecting an awareness of the very different political dynamics involved in the relationship of Europe and North Africa, on the one hand, and Europe and the Ottomans, on the other. At the beginning of the twelfth century, all eyes looked eastward, toward the holy city of Jerusalem and into the apocalyptic future to come. By the mid-fifteenth century, however, the shape of the world and the place of the Orient had come to look quite different.

---

45. A detailed account of the murky origins of the term "Saracen" and its relationship to related terms such as "Agarene" and "Ismaelite" (all of which connote both religious and ethnic difference) can be found in Beckett, *Anglo-Saxon Perceptions of the Islamic World*, 90–104. Briefer overviews can also be found in Daniel, *Arabs and Medieval Europe*, 53–54, and Tolan, *Saracens*, 10–11.

⤺ CHAPTER 1

The Shape of the World

It is commonly believed, even today, that medieval people thought that the world was flat.[1] Nothing could be further from the truth. During the Middle Ages, writers endlessly discussed the shape of the *orbus terrae* or "sphere of the world," partitioning it in many different ways. Occasionally they used the binary distinction between East and West, as in Fulcher of Chartres' famous description of the Christian crusaders in Jerusalem: "Consider, I pray, and reflect how in our time God has transferred the West into the East. For we who were Occidentals have now been made Orientals."[2] More frequently, however, medieval writers divided the world into four parts, following the four cardinal points of direction. This quadripartite structure could be readily aligned with diagrams of the four seasons, the four elements, the four humors, the four ages of the life of man, and so on—an endless series of categories that could be used to make sense of the world, facilitate memorization of its properties, and analyze the relationship of the parts to the whole. At other times, the world was understood to be

---

1. For an account of the popularization of this myth by modern historians, see Eco, *Serendipities,* 4–7.

2. "Considera, quaeso, et mente cogita, quomodo tempore in nostro transvertit Deus Occidentem in Orientem. Nam qui fuimus Occidentales, nunc facti sumus Orientales." Fulcher of Chartres, *Historia Hierosolymitana* 748 (3.27.2–3), trans. Krey, *First Crusade,* 281.

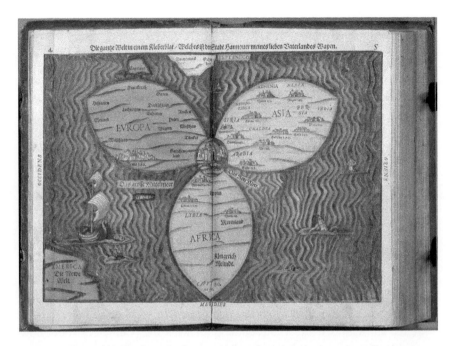

FIGURE 1. The world in the form of a flower, with Jerusalem at the center as in medieval maps, but with "America, The New World" at lower left. Heinrich Bünting, *Itinerarium Sacrae Scripturae* (Magdeburg: J. L. Siebenbürger, 1582), RES-02F-972, pp. 4–5. By permission of the Bibliothèque nationale de France, Réserve des livres rares, Paris, France.

divided into three parts: that is, the three known continents of Asia, Africa, and Europe. This schema was often integrated with the biblical account of the descent of all humanity from the three sons of Noah after the Flood, so that the tripartite division of the world provided a template for the three "races," so to speak, of mankind, as well as for the multitude of languages spoken around the world. One early modern version of the tripartite map depicts the continents in the form of a three-petaled flower, highlighting the "natural" symmetry of world geography (figure 1).[3]

The purpose of all these schemas, however variable, was to impose order on the abundant heterogeneity of creation, to gain control over the world by fitting it into an intellectually coherent system. Medieval writers would not have described their task as the "imposition" of order; rather, they would say that one "found" or "discerned" the order already imposed upon the world and its populations by God, whose foreknowledge and power of predestination were

---

3. Bünting, *Itinerarium Sacrae Scripturae,* 4–5.

understood to be absolute.[4] This erasure of human agency in the construction of systems of geographical knowledge underlines the extent to which standard categories and hierarchies were thought to be simply received from above rather than constructed on earth. The "imaginative geography" that defines the West by describing everything that it is not (that is, the Orient) provides just this sort of reassuring received knowledge in the form of what Edward Said describes as "latent" (as opposed to "manifest") Orientalism.[5] The use of geographical knowledge in the exercise of power can be seen not only in the basic, binary opposition of East and West fundamental to the manifestation of Orientalism, but also in other geographical systems. For example, the recent work of Lewis and Wigen amply illustrates how variably the boundaries of the continents have been defined, and how arbitrarily their qualities have been described.[6] By establishing a center and, consequently, a periphery, medieval maps and geographical texts both establish a hierarchy and define conceptual relationships between areas based on their physical proximity to one other. They are of interest not just for what they reveal about medieval people's efforts to understand the world as a coherent, integrated and symmetrical whole, but also for what they can tell us about how models of the shape of the world changed over time.

Among the most significant of these changes was the shift from the usual eastern orientation of medieval maps to the northern orientation normally used on modern maps, and the concomitant shift in the order of exposition in geographical prose texts. While this shift from eastern to northern orientation took place in the fifteenth century, when maps came to be used more frequently for actual navigation (rather than to illustrate an idealized, symbolic geography), it was as early as the fourth century that diagrams of the world featuring a northern orientation could be found in manuscripts of the *Saturnalia* and the *Commentary on the Dream of Scipio* written by the late antique philosopher Macrobius. These texts include diagrams of the world

---

4. This is not the place for an exposition of the often heated medieval debates on the limitations, if any, on divine foreknowledge and the power of predestination. On this topic, see the selections from pertinent philosophers in Bosley and Tweedale, "Determination, Free Will, and Divine Foreknowledge," 245–307. A more detailed survey of medieval thought on predestination (from Augustine to Ockham) can be found in Bannach, "Die Schöpfung als Abbild göttlichen Denkens," 54–275. On the received quality of medieval geographical knowledge, see the classic summary of "The Book of Nature" in Curtius, *European Literature and the Latin Middle Ages,* 319–22.

5. On "imaginative geography," see Said, *Orientalism,* 54–55; on "latent" and "manifest" Orientalism, see 206–7. An intelligent account of Said's use of geographical discourses can be found in Gregory, "Edward Said's Imaginative Geographies," 302–48. See also the introduction to this volume.

6. Lewis and Wigen, *Myth of Continents,* esp. 21–31 and 214–19.

with a northern orientation, divided into three zones: in the vicinity of the north and south poles, a "frigid zone" uninhabitable due to the extreme cold; extending north and south from the equator, a "torrid zone" uninhabitable due to the extreme heat; between them, a "temperate zone" suited to human habitation. While both the northern and the southern hemispheres, in the Macrobian schema, have a temperate zone, only the northern zone was generally held to be inhabited. Nonetheless, the southern temperate zone was in theory amenable to colonization, if only one could pass through the oppressive heat of the torrid zone. Here, according to some sources, one might find the "antipodes," the habitable lands of the southern hemisphere corresponding to the known lands of the northern ecumene.[7] Some maps, such as those accompanying many of the illuminated manuscripts of the *Apocalypse* of Beatus of Lièbana and those contained in the *Liber Floridus* of Lambert of St. Omer, include a fourth continent in the southern hemisphere, in addition to the known continents of Asia, Africa, and Europe in the north. This continent is labeled, "Unknown to us due to the heat of the sun," or "Unknown to the sons of Adam due to the heat of the sun."[8] These tantalizing rubrics suggest the exciting possibilities offered to the adventurous—or foolhardy—traveler by the as-yet-unknown territories located at the periphery of the map.

In this chapter, I will refer to maps, encyclopedias, and literary texts to illustrate medieval views of the shape of the world. What follows is far from an exhaustive survey; rather, it is a representative selection of some strategies used from the twelfth to the fifteenth centuries to impose order on an intrinsically disorderly world by defining its center, its borders, and its parts. In the first section of this chapter, "Defining the Parts," I describe how medieval cartographers and encyclopedists used the tripartite model of the world, divided into the known continents of Asia, Africa, and Europe, as a template onto which the biblical history of the three sons of Noah could be mapped. The genealogy was integrated with medieval theories regarding the natural qualities of the various regions of the world, giving rise during the later Middle Ages to something very like the modern binary of Orient and Occident. This section begins with a description of the geography of Pierre d'Ailly, whose early fifteenth-century *Imago Mundi* is a fascinating example of the variety of ways in which the world was schematized on the eve of the Early Modern period of colonization and conquest. His work, like maps of the same period,

---

7. Flint, "Monsters and the Antipodes," 65–80.

8. On the rubrics of maps showing a fourth continent, see von den Brincken, *Fines Terrae*, 50–52, 171–77, 193–202; a useful table of map rubrics appears at 149–57.

includes both the technical apparatus necessary to practical navigation and the more fanciful and symbolic features typical of earlier medieval maps.

In one sense, the conception of a tripartite world centered on Jerusalem can be described as centrifugal: this is a geographical model that envisions the whole of humanity as flowing outward into the three continents after the cataclysmic Great Flood, followed by the dissemination of a thousand different languages following the fall of the Tower of Babel. In another sense, this tripartite world is centripetal, in that the central point appears as both the point of mankind's spiritual origin and the point of return. Jerusalem thus functions as the hub of the terrestrial wheel, anchoring Christian salvation history both in its past, as the place of the Crucifixion and mankind's consequent salvation, and in its future, as the site of the first signs of Apocalypse and the gathering place for the Last Judgment. The second section of the chapter, "Defining the Center," consequently focuses on the symbolic place of Jerusalem, beginning with an account of the various world centers featured on maps and in texts—Rome, Jerusalem, Mecca, Arym—before turning to a detailed reading of *The Book of John Mandeville.* This work, which circulated widely throughout Europe in a variety of translations and adaptations beginning almost immediately upon its composition in the mid-fourteenth century, begins like many pilgrimage narratives by positing Jerusalem as both physical and spiritual center of the world.[9] Its author rapidly moves on, however, to introduce a series of what I call "shifting centers" that supplement Jerusalem without displacing it. Far from being a place conceived of as essentially "other," the Orient in *The Book of John Mandeville* proves to be a place that is variable and relative, its location defined by the position of the viewer.

↰ Defining the Parts

There are many ways to order the world: it can be divided by hemispheres, by continents, or by climatic zones; it can be mapped with its orientation toward the north, as now, or toward the east, as common in medieval maps. The work of the early fifteenth-century chancellor of the University of Paris, Pierre

---

9. *Mandeville's Travels*—more properly called *The Book of John Mandeville,* in keeping with the manuscript tradition (see Higgins, *Writing East,* 64–55 and 269n2)—survives in more than 250 medieval manuscripts. Written in French, probably in 1356, within a century it had been translated into Czech, Dutch, English, German, Irish, Italian, Latin, and Spanish. On the versions, see Seymour, *Sir John Mandeville,* 42–53; introduction by Christiane Deluz in [Mandeville, John] *Jean de Mandeville,* 28–32. Higgins provides a useful table of the versions in *Writing East,* 21–23.

d'Ailly, illustrates just this multiplicity of choices, making his work a useful introduction to the wide variety of medieval models of the world. D'Ailly's *Imago Mundi* opens with a sequence of eight diagrams, each of which depicts the world according to a different cartographic principle. Each of these diagrams, for d'Ailly, is valid, for each of them illustrates a different aspect of the structure of the world. The *Imago Mundi,* a series of astronomical treatises composed in the years 1410 to 1414, enjoyed widespread popularity: both manuscripts and early printed editions survive, including a copy with marginal notes written by the explorer Columbus.[10] Such dissemination attests to the dual function of extended geographies such as d'Ailly's. They serve both as practical guides to navigation and as books of entertainment for would-be travelers who long to see the world, but who have the opportunity to see it only through the eyes of the writer, and consequently depend upon his vision of the world.

D'Ailly is hardly the first writer to include diagrams in his prose geography; he is unusual, however, in the way in which he patterns his text around them. At the outset of his work, d'Ailly displays eight circular diagrams, each of which divides the world in a different way (figure 2a-d). Although each one uses a different organizing principle, they all have the same shape and northern orientation, which encourages the reader to compare these different models, mentally superimposing one schema upon the other. The sequence illustrates not only the continuity of different models of the world's structure, but also the continuity of the heavenly spheres with the earthly sphere itself. The first diagram shows the geocentric universe, with the earth at the center surrounded by the spheres of the various planets. Here, the center of the diagram is also the center of the world: the vertical text in the center marks the space between the North and South Poles, while the horizontal line in the center marks the equator. The second and third diagrams illustrate the alignment and movement of the stars and planets relative to the surface of the earth, while the fourth shows the elemental spheres of fire, air, and water that surround it. In the fifth diagram (figure 2a), the regions of the earth are organized according to principles derived from the earlier diagrams of the celestial regions, divided into five zones: two polar, two temperate, and one extreme or "torrid." In the sixth figure (figure 2b), d'Ailly elaborates the zonal divisions of

---

10. D'Ailly, *Imago Mundi;* on the date of composition of d'Ailly's treatises, see 1:111–12. Buron's edition is based on the incunable of 1480–83 (Louvain: Jean de Westphalie) owned by Christopher Columbus; an edition based on the manuscripts is needed. On the manuscript tradition, see von den Brincken, "Occeani Angustior Latitudo," 2:565–81, esp. 567, and Thorndike, "Four British Manuscripts."

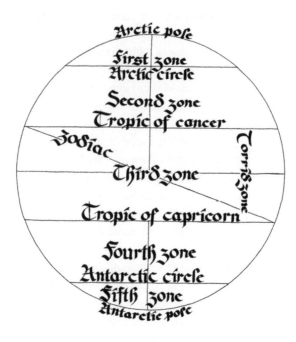

Arctic pole

First zone

Arctic circle

Second zone

Tropic of cancer

Zodiac

Third zone

Torrid zone

Tropic of capricorn

Fourth zone

Antarctic circle

Fifth zone

Antarctic pole

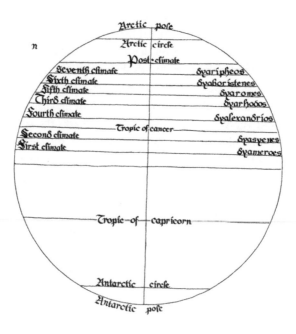

n

Arctic pole

Arctic circle

Post-climate

Seventh climate — Syaripheos

Sixth climate — Syaßoristenes

Fifth climate — Syaromes

Third climate — Syarhodos

Fourth climate — Syalexandrios

Tropic of cancer

Second climate — Syasyenes

First climate — Syameroes

Tropic-of-capricorn

Antarctic circle

Antarctic pole

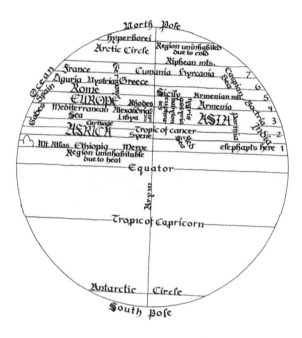

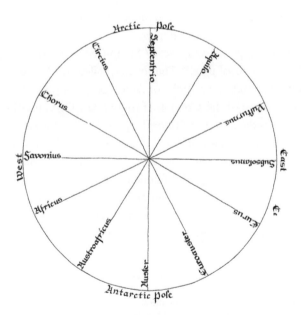

FIGURE 2. Various views of the world as outlined by Pierre d'Ailly, including (a) a Macrobian map, with five zones; (b) a map in the tradition of Albumasar (Abu Ma'shar), with seven climates; (c) an integrated map, with the five zones, seven climates, and geographical features of the traditional T-O map; and (d) a world view showing the wind directions. After Pierre d'Ailly, *Imago Mundi* (Louvain: Johannes de Paderborn, 1483). Courtesy of Yasin Akbari.

the northern hemisphere into seven subzones, each of which is named after a notable city: for example, the third zone is named after Alexandria. These subzones, derived originally from Ptolemaic geography, had a wide currency in Europe through Latin translations and adaptations of the work of the Muslim astronomer Albumazar (Abu Ma'shar).[11] The seventh diagram (figure 2c) is particularly unusual: in it, d'Ailly actually superimposes one model of the world on top of a very different one, combining the north-oriented zonal map with the east-oriented mappamundi. Many of the traditional features of the conventional world map appear here: the land mass is divided into the three known continents of Europe, Africa, and Asia; Asia is twice as large as the other two, which are confined together in the western hemisphere; the far reaches of India lie at the eastern extreme, and the pillars of Hercules in the west. D'Ailly's eighth diagram (figure 2d), again in the form of the sphere of the earth, shows the various directions of the winds. This final diagram functions in two ways, offering useful and practical knowledge for the navigator as well as a symbolic, elemental way of seeing the orderly symmetry of the created world.[12]

D'Ailly's *Imago Mundi* is a remarkable conflation of traditional ways of seeing the world and more recent scientific advances in mathematical modeling.[13] This synthesis is epitomized in the seventh diagram (figure 2c), which marries two very different cartographic conventions. The two main traditions in medieval mapping were the T-O map (also called the mappamundi) and the Macrobian zonal map.[14] The former, called the T-O on account of its shape, lent itself well to symbolic or sacred geography, for the T could be seen as representative of the Cross itself (figure 3a). Certain elaborate mappaemundi, such as the now-lost Ebstorf map, emphasize this aspect by depicting the hands, feet, and face of Jesus at the periphery of the O, reminding the viewer that the entire ecumene is, in a spiritual sense, contained within the body of Christ. T-O maps also frequently place Jerusalem at or near the center of the intersection of the T, reinforcing once more the sacred symbolism of this view of the earth. The division of the land masses into the three known continents of Asia, Africa, and Europe naturally echoes the perfect

---

11. On the knowledge of Albumazar in medieval Europe, see Lemay, *Abu Ma'shar and Latin Aristotelianism in the Twelfth Century*. On the seven subzones and the cities associated with them, see Honigmann, *Die sieben Klimata und die Poleis episemoi*.

12. Obrist, "Wind Diagrams and Medieval Cosmology," 33–84.

13. Patrick Gautier Dalché sees in d'Ailly "la volonté d'assimiler les enseignements de Ptolémée à la tradition des géographes antérieurs" (86); see "Pour une histoire du regard géographique," 77–103. For a reassessment of the significance of the late medieval rediscovery of Ptolemy's *Geography*, see Gautier Dalché, "Histoire," 85.

14. For an overview of medieval world maps, including the T-O format and Macrobian climate maps, see Woodward, "Medieval *Mappaemundi*," 286–370; Edson, *Mapping Time and Space*.

number of the Trinity. The division into three land masses also served to cate-gorize the three races of man, epitomized by the three sons of Noah. Their names even appear in place of the names of the continents in some versions of the T-O map (figure 3b).

Zonal maps are very different from T-O maps, both in their appearance and in the nature of the reality they seek to represent. Their focus is on natu-ral philosophy rather than on spiritual geography. Often called "Macrobian" due to their appearance in manuscripts of Macrobius' *Saturnalia* and *Commen-tary on the Dream of Scipio,* zonal maps divide the world according to scientific principles, based on natural phenomena such as heat and cold, and geometri-cal principles derived from Ptolemy (figure 4). The most evident difference between the T-O map and the zonal map is orientation: the T-O map is usually (though not invariably) oriented toward the east, while the zonal map (like our modern maps) is always oriented toward the north. In his *Imago Mundi,* Pierre d'Ailly is well aware that, by referring to both the zonal and the T-O map, he is synthesizing two disparate cartographic traditions: as he puts it, "now that I have divided the world according to the astrologers, now I will divide it according to the cosmographers."[15] His text includes some of the most up-to-date means of mapping the world, based on geometrical and mathematical methods. D'Ailly's most important source in this respect is Roger Bacon, who includes a description of world geography in the fourth book of his *Opus Maius,* which is dedicated to mathematics. It was Bacon who first argued that the westernmost reaches of Spain and the easternmost reaches of India were proximate to one another.[16] Pierre d'Ailly's elaboration of this argument, based on Bacon's insights, was naturally of great interest to his most famous reader, Columbus, later in the fifteenth century.

In dividing the world in these various ways, d'Ailly is one of a long line of geographers who organize the world based on mapping principles of their day. Encyclopedists such as Isidore of Seville, Bartholomaeus Anglicus, and Vincent of Beauvais all include prose geographies as part of their texts; manuscripts of Isidore, in particular, also frequently feature tripartite T-O maps. These prose texts, like medieval maps, divide, hierarchize, and order the

---

15. "Ucusque [Ut usque?] de divisione terre secundum astrologos dictunt et qui per divisionem climatum procedunt, nunc aliam divisionem quam ponunt Cosmographi posequamur" (d'Ailly, *Imago Mundi,* chap. 14 ["De divisione terre per tres partes secundum Cosmographos"], quotation from 252).

16. The city of "Arym" appears in Bacon's account of a map included in book 4 of his *Opus Maius.* The map itself does not survive, but Bacon's description indicates that it would have been north-oriented, showing the seven climates as well as lines of latitude and longitude, both of which were centered on Arym. See Bacon, *Opus Majus,* ed. Bridges, 1:300; Bacon, *Opus Majus,* trans. Burke, 1:319.

Oriens

MARE · OCCEANVS

ASIA
Sem

Mare magnum siue mediterraneum

EVROPA
Iafeth

AFRICA
Cham

Septentrio

meridies

Occidens

Sia ex noie cuiusda mu/ lieris est ap/ pellata· que apud anti/ quos imperiu orientis tenuit. Hec in tercia or bis parte disposita· ab oriente ortu solis·a me ridie·oceao·ab occiduo nostro mari finitur· a septentrione meothide lacu & tanai fluuio ter minatur. Habet autem prouincias multas et re giones·quarū breuiter nomina et situs expediam·sumpto initio a paradiso   Paradisus est locus in orientis partibus constitu/ tus·cuius vocabulum ex greco in latinum vertitur ortus. Porro hebrai e eden dicitur· quod in nostra lingua delicie interpretat quod vtrumq; iunctum facit ortum deliciarum·est enim omni genere ligni & pomiferarum arborum consitus habens· etiam lignum vite. Non ibi frigus· non estus· sed perpetua aeris tem/ peries·e cuius medio fons prorumpens·totum nemus irrigat· di uiditurq; in quatuor nascentia flumina. Cuius loci post pecca/ tum hominis aditus interclusus est. Septus est eni vndiq; rom phea flammea·id est muro igneo accinctus· ita ut eius cū caelo pene iungatur incendium. Cherubin quoq; id est angelorum presidium arcendis spiritibus malis super romphee flagrantiā ordinatum est·ut homines flamme·angelos vero malos angeli boni submoueāt·ne cui carni vel spiritui transgressionis aditus paradisi pateat.   India vocata ab indo flumine· quo ex parte occidentali clauditur. Haec a meridiano mari porrecta vsq; ad ortum solis· & a septentrione vsq;ad montem caucasum perue/ nit·habens gentes multas & oppida· insulam quoq; taprobane gemmis & elephantibus refertam. Crisam & argiram auro ar/ gentoq; fecundas·vtilem quoq; arboribus foliis nunqm caren tibus. Habet & flumina gangen & nidan & idaspen illustran tes in dos. Terra indie fauonio spiritu saluberrima. In anno bis

FIGURE 3. (a) A conventional T-O map from an early printed edition of Isidore of Seville, with the three known continents of Asia, Europe, and Africa labeled with the names of the three sons of Noah; the ocean as a circle surrounding the three land masses; and the "Great Sea or Mediterranean" forming the T at center. Isidore of Seville, *Etymologiae* (Augsburg: G. Zainer, 1472). By permission of the Library of Congress, Washington, D.C.; (b) Modern schematic of the illustration, courtesy of Yasin Akbari.

various parts of the world. They establish centers and peripheries as well as relationships between locations. At times, they even register flux and ambiguity regarding the location of a particular place: unsurprisingly, the places that are most variously located on maps and in prose geographies are generally located at the periphery of the known world. Perhaps the most variable of these is Ethiopia, sometimes placed on the continent of Africa and sometimes on that of Asia. Ethiopia is distinguished, the encyclopedists write, by the dark skin of its people, burned black—as Bartholomaeus Anglicus tells us—by the heat of the sun, "which rosteth and tosteth [t]ham."[17] The encyclopedists vary, however, in deciding where to locate these people who live

---

17. Bartholomaeus Anglicus, *De proprietatibus rerum* 15.52; quoted from the late fourteenth-century translation by Trevisa, *On the Properties of Things*, 2:754. Subsequent citations are in the text by page and chapter number.

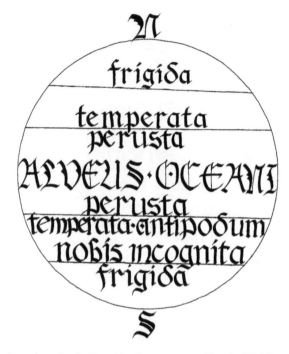

FIGURE 4. Modern schematic of a Macrobian five-zone map, with polar "frigid" zones at top and bottom, "temperate" zones in the northern and southern hemispheres, and an equatorial zone that is "burned by the sun" (*perusta*). The band of the "ocean bed" separates the northern and southern temperate zones. After Macrobius, *Somnium Scipionis* (Venice: s.n., 1492), fol. 22r. Courtesy of Yasin Akbari.

under the influence of the sun: should they be placed in Africa, near those regions which are (as the map rubrics state) "unknown to us due to the heat of the sun"? Or should they be placed in Asia, near the region labeled "regio solis," the region of the sun? The shifting position of Ethiopia is coupled with changes in the depiction of India, which in both maps and prose geographies grew in importance and in the detail of its description. As we will see in chapter 2, India increasingly became the center of attention for the late medieval geographer, replacing other traditionally central locations such as Jerusalem and the Earthly Paradise.

In Pierre d'Ailly's *Imago Mundi,* the comparatively brief treatment of India found in the works of earlier encyclopedists such as Isidore of Seville and Bartholomaeus Anglicus gives way to an elaborate description of the land that includes an account of the marvelous races, based on that found in Pliny's *Natural History* as well as the elaborations introduced in *The Book of John Mandeville.* The first indication that d'Ailly will give India special prominence appears at the outset, when he begins his description of Asia not with the rivers of Paradise, as is conventional, but with India itself. D'Ailly begins his account soberly enough by dividing the territory of India into three parts, and noting that "India is enormously large."[18] (Columbus underlines this sentence.) He goes on to state that it is possible to get there by traveling west, since the regions of Spain farthest west should, based on the principles of geometry, be proximate to the regions of India farthest east. (Needless to say, Columbus underlines this part too.) Yet d'Ailly goes on to devote another whole chapter to India, focusing now on "The Marvels of India" (chap. 16, "De mirabilius Indie"). Significantly, it is in the midst of his account of India that d'Ailly takes up the question of where the center of the world is actually located. Following Roger Bacon, d'Ailly states that the center of the world can be located geometrically, in a town called "Arym": "It is this town of Arym that the mathematicians place at the center of the equatorial habitat. This town is at an equal distance from the east, the west, the north, and the south. It is therefore false to place Jerusalem at the center of the earth, as some do based on the Psalmist's words that say that the salvation of man is located in the middle of the world."[19] This is a long way from the sacred geography of the mappamundi, where Jerusalem's centrality is less about mapping the world accurately than about mapping it faithfully.

Pierre d'Ailly goes on to amplify the importance of India even more, displacing not only Jerusalem but even the Earthly Paradise itself. His description of the rivers of Eden leads smoothly into an account of the watercourses of India, for the river Phison named in Genesis ("Pishon," Gen. 2:11), says d'Ailly, is really the Ganges. The whole first section of his chapter entitled "On the rivers of Paradise" (chap. 56, "De fluviis Paradisi") focuses on the marvels located on the banks of the Ganges, while the following chapter describes "The other rivers of Asia" (chap. 57, "De aliis fluminibus asie") beginning with the Indus, the second of the two rivers that mark the borders of India. In its emphasis on the importance of India and in its reliance on mathematical and geometrical techniques to determine the shape of the earth, Pierre d'Ailly's *Imago Mundi* marks a pivotal moment in the transition from medieval to early modern ways of ordering the world. He both dangles the lure of the marvels and riches of the Orient and tells the tantalized explorer

---

18. "Hec India valde magna est" (d'Ailly, *Imago Mundi,* chap. 15 ["De partibus Asie et primo de India"], in Buron 1:258–63, quotation from 260).

19. "Et hec est civitas Arym quam ponunt mathematici in medio habitationis sub equinoxiali. Et dista[n]t equaliter ab oriente et occidente septentrione et meridie. Unde patet falsitas cuiusdam vulgaris opinionis ponentis Hierusalem in medio terre iuxta illus psalmi operatus est salutem in medio terre" (d'Ailly, *Imago Mundi,* chap. 15, 1:262). Cf. Psalm 73:12.

how to get there, traveling to the utmost reaches of the West to discover the East.

As modern readers, we have come a long way from the simplistic belief that the medieval world model outlined in the mappamundi gave way, in a kind of cartographic Renaissance, to the Early Modern portulan-based map, with its northern orientation and its coordinates designed to facilitate the actual processes of exploration and navigation.[20] If the example of Pierre d'Ailly's *Imago Mundi* does not demonstrate this sufficiently, we have only to look at the work of Patrick Gautier Dalché, whose work on fifteenth-century geography illustrates vividly the extent to which the divide between the "medieval" mappamundi and the "modern" north-oriented map is more imagined than real. He argues that the crucial shift lies not in the image of the world presented on these maps but on the changing perspective of the maps' readers, and the increasingly pragmatic use made of them.[21] Several late medieval maps show features of the modern map, while still essentially holding to the framework of the mappamundi. Correspondingly, many maps produced during the early modern period, reflecting new discoveries and using Ptolemaic cartographic methods, retain some features of the symbolic worldview of the mappamundi. For example, the world map printed in the 1582 edition of Heinrich Bünting's *Itinerarium Sacrae Scripturae* includes "modern" features such as a northern orientation and a rubric designating "America, The New World"; it also includes, on the other hand, the three traditional continents of the mappamundi arranged in the form of a three-petaled flower, with Jerusalem as the center of the bloom (figure 1). The simplistic schematic of the T-O map continued to be reproduced well into the age of the printed book, as in copies of Isidore's *Etymologies* (figure 3).[22] The vision of the tripartite nature of the world also persisted more subtly, as in the world map found in the *Nuremberg Chronicle* (1493), which shows Noah's three sons examining a Ptolomaic world map in order to determine how best to divide up the world among themselves (figure 5).

Having used Pierre d'Ailly's *Imago Mundi* to provide a synoptic overview of the various schemas used during the Middle Ages to divide the world, I now turn to a closer examination of the parts of the world as they were presented both on pictorial maps and in discursive geographical texts. Such

---

20. On the "side by side" existence of the *mappaemundi* and portolan charts, see Woodward, "Medieval *Mappaemundi*," esp. 292, 314–15.

21. Gautier Dalché, "Histoire du regard," 100–103.

22. On the inclusion of T-O maps in manuscripts and early printings of Isidore, see Woodward, "Medieval *Mappaemundi*," 286–370.

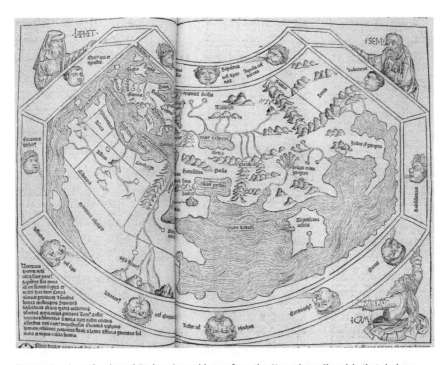

FIGURE 5. A north-oriented Ptolemaic world map from the *Nuremberg Chronicle* that, in keeping with the east-oriented Isidorean model, features the three sons of Noah: Japheth looks down on Europe and Shem on Asia, while Ham looks upward at Africa. Hartmann Schedel, *Nuremberg Chronicle* (Nuremberg: Anton Koberger, 1493), fol. 12v–13r. By permission of Lawrence University Library and Beloit College (see http://www.beloit.edu/nuremberg).

text divide the world simultaneously into three parts and into four—that is, the three known continents of Asia, Africa, and Europe, frequently associated with the three sons of Noah, and the four cardinal directions. The variety of ways in which the world could be anatomized played no small part in the development of Orientalism, because the nature of the Orient (and that of more or less eastern regions) was always contingent on the larger schema of which it was part. The binary distinction between East and West so common in modern discourse is never found on medieval maps, and only very rarely in medieval texts. These unusual cases include Fulcher of Chartres' chronicle of the First Crusade and Otto of Freising's *History of Two Cities,* both of which draw upon the notion of *translatio imperii* as presented in the *Seven Books of History against the Pagans* written by Orosius in the fifth century. Ironically, Orosius' own symbolic geography is not binary, but quadripartite: he divides up world history into four periods of domination by four different empires, located in the east, north, south, and west. Although the overall trajectory of empire is from east to west, as the mantle of power migrates from Babylon to Rome, imperial might rests temporarily in Macedonia and Carthage: Orosius states that "in the North and the South they held, for a brief time, the roles of guardian and protector."[23] The "tripertita orbus" (tripartite world), as Orosius calls it in the introduction to his chronicle, was by far the most common schema used to divide up the world, for it aligned the geographical division of the three known continents retained from antiquity with the biblical narrative of the repopulation of the earth by the three sons of Noah after the Flood. The quadripartite schema was used either separately or in conjunction with the three-part model in order to integrate principles of natural philosophy with the genealogical narrative embedded in the tripartite map.

The alternative ways in which one might divide the world (into three or four parts) is most significant for the dynamic sense of process that it created. On the one hand, the cardinal directions, a manifestation of the quadripartite system of four humors, four elements, and four seasons, generated a highly concentrated, essential notion of the Orient that could be sharply contrasted with the other three cardinal points. On the other hand, the continents could be loosely associated with the cardinal directions (Africa in the south-west, Europe in the north-west), but any simple equivalence was completely de-railed by the tremendous discrepancy in size between those two parts of the world and Asia, which encompassed the entire eastern region, extending from north to south. The tension produced between these very different modes of categorizing the East played an important role in the early development of Orientalist discourse; this tension was exacerbated by the association of the three sons of Noah with the three continents, as the migration of their descendents, chronicled in Genesis, complicated any simplistic effort to align genealogical descent with geographical region.

This alignment of the sons of Noah with the three continents, common from the seventh century onward, laid the foundations for a subsequent, more fully articulated relationship between physical geography and human geography, as theories of the relationship of climate to national properties became increasingly dominant. As we see below, medieval encyclopedists such as Bartholomaeus Anglicus played a major role in disseminating the view that qualities of a given nation were determined by climate; such views

---

23. "[A] meridie ac septentrione breuibus uicibus partes tutoris curatorisque tenuisse." Orosius, *Historiarum adversum paganos libri vii,* 3:17 (7.2.4). Translations are adapted from Arnaud-Lindet's very literal Modern French translation; a more idiomatic English translation can be found in Orosius, *Seven Books of History against the Pagans,* trans. Deferrari. For a more detailed exposition of Orosius' symbolic geography and its adaptation by twelfth-century chroniclers, see Akbari, "Alexander in the Orient," 105–26.

were further reinforced in astronomical texts that claimed that heavenly bodies also dictated national qualities. For example, the fourteenth-century astronomer John Ashenden adapted the schema of Abu Ma'shar (known to Ashenden via Latin translation) which aligned nations with heavenly bodies, inserting northern European nations (including his own homeland of England) to replace those listed in his source text. Like his near contemporary John Mandeville, Ashenden explains the propensity of his countrymen to wander by noting that England is under the influence of the moon.[24] Thus, by the late fourteenth century, national properties were thought to be dictated not only by the relative heat and cold of one's climate, but also by the nature of the land and surrounding sea, as well as by the astronomical bodies that circled the earth. Conceptions of the Orient—and of its mirror image, the West—were developed in tandem with this emergent, premodern conception of national identity, grounded in the relationship of human geography to physical geography. Moreover, the cartographic shift that took place at the end of this period, as world maps came to be oriented not to the east but to the north, participates in this new vision of the place of the individual in the world: by the mid-fifteenth century, the fixed point of Jerusalem had given way to the wandering perspective of the traveler's eye.

Mappaemundi depict the world as simultaneously whole and divided. It is whole because the known world is linked genealogically, due to mankind's common descent from Shem, Ham, and Japheth, whose names appear on world maps next to or even in place of the names of the three continents (figure 3).[25] At the same time, however, these sons of Noah epitomize the division of mankind into separate lineages following the Great Flood, a diffusion of humanity extended by the diaspora following the destruction of the Tower of Babel. In addition, the world depicted on the mappamundi is divided in another sense as well, being separated not only into three parts (the three known continents) but also into four: that is, the cardinal directions. *Oriens,* usually located at the top of the map, designates the place where the sun rises; *occidens,* where it sets; *septentrio,* the location of the north star; and *meridies,* the area closest to the equator. The primacy of the Orient on

---

24. Ashenden, *Summa judicialis de accidentibus mundi* tr. 1, dist. 8, cap. 1, in Eschuid, *Summa astrologiae judicialis,* fol. 42r; on the place of England in the astrological schemata of John Ashenden, John Mandeville, Bartholomaeus Anglicus, and Robertus Anglicus, see Akbari, "Diversity of Mankind," 156–76, esp. 162–63. For an extended study of Ashenden's life and work, see Snedegar, "John Ashenden and the *Scientia Astrorum Mertonensis.*"

25. Williams notes that this convention first appears in Isidoran world maps of the ninth century (13). Williams, "Isidore, Orosius and the Beatus Map," 7–32.

these maps is illustrated not only by their eastern "orientation," but by the illustration of the Garden of Eden frequently found at the top of the map, signaling the location of the now forbidden Earthly Paradise (figure 6).[26] Moreover, the primacy of the Oriental continent of Asia is reflected in the positioning of Jerusalem, which is often depicted prominently at or near the center of the mappamundi.

On medieval maps, the parts of the world are maintained in an orderly relation both by the stable center and by the equally fixed periphery: not the geographical features located at the margins of the world, which are often left enigmatic, but the natural climatic phenomena of the winds, which signify the elemental properties of the cardinal directions. In her study of medieval wind diagrams which, like the mappaemundi, have an eastern orientation, Barbara Obrist shows that "the main role of the cardinal winds in the medieval view was to contribute to the coherence and stability of the universe."[27] The world depicted on the mappaemundi is similarly ordered by its boundaries, marked by the four cardinal directions. The four-fold division of the earth has biblical as well as cosmological foundations: in Revelation 7:1, John relates that he "saw four angels standing on the four corners of the earth, holding the four winds of the earth." This four-fold geographical schema found its way into the medieval encyclopedic tradition as well. The natural universe was seen as fundamentally quadripartite: matter was divided into the four elements, time into the four seasons, while human health was regulated by the balance of the four bodily humors. Hrabanus Maurus bases the account of the world in his *De universo* on this four-fold schema, stating that there are four cardinal points within which the whole circle of the earth is contained. Hrabanus immediately adds that the earth can, moreover, be divided into three parts (Asia, Europe, and Africa) and also into two (Orient and Occident). Yet Hrabanus Maurus, like the other encyclopedists, fits the three continents into the four cardinal directions only awkwardly: Asia is said to extend from the south along the east as far as the north; Europe from the north along the west; Africa from the west as far as the south.[28] The uneven distribution of the three continents into the four corners of the earth is heightened in medieval accounts of the population of the continents by the sons of Noah, whose dispersal is similarly unequal.

---

26. Woodward, "Medieval *Mappaemundi*," 286–370; citation from 337.

27. Obrist, "Wind Diagrams," 84.

28. Hrabanus Maurus, *De universo* 12.2 (PL 111, cols. 9–614), col. 339B (subsequently cited in the text). Compare Isidore, *Etym.* 14.2.2 and Bartholomaeus Anglicus, *De prop. rer.* 15.1. On the place of the *De universo* in the encyclopedic tradition, see Heyse, *"De rerum naturis."*

Figure 6. Psalter map of the world, with Jerusalem at the center, East at the top, and the rivers of Eden extending downward. © World map, Psalter Map Manuscript (after 1262), London, British Library Additional 28681, fol. 9. All rights reserved.

As Benjamin Braude points out, the association of each of the three sons of Noah with each of the three known continents has been far from consistent. The assumption that Shem is to be invariably associated with Asia, Ham with Africa, and Japheth with Europe has so influenced modern readings of medieval texts that in at least one case, the readings of an otherwise authoritative manuscript of *The Book of John Mandeville* have been wrongly amended to associate the sons with their "proper" continents.[29] Braude rightly asserts that "the medieval understanding did not simply and consistently allot Africa to Ham, Asia to Shem, and Europe to Japhet."[30] Yet, as Braude himself acknowledges, many medieval texts do baldly assert the standard distribution of the three continents among the sons of Noah,[31] and, as we have seen, some medieval maps use the names of the sons interchangeably with the names of the continents (figure 3). Even as a stable one-to-one correspondence between the sons of Noah and the continents is asserted (as in the mappaemundi and general prefatory statements by the encyclopedists), more nuanced accounts of the sons' migration (as in the ninth book of Isidore's *Etymologies*) emphasize the flux and process essential to the development of nations.

The essentializing tendency evident in the one-to-one correspondence of the sons of Noah to the continents also appears in the association of one of the sons, Ham, with one of the cardinal directions, and the consequent association of his brothers with different climates. The association of Ham with heat goes back at least to Jerome: "Ham, id est callidus."[32] His etymological essentializing of Ham is repeated throughout the patristic and encyclopedic traditions. Hrabanus Maurus follows Augustine in explaining the allegorical significance of the etymology: the heat associated with Ham represents "the primordial passions of the Jews and heretics, which disturbs the peace of the holy."[33] Ham's progeny can be understood allegorically, as Hrabanus does, or literally, as in Isidore's account of the predominant distribution of Ham's offspring in the southern continent of Africa.[34] The association of Noah's other sons with other climatic conditions follows from the association of Ham with the heat of the south. Isidore identifies the regions by Japheth as

---

29. Braude, "The Sons of Noah," 103–42; citation from 116–20.

30. Ibid., 114.

31. See, for example, Vincent of Beauvais, 1.62; Bartholomaeus Anglicus, 15.1.

32. Jerome, *Liber de nominibus hebraicis* (PL 23, cols. 815–904), col. 821; echoed in Hrabanus Maurus, *Commentariorum in Genesim* 2.6 (PL 107, cols. 439–670), col. 513C.

33. Hrabanus Maurus, *Genesis* 2.9, col. 526A; cf. Augustine, *City of God* 16.2, 498–99.

34. Isidore states that three of the four sons of Ham gave rise to the nations of Ethiopia, Egypt, and Libya. The fourth, Canaan, gave rise not only to the "Afri," but also to the (Asian) Phoenicians and Canaanites (9.2.10–12).

not simply the northern continent, Europe, but the northern regions of Asia (14.3.31).[35] The offspring of Shem are not identified in terms of climate due to the much grander scale of his land allotment: his patrimony, Asia, includes both northern and southern lands.

In view of his dominant role among the sons of Noah—first-born, receiving the first fruits of the blessing of Noah (Gen. 9:26)—it is appropriate that Shem is heir to the greatest portion of the world. Bartholomaeus Anglicus emphasizes the primacy of Shem by immediately following his explanation of how each of the three sons of Noah was heir to each of the three continents with a brief account of Asia, Shem's inheritance; all the nations of the world (and the other two continents) follow, "sequendo ordinem alphabeti" (15.1, 15.2). Bartholomaeus' ordering principle gives prominence only to Asia, rather than to each of the three continents. Both Isidore, in book 14 of the *Etymologies*, and Vincent of Beauvais, in his *Speculum historiale*, treat the nations of Asia, Europe, and Africa in three separate groups, placing Asia first. For Bartholomaeus, however, Asia serves as a point of orientation according to which all other locations are ordered: Shem's portion is the greatest both in terms of size and in terms of centrality. In his twelfth-century commentary on the Pentateuch, Hugh of Saint Victor follows Isidore in assigning the sons of Japheth "the northern part of Asia and all of Europe," and the sons of Ham "the southern part of Asia and all of Africa." Shem's sons, by contrast, inherit the middle ground: "Medium autem Asiae, quae major est quam Europa et Africa, filii Sem possederunt."[36] For Hugh, Asia is "middle" in the sense that it is centrally located: it is most desirable, and is predominant in terms of size.

In Bartholomaeus Anglicus' thirteenth-century account of the division of the continents among the sons of Noah, however, the middle ground comes to seem less desirable. At the end of his chapter on "Europa," Bartholomaeus compares the three types of peoples who inhabit the known world. Following Isidore (*Etym.* 9.2.105), he states that the men of Africa are adversely affected by the heat of the sun, which discolors their bodies and weakens their spirit:

[T]he sonne abideth longe over the Affers, men of Affrica, and brennen and wasten humours and maken ham short of body, blacke of face,

---

35. Cf. Hrabanus Maurus, who states that Japheth's offspring are "Aquilonis partem habitant" (*Genesis* 2.10, col. 526D).

36. Hugh of Saint Victor, *Adnotationes elucidatoriae in Pentateuchon* (PL 175, cols. 29–86), col. 49A.

with crispe here. And for here spirites passe oute atte pores that ben
open, so they be more cowardes of herte.

An the cuntrarye is of men of the northe londe: for coldenes that
is withoute stoppeth the pores and breedeth humours of the bodye
maketh men more ful and huge; and coolde that is modir of whitnesse
maketh hem the more white in face and in skynne, and vapoures and
spirites ben ysmyten inwarde and maken hatter withinne and so the
more bolde and hardy. An the men of Asia ben meneliche disposed in
that, and here firste londe is by eeste.[37]

This passage is remarkable in a number of respects, not least because it rede-
fines the middle ground of Asia in a pejorative sense. The men of Asia are
"meneliche disposed," or, in Bartholomaeus' original Latin, "mediocriter."
The heat of southern men is expressed outwardly, leaving them "cowardes of
herte"; the heat of northern men is expressed inwardly, making them "bolde
and hardy." The visible signs of cowardice and boldness are dark skin and
white skin, for the heat of the sun makes men "blacke of face," while coldness
is the "modir of whitness."

In his account of the extremes of heat and cold and their visible manifestations in men, Bartholomaeus follows Isidore closely. His account differs, however, from that of the seventh-century bishop in the context within which
those extremes are placed: specifically, the way in which the white men of the
north and the dark men of the south are located relative to the encyclopedist's own homeland. This difference can be appreciated only in the context
of each encyclopedist's method of ordering his work. In keeping with his
method of etymological exegesis, Isidore emphasizes the interrelation of the
development of languages and the growth of nations, taking these as his dual
theme in the ninth book of the *Etymologies*. Isidore treats geography separately in the fourteenth book, though he alludes there as well to the names of
the sons of Noah and their descendants in explaining the etymological origin
of place names. The thirteenth-century encyclopedist Vincent of Beauvais
similarly conflates the origin of languages and the origin of peoples; his inno-
vations relative to Isidore take place on the level of content rather than form.
Vincent abbreviates, integrating into a single book the account of peoples
and languages and the world geography treated by Isidore separately in books
nine and fourteen of the *Etymologies*. Bartholomaeus' treatment of the material, by contrast, is more innovative: he omits the focus on the development

---

37. Bartholomaeus Anglicus, *De proprietatibus rerum* 15.50; trans. Trevisa, 752–53.

of languages central to Isidore's account. Instead, Bartholomaeus emphasizes the role of geography in generating national identity.

Isidore had stated that "nations grow out of languages, not languages out of nations." For Bartholomaeus, language is not involved at all: instead, nations grow out of the soil they are planted in. That is, for Isidore, the diversity of languages comes first; the migration of peoples follows; finally, the physical qualities of a nation are altered by the climate its members inhabit. For Bartholomaeus, however, climate is the only factor that determines the characteristics of a nation. Yet the most important difference between Isidore's and Bartholomaeus' accounts of the effect of climate upon nations can be found in the context in which each encyclopedist embeds the comparison of northerners and southerners. In his account of the white-complected Gauls and the dark-skinned Mauritanians, Bartholomaeus follows Isidore closely. Gaul has its name due to the "whittenes of men. For *Gallia* is grew [Greek] and is to menynge 'melke.'" Galicia is similarly named after the "wytnes of men, for they ben more wyte than men of the othere cuntreis of Spayne" (15.66; p. 763). Just as the Gauls are named on account of their milky white skin, so the Mauritanians are named after their black skin: "Mauritania hath that name of the colour of men, as it were to menynge 'blacke.' For as Fransshe men ben yclepede Galli and han that name of whitnes of men, so men of this londe ben yclepede Maury and han that name of blacke colour" (15.93; p. 780). These etymologies are based on Isidore (9.2.104, 14.4.25; 9.2.122, 14.5.10), and Bartholomaeus explicitly cites the ninth book of the *Etymologies* in explaining how the qualities of the people of a nation are determined by its climate: "For by the dyversite of hevene, face and colour of men and hertes and witte and quantite of bodyes ben dyvers. Therefore Rome gendreth hevy men, Frece lit men, Affrica gyleful men, and Fraunce kyndeliche fers men and sharpe of witte" (15.67, p. 763; cf. Isidore 9.2.105). Bartholomaeus expands upon Isidore's account of the effect of the climate of a land on the physical traits of its inhabitants, as when he describes how the Ethiopians are darkened by the sun; his fourteenth-century translator, Trevisa, in one of his relatively few departures from literal translation, amplifies this aspect even further, stating that the sun "rosteth and tosteth ham [them]" (15.52; p. 754).[38]

Of the several significant differences that separate Bartholomaeus from Isidore, one of the most striking is the way in which each encyclopedist posits his points of reference: for both, these points of reference include, first, the

---

38. On the consistently literal fidelity of Trevisa's translation, see Greetham, "Fabulous Geography," 261.

rising sun and, second, his own homeland. The way in which each positions these points of reference, however, is strikingly different. Unlike Bartholomaeus, Isidore describes the geography of the world as though he were following the contours of a map: he enumerates the lands of Asia, beginning in the farthest east with Paradise (14.3.2), India (14.3.5), and Parthia (14.3.8), in that order. His account of Asia finishes up in the north-east, and resumes with Europe, beginning with Scythia (14.4.3) in the easternmost part of Europe and ending with Spain (14.4.28). An account of Africa follows, moving from Egypt to the farthest regions, "unknown to us due to the heat of the sun" (14.5.17). In Isidore's descriptive geography, lands are consistently located relative to their proximity to the sun. This is seen both in the descriptions of the peoples, variously disposed both physically and mentally depending on their climate, and in the description of where the lands are to be found. The people in the farthest north are least marked by the heat of the sun, while those farthest south are most marked: "Ethiopia has its name from the color of the people, who are scorched by being so near to the sun" (14.5.14). The sun serves as an ordering principle that allows the encyclopedist to differentiate between peoples and between disparate territories. Isidore's geography is schematized according to the principle of the sun. He begins with Paradise, located in "Oriens" itself, where the sun rises; India is placed near it, enclosed on the west by the river Indus (14.3.5); Parthia extends from India as far as Mesopotamia (14.3.8), and so on. The area farthest east is defined as the land most proximate to the sun (Asia is "ab Oriente ortu solis" [14.3.1]), but so is the area farthest south: Africa is said to have its name from "*apricam,* that is, open to the sky and the sun, and without any bone-chilling cold" ("sine horrore frigoris" [14.5.2]). Ethiopia, located "circa solis ardorem" (14.5.3), is said to have two parts, one nearer Mauritania, one located "circa solis Ortum" (14.5.16), that is, "toward the East" or "toward the rising of the sun." That further Ethiopia is "exusta solis ardoribus" (14.5.17), scorched by the heat of the sun; in Trevisa's translation of Bartholomaeus Anglicus, this region is said to be located "aens the cours of the sunne, in the southe" (15.52; p. 754). This land is doubly marked by the effects of the sun, by its southern exposure as well as its eastern orientation.

For Isidore, the sun is a temporal reference point, with the "ortu solis" marked at both the beginning and the end of his geographical survey: first, in the easternmost region of Asia, and finally in the extreme south-eastern reaches of Ethiopia located "circa solis Ortum" (14.5.16), beyond which lie only lands "unknown to us due to the heat of the sun" (14.5.17). Such ordering gives Isidore's world geography a circular structure patterned about the location of the sun; simultaneously, however, it defines the location of the sun in a double way. The Orient, location of the rising sun (*sol oriens*), is the farthest east; yet the region most visibly scorched, both in its desert land and in the blackened faces of its people, is the southern extreme of Africa. The former region of the sun is the place of origin not only for the sun but also for humanity itself, because Eden, mankind's ancient cradle, is located there. The latter region of the sun is a place currently unknown, knowledge of which lies at some unspecified point in the future, if at all: the "fabled Antipodes," as Isidore calls them (14.5.17), await exploration. Yet the distant lands of Africa, for Isidore, are not so distant as they may at first seem. Isidore concludes his survey of the three known continents with a summary: "Mauritania is the nearest to Spain, then Numidia, then the area of Carthage, after that we find Getulia, and thereafter Ethiopia, that place scorched by the heat of the sun" (14.5.17). The dark-skinned Mauritanians, for the Spanish bishop, lie just to the south; the fair-skinned Gauls and Galicians, just to the north. In this way, Isidore's own homeland of Spain appears as a kind of microcosm of the great world all around.

Bartholomaeus Anglicus' adaptation of Isidore's schema departs from his model in several respects. Bartholomaeus' alphabetical ordering, while facilitating the use of his encyclopedia as a reference tool,[39] omits the map-like survey of the world employed by Isidore and followed by Vincent of Beauvais.[40] Bartholomaeus does not move smoothly from east to north and down into the south; instead, his alphabetical geography skips about, ranging from Aragon to Babylon to Crete. Significantly, where Isidore had discussed the islands of the world in a separate section, Bartholomaeus integrates them into his alphabetical schema, allowing him to give the same prominence to "Anglia" that he does to, for example, "Italia" or even "Europa" itself. He notes Isidore's etymology of "Anglia" as "*angulo* 'a corner' as it were a londe ysette in the eends or a cornere of the worlde" (15.14; p. 733). But, says Bartholomaeus, the fabulous etymology of Angles/angels in the story of Pope Gregory more accurately reveals the extraordinary quality of the nation. If it is a corner, says Bartholomaeus, "Inglonde is a stronge londe and sterne and the plenteuouseste corner of the world" (15.14; p. 734). For Isidore, the extremes of heat and cold function as an ordering principle that does not, however, geographically alienate those lands from his own homeland: the white-skinned Galicians inhabit one portion of Spain, while the black-skinned Mauritanians inhabit the southern land nearest Spain. Isidore's own space is a mean, but

---

39. On the independent use of book 15 of the *De proprietatibus rerum*, see ibid., 188.

40. See also Hugh of Saint Victor's *Descriptio mappe mundi,* which, Gautier Dalché has argued, follows very closely a particular *mappamundi*. See *La Descriptio mappe mundi de Hugues de Saint-Victor.*

one surrounded closely by climactic extremes, with Spain being a kind of microcosm that enfolds within it the diversity of the earth.

Like Isidore, Bartholomaeus positions his own homeland as a secondary point of reference in his schema of the earth: while England is just a little "corner" of the earth, it is nonetheless a fountain of abundance and wealth. Unlike Isidore, however, Bartholomaeus does not depict a homeland characterized by climatic extremes. Instead, Bartholomaeus emphasizes the ways in which climatic extremes endow the various regions of the world with distinct features, imbuing the people with specific national features, and the broader regions with strongly defined qualities. In his chapter on "Europa," Bartholomaeus suggests that Europe, not Asia, is the dominant continent, for its people are better formed by their native climate "thanne men of the cuntres and londes of Asia other of Affrica" (15.50; p. 752). The cold northern climate of Europe breeds men who are physically "more ful and huge" and, in spirit, "more bold and hardy" (15.50; p. 753). This development of a cold, northerly European identity marks a crucial point in the development of an Occident that mirrors the Orient. The northern chill produces white-complected men whose bodily heat, says Bartholomaeus, is turned inward to produce men who are "bold and hardy." Asian men, by contrast, are "meneliche disposed in that": they have some interior heat, some exterior, only moderate boldness, and are only moderately marked by the heat of the sun. Bartholomaeus' Asia is still central in that its people are "meneliche disposed"; yet the virtues of being in the "middle" are appropriated by the men of the north praised by Bartholomaeus. Asia is primary ("regio prima est"), but the Asians are "mediocriter."

In John Gower's *Confessio Amantis,* written during the last decades of the fourteenth century, a brief descriptive geography appears that is worth comparing to Bartholomaeus' depiction of the bold, white European men of the north. Gower declares that his geographical description is "after the forme of Mappemounde" (7.530)[41] and, accordingly, Gower follows the conventional tripartite division of Asia, Europe, and Africa, distributed among the three sons of Noah. As in the encyclopedias, Asia is the largest portion ("double as moche as othre two" [7.559]), and thus belongs by rights to the eldest son (7.557). The continent of Asia is, as usual, defined in terms of the sun, and—unusually—is defined as coterminous with the Orient itself: "Asie...lay to the Sonne / Upon the Marche of orient, / ... / And schortly for to speke it so, / Of Orient in general / Withinne his bounde Asie hath al" (7.554–55;

---

41. In volume 3 of *Complete Works of John Gower;* cited in the text.

572–74). The other continents are subsequently defined in terms of direction, the western continents of Europe and Africa:

> And thanne upon that other side
> Westward, as it fell thilke tyde,
> The brother which was hote Cham
> Upon his part Aufrique nam.
> Japhet Europe tho tok he,
> Thus parten thei the world on thre.
>
> (7.575–80)

So far, Gower's account is in keeping with the basic division of the world among the sons of Noah found in the encyclopedias. The world is in three parts, the continents; but it is also divided into two parts, as Augustine, Isidore, Hrabanus Maurus, Vincent of Beauvais, and Bartholomaeus Anglicus all declare. The two parts are, of course, Orient and Occident, occupied by Asia, on the one side, and Europe and Africa on the other. This two-part division of East and West is in tension with the competing binary opposition of frigid north and torrid south.

From Isidore's seventh-century *Etymologies* to the massive thirteenth-century compilations of Bartholomaeus Anglicus and Vincent of Beauvais, medieval encyclopedias disseminated a view of the world that held it to be composed of two symmetrical parts: northern Europe, inhabited by fair-skinned men, and southern Africa, inhabited by dark-skinned men. For Isidore, these diverse peoples are proximate to his own location in Spain, while for Bartholomaeus these peoples are more distant, and the northerly climate of Europe is explicitly stated to breed men who are more "bolde and hardy" due to their inwardly directed heat. Bartholomaeus thus claims that not the East but the north-west is the place of greatest potency, setting the stage for Gower's extraordinary recasting of the "forme of Mappemonde." Gower concludes his brief geography by evoking the two-part division of the world into East and West:

> Bot yit ther ben of londes fele
> In occident as for the chele,
> In orient as for the hete,
> Which of the poeple be forlete
> As lond desert that is unable,
> For it mai noght ben habitable.
>
> (7.581–86)

To a modern reader, it may not seem peculiar to associate the Orient with heat. But as we have seen, medieval encyclopedias universally describe the south in terms of the sun's heat, its people blackened and its earth scorched. While the encyclopedias naturally define the Orient in terms of the sun, the quality of heat is associated with the south rather than the east.

This pattern can be found, for example, in medieval allegory, both sacred and profane. One twelfth-century account of the north and south winds identifies the latter with "the throne of the Almighty," where "the flame of love" ("ardor") is found: "the south wind denotes the grace of the Holy Spirit...the warmth [Its] love" ("calor amor").[42] Similarly, the description of the Castle of Love in Andreas Capellanus' twelfth-century *Art of Courtly Love* includes an account of the moral character of the ladies at each of the four gates. Unsurprisingly, it is the ladies at the south gate who "always linger around the open door" and are receptive to love: "Those at the south, then, are those women who wish to love and do not reject worthy lovers; this is proper since, being all in the south, they are worthy to be illuminated by a ray from Love himself who lives in the east."[43] It is only in the fourteenth century, as seen here in Gower's account, that the Orient comes to be known as a place of overwhelming heat, understood in both a literal and a moral sense. By characterizing the Orient in terms of (formerly southern) heat, it becomes possible to characterize its opposite, the Occident, in terms of (formerly northern) cold. It is thus only during the late fourteenth century that something like the modern notion of a European "West" appears in literature: an Occident characterized by cold, and the external whiteness and internal fortitude born of it.

It is therefore unsurprising that modern readers have tended to read medieval texts in terms of the modern dichotomy of Orient and Occident.[44] This tendency is the result not only of the centrality of that dichotomy in more modern manifestations of Orientalism, but also of the participation of certain late medieval texts in the construction of a cold, dispassionate, northerly Occident. The formation of this Occident can be witnessed in Bartholomaeus Anglicus' comparison of the "bolde and hardy" white men of the north with the southern men, "blacke of face," who are "cowardes of herte"; in Gower's opposition of deserts found "in occident as for the chele, / In orient as for the hete"; and in Chaucer's contrast of the setting of the Squire's Tale with that of the Franklin's Tale. In the former Tale, the sun, "ful

42. Hugh of Fouilloy, *Medieval Book of Birds,* 138–39 (chap. 14).
43. Capellanus, *Art of Courtly Love,* 73–74 (fifth dialogue).
44. Chism, "Too Close for Comfort," 116–39, esp. 121; Lynch, "East Meets West," 547.

joly and cleer," causes "lusty . . . weder" (V.48, 52), while in the latter, the sun is "hewed lyk laton" and "shoon ful pale" (V.1245, 1249), coldly illuminating a world where fraternal exchange takes precedence over carnal desire. Throughout the *Canterbury Tales,* the reader is 'oriented' by the sun which, as it were, rises in the Squire's Tale, where the steamy "vapour" rising from the earth causes "the sonne to seme rody and brood" (V.394). The Oriental sun is reflected in those who inhabit its regions, so that the movement of "Phebus" is simultaneous with the movement of the "Tartre kyng" (V.263–67), while his daughter Canacee rises "As rody and bright as dooth the yonge sonne" (V.385). According to Bartholomaeus Anglicus, the people of the Orient are "disposed meneliche," characterized by neither of the extremes of hot and cold; in the Squire's Tale, however, the east rather than the south is the location of "lusty . . . weder" (V.52), where "dauncen lusty Venus children deere" (V.272). They are shaped by the heat of the sun.[45]

The development during the fourteenth century of an idea of the Occident that is the mirror image of the Orient is accompanied by a concomitant change in the figurative meaning of the cardinal directions. The north had long been associated with evil, based on the biblical tradition identifying it with the realm of Lucifer (Jeremiah 1:14, 6:1; Isaiah 14:13). In his twelfth-century *De naturis rerum,* Alexander Neckam explains the allegorical significance of the magnetic compass, which points to the North Pole:

> Sailors crossing the sea . . . put a needle above the lodestone; and the needle revolves until, after its motion has stopped, its point faces due north. So should a prelate guide his subjects in the sea of life, so that his reason may set them facing that north of which it is written, "From the North is all evil spread" [Jeremiah 1:14].[46]

With the increasing practical use of the magnetic compass during the thirteenth and fourteenth centuries, however, the cardinal direction north came to be representative not of the presence of evil, but of locatability. This shift is most clearly visible in the transition from mappaemundi to more modern-looking, north-oriented maps influenced by portolan charts. It would be an oversimplification to suggest that a linear progression from one kind of map to the other took place; as Friedman, among others, has pointed out,

---

45. On Orientalism and national identity in the Squire's Tale, see Akbari, "Orientation and Nation," 102–34.

46. *De naturis rerum* 2.98, 183. Translated in Smith, "Precursors to Peregrinus," 21–74; citation from 37.

conventional mappaemundi are "works of art of a didactic and cultural sort, rather than rigid and unsuccessful attempts to portray geographical features,"[47] while portolan-influenced maps function as practical guides to navigation. Yet the portolan-influenced map is, like the mappamundi (and, indeed, every map), also a symbolic image of the world. This symbolic value is evident in the ornate presentation copies of some portolan-influenced maps, where compass roses appear in which the arrow pointing north is richly embellished.[48] The shift from maps oriented toward the east to those oriented toward the north is therefore very meaningful. It illustrates a transition from a view of the world based on sacred geography, which tells you mankind's collective destination (Jerusalem), to a view of the world that tells you individually where you are, and hence enable you to choose where to go and how to get there. The transition from east to north thus marks a transition from the primacy of the sacred object to the primacy of the seeing subject.

✦ Defining the Center

Having outlined the parts of the world described on medieval world maps, including not only the three known continents but also the four cardinal directions, I turn now to the central point of the map, the anchor about which the parts were arranged. Especially after the beginning of the crusades in 1095, Jerusalem was often depicted at or near the center of the mappamundi.[49] On these maps, Jerusalem appears both as a point of origin and as a place of return, the objective of every assault on the Holy Land and the conjectured site of the Last Judgment.[50] In this context, it is interesting to note that the map of the Holy Land included in Matthew Paris' *Chronica majora* (ca. 1270) emphasizes the centrality not of Jerusalem, but of the last crusader stronghold of Acre (lost in 1291), signaling the imperative of conquest essential to the mappaemundi created during the Crusades.[51] The

47. Friedman, "Cultural Conflicts," 64–95; citation from 64.

48. See Woodward, "Medieval *Mappaemundi*," 315 and plate 17. Increasingly striking examples appear during the course of the fifteenth century; see Campbell, "Portolan Charts," 371–463; citation from 396.

49. Woodward, "Medieval *Mappaemundi*," 341–42.

50. More specifically, the Valley of Josaphat, based on Joel 3:12, identified after the fourth century with Cedron, located just outside the walls of Jerusalem. See *The Catholic Encyclopedia,* vol. 8, "Josaphat," 503; also J. Rivière, "Jugement," *Dictionnaire de Théologie Catholique,* vol. 8, part 2, col. 1721–1828, esp. col. 1819.

51. Woodward, "Medieval *Mappaemundi*," 341–42; noted in Iain Higgins, "Defining the Earth's Center," 29–53; citation from 49.

centrality of Jerusalem is repeatedly affirmed in the descriptive geographies of medieval encyclopedias. Isidore of Seville writes that Jerusalem is located at the center of the province of Judea, "quasi umbilicus regionis totius" (as if it were the navel of the whole region).[52] His assertion is based on biblical references to the city's position "in the middle of the earth" (Psalm 73:12; cf. Ezekiel 5:5), emphasized in the early fifth-century commentary on Ezekiel written by Jerome.[53] Isidore's statement is echoed by other encyclopedists, including (in the ninth century) Hrabanus Maurus and (in the thirteenth century) Vincent of Beauvais and Bartholomaeus Anglicus. Hrabanus Maurus amplifies Isidore's statement that Jerusalem is, as it were, the navel of the region of Judea, stating that it is the navel "of the region and of the whole earth" ("quasi umbilicus regionis et totius terrae" [12.4; 339C]). Vincent of Beauvais follows Isidore closely,[54] as does Bartholomaeus Anglicus: "In the myddel of this Judea is the cite of Jerusalem, as it were the navel of all the cuntrey and londe" (15.58; 772).

The identification of such a sacred center or *umbilicus* (literally, navel) is not uncommon. The ancient Greeks placed theirs at Delphi, the site of the sacred oracle, while Muslims since the lifetime of Muhammad have directed their daily prayers and annual pilgrimage toward the Ka'aba at Mecca. Other texts, however, establish a center without necessarily justifying its position in terms of sacrality: for example, some ancient maps place Rome at the geographical center of the world in order to affirm the city's symbolic role as the site of civic and political origins and the seat of imperial power.[55] Maps produced in the Islamic world similarly place Mecca at their center, illustrating its position as the site of the foundation of the first Muslim community. The placement of Mecca at the map's center has, in addition, a religious significance, marking its role as the spiritual focus or *qibla* of all Muslims' daily prayers as well as the annual *hajj* or pilgrimage.[56] Still other maps, produced both in the Islamic world and in western Europe, include the imaginary

52. Isidore, *Etymologies* 14.3.21, cited from *Isidori Hispalensis Episcopi Etymologiarum sive Originum Libri XX;* subsequently cited parenthetically in the text.

53. Jerome, *Commentariorum in Ezechielem* (PL 25), col. 52.

54. Vincent of Beauvais, *Speculum historiale* 1.67; cited from vol. 4 of *Speculum quadruplex sive Speculum maius,* 25.

55. On the appearance of Rome as a central point in ancient and some medieval world maps, see Woodward, "Medieval *Mappaemundi.*"

56. David A. King has written extensively on Mecca-centered cartography: see "Weltkarten zur Ermittlung der Richtung nach Mekka," 1:167–71 and 2:689–91; "Two Iranian World Maps," 1–20; "Islamische Weltkarten mit Mekka als Mittelpunkt," 93–107; and *World Maps for Finding the Direction to Mecca.* An overview of the subject, written at an earlier stage of King's research, can be found in King and Lorch, "Qibla Charts, Qibla Maps, and Related Instruments," 189–205.

city of Arym at their center.[57] Here, the fixed point functions primarily as a geometrical point of reference, facilitating the ordering of the world into its several climates and the accurate measurement of the world sphere. In each of these examples, the establishment of a central geographical point, whether pictorially on the map or verbally in the written text, does not serve as an end in itself. Instead, the fixed point serves as an anchor about which the parts of the world are arranged, deriving their significance from their distance from and relationship to the central point.

Some medieval texts, however, posit more than a single fixed point, moving from one center to another in a demonstration of the dynamic quality of symbolic geography. On world maps, this can be seen in the prominent position given to the Earthly Paradise: located in the extreme east, its rivers extend throughout the world, eternally linking the populated world to the now-forbidden Garden (figure 6). Its prominence on the map is rivaled, however, by the detailed depiction of Jerusalem at the center of the map. Both the site of mankind's physical birth (Eden) and spiritual rebirth (Jerusalem) qualify as focal points on the map, for both are sacred locations due to their status as not only sites of origin, but also sites of apocalyptic return. An even more elaborate use of multiple geographical focal points can be found in the shifting centers of *The Book of John Mandeville*. Although Jerusalem's centrality is an important theme in the opening sections of Mandeville's book, which at the outset follows a conventional pilgrim itinerary,[58] in the later sections India (particularly Prester John's Land) is presented as an attainable and desirable goal. It is the place where spiritual renewal can more aptly be sought, and where the adventurous traveler can expect to find both material wealth and spiritual gifts. Between Jerusalem and Prester John's Land appears another central point, one whose focal nature depends less upon geographical convention than upon the narrator's self-presentation as an Englishman traveling in strange lands. His conversation with the Sultan of Babylon, carried out in great secrecy in the ruler's private chamber, marks a transitional moment in which the familiar and the strange are uncannily interchanged. Finally, England itself appears as an additional central point in the course of Mandeville's elaborate account of the shape of the world and the way in which each territory has its counterpart at the other extreme of

---

57. On Arym-entered maps, see Woodward, "Medieval *Mappaemundi*"; King, "Qibla Charts"; Honigmann, *Die sieben Klimata.*

58. On Mandeville's Jerusalem and pilgrim itineraries, see Howard, *Writers and Pilgrims;* Yeager, "Remembering the Passion," and Yeager, *Jerusalem in Medieval Narrative.*

the globe. Prester John's Land, we discover, has its mirror image in the very island that Mandeville calls home.

The *Book* begins with the narrator's claim of first-hand experience: "Jeo Johan Maundeville chevaler...neez et norriz d'Engleterre de la ville de Seint Alban...et qe depuis ai esté outre mer par long temps, et ai veu et environé moint pais et mointes diverses provinces et mointes diverses regiouns et diverses isles...[dont] jeo parleray plus plenerement et diveseray ascune partie des choses qe y sont" (I, John Mandeville, knight...born and brought up in England, in the town of Saint Albans, and who since then have been overseas for a long time, and have seen and gone all around many lands, and many diverse provinces, and many diverse regions and diverse isles...[of which] I will speak more fully and describe some part of the things that are there [Prol.; 92–93]).[59] It is now known that this claim to have had such first-hand experience is false, as is, perhaps, the claim of English nationality.[60] The identity of the narrator in the text is very self-consciously fashioned: it is clearly important to the author that the narrator be identified by the reader as an Englishman. This is made evident not only in the *Book*'s opening lines but in the repeated references to specifically English things—to the barnacle geese who grow on trees found in the British Isles, to the thorn and yogh used in writing English. As has often been observed, these references could easily have been derived from written sources and in themselves constitute no proof of the writer's national origin.[61] They do demonstrate, however, the author's self-conscious determination to present himself as an Englishman, and his intention to address a community of Christian readers who also identify themselves as inhabitants of England.

The Book of John Mandeville features several scenes in which the character of western European Christendom is illustrated not just by direct description, but by its reflection in the mirror of alien cultures. These cultures may be proximate to the Christianity of Rome, as when Mandeville recounts the

---

59. *The Book of John Mandeville* is quoted here in the edition of the Insular version prepared by Deluz, *Jean de Mandeville,* with chapter and page number cited parenthetically in the text. Translations are my own.

60. Because the sources of *The Book of John Mandeville* include texts likely to have been found only in France during the mid-fourteenth century, Seymour has argued that the author could not have been an Englishman (Seymour, *Sir John Mandeville,* 1–64). As Deluz points out, however, this constitutes proof that the author prepared his book on the Continent, not proof of his national origin (Deluz, "Introduction," 7–14). Most recently, John Larner has suggested that *The Book of John Mandeville* may have been composed by Jan de Langhe; see "Plucking Hairs from the Great Cham's Beard," 133–55.

61. The barnacle geese are described in the *Topographia Hiberniae* of Gerald of Wales, *The History and Topography of Ireland,* 41–42.

exchange between the Orthodox Christians of Greece and the Roman pope, or far distant from the familiar spaces of Europe. The most striking of these moments of self-definition, in which the state of contemporary Christianity is reflected in the mirror of alien cultures, appears in the narrator's private audience in the chamber of the Sultan of Babylon.[62] In the course of his travels, the narrator of the *Book* tells us, he developed a close relationship to the Sultan: "Jeo le doy bien savoir qar jeo demorray soudeour ove luy en ses guerres grant piece de temps encontre les Bedoins" (I should know [his court] very well, for I stayed there with him a long time as a soldier in his wars against the Bedouins [chap. 6; 134]). The intimacy of 'John Mandeville' (the author's fictitious persona) and the Sultan of Babylon is a microcosm of the close relationship of Christianity and Islam as described in the *Book*. Here, Islam is not the polytheistic idolatry of the Saracens of the *chansons de geste* and their Middle English romance adaptations, where monstrous Saracens swear by their lord "Mahoun." Instead, in *The Book of John Mandeville,* Islam is a religion which so closely resembles Christianity that the English redactor of the Egerton version found it necessary to pause several times in the course of the description to point out differences: "This Christians do not believe," he interjects or, on a certain point of Islamic theology, "it is they that are wrong." His account of the Saracens and their belief concludes with a scene of remarkable intimacy in which the Sultan of Babylon sends his retainers out of the room and, in a private audience with the narrator, discusses the state of Western Christendom and the prospects for a Western victory in the Crusades. It is striking that, at this moment, when it seems that the narrator has penetrated into the center of the mysterious East, what he learns about is not the East, but the West.

This search for Western identity through the medium of the Islamic world appears in a number of medieval texts. A useful comparison can be made with the fourteenth-century Middle English *Siege of Melayne,* in which a pivotal scene is staged (as in *The Book of John Mandeville*) in the privacy of the Sultan's chamber. The depiction of Islam and of Muslims is venomous and parodic in the *Siege of Melayne,* in keeping with the practice of the *chansons de geste* and their Middle English adaptations, and is in this respect very different from the more even-handed, tolerant view of Islam presented in *The Book of John Mandeville.* Both texts share, however, a crucial scene staged in the chamber

---

62. Medieval texts frequently conflate the biblical Babylon, located in Mesopotamia, with Cairo, seat of the caliphate. Deluz notes that this results from the confusion of the name "Babylon" with the other name of Cairo, "Pi-Hapi-n-On" (the city of On, located on the Nile); see Deluz, *Merveilles,* 146n3.

of the Sultan in which the contest of Christianity and Islam is waged in microcosm. The Sultan, who has seized the city of Milan, has the Christian heroes Roland and Oliver taken to his private chamber ("sowdane chambir" [385])[63] in order to demonstrate the futility of the Christian faith: he orders that "one of theire goddis" (421) be brought to his chamber and burned. Its destruction, says the Sultan, will prove the impotence of the Christian God: if this image burns, "all other sett att noghte" (423). Predictably, the crucifix brought into the Sultan's chamber for this test does not burn; instead, its miraculous preservation provides the means for the escape of the Christian knights and, consequently, a Christian victory at the disputed city of Milan. A fire bursts out from the crucifix that blinds and paralyzes the Saracens present in the chamber, including the Sultan himself. Then, the Christian knights throw the immobilized Saracens into the fire: unlike the crucifix, they burn (469–72, 487–88). In both the *Siege of Melayne* and *The Book of John Mandeville,* the Sultan's chamber is the location where the conflict of Muslim and Christian, experienced on the broad stage of the Crusades, is enacted on a smaller, more intimate scale. The Sultan's chamber acts as a kind of crucible that yields evidence regarding the righteousness of the Christian effort to take Jerusalem.[64]

The encounter in the Sultan's chamber in *The Book of John Mandeville* is, as in the *Siege of Melayne,* a moment in which the superiority of Christianity is displayed. Yet, in each text, that superiority is displayed not in public but in private: not for a large, heterogeneous audience, but for a rigidly limited group and even, in Mandeville's *Book,* for an audience of just one.[65] In the Sultan's private audience with the narrator, intimacy and secrecy are paramount: "Il fist voider sa chambre de toutes maneres des gentz, sires et autres, pur ceo qil vouloit parler au moy au consil" (chap. 15; 278). [He made everyone else leave his chamber, both lords and others, because he wanted to speak with me privately.] One might imagine that the Sultan desires privacy so

---

63. Quotations from the *Siege of Melayne* are taken from *Six Middle English Romances* and are cited parenthetically in the text.

64. On the scene on the Sultan's chamber, see Akbari, "Incorporation in the *Siege of Melayne,*" 22–44, esp. 28–30.

65. The narrator of Mandeville's *Book* has previously prepared the reader to think of the Sultan's chamber as a private space by earlier describing how, when the Sultan sees a desirable woman, "homme la meigne baigner et vestir et asseiner noblement, et la noit homme la meigne en sa chambre" (someone takes her to be bathed and clothed and perfumed sumptuously, and at night someone takes her to his [i.e., the Sultan's] chamber [chap. 6; 139]). While one might reasonably suggest that the "chambre" in which the Sultan meets his paramours is different from the one in which he meets his valued retainers (and indeed, the modern translation paraphrases in order to make that distinction), the medieval texts use the same phrase to describe the room in each case.

that his Saracen lords will not be disheartened by the admission the Sultan makes to the narrator, that he knows "qe christiens regaigneront ceste terre quant ils serviront lour Dieu plus devotement" (that Christians will regain this land when they serve their God more devoutly). Yet, as the Sultan himself emphasizes, this is common knowledge among his people: we know this very well (bien de voir), we know it well by our prophecies (si savoms bien par noz prophecies) (chap. 15; 279). Instead, the privacy of the Sultan and the narrator serves a more subtle purpose, setting the stage for a spectacle of surprising intensity. When the two men are alone, the Sultan asks the narrator how Christians behave in their own countries. This seems to be a request for information, where the Sultan is asking the narrator, as a representative of the Christian West, for an account of lands that are unfamiliar to the eastern ruler. Instead it proves to be, like the comparable scene in the Sultan's chamber in the *Siege of Melayne,* a test. To Mandeville's answer that Christians conduct themselves at home "bien, Dieu Graciez" (very well, thanks to God), the Sultan answers curtly: "Et il me dit qe veraiment qe noun font" (And he said to me that, truly, it was not so) (chap. 15; 278). He goes on to tell the narrator precisely how Christians have fallen away from their first fidelity to God, and are instead drawn to gluttony, covetousness, and lechery. It is because of their sins, says the Sultan, that "ount ils perdu toute ceste terre qe nous tenoms" (they have lost all this land that we now hold) (chap. 15; 279).

When the narrator, amazed, asks the Sultan how he knows so much about the behavior of contemporary Christians, the Sultan explains that he sends out messengers, disguised as merchants, to Christian lands in order to gather information. As proof, the Sultan calls his lords back into the chamber to tell the narrator of their first-hand knowledge not only of the narrator's own homeland but also of "les autres païs de christieneté aussy bien qe s'ils fussent del païs" (other Christian lands as well as if they had been from those same countries). Finally, the Saracen lords (and the Sultan himself) demonstrate that they speak French perfectly, at which, says the narrator, "jeo me merveillay moult" (I marvelled greatly [chap. 15; 280]). In this complex scene, what begins as a request for information turns out to be a test designed to reveal the defects of Christian belief; so far, the scenario is similar to that in the *Siege of Melayne.* Yet, in Mandeville's *Book,* the defects of Christianity are not permanent, but temporary. What is superficially an indictment of Christianity is in fact only an indictment of remediable sinful behavior. The seeming indictment is instead an endorsement of Christianity and a promise that Christian victory, however far off, is inevitable. Finally, the scene concludes by at last offering the revelation of Oriental mystery that one might have expected to find in the intimate setting of the chamber of the Sultan of Babylon: disguised as "marchantz des pieres preciouses" (merchants of precious stones [chap. 15; 279]), the Sultan's spies circulate throughout Europe, clothed like Christian men and speaking good French. Paradoxically, this final moment, in which we expect at last to catch a glimpse of the heart of the enigmatic Orient, displays as if in a mirror the narrator's own identity. Earlier in the text, the narrator mentions that attendance upon the Sultan requires that one be dressed "en la guyse qe les Sarazines sont vestuz" (in the manner that the Saracens are clothed [chap. 6; 139]); presumably the narrator, accustomed to the Sultan's service, conforms to this requirement. Similarly, in the scene in the Sultan's chamber, when the lords and the Sultan himself begin to speak French, the narrator and the Sultan must presumably have been speaking what the *Book* calls "the Sarazine langage." From this point of view, the narrator standing in the Sultan's chamber, dressed in Saracen clothing and speaking the local tongue, appears to be the counterpart to the Sultan's spies roaming abroad in Europe. In the encounter with the Islamic world, as well as during the journey further abroad, knowledge of the East is simply the vehicle by means of which knowledge of the West is conveyed.

This cross-dressing of the narrator and the Sultan's spies illustrates how deceptive external appearances can be in distinguishing between Christians and Saracens. The account of Islamic theology that immediately precedes the audience with the Sultan illustrates, in addition, the porousness of the boundary separating Christianity and Islam. The account here, strikingly different from the typical representation of Muslims as polytheistic idolaters, emphasizes the congruence of the two religions. The detailed description of Islamic theology notes more similarities than differences, with the purpose of reinforcing the inevitability of the final victory of Christianity explicitly promised in the Sultan's chamber. "Et pur ceo q'ils vont si près de nostre foy sont ils de legier converty a christienne loy" (And because they come so near to our faith, they can easily be converted to the Christian law [chap. 15; 276]). He concludes by reiterating this proximity, stating that "ils ount plusours bons articles de nostre foy et de nostre creaunce, come bien qe ils n'aient loy parfaite et foy selonc christiens, et sont de legier convertyz" (they have many good articles of our faith and our belief even though they do not have the perfect law and faith as the Christians do and therefore they can easily be converted" [chap. 15; 277]). The suggestion that Muslims can be converted to Christianity is not an unusual one; what is far more remarkable is the observation that the porousness of the boundary separating Christianity and Islam makes it possible for conversion to operate in the other direction. The author of the *Book* is prepared to admit that some Christians convert, though not frequently, and only when no other choice seems possible: "Il avient sovent qe ascun christien devient sarazins ou par simplece ou poverté, ou par malveisté" (It sometimes happens that a Christian becomes a Saracen, either out of foolishness or poverty, or out of wickedness [chap. 15; 283]). The narrator himself is tempted to convert when the Sultan promises him great rewards: "[il] me eust mariez moult hautement au fille du prince terrien et doné des grantz heritages si jeo vousisse avoir renoié moun creatour. Mes jeo n'avoy talent pur nul avoir qe il me poait promettre" (he would have arranged a very advantageous marriage for me with the daughter of a wealthy prince, and given me great properties if I had been willing to renounce my Creator. But I did not want to, not for any wealth that he could offer me [chap. 6; 134]). Prepared to wear their clothes and speak their language, the narrator will not go so far as to take on the Saracen "law" (chap. 15; 272).

Although the scene in the Sultan's chamber is the symbolic center of the text, the mirror in which the Christian West sees itself, it is only one of several competing centers in *The Book of John Mandeville*. The most prominent of the text's many centers is, of course, Jerusalem. The author affirms several times that the holy city is the center not only of his text, but of the world itself. He opens his book by naming "Jerusalem qe est en my lieu de mounde" (Jerusalem, which is at the middle of the world [Prol.; 90]), and goes on to specify that the spot in Jerusalem where Joseph of Aramathea placed the dead body of Christ "est droitement en mylieu de mounde" (is rightly at the middle of the world [chap. 10; 192]). He repeats this assertion throughout the *Book*. As Iain Higgins has pointed out, this claim is far from universal, and he argues that the Mandeville-author "takes the idea of Jerusalem's centrality...much more seriously than his predecessors did."[66] This prompts the question of what purpose the claim for Jerusalem's centrality serves in the text and, moreover, what its status is with regard to the other geographic centers posited later in the text: the Earthly Paradise, Prester John's Land, and England itself. These locations serve as alternative centers for organizing a world that was increasingly seen not as ordered about one point, but as fanning outward to new horizons for exploration and conquest.

As modern readers of the *Book* have observed, the narrative initially follows the conventional itinerary of the pilgrimage to the Holy Land, which has its end and climax in reaching Jerusalem; yet the *Book* soon leaves behind that apparent "end," moving beyond Jerusalem in what Iain Higgins (borrowing a term from the cartographer Tony Campbell) has called a "speculative fashion."[67] Higgins has called attention to the way in which the *Book*'s movement beyond Jerusalem does not simply leave behind the pilgrimage itinerary

---

66. Higgins, "Defining the Earth's Center," 29–53, quotation from 44.
67. Zacher, *Curiosity and Pilgrimage,* 140; Greenblatt, *Marvelous Possessions,* 29; noted in Higgins, "Defining the Earth's Center," 40; "speculative fashion," 49.

in favor of exploring, as Stephen Greenblatt puts it, "the bewildering variety of 'marvellous things'"; instead, Higgins argues, Jerusalem's geographical and spiritual centrality continues to inform the depiction of the world even as the narrative moves further and further eastward. Jerusalem is, as it were, the first center, which continues to be primary as the text moves along; but it is nonetheless also the first in a series of centers about which the world is pro-visionally and temporarily centered. These centers include not just Jerusalem but also the Sultan's chamber in Babylon, Prester John's Land, the Earthly Paradise, and England itself, which the fictitious John Mandeville claims as his homeland. Each of these locations offers, as it were, a double view: it displays an alien place and, simultaneously, displays a mirror image of the viewer's own location. In the scene in the Sultan's chamber, one learns about the Christian West both directly, in the Sultan's commentary on the state of contemporary Christianity, and indirectly, by observing how the narrator becomes, albeit temporarily, a member of the alien community of Babylon.

These centers are linked by their identification, each in turn, with the site of origins: that is, Paradise. The account of Islamic theology that pre-cedes the narrator's audience with the Sultan begins with an appealing ac-count of Muslims' notion of Paradise: it is "un lieu de delices" (a place of delights), having "maisouns beles et nobles...faites des pieres preciouses et d'or et d'argent" (beautiful and stately houses...made of precious stones and of gold and silver). These delights extend beyond the beautiful exteriors of the houses, for in this place, "chescun avera IIIIxx femmes toutes pucelles, et avera touz les jours affaire a elle, et toutdis les trovera pucelles" (every man will have twenty-four women, all virgins, and he will have intercourse every day with them, and nonetheless he will always find them still virgins [chap. 15; 272–73]). (Fearing perhaps to have tempted his reader too much with such a description, the redactor of the Egerton manuscript hastens to add, "This is against our creed.") This relentlessly literal reading of the Qur'anic account of heaven is clearly an image of a false Paradise, one to which we return in the closing chapter of this volume to discuss in detail. The rivers of this Eden transmit not spiritual blessings but sensuous pleasures, "corantz de lait et de mel et de vin et de douce eawe" (running with milk and honey and wine and sweet water [chap. 15; 273]). The rivers of Paradise are also, in part, the source of the holiness of Jerusalem itself. Jerusalem is sanctified as the place of Christ's sacrifice, visible in the circle on the floor that marks the place where his body was laid after the deposition, the fixed point that marks the geographical center of the world. Yet just as the dead body of Adam provided the nourishing soil in which grew the tree that became the Cross, as the narrator reminds us (chap. 2; 102), so too the rivers of Eden water Jerusalem. In his tour of the holy places, the narrator notes that "en l'angle de la cité est ly bain Nostre Seignur. En ceo bain soloit entrer l'eawe de Paradis et unqore elle degoute" (in the corner of the city is the bath of Our Lord. In that bath the water of Paradise used to flow, and even now it still drips there [chap. 11; 205]).

Eden, the Earthly Paradise, is the place of origins and mankind's first home. It ceased to be home, however, with the Fall and the consequent expulsion of man. There was no going back to Paradise, no chance of pilgrimage to that holy place: as the narrator reminds us, "nul homme mortel ne poait aler ne approcher a ceo Paradiz" (no living man may go to or approach Paradise [chap. 33; 470]). After the Fall, Paradise remained a center, but an inaccessible one. It was still an *umbilicus,* a marker of the place of birth. Because mankind had become cut off from it, however, a new *umbilicus* came to take its place as center of the world: Jerusalem, which the encyclopedists refer to as being at the middle of things, "quasi umbilicus regionis totius." Eden is supplanted by Jerusalem; but Jerusalem in its turn, worn down by centuries of pilgrimage, is ripe for replacement. In the journey beyond Jerusalem carried out in *The Book of John Mandeville,* an effort is made to return to the original center by navigating the waters of the rivers of paradise.

In his essay on the ongoing importance of Jerusalem's centrality throughout the *Book,* Iain Higgins issues an important corrective of earlier readings which had suggested that the Mandeville author's description of the Earthly Paradise, which appears near the end of the text, is the real end and climax of the journey.[68] I would suggest that, while the Earthly Paradise does not supplant Jerusalem as the center of the world, it does act as a supplement. Eden is, in Mandeville's *Book,* the source one must look to in order to find a new sacred place to restore the vitality of a Jerusalem ravaged by time. Jerusalem is worn down by innumerable visits from eager pilgrims, with shrines newly enclosed by walls because "chescun qe y aloit se penoit de prendre de la piere ou piece, ou poudre" (some men who went there used to take away bits of the stone or dust [chap. 10; 188]). Jerusalem is altered not just by the presence of pilgrims but by the passage of time, as the reader is constantly reminded: here used to stand this, and there formerly was that. A church that formerly was at ground level is now below it "pur ceo qe Jerusalem ad esté plusours foiz destruit et les murs abatuz, qe ly murs soient cheux et tombez en la vallee" (because Jerusalem has been often destroyed and the walls broken down, so that the walls were tumbled down into the valley [chap. 11; 213]). Only the Earthly Paradise stands outside time, its bounty endlessly renewed as its four rivers

---

68. Zacher, *Curiosity and Pilgrimage,* 151; Campbell, *Witness and the Other World,* 160.

flow outward into the world bearing "moultz des preciouses pierres et moult de lignum aloes et mult de gravele d'or" (many precious stones and much *lignum aloes* and much gravel of gold [chap. 33; 468]). These jewels are relics whose beauty is not accidental but essential, because their source is divine.

The sacrality of Prester John's land, described at length in *The Book of John Mandeville,* is in no small part based on its geographical and spiritual proximity to the Earthly Paradise. The waters that divide his kingdom, India, into separate islands are the "granz fluvies qe viegnent de Paradis" (great rivers which flow out of Paradise [chap. 30; 433]). His own land is thick with gold and precious stones which flow out, carried upon "une fluvie qe vient de Paradiz" (a river that comes from Paradise [chap. 30; 436]). Yet the purposes to which these riches are put serve to distinguish significantly between Prester John's Land and that other alien culture defined in terms of the abundance of Paradise: that is, the Islamic world described earlier in the *Book* in connection with the encounter with the Sultan of Babylon. In Prester John's kingdom, the material riches embodied in jewels are appropriately subordinated to the spiritual riches of heaven: in processions, the narrator tells us, Prester John has carried before him a "vesseal d'argent ovesqez nobles joiaux d'or et des pierres preciouses" (silver vessel full of splendid jewels, gold, and precious stones). But this vessel is preceded by "une plateal d'or plein de terre, en memorie qe la noblesse de ly, sa puissance et sa char devendront et retorner-one en terre" (a golden plate full of earth, as a reminder that his nobility, his power, and his very flesh came from the earth, and will return to the earth). That plate, in turn, is preceded by "une croiz simple de boys sanz peintures et sanz or et sanz pierres preciouses" (a simple cross of wood, without painting and without gold and without any precious stones [chap. 30; 438]). In Prester John's Land, abundance is always subordinated to humility.

Such subordination of the external trappings of wealth to those things of spiritual value is perhaps most striking in the description of Prester John's bed, the frame of which is made "de fins saphirs bendez d'or" (of fine sapphire set in gold [chap. 30; 439]). This image evokes the material wealth associated with the Muslim East in a variety of medieval texts, as well as the luxuriousness and sexual license particularly prominent in Western medieval lives of the Prophet Muhammad. (One thinks, in particular, of the gem-encrusted bed, heaped with gold and pearls, which Saladin uses to magically send his friend, Messer Torello, home to Italy in Boccaccio's *Decameron*.)[69] Yet while the appearance of Prester John's sapphire and gold bed evokes comparable characterizations of the Muslim East, the purpose to which the

---

69. Boccaccio, *Decameron* 10.9, trans. MacWilliam, 764–83. See Kirkham and Menocal, "Reflections on the 'Arabic' World," 95–110.

gems are put distinguishes it sharply from the licentiousness associated with Islam: the bed is made of sapphire in order "pur le faire bien dormer et pur sa luxurie refrener, qar il ne voet coucher ovesqes ses femmes qe IIII foiz l'an solonc les IIII seisouns. Et c'est soulement pur enfanz engendrer" (to make him sleep well and to restrain his lust, because he wants to sleep with his wives only four times a year, according to the four seasons. And this is only to engender children [chap. 30; 439]). The austerity underlying the apparent luxury of Prester John's realm reveals a spiritual purity that is also manifested in the Christianity practiced there: "[Ils] ount comunement lour chapelleins qe chauntent la messe... mes ils ne dient pas tantz des choses a la messe come l'em fait par decea" (They have priests among them who sing Mass for them... but they do not say their Mass in exactly the same way that one does here). The difference seems to be the result not of their inadequacy but of our excess, for "nous avoms plousours addiciouns qe ly papes ount depuis faites dont ils ne scievent rienz" (we have many additions that the popes have made, of which they know nothing [chap. 32; 463]). The implication is that contemporary western Christian practice is degenerate, fallen away from the ideal preached by Jesus and promulgated by his apostles. The ideal is preserved far away in Prester John's Land.

Prester John's Land is a place of origins, linked both to Paradise (by its geographical proximity to Eden) and to the spiritual ministry of Jesus' own day (by its people's rejection of theological and liturgical innovation). Simultaneously, however, Prester John's Land is a place of great contemporary resonance, for it represented, to the medieval Western Christian, the last great hope for a military victory in the Holy Land. The apocalyptic context of writings about Prester John, beginning with the eponymous letter which appeared in Europe during the twelfth century, is preserved in *The Book of John Mandeville* in its account of the fierce nations of Gog and Magog that adjoins the account of Prester John. Through its association with Eden and early Christian practice, Prester John's Land is a place of origins; through its apocalyptic context, Prester John's Land is a place located at the end of things, involved in the Last Judgment. Yet, in *The Book of John Mandeville,* the reconquest of Jerusalem to be facilitated by knowledge of Prester John is not military, but spiritual. As in the private audience in the Sultan's chamber, the encounter with Prester John teaches the narrator (and, consequently, his readers) that spiritual reform must precede military victory. The place to direct one's sights is not Jerusalem, but home.

With this in mind, it is unsurprising that Prester John's Land is juxtaposed by the author of the *Book* with the narrator's own avowed homeland, England: "solonc ceo qe jeo puis perceivoir et comprendre, les terres

Prestre Johan emperour de Ynde sont dessouz nous. Qar en alant d'Escoce ou d'Engleterre vers Jerusalem homme mounte toutdis, qar notre terre est en la basse partie de la terre vers occident, et la terre Prestre Johan est la basse partie de la terre vers orient.... Et ceo qe l'em mounte al une coustee l'em avaloit al autre" (as far as I can see, the lands of Prester John, Emperor of India, are directly beneath us. For in going from Scotland or England toward Jerusalem, one climbs upward, because our land is in the lowest part of the earth toward the west, while the land of Prester John is in the lowest part of the earth toward the east.... And just as far as a person would climb up on one side, he would descend as far upon the other side [chap. 20; 336]). In this striking image, Jerusalem acts as a fulcrum with England on the one side, balanced by Prester John's Land on the other. Prester John's Land is "directly beneath us": opposite but, like one's inverted image in a mirror, the same. To make the point clear, the Mandeville author adds a brief anecdote concerning a man who traveled so far abroad "q'il troeva un isle ou il oÿ parler soun langage... disant tieles paroles come l'em fait en son pays dont il s'enmerveilla moult" (that he found an island where he heard his language being spoken... using the same words that one does in his own land, at which he marvelled greatly [chap. 20; 337]). The narrator adds, however, that "jeo dy q'il avoit tant irré par terre et par mer q'il avoit environé toute la terre, q'il estoit revenuz envyronant jusqes a ses marches, et s'il vousist avoir passé avant q'il eust troevé et sons pays et sa conissaunce" (I think that he had wandered so far by land and by water that he had circled the whole earth, so that he had come around as far as his own borders, and if he had gone a little farther he would have discovered his own familiar land [chap. 20; 337]). This passage suggests that, if the traveler ventures far enough into alien territory, he finds himself at home: to put it another way, a close look at the Other shows the self. This is why the narrator's conversation with the Sultan reveals not the heart of Oriental mystery but the spiritual defects of western Christendom; why the idiosyncrasies of the Saracen alphabet are explained by the fact that, in English, we similarly have strange characters, the thorn and yogh (chap. 15; 283), and why the exotic hybrid creatures found abroad are no more strange than the barnacle geese of the British isles (chap. 29; 427).

The shifting centers that order the narrative of *The Book of John Mandeville* can be fruitfully compared to the way in which descriptive geographies, found in the writings of medieval encyclopedists, structure the world. As noted earlier, such geographies are, at least in rough outline, based on the tripartite division of the continents found in the medieval T-O map. It is useful to recall here how two of these encyclopedists, Isidore of Seville and Bartholomaeus Anglicus, organize their descriptive geographies. Inevitably, Asia is their starting point due to its prominence on the world map both by virtue of size and because it contains the locations of mankind's physical birth—Eden—and spiritual rebirth—Jerusalem. Yet both descriptive geographies have what one might call a secondary center, an implicit point of reference about which descriptions of other, more distant parts of the world are ordered. For Isidore, this secondary center is Spain; for Bartholomaeus, it is England. For Isidore, the climatic extremes of north and south serve to define the location of what one might call his personal world center—that is, Spain. The Galicians, whose name is derived from their milky-white complexion (*Etym.* 9.2.104, 14.4.25), are located just to the north while the Mauritanians, so-called after their dark skins, are at the southern border (9.2.122, 14.5.10). For Isidore, the northern and southern extremes used to establish the centrality of Spain are proximate locations; conversely, Bartholomaeus emphasizes the remoteness of the climatic extremes that make distinct the various parts of the world. In this schema, England appears as a little corner ("angulo") of the world, but one distinguished by its plenty and its beauty. In this respect, Bartholomaeus resembles his countryman Robertus Anglicus, who in his commentary on Sacrobosco's *De Sphaera* includes an encomium to England in the midst of a discussion of the climates of the world.[70]

In spite of arguments by scholars such as M. C. Seymour and John Larner that the author of *The Book of John Mandeville* must have been French or Flemish, it is undeniable that the claim of English nationality is fundamental to the narrative.[71] This is evident not only in what Christiane Marchello-Nizia and Christiane Deluz have identified as the "juridical" opening statement of the *Book* ("I, John Mandeville...")[72] but in its geographical structure, where the imagined utopia of Prester John's Land and the lived experience of England mirror one another, each oriented toward the focal point of Jerusalem. Like Bartholomaeus Anglicus and Robertus Anglicus, the author of *The Book of John Mandeville* offers both a panoramic view of the scope of creation and an intimate, even loving portrait of his homeland—"the plenteuouseste corner of the world," as Bartholomaeus calls it. The world has an absolute center: that is, in spiritual terms at least, Jerusalem. But it also has a personal center, the place in which one stands, as it were, to survey the world. For these

---

70. On cosmography and English nationalism in Bartholomaeus Anglicus, John Trevisa, and Robertus Anglicus, see Akbari, "The Diversity of Mankind," 156–76.

71. On Continental authorship of *The Book of John Mandeville,* see Seymour, *Sir John Mandeville;* Larner, "Plucking Hairs."

72. On the "juridical" formula in *The Book of John Mandeville,* see Marchello-Nizia, "Entre l'Histoire et la poétique, le Songe politique," 39–53, and "L'historien et son prologue," 13–25. See also Deluz, "Introduction," 13–14.

writers, that place is England. In *The Book of John Mandeville,* England is the last in a series of transitory centers—the Sultan's chamber in Babylon, Jerusalem, Paradise, Prester John's Land, England—each of which enables a moment of clear vision. In the Sultan's chamber, the narrator comes face to face with the defects of western Christendom and learns how to correct them. In Jerusalem, he looks back into the past, at the circle on the floor of the Church of the Holy Sepulchre that marks the site of mankind's spiritual rebirth. He seeks Paradise but, since no one may reenter Eden, he contents himself with describing the spiritual and material riches that continue to flow out from the Garden, nourishing the four corners of the world. Prester John's Land offers a glimpse of what a reformed Christendom might look like, spiritually cleansed in preparation for the reconquest of Jerusalem and blessed with luxurious material wealth in recognition of its spiritual abundance. It points the way to its counterpart, England, the place where the utopian vision might take root and, eventually, flourish.

The shifting center of *The Book of John Mandeville* is no small part of what makes the work so appealing to its audience, whether in the fourteenth century or today. The reader is oriented and reoriented again—toward Jerusalem, toward Eden, toward Prester John's Land, and finally toward home. The Orient, place of the rising sun, is in the end no fixed point at all. The narrator says that to the east of Prester John's Land is wasteland that is "vers orient al comencement de la terre. Mes ceo n'est mie notre orient de cea qe nous appellomz orient, la ou le solail leve a nous, qar quant ly solail est orient vers celles parties de Paradis, il est adonques mie nuyt en notres parties de cea pur la reondese de la terre" (toward the east, at the edge of the earth. But that is not the same as our orient here, what we call 'the orient,' where the sun rises for us; for when the sun rises in those regions near Paradise, it is the middle of the night in our regions here, due to the roundness of the earth [chap. 33; 467]). By declaring that that east "is not *our* east," the author asserts that the Orient is everywhere and, in a sense, nowhere.

In *The Book of John Mandeville,* balance is the fundamental ordering principle of the world. Each part of the world has its opposite, which corresponds to it exactly. The incredible diversity of the world, including the many bizarre "monstrous races" that so appealed to medieval readers of the *Book,* is not indicative of chaos: on the contrary, each part is balanced—heat and cold, dryness and moisture, light and dark, orthodoxy and religious deviance, monstrosity and normalcy. In another kind of text, such a series of binary oppositions might create a kind of Manichean opposition, where Christian and pagan, European and foreigner, are locked in an eternal battle that only one of them can rightly win. In *The Book of John Mandeville,* however, these oppositions are in the service of a larger system, one that enfolds within it the full range of natural, cultural, and geographical diversity.[73]

It is almost a cliché to compare the world depicted in *The Book of John Mandeville* to the world depicted pictorially on the mappamundi. It is nonetheless useful to ask whether the world of Mandeville's *Book* is the same as the world depicted on the medieval map; or, to ask the question in a more useful way, Is the world of Mandeville's *Book always* the world that we see on the map? In the journey to Jerusalem, in the first fifteen chapters of the text, we are surely in the geography of the mappamundi, where all roads inexorably lead to the center, which is also the point toward which all eyes are turned. In the latter chapters, however, are we in this same world? In the discussion of the relative positions of England and Prester John's Land, especially, we look at the world as if we were not in it at all: the earth and sea are round, one part illuminated, the other in darkness. Centrality, then, for Mandeville, is variable: Jerusalem is surely the center of the world, at least as long as one treads the path of the pilgrim. After that, however, it functions as a central point in a rather different way: Jerusalem now acts as the fulcrum that is absolutely necessary to the overall balance of the world—Prester John's Land on this side of the scales, England on the other. From this point of view, the reader, guided by the narrator, can stand back and see the panorama of the world all at once.[74] Jerusalem remains the central point, as in the mappamundi; but it is also a point of departure, from which one takes stock of the rest of the world. The description of Paradise is similar in that it too is both a point of return and a point of departure: the narrator recounts his unsuccessful effort to reach Eden, stating "de cel lieu ne vous saveroie jeo plus qe dire ne diviser et pur ceo me taray atant et me retorneray a ceo qe j'ay veu" (of that place I do not know any more that I can speak of or describe; and therefore I will keep quiet and return instead to those things that I have seen [chap. 33; 470]). He will turn around, and go back: drawn in by the attractions of Paradise, and spun around again, back into the world, by the impossibility of entering into it. In this moment of almost simultaneous attraction and repulsion, the centripetal model of the world is transformed into a centrifugal model, spinning the imaginary traveler outward toward the edges of the map in search of new sites of exploration and conquest.

---

73. On balance and symmetry in the geography of Bartholomaeus Anglicus and *The Book of John Mandeville,* see Akbari, "Diversity of Mankind."

74. Compare the development of "bird's eye views" of cities during the late fifteenth and sixteenth centuries, described in Hillis, "Power of Disembodied Imagination," 1–17.

✦ CHAPTER 2

From Jerusalem to India

In the previous chapter, we examined views of the world that emphasize symmetry, balance, and the stability of a focal center—Jerusalem—which serves to anchor the world both in space (as the geographical center of many medieval maps) and in time (as the fulcrum of Christian salvation history). This might be described as a fundamentally centripetal view of the world, where the constituent parts revolve around a fixed center, drawing their own significance from their relationship to that focal point and consequently, over time, investing it with layer upon layer of accreted spiritual and symbolic weight. The centrifugal flow of mankind— the ejection of Adam and Eve from Eden, the dispersal of the descendants of Noah following the flood, and the scattering of nations after the fall of the Tower of Babel—is countered, in this worldview, by the anchoring presence of Jerusalem as the site of mankind's spiritual rebirth. Its place in salvation history as both point of origin (the Crucifixion) and point of return (the Last Judgment) causes it to be identified repeatedly by medieval writers as the center of the world. The present chapter focuses more closely on the centrifugal aspects of medieval views of the world, where the mysterious and excessive elements located at the fringes of the ecumene take on a special resonance, seen as the wellsprings of marvelous manifestations of the extremes of nature. These feature, most prominently, the "monstrous races," but also include other phenomena that seem to defy the norms of creation, such as chimerical animals or rivers flowing with fire instead of water. In this centrifugal model of the world, geographically marginal locations reach out across time, as does the sacred center of Jerusalem in the centripetal model seen in the texts described in the previous chapter. They harbor both the mysteries of the distant past and the still-veiled promise of the apocalyptic future.

For medieval Europeans, the unknown margins of the world extended across all four of the cardinal directions, and so wondrous phenomena and monstrous races were described in a variety of locations: Gerald of Wales, for example, chronicles the extraordinary sights to be seen in the north-west of Europe in his *Chronica Hibernica,* while the *Cosmographia* of Aethicus Ister suggests that the far northern realms are the home of bizarre species of mankind. Yet no regions were so consistently and so vibrantly characterized in terms of monstrous excess and marvelousness as the south-eastern realms of Ethiopia and India. While these two regions are distinct in modern geography, they were often conflated in medieval texts and on maps. Both India and Ethiopia are defined by medieval encyclopedists in terms of their proximity to the sun. Isidore of Seville, for example, states that India lies closest to the "ortum solis" (where the sun rises), while Ethiopia is located "circa solis ardorem" (where the sun's heat is greatest)" (*Etym.* 14.3.5, 14.5.3, 14.5.14). These locations are "oriental" in the most fundamental sense, dominated by the nourishing—and desiccating—presence of the sun.

Both India and Ethiopia are also described as multiple. There are several Indias and several Ethiopias; there is an Ethiopian India, sometimes located in Asia, sometimes in eastern Africa.[1] This confusion appears as early as the seventh century, when Isidore states in one chapter of his *Etymologies* that there are two Ethiopias, one to the west and one "circa ortum solis" (14.5.16), but elsewhere he says that there are three races of Ethiopians, one of which (the "Indi") lives in the east (9.2.128).[2] Moreover, says Isidore, beyond the two parts of Ethiopia lies a fourth part of the world that "solis ardore incognita nobis

---

1. Von den Brincken notes that "India prima," "India secunda," "India tertia," "India superior," and "India inferior" are generally placed in Asia, while "India Aegypti" and "India Aethiopie" usually appear in eastern Africa (*Fines Terrae,* 162). As early as Jerome, the overlap of India and Ethiopia is evident: "Aethiopum regio ab Indo flumine consurgens, juxta Aegyptum inter Nilum et oceanum, et in meridie, sub ipsa solis vicinitate jacet." Jerome, *Liber nominum locurum et aetis,* PL 23, col. 1298.

2. Isidore's account is based on Pliny's *Historia naturalia,* but differs from it in several ways. Pliny describes four Ethiopian peoples: the White Ethiopians ("Leucoe Aethiopes"), the Nigritae (named after the river Niger), the Pharusian Gymnetes, and the Perorsi, as well as several smaller tribes. Pliny credits Homer with the observation that there are two Ethiopias, one eastern and one western (*Historia naturalia* 5.8.43). Like Pliny, Isidore says that there are two Ethiopias, but describes only three Ethiopian peoples, omitting the White Ethiopians and renaming the other three groups (from west to east) the Hesperi, the Garamantes, and the Indi. Pliny, *Historia naturalia,* 2:248–51.

est" (is unknown to us due to the heat of the sun [14.5.17]). Here, according to Isidore, the Antipodes can be found. Some encyclopedists, such as Vincent of Beauvais, follow Isidore very closely, reproducing his ambiguity regarding the number of Ethiopian territories.[3] Vincent's contemporary Bartholomaeus Anglicus, however, alters Isidore's account to state that there are not two but three Ethiopias: one toward the west, one toward the east, and a third that is (in the translation of Trevisa) "Ethiopia adusta, that is, ybrent" (De prop. rerum 15.52). Here, says Bartholomaeus, lie the Antipodes. In this passage, Bartholomaeus assimilates the unknown fourth continent mentioned by Isidore to Ethiopia itself, avoiding the contentious notion of a continent lying outside the ecumene. Like Ethiopia, India is always described as plural: Isidore notes the many rivers that divide it (Etym. 14.3.5–7), while Bartholomaeus relates that India has "many wondres in longe space toward Ethiopia" and still more marvels "in the eende of eeste Inde" (De prop. rerum 15.75). The multiplicity of India is also evident on maps, which usually label three Indias, in keeping with the literature of the Alexander legend and apostolic histories, but sometimes considerably more than three.[4] (An example can be seen on the world map of Lambert of St. Omer [figure 7].) In sum, the region of the sun is a location of multiplicity and uncertainty, where borders are extremely variable.

Ethiopia and India are, however, linked by more than their south-eastern location and their variable multiplicity. Both are also depicted as repositories of supernatural and arcane knowledge, and both are characterized in terms of abundant wealth and luxury, a means of acquiring great profit yet simultaneously a source of potential danger to the unwary traveler. These extraordinary qualities are linked to their proximity to the sun, which imbues them with both marvelous virtues and great perils. The region of the sun—labeled variously as the "ortum solis," "vicina solis," "insula solis," or lands "circa solis ardorem"—appears frequently on medieval maps in the south-eastern location lying between India and Ethiopia.[5] For example, maps illustrating Beatus of Lièbana's eighth-century commentary on the Apocalypse include the "ortum solis" in the form of an island shape labelled "Hic ortus sol." It is located close to an illustration of the hot sun beating down upon a sciopod,

---

3. Vincent of Beauvais, Speculum Historiale 1.77.

4. For example, in the mid-twelfth century, Orderic Vitalis states that "Indiae tres esse.... Prima India ad Aethiopiam mittit, secunda ad Medos, tertia finem facit." Orderic Vitalis, Ecclesiastical History 2.15, PL 188, col. 165B. The main source for this description of the three Indias is the apocryphal Passion of St. Bartholomew, 128. On the variable number of Indias on medieval maps, see von den Brincken, Fines Terrae, 162–63. On the various Indias on the map associated with the Descriptio mappe mundi attributed to Hugh of St. Victor, see La Descriptio mappe mundi de Hugues de Saint-Victor, 78–79.

5. See von den Brincken, Fines Terrae, 2, 29, and fig. 32.

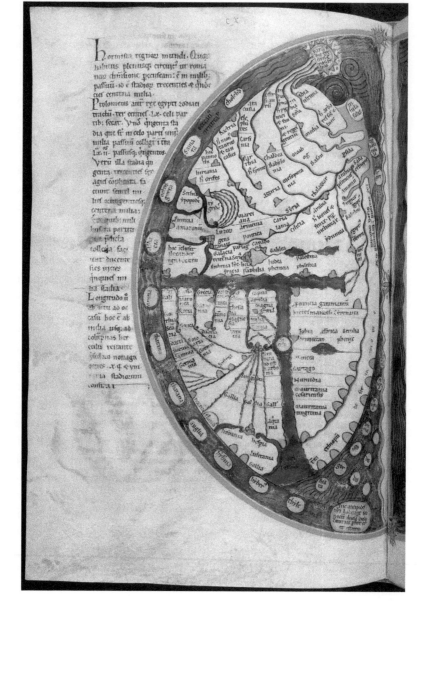

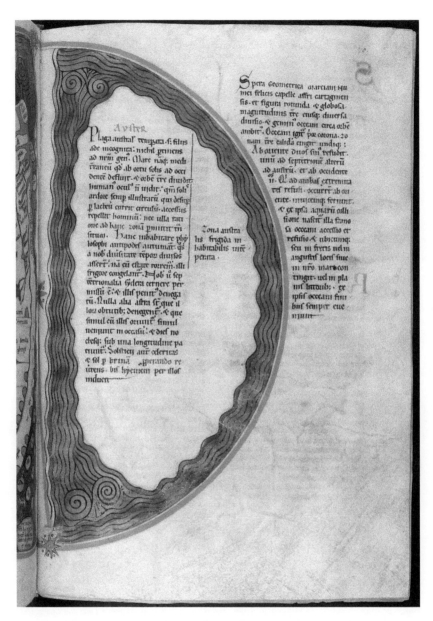

FIGURE 7. World map of Lambert of St. Omer, featuring the oriental "island of the sun" slightly below and to the right of Eden (at the top), with the island of Taprobana just below. A fourth continent appears in the southern hemisphere (at right), cut off by the equatorial torrid zone and consequently "unknown to the sons of Adam." Lambert of St. Omer, *Liber Floridus,* Wolfenbüttel, Herzog August Bibl, Cod. Guelf. I, Gud. Lat. I, fol. 69v–70r (c. 1180). By permission of the Herzog August Bibliothek, Wolfenbüttel, Germany.

one of the monstrous races inhabiting the southern continent, a "region unknown to us due to the heat of the sun" (figure 8).[6] Similarly, a twelfth-century map illustrating Jerome's *Liber nominum locorum* includes a "solis insula," located at the south-eastern extreme of the world.[7] As on the Beatus map, the region of the sun closely borders the island of Taprobana, which is located slightly north of the "ortus sol." This island, known to medieval mapmakers through Solinus and Pliny, became increasingly well known for its abundant wealth, described in detail in later medieval versions of the Alexander legend. The twelfth-century map illustrating Lambert of St. Omer's *Liber Floridus* (figure 7) also depicts the "insula solis," but places it slightly north of Taprobana, very close to the enticing but forbidden Earthly Paradise. Like the Beatus map shown in figure 8, Lambert's map includes a fourth continent "unknown to the sons of Adam."[8] Unlike the illustrator of the Beatus map, however, Lambert does not dismiss this fourth continent as torrid and uninhabitable by any men other than the monstrous races. Instead, Lambert indicates the presence of torrid, temperate, and frigid zones in the southern hemisphere, corresponding to the zones found in the northern hemisphere, as could be inferred logically from Macrobian zonal maps (which Lambert depicts elsewhere in his *Liber Floridus*).

Like maps, accounts of world geography in medieval encyclopedias emphasize the role of the sun in defining the scope and nature of oriental regions. They usually begin with the easternmost locations on the map, in Asia, and then move through the other two known continents of Europe and Africa. The extreme south-eastern reaches of Africa treated at the end of the encyclopedic accounts, like the extreme eastern reaches of Asia with which the accounts begin, are defined in terms of the sun.[9] The accounts of Asian geography in the encyclopedias correspond in many respects with the features appearing on the world maps. Eastern locations connected with the Alexander legend, however, such as the "arbor solis" and "arbor lunae" (tree of the sun, tree of the moon) and the "columpne Alexandri" (pillars of Alexander)

6. "Hec regio ab ardore solis incognit. nobis et inhabitabilis...." Beatus de Lièbana, Cathedral of Burgo de Osma, Cod. 1, ff. 34v–35r (c. 1086); reproduced in Edson, *Mapping Time and Space,* 152. A schematic for this map can be found in Williams, "Isidore," 8.

7. The map illustrating Jerome's *Liber nominum locorum* appears in BL Add. MS 10049, fol. 64r; reproduced in Edson, *Mapping Time and Space.*

8. "Plaga australis temperata. Sed filiis Ade incognita...." *Liber Floridus,* Wolfenbüttel, Herzog August Bibliothek, MS Gud. lat. 1, ff. 69v–70r (c. 1180). A transcription of the map legends and schematic can be found in Lecoq, "La Mappemonde du *Liber Floridus* ou La Vision du Monde de Lambert de Saint-Omer," 9–49, esp. 17.

9. On the overlapping treatment of the east and the south, see von den Brincken, *Fines Terrae,* 158, 171.

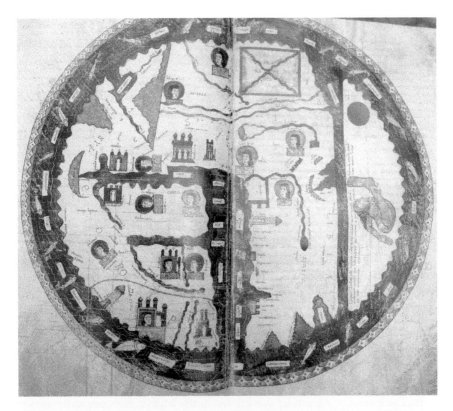

FIGURE 8.   World map of Beatus de Lièbana, with Eden depicted as a square at the top and the sun and "ortus sol" at top right, with a monstrous sciopod just below. Beatus de Lièbana, *Apocalypse*. Cathedral of Burgo de Osma, Cod. 1, fol. 34v–35r (1086 c.e.). By permission of Vicent García Editores, S.A., Spain.

usually do not appear in the geographical sections of the encyclopedias even though they are prominent on the maps. The Alexander material instead appears in other sections of some of these encyclopedic compilations, including the *Speculum Historiale* of Vincent of Beauvais and the *Liber Floridus* of Lambert of St. Omer.

Because of the ubiquity of landmarks associated with the history of Alexander in the oriental regions of medieval maps, the literary texts chosen to anchor this chapter are drawn from the Alexander romances of the twelfth through fourteenth centuries. The romances form a rich yet unwieldy tradition, involving not just numerous sources but also a very great degree of overlap and mutual influence. The manuscript evidence adds further layers of complexity, as redactors of one version of the Alexander romance draw upon the conventions of quite another strand in order to embellish and enrich their narrative. This chapter focuses on three examples, related by their common use of one of the two main sources of the history of Alexander (the account of Julius Valerius), but differing significantly with regard to the emphasis they place on various aspects of the legend. They include the Alexander material collected in the encyclopedic *Liber Floridus,* compiled by Lambert of St. Omer in the early twelfth century; the *Roman de toute chevalerie,* written by Thomas of Kent in the last decades of the twelfth century; and the early fourteenth-century *Kyng Alisaunder,* freely adapted from Thomas' Anglo-Norman poem by an anonymous English writer. The apocalyptic content of the Alexander story, essential to Lambert's presentation of the material and dramatized at length by Thomas, is significantly diminished in the Middle English adaptation. The interest in the role of climate in the generation of physical wonders at the margins of the world reaches its zenith in the *Roman de toute chevalerie,* but becomes inconsistent and confused in *Kyng Alisaunder.* Simultaneously, however, the luxurious nature of the Orient and the riches to be acquired there are amplified in the fourteenth-century text; the accessibility and portability of eastern wealth is emphasized, rather than simply its wondrous nature.

Before turning to a closer examination of the *Liber Floridus,* the *Roman de toute chevalerie,* and *Kyng Alisaunder,* I give a brief account of the medieval development of the Alexander story and the place of these selected texts within it. The legend of Alexander was known in the Middle Ages primarily in two versions, both Latin adaptations derived from the third-century Greek account of pseudo-Callisthenes.[10] These include the fourth-century *Res Gestae Alexandri Macedonis* of Julius Valerius and the mid-tenth-century version of Leo of Naples (also called Archpresbyter Leo). The latter account, known to future generations as the *Historia de Preliis,* was the basis for many versions of the Alexander romance, including the Old French prose *Alexander* and the Middle English *Wars of Alexander.* The version of Julius Valerius, primarily transmitted in the form of a ninth-century abbreviation known (after its nineteenth-century editor) as the Zacher Epitome, gave rise to a number of other accounts, including the three examined in this chapter.

The *Liber Floridus* juxtaposes a short version of Julius Valerius, drawn primarily from the Zacher Epitome, with other materials associated with Alexander, including the *Letter of Alexander to Aristotle* and the *Correspondence with*

---

10. Note also the history of Alexander by Quintus Curtius, transmitted through the *Alexandreis* of Walter of Châtillon and its many translations and adaptations: *Galteri de castellione Alexandreis; Alexandreis of Walter of Châtillon.* On vernacular translations of the *Alexandreis,* see Cary and Ross, *Medieval Alexander.*

Didymus. Thomas of Kent bases the framework of his *Roman de toute chevalerie* on the account of Julius Valerius found in the Zacher Epitome, but enriches the narrative enormously by assimilating within his poem not only the *Letter of Alexander to Aristotle* but also a variety of works of natural philosophy, including Pliny's *Historia naturalia,* Solinus' *Collectanea rerum memorabilium,* and Aethicus Ister's *Cosmographia.*[11] The author of *Kyng Alisaunder* bases his work on the *Roman de toute chevalerie,* but alters the narrative substantially in order to increase the smoothness of the plot and to diminish what he apparently perceived as unnecessary digressiveness concerning the marvels to be found at the extreme margins of the world. As part of this effort to achieve greater coherence, he also draws upon other strands of the Alexander legend, including the *Alexandreis* of Walter of Châtillon.[12] In sum, the three texts highlighted here offer a unified yet divergent view of the complex Alexander romance tradition. Related closely, yet differing significantly, they reveal how the Alexander legend participated in the development of ideas of the Orient that highlighted its seductive yet dangerous nature—seductive, because fabulous wealth and fascinating marvels could be found there; dangerous, because the far reaches of the east prove to be a place from which one returns profoundly changed, if one returns at all.

↞ The *Liber Floridus*

The *Liber Floridus* is an encyclopedic work, but of a peculiar kind. Like the great compilations of the thirteenth century assembled by Bartholomaeus Anglicus and Vincent of Beauvais, it offers a comprehensive overview of the world—historical, cosmological, and theological. Unlike the *De proprietatibus rerum* or *Speculum Maius,* however, the *Liber Floridus* does not synthesize its disparate elements into a coherent, linear narrative. Instead, its compiler Lambert, a canon of the Church of Our Lady at St. Omer in Flanders, juxtaposed a range of materials in such a way as to indicate relationships without explicitly articulating the connection between them. It is a highly idiosyncratic work, written in poor Latin, grouping an extremely heterogeneous collection of texts and images—these last often strikingly beautiful, as many

---

11. On the sources of the *Roman de toute chevalerie,* see Weynand, *Der "Roman de toute chevalerie" des Thomas von Kent in seinem Verhältnis zu seinen Quellen.*

12. On the supplementary use of the *Alexandreis* by the author of *Kyng Alisaunder,* see G. V. Smithers' introduction to his edition of the poem, *Kyng Alisaunder,* 2:15–16. All quotations from *Kyng Alisaunder* are cited in the text by line number.

readers have remarked.[13] On first reading, the *Liber Floridus* seems repetitive, but this initial impression soon gives way to the realization that the work actually circles back, as it were, on the same territory, providing slightly different perspectives on history with each successive cycle. For example, the *Liber Floridus* includes several different genealogies, some beginning with Adam, some with the sons of Noah, as well as lists of names of significant historical figures arranged in chronological order but lacking a paternal lineage. While elements of the genealogies are repeated, especially in the ancient periods, the historical overview presented by the list varies with each entry.

While earlier scholars saw the *Liber Floridus* as fundamentally incoherent, lacking any unified structure, more recent critics have looked deeper.[14] Harry Bober was among the first to argue that the *Liber Floridus* is far from being "a chaotic and totally disorderly composition." Instead, he suggested, the *Liber Floridus* has "a dual aspect," being "a traditional body of encyclopaedia materials, composed and reorganized around…a specific historical and local occasion"—namely, the Christian victory of the First Crusade and the special role of the Counts of Flanders in the establishment of the Latin Kingdom of Jerusalem.[15] Building on the foundations laid by Bober, Derolez has more fully illuminated the text's conceptual framework. His analysis of the complex and irregular quire structure of the autograph manuscript of the *Liber Floridus* demonstrates that Lambert "has been *organizing* his materials, instead of simply copying extracts from his sources as he encountered them."[16] Derolez emphasizes the extent to which the *Liber Floridus,* compiled between 1112 and 1121, is the product of the time following two historical climaxes: the Norman Conquest of 1066 and the Christian conquest of Jerusalem in 1099. He argues that the impact of these two events, which saw Flanders rise in power and influence, serves to explain the predominance of "unusually strong historical and eschatological components" in the *Liber Floridus,* which are integrated within an encyclopedic view of the world

---

13. On the illustrations of the *Liber Floridus,* see Derolez, *Autograph Manuscript of the "Liber Floridus."*

14. Delisle, "Notices sur les manuscrits du *Liber Floridus* de Lambert, chanoine de Saint-Omer," 577–791, esp. 577; Lefèvre, "Le *Liber Floridus* et la littérature encyclopédique au moyen âge," 1–9, esp. 8.

15. Bober, "Structure and Content." A more adventurous (but not widely accepted) hypothesis can be found in Tuttle, "Analysis of the Structure of the *Liber Floridus.*" Tuttle argues that the *Liber Floridus* is composed of twelve sections that correspond to the twelve books of the eighth-century commentary on the Apocalypse written by Beatus of Lièbana.

16. Derolez, *Autograph,* 18. On the relationship of Bober's initial studies of the quire structure to Derolez's work, see *Autograph,* 17.

drawn primarily from the writings of Isidore of Seville.[17] One might go so far as to say that the *Liber Floridus* is the product of an extraordinary time, a kind of golden age for European Christians punctuated by the conquest of Jerusalem in 1099 and the fall of Edessa to the Muslims in 1144, a period when it really seemed as though the end of things was near at hand. The abundant eschatological materials found in the *Liber Floridus,* including the *Revelations* of pseudo-Methodius and Adso's *De Antichristo,* testify to the zeal with which the compiler awaited the promised Apocalypse, while almost every entry concludes with a calculation of dates based on the age of the world, measuring the short period left before the end of time. This eschatological focus permeates the work, so that (for example) the bestiary included in the *Liber Floridus* (61r–62v)[18] closely follows the catalogue of animals found in Isidore's *Etymologies* (12.6), until it concludes with a passage describing the behemoth and the leviathan, punctuated by an almost full-page illustration of Antichrist mounted on his beast.

The *Liber Floridus* includes an extraordinarily diverse range of materials, including genealogies, chronologies, historical chronicles, and scientific writings, as well as vivid illustrations, maps, and schematic diagrams. The Alexander legend occupies a central place in the *Liber Floridus,* intersecting with a variety of its heterogeneous elements.[19] It fits in smoothly with the historical chronicles, as Derolez points out in his discussion of why Lambert originally placed the chronicle of the First Crusade written by Fulcher of Chartres immediately before the history of Alexander.[20] Yet the Alexander material is also closely affiliated with other genres found in the *Liber Floridus:* maps and climate-related scientific texts come to life, as it were, in the catalogue of marvels appearing in the *Letter of Alexander to Aristotle.*[21] The apocalyptic texts included by Lambert (Adso's *De Antichristo* and the *Revelations* of pseudo-Methodius) are even more intimately related to the Alexander material, for the enclosure of the unclean tribes of Gog and Magog at the hands of Alexander,

---

17. Derolez, *Autograph,* 181. On the dates of composition of the *Liber Floridus,* see Derolez, *Autograph,* xx.

18. Citations of the *Liber Floridus,* which appear in the text noted by folio number, are based on Albert Derolez's facsimile edition of the autograph manuscript, *Lamberti Sancti Audomari Canonici Liber Floridus Codex Autographus Bibliothecae Universitatis Gandavensis.*

19. As Lecoq notes, Alexander occupies "une place prépondérante dans le *Liber Floridus,* qu'il fait partie de ces personnages autour desquels s'articule, en quelque sorte, la vision du monde de Lambert de Saint-Omer" ("*Liber Floridus,*" 21). Penelope C. Mayo also points out Alexander's role as one of a series of divinely appointed world rulers in "Crusaders under the Palm," 29–67, esp. 62n117.

20. Derolez, *Autograph,* 122. Derolez notes that Lambert's abbreviation of the chronicle is based on the earliest version of Fulcher's work (*Autograph,* 117).

21. On the correspondence of marvels depicted on the maps of the *Liber Floridus* to the Alexander texts, see Lecoq, "*Liber Floridus,*" 26.

widely known from the detailed account of pseudo-Methodius as well as numerous intermediaries, was probably the most widely known aspect of the whole legend concerning the life of Alexander.[22] The Alexander material in the *Liber Floridus* is thus a kind of nexus of the work as a whole, marking the point of intersection of many of its central themes. Perhaps the only aspect crucial to the *Liber Floridus* not addressed by the Alexander material is the specific, regional focus on Flanders; this aspect emerges in the local genealogies integrated throughout the work, including Lambert's own maternal genealogy (154r).[23]

Lambert's version of the Alexander legend is unusual in that it represents a transitional state between the simple compilation of assorted Alexander texts in a single manuscript and the full integration of such texts into a unified narrative, as found in the later twelfth-century works of Walter of Châtillon, Alexandre de Paris, and Thomas of Kent.[24] Lambert collects several texts concerning the life of Alexander into a single chapter titled "De Alexandro Magno" (chap. 132), abridges them, and juxtaposes them in a way that encourages the reader to assimilate these disparate narratives into a coherent view of the great ruler. The sequence begins with an abbreviated version of the life of Alexander found in the Zacher Epitome (itself based on Julius Valerius), followed by a full-page illustration of Alexander mounted on horseback captioned with extracts from Julius Valerius and Orosius (153r–153v; includes an additional leaf, 153', pasted on the right margin). Already in the midst of the abbreviation of the Zacher Epitome, Lambert had made reference to the catalogue of oriental marvels to be found in the *Letter of Alexander to Aristotle,* advising the curious reader "in epistola Aristotili, quae sequitur, cognoscere poteris" (you can learn more about this in the *Letter to Aristotle,* which follows, 153'v). Appropriately, this letter appears next in the *Liber Floridus* (156r–161r), followed by a shortened version of the *Correspondence with Didymus* (161v–162r) and, finally, a brief description of the twelve cities founded by and named after Alexander, drawn from the Zacher Epitome

---

22. On the apocalyptic texts of the *Liber Floridus,* see Verhelst, "Les textes eschatologiques dans le *Liber Floridus,*" 299–305. Verhelst's edition of Adso includes the abbreviated version composed by Lambert: *De ortu et tempore Antichristi: necnon et tractatus qui ab eo dependunt.* On the wide knowledge of the enclosure of Gog and Magog by Alexander, see Pfister, "Alexander der Grosse in der Sage," 1–35, esp. 10; Gow, "Gog and Magog on *Mappaemundi,*" 61–88, esp. 62–63.

23. On Lambert's maternal genealogy, see Derolez, *Autograph,* 180. On Flanders, see van Caenegem, "Sources of Flemish History," 71–85.

24. Several examples of Latin compilations of Alexander texts are noted by W. Walther Boer in the introduction to his edition of the *Epistola* (or letter) of Alexander to Aristotle. *Epistola Alexandri ad Aristotelem ad Codicum Fidem Editit et Commentario Critico Instruxit.*

(162r).[25] The brevity of the abridged materials facilitates their integration in the mind of the reader, who is encouraged to assimilate them into a unified narrative not just by intertextual references but also by the inclusion of additional sources within the texts (Josephus within the Zacher Epitome, Orosius in the caption to the portrait of Alexander) and the combination of all of these diverse Alexander texts into a single chapter of the *Liber Floridus.*

The position of the Alexander materials within the *Liber Floridus,* moreover, adds to the reader's understanding of the significance of Alexander within history—a history that, in Lambert's view, includes both the historical past and the eschatological future. The chapters preceding "De Alexandro Magno" in the *Liber Floridus* raise themes that subsequently emerge within the Alexander materials, investing them with a kind of typological significance. The "Genealogia Mundi" (chap. 123), along with the following chapter with which it is closely linked, is what might be described as an integrated chronology, organized according to the ages of the world. Though Lambert almost always modifies (usually abbreviating) texts included in his compilation, he rarely composes them; the integrated chronology is one of his rare compositions.[26] Its temporal framework, based on that found in apocalyptic works such as the *Revelations* of pseudo-Methodius, provides the basis for a chronology that ranges through Jewish, Trojan, and Roman history. The first age, naturally, begins with Adam and Eve, while the second begins with the repopulation of the earth following the deluge by the sons of Noah; both of these lists are said to be "secundum Genesim" (136v).

The third age, which begins with Abraham and goes on to take note of Joseph's residence in Egypt, seems to continue along the standard path of biblical history. Lambert takes an abrupt turn in the third age, however, to describe the fall of Troy: "In hac aetate subversa est Troia est Eneas fugit in Italiam" (137r). The fourth age is similarly composite, including not only the descendants of King David and the Babylonian Captivity but also the population of Italy by the Trojans, the birth of Romulus and Remus and the subsequent foundation of Rome, along with the names of its first rulers. In his chronology of the fifth age, Lambert notes the genealogy of the Jewish patriarchs which, as he notes, runs concurrently with the first consuls of Rome: "In hac aetate Romae regnaverunt consules. Primus consol [*sic*] Brutus..." (137r). Here, he inserts the heading for a new chapter, numbered

---

25. See the detailed account of these in Derolez, *Autograph,* 131–34. A new edition (with modern German translation) of the *Correspondence with Didymus* (*Collatio Alexandri et Dindimi*) can be found in *Die "Collatio Alexandri et Dindimi."*

26. Derolez, *Autograph,* 125.

124 and titled "Nomina Consulum." In spite of the apparent break, however, the chronology continues on from when it left off, in the midst of the fifth age. The chapter break signals not so much an interruption in time (which continues to unfold seamlessly) as an interruption of genre, as Lambert moves from the mode of genealogy to a purely chronological mode.

A list of Roman consuls is followed by a list of the kings of Persia, including a short description of the Babylonian Captivity of the Jews under Cyrus and the rebuilding of the Temple in Jerusalem (based mainly on Josephus and the book of Maccabees), an account of the Punic Wars, and the campaigns of Julius Caesar in Gaul, Germania, and Britannia. The fifth age draws to a close with the reign of Augustus Caesar, the ruler of the world destined to yield his empire, in Lambert's account, to the one true King. Lambert, following the Orosian account of imperial history, describes how the Roman Empire had been expanded to its utmost bounds by Julius Caesar ("regna Orientis et Meridiani ac Septentrionis occidentisque et provintias insulasque"; 138v), creating an expansive realm to be subsequently ruled by his heir, Octavian. He illustrates this with a portrait of the young Octavian, enthroned, with a sword in the right hand and an orb in the left. This orb is no simple spherical image of the world, but an actual map, with the three known continents of Asia, Europe, and Africa depicted on it.[27] The sixth age begins, paradoxically, with the Roman Empire at the pinnacle of its might, yet bearing within it the seeds of its own destruction: that is, the birth of Christ, forecast by miracles seen in Rome itself and abroad ("signo in caelo et in terra prodigia"; 139r). At this moment, secular chronology gives way to sacred chronology, as Jesus is born in the year 752 (dated from the founding of Rome), marking the first year of the Christian era: "Anno itasque ab Urbe condita DCCLII Cesar Augustus ab Oriente in Occidentem, a Septentrione in Meridiem ac per totum Oceani circulum cunctis gentibus una pace compositis, Christus Dei filius in Iudea nascitur." From this moment, history speeds (in sixteen lines!) to its inevitable climax, with the advent of the "filius perditionis Antichristus," who will reign for a short time and, so, "mundus iste finietur" (139r).

It is easy to see how the history of Alexander both fits within this chronology (in a short passage embedded within an account of the reign of the Persian king Darius) and, in a sense, emblematizes it. Like Octavian, Alexander rules the whole known world, uniting it into a brief moment of universal harmony; like Rome, Alexander's empire is divinely sanctioned, his actions (especially the enclosure of the unclean tribes of Gog and Magog) directed

27. On this imposing illustration, see Derolez, *Autograph,* 125–26.

by the hand of God. Like Christ, however, Alexander is a hybrid creature: not God and man, precisely, but something other than a normal man, as is emphasized in the opening pages of his history, which Lambert prefaces with the rubric "De Nectanebo." In the account of Julius Valerius, Nectanebus was an Egyptian sorcerer who, disguised as the god Ammon, deceived the Macedonian queen Olympia by taking on the form of her husband, Philip, and fathered Alexander. Alexander is thus, depending upon how you look at it, half-divine (fathered by Ammon) or simply a half-breed bastard (fathered by the Egyptian sorcerer Nectanebus). The various lives of Alexander play on this ambiguity, investing him with god-like qualities of strength, wit, and physical beauty, but bringing out the very human frailties that lead inevitably to his downfall.

Between the integrated chronology and the lengthy chapter on Alexander, Lambert includes several short materials that also anticipate the Alexander story. The most prominent of these is an adaptation of Anselm's *Cur Deus Homo,* which immediately precedes the Alexander material. Though Derolez states that the link between Anselm's treatise and the Alexander chapter remains "one of the weak points" of the book, the closing lines of the integrated chronology (emphasizing the Incarnation) make clear its place in the sequence.[28] A few short texts are placed between the integrated chronology (chaps. 123–24) and the *Cur Deus Homo* (chap. 131): these include illustrations of the beatitudes in the form of trees (chap. 125) coupled with a short herbal (chap. 126), excerpts from Josephus on Moses and John the Baptist (chaps. 127–28), Bede on Herod (chap. 129), and Gregory the Great on the choirs of angels (chap. 130). As Penelope Mayo has shown in her lucid study of the interrelation of the *Liber Floridus'* texts and images, the Beatitude trees can be understood neither in isolation, nor in the context of the iconographic tradition of using trees to emblematize intellectual ascent. Rather, the Beatitude trees must be recognized as a single stage in a series of depictions of trees throughout the *Liber Floridus,* whose purpose is to illuminate the central role of Jerusalem in salvation history, as both the geographical destination of contemporary crusaders and the spiritual goal of every Christian soul. They are, in Mayo's words, typical of Lambert's "integrated, multi-level thinking."[29] The apparent shift in genre with the herbal (chap. 126) is elided as the text begins by enumerating the very same trees used in the preceding chapter to emblematize the beatitudes. Significantly, the chapter on Alexander will also include an extended description of trees—the oracular trees of the sun and

---

28. Derolez, *Autograph,* 133. On Lambert's adaptation of Anselm, see *Autograph,* 129.
29. Mayo, "Crusaders Under the Palm," 47.

moon—in one of the rare passages not to undergo substantial abbreviation by Lambert in his adaptation of the *Letter of Alexander to Aristotle.*

The single element that interrupts the continuity of the sequence is actually embedded within chapter 132 itself, among the cluster of texts concerning Alexander: it is yet another one of Lambert's chronologies, this one a genealogy beginning with Adam. The intended position of these leaves (154r–155v) is a vexed question. They currently appear, in accord with their twelfth-century pagination, within chapter 132, but were earlier bound at the end of the volume. On the basis of codicological evidence, Derolez concludes that these leaves were intended by Lambert to appear at the end of the volume; at some earlier point in the development of the *Liber Floridus,* however, they definitely appeared within the Alexander section, as evidenced by a marginal note in Lambert's own hand which states that the genealogy appearing on those manuscript leaves are "juxta Alexandro" (that is, "beside" either one of the texts or the full-page illustration). To complicate matters, however, the same note adds that the leaves are "in fine iste libro" ("at the end of this book").[30] Perhaps this note reflects a stage in the work's history when the Alexander chapter actually concluded the *Liber Floridus.*[31]

While this genealogy may ultimately belong at the end of the *Liber Floridus,* its original position within the Alexander chapter was by no means incoherent, for it juxtaposes Alexander's travels in the distant east with another figure associated with the same region: Jonitus, the fourth son of Noah. During the twelfth century, writers such as Lambert of St. Omer and Peter Comestor sought to integrate biblical history with that gleaned from other sources. Accordingly, they combine the conventional tripartite division of the world among the three sons of Noah with the alternative genealogy found in the *Revelations* of pseudo-Methodius, an eighth-century apocalyptic universal history extending from the creation of mankind to the advent of Antichrist. In his *Historia Scholastica,* Peter Comestor integrates pseudo-Methodius' account of the fourth son of Noah into the conventional biblical story:

---

30. The marginal note pertaining to the genealogy appears on fol. 105r. On the placement of fol. 154r–155v, see Derolez's introduction to the facsimile of the *Liber Floridus* (where he concludes that the leaves appeared at the end of the book by the thirteenth century; *Facsimile,* x), and Derolez's more recent study (where he concludes that Lambert himself may have shifted the leaves; *Autograph,* 179–80).

31. In his description of the table of contents found in the autograph manuscript of the *Liber Floridus,* Derolez notes that the Alexander chapter is set out as a new beginning to the table of contents. This may suggest that the Alexander material, formerly at the end of the compilation, was recast by Lambert as the beginning of a new movement in the compilation. The genealogical and computational material appearing on fol. 154r–155v would then logically have been moved to the new end of the compilation.

"the sons of Noah," he recounts, "were disseminated into the three parts of the world. Shem went to Asia, Ham to Africa, and Japheth to Europe.... In the third age," he adds, citing pseudo-Methodius, Noah had "another son, of whom Moses does not speak." This son, Jonitus, "received wisdom from God, and discovered astronomy."[32] In pseudo-Methodius' account, the fourth son of Noah, born after the Great Flood, was imbued with an arcane wisdom he shared with the descendants of his brothers—most notably, Nimrod. His dwelling was in the region closest to the sun, in the furthest east. The ninth-century Latin translation of the Syriac text (via a Greek intermediary) renders the name of Jonitus' land as "Eocham, id est, regio solis" ("Eocham, that is, the region of the sun," translating the Greek "helios chora").[33] The manuscript tradition of pseudo-Methodius renders this place name variously, sometimes as "Eocham" but often as "Eoam" or "Ethan," and the same variations are found in the texts that make use of pseudo-Methodius, such as the *Historia Scholastica* and the *Liber Floridus*.[34] It may be that the name given

---

32. Peter Comistor, *Historia Scholastica,* cap. 37; PL 198, cols. 1087D–88C; newly edited by Agneta Sylwan, *Scolastica historia. Liber Genesis.*

33. See *Die Apokalypse des Pseudo-Methodius die ältesten griechischen und lateinischen Übersetzungen.* The birth of Jonitus to Noah, his reception of the eastern land of "Eocham" or "Eoam" (the "regio solis"), and education of Nimrod appears in chapter 3.2–5 (1:81). Aerts and Kortekaas' introduction includes a useful overview of the history of the Latin translations of pseudo-Methodius. Another edition is promised by Laureys and Verhelst in "Pseudo-Methodius, *Revelationes,*" 112–36. A useful overview of pseudo-Methodius' scope and influence can be found in McGinn, *Visions of the End,* 70–73.

34. The ninth-century Latin translation edited by Aerts and Kortekaas renders the name as "Eoam," corresponding to the Greek εώαν of the translation's source text: "Ionetus autem filius Noe introivit in Eoam usque ad mare, qui vocatur 'Hiliu Chora,' id est 'Regio Solis,' in quo solis ortum fit et habitavit ibidem" (chap. 3.4; 1:81). Other pseudo-Methodius redactions render the name as Eocham, Eoum, or Ethan; see notes to this passage in the edition of Aerts and Kortekaas. In his *Historia Scholastica,* Peter Comestor renders the term as "Ethan" (PL 198, col. 1088B); a similar variant appears in one of the manuscripts of the fourteenth-century English translation of pseudo-Methodius formerly attributed to John Trevisa. One manuscript (Additional 37049) renders the term as "Etham" or "Eotham," the other (Harley 1900) as "Eocham"; see pseudo-Methodius, "Bygynnyng of the World and the Ende of Worldes," 94–112; the two manuscript readings appear on 97–98.

An interesting variation appears in the twelfth-century *Imago Mundi* of Honorius of Autun, reflecting the conflation of India and Ethiopia, located on different continents but both identified as borders of the "region of the sun." Honorius states that the Ethiopians have their name from "Ethan" (the variant spelling of Eocham in some pseudo-Methodius manuscripts): "Aethiopia, ab Ethan dicta" (PL 172, col. 131). (Isidore, of course, had influentially stated that the Ethiopians have their name from Chus, whose name is "Aethiops" in Hebrew [*Etym.* 9.2.127].) Honorius' error may be due to the fact that Isidore immediately goes on to mention the Indian population of Ethiopia, which later cartographers will call "India Ethiopie" (9.2.128); where better than on the nebulous border of India and Ethiopia to locate the "regio solis," which Honorius may have known from pseudo-Methodius. (He includes a brief account of Gog and Magog [book 1, chap. 11, col. 123D], which appears to be derived from the *Revelations.*) Honorius' substitution may have found its way into the insular manuscript tradition of Bartholomaeus Anglicus, because the English manuscripts

to the eastern ocean, Eos (in the accusative, "Eoum"), in classical and late antique texts such as Pliny's *Historia naturalia* and Orosius' *Seven Books of History against the Pagans* influenced the scribal tendency to render "Eocham" as "Eoam," since both the eastern ocean and the land of the "regio solis" were said to be located in the extreme Orient. In fact, in Peter Comestor's account, the phrasing is so ambiguous that "regio solis" may denote either the territory received by Jonitus or "the eastern sea" itself.[35]

Like Comestor, Lambert's interest in the *Revelations* was stimulated by the fortunes of the crusades during the twelfth century; unlike Comestor, however, Lambert was writing at a pivotal moment in the history of efforts to establish European, Christian rule in Jerusalem. Accordingly, Lambert's encyclopedic compilation is centered on the apparent culmination of world history in his own time, and the role of Flanders in establishing Christian rule in Jerusalem. Jonitus appears several times in Lambert's compilation: first, in the first few lines of the first page, as the discoverer of astronomy, in a list of the great inventions and accomplishments of world history. Jonitus appears near the head of the list, among the inventors of metalwork and language.[36] The list closes with Godfrey of Bouillon, who captured Jerusalem, and Robert, count of Flanders, whose accomplishment was to set the Christian king of Jerusalem on his throne following the success of the First Crusade. In this list, the arcane oriental knowledge of Jonitus is the first link in a chain that ends by highlighting Flanders' role in Christian history.[37] Jonitus is, of course, featured prominently in pseudo-Methodius' *Revelations,* an abbreviation of which is included in the *Liber Floridus,* and Jonitus reappears in the genealogy of mankind sandwiched in the midst of the chapter devoted to Alexander the Great.

---

of his *De proprietatibus rerum,* in the description of Ethiopia, relate that the people are named after Chus, who "is yclepede Evas in the langage of Ethiopia" (15.52). Greetham states that all the English manuscripts (both Latin and Middle English) have this misreading. See Greetham, "Fabulous Geography," 330–31.

Another twelfth-century example appears in the *Arca Noe Mystice* of Hugh of St. Victor, in which the parts of Noah's ark are associated with the cities of the world. One of these, called "Etham," corresponds to the city that Hugh refers to as "Heliopolis" in his *Descriptio Mappe Mundi.* See Hugh of St. Victor, "De Arca Noe" (PL 176; new ed. P. Sicard); Gautier Dalché, *Descriptio Mappe Mundi.*

35. "Trecentismo anno dedit Noe donationes filio suo Jonitho, et dimisit eum in terram Ethan, et intravit eam Jonithus usque ad mare orientis, quod dicitur Elioschora, id est solis regio." Peter Comestor, *Historia Scholastica* (cap. 37), PL 198, col. 1088B.

36. "Ionitus filius Noae primus astronomiam invenit et sydera caeli cognovit" (1v). Jonitus appears fourth on the list, which begins as follows: Cain (city), Tubal (music), Obal (ironwork), Ionitus (astronomy), Abraham (astronomy), Ninus (idolatry), Isis (letters).

37. On the prominence of Flemish history in the *Liber Floridus* and its relationship to the work's eschatological focus (and the opening list in particular), see van Caenegem, "The Sources of Flemish History," 71–85, esp. 83.

Lambert gives several accounts of the genealogy of mankind in the *Liber Floridus*. In those which are, in his words, "secunda secundum Genesim" (e.g., 136v), only the three sons found in the biblical account appear; in this genealogy (154v), however, Lambert integrates the conventional tripartite division of the world among the three sons of Noah with the account of Jonitus found in pseudo-Methodius, very much as Comestor would go on to do fifty years later in his *Historia Scholastica*.[38] He repeats the conventional allotment of the three known continents of Asia, Africa, and Europe to Shem, Ham, and Japheth, then goes on to add that Jonitus received "terram Eocham ad Orientem" (the land of Eocham, toward the east, 154v). In his abbreviation of pseudo-Methodius' *Revelations* (217r–219v), Lambert omits the account of Alexander in the "regio solis," leaping instead from the early ages shortly after the deluge to the last years of world history.[39] This is in keeping with Lambert's usual editorial practice, where large sections of selected works in the compilation are omitted, not because of their irrelevance but because they are dealt with comprehensively elsewhere in the *Liber Floridus*.[40] Alexander's advance into the "regio solis" instead appears elsewhere, grouped among the Alexander texts of the *Liber Floridus*.

In the *Letter of Alexander to Aristotle*, the Macedonian reflects on his ability to "penetrate" the remotest parts of the Orient: "Indi enim sacra deorum ad oceanum colentes dicebant me quoque esse immortalem, qui usque eo penetrare potuissem. Quibus ego, quod de nobis opinarentur insinuans, gratias agebam" (In fact the Indians, who tend the shrines of the gods towards ocean, said that I was also immortal since I was able to penetrate all the way to that point. Putting in my bosom what they believed about me, I thanked them).[41] In this passage, "to that point" translates "eo," that is, as far as the eastern ocean. The manuscript tradition of the *Letter*, however, sometimes

---

38. "NOE genuit Sem, Cham, et Iaphet....Sem filius Noe cum generatione sua obtinuit Asiam ab Eufrate usque ad Oceanum. Cham cum filiis suis obtinuit terram a Philadelfia quae est in Arabia usque ad montem Lybanum. Iaphet cum progenie sua obtinuit regiones Asiae a monte Tauro usque ad flumen Tanay et Magog in terra Scytarum et omnes fere insulas usque ad Oceanum Britannicum. Tricentismo anno post diluvium genuit Noe filium nomine Ionitum, cui dedit terram Eocham ad Orientem. Iste Ionitus nutrivit Menbroth gigantem, qui edificavit turim Babel in campo Semnaar" (154v). Compare Comestor's later account in the *Historia Scholastica* (cap. 37, cols. 1087D–88C).

39. On the version of pseudo-Methodius likely to have been used by Lambert, see Verhelst, "Les textes eschatologiques dans le *Liber Floridus*."

40. On Lambert's practice of abbreviating his sources, see Derolez, *Autograph*. Friedrich Pfister notes that the section deleted by Lambert from the *Revelations* of pseudo-Methodius—the section on Alexander's enclosure of the savage tribes of Gog and Magog—was the most widely known and most broadly disseminated aspect of the Alexander stories ("Alexander der Grosse," 10).

41. *Epistola Alexandri ad Aristotelem ad Codicum Fidem Edidit et Commentario Critico Instruxit*, 53; [Epistola], *Alexander's Letter to Aristotle about India*, 154–55.

renders the term as "eoum," reflecting the scribes' knowledge of the name of the eastern ocean ("Eos," "Eoum") appearing in the work of such widely read authors as Pliny and Orosius.[42] This same knowledge is apparent in Lambert of St. Omer's rendition of the passage, which reads, "Indi enim sacra deorum ad Oceanum colentes me quoque parumper inmortalem esse dicebant, qui usque Eoum penetrare potuissem. Quibus ego, quod de nobis talia opinarentur, gratias agebam" (161r). This interest in the mysterious eastern extremes reached by Alexander is also evident in the magnificent world map prepared by Lambert to accompany his text, in which the oriental regions visited by Alexander are featured prominently. These include the "arbor solis," one of the oracular trees consulted by Alexander in the farthest reaches of his travels and, just beyond it to the east/south-east, the "insula solis," or island of the sun (figure 7). Lambert's region of the sun is thus located both in the historical past and in the apocalyptic future: it is not only the furthest limit of Alexander the Great's journey east but also the dwelling place of Jonitus. It is a repository of arcane knowledge drawn upon in the past and—presumably—to be drawn upon in the future.

Later writers, such as Vincent of Beauvais writing in the mid-thirteenth century, treat the story of Jonitus and the "regio solis" far more gingerly. Like Lambert of St. Omer and Peter Comestor, Vincent adds to the conventional account of the three sons of Noah, whose descendants populate the three continents, a fourth son "de quo Moyses tacit" (of whom Moses does not speak, *Spec. Hist.* 1.24). Vincent adds nothing more about Jonitus, although he continues to draw upon pseudo-Methodius in his account of the enclosure of the tribes of Gog and Magog. In the twelfth century, however, the figure of Jonitus served as the focus for aspirations to achieve Christian control of the Holy Land and thus precipitate the events leading to the Last Judgment. We see this not only in the *Liber Floridus* but also in the rise of the legend of Prester John, which first appeared in 1122, just after Lambert's work had been brought to completion in 1120. In that year, a messenger was said to have come to the court of the pope (Calixtus II) and told of a Christian king located far to the east who wished to come to the aid of the Crusaders.[43] In the chronicle of Otto of Freising, in the entries for the year 1145, the legend appears in a more richly elaborated form: Otto states that a bishop who came to Rome to report on the state of affairs in the Holy Land

---

42. Boer notes the reading "eoum" in Oxford, Corpus Christi College MS 82, a collection of Alexander materials including not only the *Letter to Aristotle* but also the biography according to both Quintus Curtius and Julius Valerius, Alexander's exchange of letters with Didymus, and the *Itinerarium Alexandri ad Paradisum.* De Boer, ed., *Epistola Alexandri ad Aristotelem,* 53n and xvi.

43. Noted in Gautier Dalché, *Descriptio,* 80.

brought news of a Christian king who had defeated a Muslim army, and who had been prevented from coming to liberate the Holy Land itself only by his difficulty in crossing the Tigris River.[44] The letter of Prester John, which began to circulate by 1165, amplified this legend, incorporating elements from Marvels of the East literature into a text that affirmed that the climactic events of world history were at hand. The letter served as a kind of magnet for all kinds of apocalyptic longings: by the end of the twelfth century, details regarding the enclosed tribes of Gog and Magog (taken from pseudo-Methodius)[45] had been incorporated into the letter, and some later vernacular versions amplify the apocalyptic content even more.[46]

The apocalyptic basis of the Prester John story has long been noted: Kampers suggests that it is closely connected with sybilline prophecies regarding a long-lost king who will, inevitably, return.[47] I would suggest, more specifically, that the legend of Jonitus provided a rich source for the legend of Prester John as it developed in the early twelfth century, while the apocalyptic orientation of Otto of Freising's chronicle made it a particularly appropriate venue for the early dissemination of the legend.[48] The figure of Prester John mingles the magnificent royal power of Alexander with the arcane wisdom of Jonitus; like Prester John, Jonitus is said to have written a letter that foretells the victory of the descendants of Japheth over the descendants of Ham;[49] finally, both are said to inhabit the most distant reaches of the Orient, the "regio solis" which, in several texts, is identified with the remotest part of India.[50] In the *Liber Floridus,* Lambert modifies pseudo-Methodius' text

---

44. *Chronica* 7.33, in *Ottonis Episcopi Frisingensis Chronica sive Historia de duabus civitatibus,* 363–67; *The Two Cities.*

45. Anderson, *Alexander's Gate,* 48.

46. On the apocalyptic content of the Occitan version, see Gosman, *La lettre du prêtre Jean.*

47. Kampers, *Alexander der Grosse und die Idee des Weltimperiums in Prophetie und Sage,* quoted in Gosman, *Lettre,* 27; cf. Gosman, *Lettre,* 44.

48. The most important source of Otto of Freising's apocalyptic historiography is Adso's *Libellus de Antichristo,* which integrates the Holy Roman Empire into the succession of empires as formulated by Orosius (see *De ortu et tempore Antichristi,* ed. Verhelst). For an overview of Adso's scope and importance, see McGinn, *Visions of the End;* on the relationship of Adso's apocalypticism to Otto's chronicle, see Sumption, *Pilgrimage.* Thanks to Suzanne Yeager for the last of these references.

49. For pseudo-Methodius' account of Jonitus' letter to the sons of Japheth, see the edition of Aerts and Kortekaas.

50. It has been suggested that the name "Prester John" is based on a reference to a "presbyter Iohannes" in Rufinus' Latin translation of Eusebius (Helleiner, "Prester John's Letter," 47–57; noted in Gosman, *Lettre,* 45). If, as I suggest, Prester John is a later medieval interpretation of the figure of Jonitus, the forename "Prester" may refer originally not to clerical status but rather to the legend "prester" found in the southernmost region of maps such as that associated with Hugh of St. Victor's *Descriptio mappe mundi* and in Hugh's text itself. In Hugh's text (as in his source, Isidore), "prester" refers to a variety of serpent, creatures that were, according to medieval bestiaries (including that in Lambert's *Liber Floridus*), found only in the hottest regions of the east and south; for a useful overview of the animals of the torrid climates, see Gravestock, "Did Imaginary Animals Exist?" 119–40.

to associate the two, when he relates that Samisab, king of the "regio solis," adds to his realm "the kingdom of the third India."[51] Similarly, in his own adaptation of pseudo-Methodius, Godfrey of Viterbo glosses the realm of the "regio solis" as "finibus Indorum."[52] This remotest part of India was precisely the home of Prester John, who (according to his letter) ruled over a land extending from "the end of the Orient . . . to the Tower of Babel."[53] The land of Prester John continued to be identified as India through the early fourteenth century. It last appears in India on the map of Paulinus Minorita, drawn around 1320,[54] where it appears in the easternmost location, the place which had conventionally been allocated to the Earthly Paradise on medieval maps. Thereafter, cartographers would place the land of Prester John in Ethiopia, on the African continent. This change reflected both the development of actual exploration of these regions at the dawn of the early modern period, and the age-old blurring of the distinction between India and Ethiopia, the regions furthest east and south-east, both dominated by the sun.

For Lambert of St. Omer, the figure of Jonitus held all the embryonic promise that would be fulfilled in the legend of Prester John later in the twelfth century. Now that Jerusalem was finally ruled by a Christian king, the last days could not be far off. In this context, the legend of Alexander reproduced in the *Liber Floridus* had an important didactic function: the fate of Alexander was a warning to the ruler who might reach too far in his quest for knowledge and power and pay the price of his life. While Lambert abbreviates the already-shortened source version of the *Letter of Alexander to Aristotle,* he does not shorten the account of Alexander's journey into the regions furthest east, including a remarkably detailed rendition of his encounter with the oracular trees of the sun and moon. Here, Alexander comes face to face with the arcane knowledge to be found in the furthest reaches of the Orient; the message they reveal, however, is a prophecy of Alexander's own death.

Lambert's awareness of the relevance of the Alexander legend to the Christian conquest of Jerusalem led him to make another significant alteration in

---

According to Hugh of St. Victor, "prester" can be glossed as a "fiery hot wind," which may also be an element in the development of the legend of Prester John.

51. "Samisab rex de Eocham" adds to his realm "regno tertio Indorum" (f.218r).

52. The variation in Godfrey of Viterbo is noted in Anderson, *Alexander's Gate,* 74–76. A similar identification of the "regio solis" with India appears in the Middle English metrical translation of pseudo-Methodius, where Jonitus' land, placed in "the oryent the est syde" (165, line 347) extends "thorow-owt all the heye Ynde" (167, line 425); the text appears in d'Evelyn, "Middle-English Metrical Version," 135–203.

53. "[L]a fin de l'Orient. . . . Juste la tur Bable nomé" (lines 151, 155; Gosman, *Lettre,* 124).

54. A reproduction of Paulinus Minorita's map, showing the land of Prester John in India, can be found in von den Brincken, *Fines Terrae,* plate 40.

his retelling of the life of the Macedonian. Into the account found in the Zacher Epitome, Lambert inserts the account of Alexander's entry into Jerusalem and encounter with the high priest of the Jews found in Josephus.[55] This passage from the *Bellum Judaicum* is commonly inserted into lives of Alexander; these are the versions based on the account found in the *Historia de Preliis,* however, not the account of Julius Valerius on which the Zacher Epitome is based. Moreover, the Josephus episode is inserted at an entirely different point in the history of Alexander's conquests.[56] Lambert places the episode at the pivotal point between Alexander's entombment of the Persian king Darius and the beginning of his journey into India in the company of King Porus, reinforcing the central place of Jerusalem in Alexander's path of imperial expansion. Alexander's time in Jerusalem foreshadows the rule of the Christian kings of Jerusalem in the twelfth century. His conquest of Darius the Persian is echoed in the crusaders' defeat of the Saracen armies, while his exploration of India is reflected in the apocalyptic future that, from Lambert's point of view, would surely follow on the heels of the Christian conquest of Jerusalem. The placement of the Josephus episode at this point in the Alexander narrative is uniquely found in Lambert; in the late twelfth century, however, it reappears in Thomas of Kent's *Roman de toute chevalerie.*[57] Lambert's addition serves to highlight the role of Alexander at this crucial point in the history of the Western effort to reclaim Jerusalem, for Alexander appears both as a figure of the exemplary ruler and as a negative exemplum of the terrible dangers awaiting the man who ventures too far into the dangerous region of the sun. It is striking that the Jews depicted in Lambert's version of the Alexander story are not demonized, as they are in later medieval texts that go so far as to identify the unclean tribes of Gog and Magog, enclosed in the far north by Alexander, as the twelve tribes of Israel.[58] Instead, their conversion and integration into the community is the long-awaited signal of the arrival of the last days and the approach of the apocalypse.

---

55. Josephus, *Ant. Jud.* XI.8.5, 472–79.

56. On the incorporation of Josephus' account of Alexander's visit to Jerusalem, see *Historia Alexandri Magni.* On the independent circulation of the excerpt from Josephus, see Hamilton, "Quelques notes sur l'histoire de la légende d'Alexandre le Grand en Angleterre au moyen âge," 200.

57. In the introduction to his edition of the *Roman de toute chevalerie,* Brian Foster argues that the Josephus material is unique to the fourteenth-century Durham manuscript (98 [note to line 3777]); see also the comments of Maria-Rosa Lida de Malkiel, "Alejandro en Jerusalén," 186n2, as well as the discussion below.

58. On the identification of the tribes of Gog and Magog with the twelve tribes of Israel, see Gow, *The Red Jews,* 37–63; Westrem, "Against Gog and Magog," 54–75, esp. 65–66. A fuller discussion of apocalypticism in connection with the perceived threat to Christendom posed by Muslims and Jews appears in chapter 3, 135–40.

↢ The *Roman de toute chevalerie*

The *Liber Floridus* of Lambert of St. Omer and the *Roman de toute chevalerie* of Thomas of Kent are closely related branches of the same tree. Although one is a compilation of heterogeneous materials compiled in Flanders during the early twelfth century and the other an elaborate Anglo-Norman romance written in northern England at least fifty years later, they share a common vision of Alexander and his place in the conquest and exploration of the Orient. They also share, as noted briefly above, the unusual integration of Josephus' account of Alexander's entry into Jerusalem into the Julius Valerius Epitome at the crucial point between the entombment of Darius and the journey into India with Porus. This could suggest that Thomas of Kent was familiar with the account of Alexander appearing in the *Liber Floridus;* alternatively, since the episode in Jerusalem appears only in the Durham manuscript of the *Roman de toute chevalerie,* it could have been interpolated by a knowledgeable scribe.[59] The encyclopedic impulse so vividly demonstrated in the *Liber Floridus* is also evident in the *Roman de toute chevalerie,* which brings together a variety of geographical and anthropological texts within its heroic narrative, including Pliny's *Historia naturalia,* Solinus' *Collectanea rerum memorabilium,* and Aethicus Ister's *Cosmographia,* as well as the "Wonders of the East" material associated with the *Letter of Alexander to Aristotle.*[60] The skillful integration of the various Alexander materials in the *Roman de toute chevalerie* is the culmination of the tendency to include a sequence of texts devoted to the Macedonian within a single collection or even, as in Lambert's work, within a single chapter. Several manuscript compilations from the twelfth century survive that couple one or more versions of the life of Alexander with the *Letter to Aristotle,* the exchange with Didymus, and other Alexander texts.[61] The *Liber Floridus* goes one step beyond such compilations, uniting these disparate parts into a single chapter titled "De Alexandro." The

---

59. On the manuscript tradition of the *Roman de toute chevalerie,* see Bunt, *Alexander the Great,* 19–20. See also Brian Foster's introduction to his edition of the *Roman de toute chevalerie,* prepared together with Ian Short: *Anglo-Norman "Alexander,";* also the introduction to the modern French translation of the *Roman de toute chevalerie* (which reproduces Foster and Short's edition), *Le Roman d'Alexandre ou Le roman de toute chevalerie.* Quotations from the *Roman de toute chevalerie* are cited in the text; translations are my own. On the use of Josephus, whether in the original version of the *Roman de toute chevalerie* or in the Durham manuscript, see Weynand, *Der "Roman de toute chevalerie" des Thomas von Kent,* 70.

60. On the use of these sources in the *Roman de toute chevalerie,* see Weynand, *Der "Roman de toute chevalerie" des Thomas von Kent.*

61. Some of these manuscript compilations are noted in De Boer's edition of the *Letter of Alexander to Aristotle.*

Roman de toute chevalerie, in turn, goes one step further, integrating these materials into a single—albeit expansive—narrative.

Despite the apparently innovative nature of Thomas' enterprise, it is widely
believed that the integration of the *Letter of Alexander to Aristotle* with the
account of Julius Valerius had taken place at an earlier date. Several scholars
working on the twelfth-century Alexander romances have posited a now-lost
Old French original, hypothetically titled *Alexandre en Orient,* which provided
a common source of parallel passages in the two main Alexander romances
of the twelfth century, the *Roman d'Alexandre* and the *Roman de toute chevalerie.*[62] There are several problems with this hypothesis, among them the fact
that the author of the *Roman d'Alexandre* refers to a vernacular ("romans")
antecedent, while Thomas of Kent refers to a Latin source: "d'un bon livre
en latin fist cest translatement" (I made this translation from a good book
in Latin [P21]).[63] More significant than the (probably insoluable) question
of whether the *Alexandre en Orient* really existed is the fact that Thomas
self-consciously presents his *Roman de toute chevalerie* as a work of translation
("cest translatement"). The fictitious assertion of a Latin source appears to
be an effort to claim greater authority for Thomas' narrative, giving the vernacular romance a stabilizing foundation in an ancient text.[64]

The *Roman de toute chevalerie* is, in one sense, the portrait of a single man,
a hero whose journeys of exploration and conquest are exemplary both in
their triumphant demonstration of the abilities of the perfect knight (that is,
Alexander's "chevalerie") and in their implicit warning of the dangers that
await the man who ventures too far. In another sense, however, the *Roman de
toute chevalerie* is a cosmography, for between the account of the magnificent
sarcophagus of the fallen Persian king Darius and the description of the death
of Alexander lies a sprawling account of the marvels of the world, as the
Macedonian ventures into the furthest regions of the east, north, and south
in his passionate endeavor to explore everywhere and conquer everything.
The magnificent mappamundi that adorns Darius' tomb in another twelfth-
century life of Alexander, the *Alexandreis* of Walter of Châtillon, seems to
come alive in the *Roman de toute chevalerie*'s account of the abundant luxuries

---

62. On the conjectural *Alexandre en Orient,* see Armstrong's comments in Alexandre de Bernay,
The Medieval French, vii and 22 ff.

63. Ibid., 88–89 (line 15 in the version of Alexandre de Paris). Note that Foster and Short's edition of the *Roman de toute chevalerie* numbers the lines of the poem according to manuscript D; where
D lacks an episode, they restart the numbering, adding the letter of the supplementary manuscript.
Hence lines P1–178 follow line 3921 in D. On the limitations of Foster and Short's edition, see Gosman, *La légende d'Alexandre le Grand dans la littérature française du 12e siècle,* 290–92.

64. On the use of Latin and the position of Rome in the *Roman de toute chevalerie,* see Akbari,
"Alexander in the Orient," 105–26, esp. 112–13.

found in the "fin d'Orient," the hideous tribes of Gog and Magog found in the northern wastes, and the monstrous races populating the torrid regions of the south. Significantly, the trajectory of Alexander's route of exploration and conquest—east, north, and south—follows that found in Orosius' universal chronicle, as the Persian Empire gives way to Macedonia and then to Carthage, before it reaches the end of its trajectory in Rome. Alexander thus embodies the spirit of conquest, summing up the path of *translatio imperii* in the life of a single man.

The *Roman de toute chevalerie* differs from earlier accounts of Alexander, including the sequence of materials found in the *Liber Floridus,* in several ways. Most prominent among these is Thomas' organization of the path of Alexander's conquest. While following the basic trajectory of conquest outlined in the Julius Valerius Epitome, Thomas maps out the world brought under the yoke of Alexander in terms of the cardinal directions: Alexander ventures into the regions furthest east, north, and then south, following the Orosian model of *translatio imperii.*[65] Thomas places this path of conquest, moreover, within an elaborately developed quadripartite model of the world, drawn mainly from the *Cosmographia* of Aethicus Ister. This allows Thomas to rationalize and explicate the nature of the wonders to be found as one approaches the limits of each cardinal direction in terms of climate theory. A second feature specific to Thomas' version of the Alexander narrative concerns the dangers met by the Macedonian at the furthest points of exploration, and the way in which Alexander compares his own accomplishments to those of Hercules, the last hero to venture as far as the edges of the earth. Alexander's destruction of the "mercs" or pillars of Hercules and replacement of them with monuments of his own is at once testimony to Alexander's greatness and evidence of his hubris. Third, liminal points found in the distant Orient, such as the eastern ocean, the oracular trees of the sun and moon, and the exotic island of Taprobana, are described in terms of luxurious excess in more detail than they had been in the *Epistola.* In the *Roman de toute chevalerie,* these sites are both intensely alluring and profoundly dangerous. Finally, Thomas devotes a great deal of space to the apocalyptic aspect of the Alexander story concerning the enclosure of the unclean races of Gog and Magog in the remote north, drawing upon not only the account found in the *Cosmographia* of Aethicus Ister but also that appearing in the *Revelations* of pseudo-Methodius (which had itself been a source for the *Cosmographia*). This emphasis on apocalypse, shared by Lambert of St. Omer, reaches its

65. On the absent west in Alexander's path of conquest as presented in the *Roman de toute chev- alerie,* see ibid., 120–23.

height in the account of Thomas of Kent; later vernacular versions of the Alexander romance sharply reduce the apocalyptic import in favor of an Alexander whose exemplary status is social and political rather than eschatological.[66] In order to appreciate these four distinguishing features of the *Roman de toute chevalerie,* it is helpful to follow the sequence of Alexander's path as presented in the romance. Each region—east, north, and south—has qualities proper to it, and each in turn is explored by Alexander, adorned with monuments marking the limits of conquest.

Alexander's voyage into the east is characterized in terms of doubleness. The land itself is double, for India is divided into two parts: "En la fin d'orient, de Inde i ad deus paire, / Inde superior e Inde la maire" (In the furthest east, there are two Indias, Upper India and Greater India [4601–02]).[67] This doubling has a temporal dimension as well, for there are two summers and two harvests (4619–20). The resulting plenty extends not just to the abundant crops but also to the numerous cities and great number of "diverses genz" (diverse peoples [4623]). The east is filled with "merveiles" (4626), as Thomas illustrates in his long catalogues of the various peoples and wondrous animals to be found in India. When Alexander encounters the Indian king Porus, he has only one demand: he asks Porus to take him to the "fin d'orient" (5359), as far as the "mercs" left by Hercules long ago (5377). There, an aged native comes up to Alexander to tell him about the further marvels to be found further east, beyond the pillars of Hercules, in the land of Taprobana.[68] Predictably, Alexander insists on going "ou Hercules n'osa" (where Hercules did not dare [5484]). In Taprobana, the doubleness of the east is reinforced, for there are not only two summers and two harvests, but two winters as well. In this easternmost region, Alexander encounters further marvels, exploring until there is no more to be found: "Par tote [Ynde] est alez cerchant la region" (He went throughout all India, exploring the region [5938]).

Alexander's exploration of the Orient is interrupted when a messenger comes down from the north, begging the conqueror to come back with him to deal with the hideous tribes of Gog and Magog, who live "vers aquilon" (in the place of the north wind). This horrible "nacion" is "vers humeine

---

66. On Alexander as a "chivalric model" (118) in the Middle English alliterative *Wars of Alexander,* see Chism, "Too Close for Comfort," 116–39, esp. 118–19, 137.

67. On maps and in prose geographies, India is divided into two, three, or even more parts. See von den Brincken, *Fines Terrae,* 162.

68. In connection with the figure of the local informant, a native who offers direction and information in an unfamiliar territory, compare Ora Limor's description of the "knowing Jew" in "Christian Sacred Space and the Jew," 55–77.

nature" (against human nature): their favorite food is "char d'ome" (human flesh), but they also eat dogs in place of venison, as well as serpents, toads, frogs, and slugs (5961–70). The uncleanliness of these tribes is manifested not just in their cannibalism (and in eating man's best friend), but also in their consumption of foods that are unclean because they fall outside normal categories, such as frogs and toads.[69] The tribes of Gog and Magog are, in some ways, homogeneous: Thomas describes them as a single "nacion" (5961), united in their unclean behaviors and in their common descent from Nimrod ("Nembroth le traitur" [5980]).[70] In spite of this apparent homogeneity, however, the northerners prove to show a range of diversity similar to that encountered earlier during Alexander's travels throughout the east. One group lives on the sea and eats human flesh; another eats mice; still another is made up of metalworkers, and so on. Among this diverse lot, Thomas gives special emphasis to the Turks, who eat both humans and dogs, "char vive" (living flesh) and "ordure" (filth [6021]). They are "cruel e dure" (cruel and hard), given to "lecherie e chescune luxure" (lechery and every wanton behavior [6019–20]). Thomas goes beyond his source, the *Cosmographia* of Aethicus Ister, in his emphasis on the Turks and in his description of the climatic qualities associated with the northern region they inhabit. In this chilly, arid land, "Il n'i put nul blé crestre, ne nul fruit n['i] m[e]ure; / En esté, en yver ont toz jors la froidure" (no wheat can grow there, nor any fruit or berry; in summer and in winter, they have constant cold [6048–49]).[71]

The catalogue of the tribes of Gog and Magog goes on to include those who swim in the sea, those who build "estranges nefs" (strange boats [6057]) that travel underwater for up to four months, unnamed dwarves, and "Rifaires" who constantly fight "vers autres Sarazins" (against other Saracens [6090]).[72] Alexander determines that his role as conqueror demands that he take on the task of preserving the world from the tribes of Gog and Magog, stating "De cest[e] ordure est trestuit le mond soillez" (The entire world is made dirty by this filth [6338]). Because the tribes consume unclean things,

---

69. See Douglas, "Forbidden Animals in Leviticus," 3–23.

70. This unusual detail comes not from the *Cosmographia* of Aethicus Ister, the source for much of Thomas' account of Gog and Magog, but from the *Apocalypse* of pseudo-Methodius; noted in Smithers' edition of *Kyng Alisaunder* 2:135–36 (note to line 5954).

71. Compare the source passage in the *Cosmographia* of Aethicus Ister, where the chill of the northern climate is not emphasized, and the natives even celebrate a late-summer religious festival. *Die Kosmographie des Aethicus,* 120–21 (chap. 4).

72. Thomas of Kent uses the term "Sarazin" to refer to pagans in general, not just those found in the Orient, and also applies it to the pre-Christian period. Diane Speed suggests that such generic usage of the term was standard in twelfth- and thirteenth-century England; see "Saracens of *King Horn,*" 564–95, esp. 566–67.

they themselves become a source of uncleanliness. Having established the borders of the known world through conquest, Alexander also must bear the burden of maintaining the order of his territory within. Accordingly, he withdraws to Mount Chelion to make sacrifices, where he hears the voice of God telling him how to enclose Gog and Magog. Forging columns of metal, reinforced with bitumen, Alexander seals up the unclean tribes in an enclosure from which they will emerge only in the time of Antichrist.[73]

> Enclos ad Taragonce e les Magogetas,
> E les Turcs e les naims, Chanalius e Egetas,
> E vint e deus poples en ces regnés plus bas.
> Ainz le temps Antecrist n'istront il pas.
> Merveillus fu Alisandre qe unques ne fu las.

> He enclosed Taragonce and the Magogetas [Gog and Magog],
> the Turks and the dwarves, the Chanalius and the Egetas,
> and the twenty-two peoples of the realms below.
> They will never emerge, up until the time of Antichrist.
> Alexander was marvelous, he who ever was tireless.
>
> (6574–78)

It is this accomplishment, for Thomas, that makes Alexander "the Great," himself as marvelous as the marvels he discovers.

Having swept through the regions of the east and north, Alexander turns his glance southward: "Les deus parties del mond ad pres environé, / ... / Al regné de Ethiopie ad il ost mené, / E veu tel[es] choses qe point nen ay conté" (He surrounded two parts of the world...and turned his host toward the kingdom of Ethiopia, and saw such things as I have not yet begun to tell [6637–40]). Ethiopia—used here, as usual in twelfth-century maps and geographies, to represent the southernmost habitable region[74]—is replete with marvels and marvelous diversity. Its many kingdoms are filled with "Gent de meintes maneres e de diverse colur: / Aquanz i sunt noir, autres blanc cum flur, / Aquanz sunt coloré, aquant ont palur" (people of many different characters and of different colors: some there are black, others white as

---

73. The standard source on the tradition of the encounter of Alexander with the tribes of Gog and Magog is Anderson, *Alexander's Gate*. See also Gow, *The Red Jews* and "Gog and Magog"; Westrem, "Against Gog and Magog."

74. Compare the climatic maps that illustrate Isidore, *Etymologiae* 13.6, in which the northern habitable extreme is labeled with the Riphaean Mountains and the southern extreme with Ethiopia; examples in von den Brincken, plates 13–15.

a flower; some are ruddy, others pale [6681–84]). Unlike medieval encyclopedists, who attribute the racial diversity of the southern regions to the effects
of climate, Thomas describes it as the consequence of their unusual behavior:
"En Ethiope ad gent de diverse nature, / De diverse lignee, de diverse par-
leure, / Car trestoz en sunt de diverse engendrure" (In Ethiopia are people
of diverse natures, of diverse lineages, of diverse languages, because everyone
there is diversely engendered [6702–04]). Thomas explains that Ethiopians'
great diversity is due to their sexual promiscuity, such that no man knows
his father, nor any father his sons: "Tuit sunt commun entr'els cum bestes en
pasture" (All is common among them, like beasts in the field [6708]). As in
the regions of the east and north, the southern expanse contains a numerous,
heterogeneous collection of peoples: some who have a dog for their king,
others who have four eyes and worship Mercury; those who eat lions and
have one eye, those who bark like dogs, those who ride elephants, those who
have no mouths and communicate by sign language, and so on.

As Alexander moves through Ethiopia, its resemblance to the Indian regions where he began becomes more evident. The marvelous races, the wondrous animals, and even the land itself recall the India he left behind, for there
are said to be two Ethiopias ("Deus Ethiopes sunt," 6776), just as there were
two Indias (4601). In a reenactment of his behavior in the northern wastes,
Alexander withdraws to a mountain to make a sacrifice. A voice speaks to
him once again, but this time it tells him that he will never return, that his
insatiable thirst to see the world will end not in the safe haven of home but
abroad. At last, Alexander has received tribute from every nation, and seen
everything there is to see: "Ne remeint a veer nule merveille seue, / De
mostre ne d'engin ne de beste mue" (No more marvels remained to be seen,
neither monsters nor quaint inventions nor crouching beasts [6923–24]).
Therefore, Alexander decides to turn back; but in returning home, he turns
his steps not toward Macedonia but toward "Inde majur" (6929). In a curious sense, the Orient has itself become home to this king of the Orient.
It is therefore unsurprising that the two major episodes remaining in the
romance focus on Alexander's identity and his ultimate fate, as he encounters the oracular trees at the very farthest limits of the east and is entertained
by the Oriental queen Candace in her private chamber. Both the grounds
surrounding the trees and the chamber of Candace are said to be enclosures;
these enclosures, however, represent not the secure, domestic spaces of home
but instead unsettling locations where identity is revealed to be contingent,
and danger is close at hand.

The haunting, fearsome quality of Alexander's encounter with the oracular trees is signaled from the outset of the episode, as the conqueror enters

into a dark land ("lande oscure" [7019]) where he stumbles upon two old men. Alexander, as usual, inquires whether they have heard of "Nul[e] estrange merveille en ices regnez" (any strange marvel in this kingdom [7026]). The men tell him about two marvelous trees, one male and one female, that speak both Indian and Greek; these trees are oracular, able to reveal the future to anyone who asks. His interest awakened, Alexander heads eastward. He sees many marvels along the way, none more remarkable than the man who guards these trees "a la lune e al soleil sacrez" (sacred to the moon and sun [7069]): he is ten feet tall, with a black body and dog-like teeth, dressed in the skins of white lions and tigers. As Thomas puts it, "bien semblot enemis" (he looked very much like an enemy [7106]). His repellent appearance, however, is belied by the attractive atmosphere that surrounds him: "Flairist i ly balmes, la mirre e ly [en]sens, / Car les cher[e]s espi[c]es i cressent tot temps" (balm, myrrh, and incense gave off a wonderful odor there, for these precious spices flourished there constantly [7132–33]). This fearsome man is no savage guardian barring the way to the oracle; rather, he is a cleric, the "ercevesque" (archbishop [7102]) who attends the sacred trees. In a detail found in none of his sources, Thomas states that the name of this strange "prestres" is "Longis" (priest [7135, 7141; 7102]).[75] Like Prester John of the eponymous letter, like Jonitus, the fourth son of Noah who inhabits the distant "regio solis," this "prestres" who attends the trees of the sun and moon is a liminal figure who embodies both the exotic allure of the Orient and its frightening danger.

The location attended by this strange "priest" has the qualities of both interior and exterior spaces. Although the sacred trees (being trees) are out in the open, they are said to be within an enclosure: "Enclos est tot entur" (it is entirely enclosed all around [7134]). Like a church, the proper domain of a priest, this place is a "leu sacré" or a "seint l[e]u" (7100, 7136, 7162); at the same time, however, the sacred trees are constantly bathed in the rays of the sun and the moon. The scent of incense and perfumed candles normally found in a church are the product here not of art but of nature, for the trees are located within a realm abundant in these luxurious goods: "Mult fu le regné

---

75. It is tempting to speculate that the name "Longis" is to be associated with Longinus (also rendered as "Longis" in Old French texts), the name of the soldier and subsequent Christian convert whose lance was used to pierce the side of Jesus on the Cross, making the lance among the holiest relics in Christendom. (It turns up, among other places, in the pommel of Charlemagne's sword, according to the Chanson de Roland.) See, for example, "Longis" (for Longinus) in La Novele Cirurgie, ed. Constance B. Hieatt and Robin F. Jones (London: Anglo-Norman Text Society, 1990), 8 (III.1). This identification, combined with the evocation of Prester John in the same passage, would reinforce the specifically Christian, redemptive apocalypticism of Alexander's journey into the Orient.

beaus, riches e plentifs, / D'encens et de balme, d'olive e de vins, / De dates
e de gelofre, de poivre e d'anis. / Des espices preciouses ert tot le regne assis"
(the realm was very beautiful, rich and plentiful with incense and balm, with
olives and grapes, with dates and ginger, with pepper and anise. The whole
realm was full of precious spices [7094–97]). Located in a space that is neither fully interior nor fully exterior, the sacred trees inhabit a liminal position,
in between two states of being.

Moreover, the trees' own liminality is projected upon those who encounter the oracle, including not only the strange "prestres" who has the appearance of both man and beast but also Alexander himself. This strange place
replete with beauty and luxury marks the beginning of Alexander's end, not
only in the sacred trees' explicit prophecy of his doom but in the nature of
their response to his query. "[P]ensez vostre voleir," the priest says to the
ruler, "Tost en averez respons par mult apert langage" (Think of your desire;
right away you will have your response in very clear language [7147, 7150]).
Alexander kneels and kisses the tree of the sun; within a few moments, the
tree speaks "en indiene parole" (in Indian language [7178]), declaring that
the Macedonian will never see his mother or sisters again. Alexander returns
at night to hear the verdict of the tree of the moon. Speaking "en griu" (in
Greek" [C41]), the tree confirms Alexander's doom. The two languages of
the trees—Indian and Greek—reflect Alexander's two natures, his origin as
king of the Greek-speaking nations and his new role as ruler of India. Divided in this way, Alexander cannot endure; therefore it comes as no surprise
that his end comes soon after the prophecy of the oracle.

In the *Letter of Alexander to Aristotle,* the encounter with the oracular trees
of the sun and moon appear near the end of the text; in the version found in
the *Liber Floridus,* the climactic nature of the scene is enhanced by Lambert's
extreme compression of the episodes preceding and following the encounter
with the trees. In the *Roman de toute chevalerie,* however, the placement of
this encounter is quite different. While the trees of the sun and moon appear following Alexander's exploration of the furthest reaches of the earth,
and thus represent both the culmination of his endeavors and the signal of
the conqueror's own imminent mortality, they are followed by an elaborate
rendition of the meeting of Alexander and Candace. Though the *Roman de
toute chevalerie*'s version is based on the account found in the Julius Valerius
Epitome, Thomas embellishes it in many ways, making the realm of Candace
into an ambiguous space that epitomizes at once the familiar comforts of
home and the exotic and erotic excess of the Orient.

Initially, Alexander's encounter with Candace seems as though it could
have taken place in the courts of France or England. This Oriental queen is

"bele e blanche" (6943; cf. 7751), fair-skinned and blonde as any European. As Alexander approaches the queen's palace, disguised as a messenger called Antigone, she listens to her minstrels play "un nouvel son / Coment danz Eneas ama dame Didon" (a new song of how Lord Aeneas loved Lady Dido [7650–51]).[76] Perhaps remembering the fate of Dido, "Pensive en est Candace del torn de l[a] chançon" (Candace is made thoughtful by the refrain of the song [7655]). Thomas of Kent's characterization of Candace as an Oriental queen who is most European is at odds with other renditions of Alexander's life written both before the *Roman de toute chevalerie* and after it. In the versions of the Latin text preceding Thomas, Candace's realm is said to be located in the south-east, contiguous with Ethiopia. Accordingly, she is an exotic ruler, able to offer Alexander rich gifts and luxurious goods, more reminiscent of the biblical Queen of Sheba than of a courtly *demoiselle*. The same characterization is found in the Middle English *Kyng Alisaunder*, adapted from the *Roman de toute chevalerie:* returning to the Latin tradition, Candace's realm is explicitly called "Saba," and her character modeled on Sheba herself.[77]

Showing a passivity rarely found in a conqueror of the world, Alexander does not approach Candace first; instead, she approaches him, sending messengers bearing luxurious gifts ranging from camels loaded with baskets of emeralds to a thousand armed "white Ethiopians" (6971). The inclusion of Ethiopian soldiers in the tribute offered by Candace is utterly conventional; what is very peculiar is their description as "blans," or white.[78] It is clear that their skin color is meant, because Thomas goes on to reiterate that "Il sunt plus blanc qe neif e plus qe lion fier" (They are whiter than snow and fiercer than lions [6976]). This is unusual precisely because Thomas has so elaborately embellished the text of his romance with allusions to how climate affects the flora and fauna of a land. Medieval scientific texts and encyclopedias point out that different climates give rise to different species: accordingly, creatures of the north tend to be larger and whiter, while creatures of the south tend to be smaller and darker.[79] White Ethiopians, then, are not just an anomaly, but a paradox, emblematic of this land located in the remotest Orient though with all the trappings of the cultured West. They are of the realm most fully marked by the heat of the sun, yet bear no markings of it on their milky bodies.

---

76. This may refer to the twelfth-century romance of *Eneas;* see Foster and Short, 2:73.
77. Compare *Kyng Alisaundre*, line 7616, and the discussion below.
78. For the source in Pliny's *Historia naturalia*, see note 2 above.
79. Akbari, "Diversity of Mankind," 249–77, esp. 252–58.

Candace's purpose in sending this collection of sumptuous gifts is not merely to propitiate Alexander: she also sends an artist along with her delegation, commissioned to make a portrait of the Macedonian. On his return, the portrait is used as a model for the construction of a life-size statue which will greet the conqueror during his encounter with Candace, which immediately follows his visit to the oracular trees of the sun and moon. After displaying all her rich treasures, Candace confronts Alexander with the truth of his identity: "Vous estes Alisandre; le non por quei changez?" (You are Alexander; why have you changed your name? [7685]). Alexander insists that he really is just "Antigone," the king's messenger, whereupon Candace takes Alexander off to a "privé manage" or private room (7698): "Alisandre," says Candace, "veez cy vostre ymage" (Alexander, see here your image [7699]). By not only tricking Alexander, but actually trapping him alone in her private room, deep within the palace walls, Candace gains ascendency over Alexander. Generously, however, Candace tells him not to be ashamed, because "tuit temps est usage / Qe femme deceit homme" (it always happens that woman deceives man [7710–11]). Now that you are under my "discipline," says Candace, "Aloms ore juer suz cele cortine" (Let's go play now behind those bed-curtains [7748–49]). They go "desur le lit parler d'amur fine; / Recordent la lesçon qu'afiert a tel doctrine" (onto the bed to speak of "fine amour," to rehearse the lesson that goes along with that doctrine [7755–56]). Alexander has entered a kind of carnal paradise, where the deceptive nature of woman renders man powerless, and where no secrets can be held back.

Several scenes of enclosure punctuate Alexander's journeys throughout the world, ranging from the walling up of the tribes of Gog and Magog in the north, to the oracular cave in the deepest south, to the grove containing the trees of the sun and moon in the land furthest east, which is said to be "enclose . . . tot entur" (entirely enclosed [7134]). Like the grove of trees, where "flairent . . . les espices cum ceo fust Paradis" (the spices smelled as fragrant as if it were Paradise [7101]), Candace's bedchamber is a location which is at once paradise-like and threatening, offering both sensuous pleasure and imminent danger. The series of enclosures near the end of the narrative, including the grove of trees and the bedchamber of Candace, will end with a final enclosure: the "sarcu de fin or" (7982) that encloses Alexander's dead body, like the one in which he enclosed the body of his predecessor, Darius. The private room in which Alexander and Candace meet is a place which is at once strange and familiar: strange, because it is located in an eastern locale, decorated with curious and rare treasures, but familiar because it is a place where the knight Alexander can play at "fine amour" with a lady who is both "beautiful and white." The distant center of oriental luxury proves to epitomize the courtly ideal found (for the European reader) at home. In spite of its reassuring familiarity, this locale proves to be dangerous, for here Alexander's own identity becomes peculiarly fluid. In Candace's realm, he is known as Antigone, the messenger of Alexander, in order to protect himself from enemies in this alien land. Only in the queen's bedroom is he known by his right name, for she alone knows his true identity. He wavers between being Antigone and Alexander, messenger and king, depending upon his location.

The enclosed spaces of Candace's chamber and the grove containing the oracular trees can be described as places of "danger," in the sense used by cultural anthropologists such as Mary Douglas.[80] These spaces are liminal in the sense that they mark transgressive moments, where powerful knowledge—of one's fate, in the case of the oracular trees; of one's identity, in the case of Candace's chamber—is revealed. Because they are enclosures, however, these spaces represent thresholds only in a symbolic sense, rather than a spatial sense. One cannot pass beyond the trees, or beyond Candace's chamber; these are spaces to be entered and then exited, transformed by the experience that takes place within the enclosure. The spatial sense of the threshold is instead projected outward, to the "mercs" or boundary markers delineating the furthest geographical point reached by those who, like Hercules and Alexander, dare to explore more distant locations than anyone had done before. The effort to push outward the boundaries of human knowledge and power ends, inevitably, in the containment, transformation, and (ultimately) destruction of the one who dares to venture too far.

The enclosed spaces of the grove and chamber depicted in the *Roman de toute chevalerie* can be fruitfully compared with the *regio solis* or "region of the sun" central to the story of Jonitus, the fourth son of Noah. In the version recounted by Lambert of St. Omer in his *Liber Floridus,* Jonitus is said to inhabit the eastern land of Eocham ("terram Eocham ad Orientem" [154v]), a location which Lambert (like Peter Comestor) clearly associates with the eastern ocean of Eoum (161r) explored by Alexander. On the world map included by Lambert in his *Liber Floridus,* this region is depicted in still a third way, as the enigmatic "insula solis" located at the point of land furthest east, just before the inaccessible earthly paradise of Eden (figure 7). This "region of the sun" is both a place of origins and a place of uncertainty. Placed at the gates of Eden, it heralds the rising of the sun and houses the fourth son of Noah; it nonetheless remains indefinable, comprising territory, ocean, and

---

80. "[I]deas about separating, purifying, demarcating and punishing transgressions have as their main function to impose system on an inherently untidy experience." Douglas, *Purity and Danger,* 5.

island. It is both multiple and singular, the *regio solis* or "region of the sun." The Latin translator of pseudo-Methodius uses this phrase to translate the Greek term "helios chora." Like *regio, chora* denotes a place; the same term, however, was used by Plato and Aristotle in the metaphysical sense to describe the space within which things come into being. For Aristotle, the *chora* was to be identified with matter itself, which upon being impressed with form comes into being. For Plato, however, the spatial aspect of the *chora* remained primary; in the *Timaeus,* he defines it as the space in which the generation of forms takes place.[81] Something of this metaphysical sense of the *chora* persists in the medieval traces of the *regio solis,* for it too takes up space without having a clearly defined ontology. It is the mysterious and dangerous heart of the Orient, which no one can locate even though everyone knows that it is there.

⤺ *Kyng Alisaunder*

After the arcane apocalypticism of the *Liber Floridus* and the exotic heterogeneity of the *Roman de toute chevalerie,* the relatively straightforward adventures of *The Romaunce of Kyng Alisaunder* may seem rather anticlimactic. Like the *Roman de toute chevalerie,* on which it is closely based, *Kyng Alisaunder* presents an anachronistically chivalric world in which Alexander represents the epitome of medieval knighthood. It differs, however, from the *Roman de toute chevalerie* in several ways, most notably in the extent to which it subdues the exuberant exoticism of Thomas of Kent's poem. The anonymous writer of *Kyng Alisaunder* simplifies the elaborate catalogues of fantastic beasts and marvelous races, and shortens and makes more coherent Thomas' often convoluted account of Alexander's efforts to enclose the unclean tribes of Gog and Magog. He also largely ignores the cosmographical dimension of the *Roman de toute chevalerie,* where the four-fold division of the world into its cardinal directions, each with its special properties, provides the geographical framework for Thomas' presentation of Alexander's path of conquest. Moreover, the apocalypticism crucial to the Alexander story as recounted in the *Liber*

---

81. "[A] third kind [of form] is ever-existing place, χώρασ which admits not of destruction, and provides room for all things that have birth...when we regard this we dimly dream and affirm that it is somehow necessary that all that exists should exist *in* some spot and occupying some *place,* and that which is neither on earth nor anywhere in the Heaven is nothing." Plato, *Timaeus* 52a–b, 122–23; compare the Latin translation in *Timaeus a Calcidio Translatus commentarioque instructus,* 50 (at 52a–b). For a provocative overview of the intellectual history of the *chora* ranging from Plato and Plotinus to Derrida, Irigaray, and Kristeva, see Butler, *Bodies That Matter,* 39–48 and 254n28.

Floridus and the *Roman de toute chevalerie* is largely absent from *Kyng Alisaunder.* Finally, the depiction of Candace is also different from that found in the Anglo-Norman poem, for the alluring, enigmatic Oriental ruler of Thomas' romance is replaced by a more mature, wise, and articulate queen who is said to rule over the Ethiopian realm of Sheba.

In general, the procedure of the anonymous writer of *Kyng Alisaunder* is to translate the text of the *Roman de toute chevalerie,* tightening up Thomas' sometimes too expansive account of the heterogeneous wonders of the world, not so much by reducing the number of lines but by increasing the narrative coherence of the work wherever possible, often by resorting to other sources of the Alexander narrative. This procedure can be seen in the catalogues of fantastic beasts and marvelous peoples found in *Kyng Alisaunder.* In general, they follow the order found in the *Roman de toute chevalerie,* as for example in the account of the monstrous races of India (*KA* 4771–5032). Interestingly, the catalogue of the peculiar animals of India that immediately follows the listing of monstrous races is reworked in the Middle English version: the simple, straightforward list of beasts found in the *Roman de toute chevalerie* (4928–5228) is transformed into a narrative describing Alexander's journey, naming the various animals seen by the Macedonian as he proceeds along his route of conquest (*KA* 5157–5446).

A similarly creative handling of Thomas' tendency to produce long lists of marvels appears later in *Kyng Alisaunder,* where one of Thomas' catalogues is actually increased in length; here, the writer resorts to Thomas' own source, Solinus, in order to restore order and coherence to a fragmented, somewhat rambling passage describing the monstrous races of Ethiopia (*KA* 6288–6615). The *Roman de toute chevalerie's* disorderly, almost random description of the southern races (6637–6879) is carefully divided, in the Middle English poem, into the races found "in the west half" (6340) and those "in the est" (6364). The editor of *Kyng Alisaunder,* G. V. Smithers, suggests that the fuller version of the passage found in the Middle English poem simply reflects the use of an Anglo-Norman source text better than any of the manuscripts of the *Roman de toute chevalerie* that currently survive.[82] The alternative explanation, however, is entirely in keeping with the editorial procedure followed elsewhere by the author of *Kyng Alisaunder;* as Smithers points out, he sometimes uses the *Alexandreis* of Walter of Châtillon in order to correct inconsistencies in Thomas of Kent's narrative, or to provide character names where they are

---

82. Smithers, *Kyng Alisaunder* 2:18–20.

lacking.[83] In addition, the passage in *Kyng Alisaunder* describing the eastern range of Ethiopia includes a detailed account of "Saba," the home of the biblical Queen of Sheba beloved by Solomon (6364–95). This passage is particularly prominent and detailed in the version found in *Kyng Alisaunder,* perhaps because the analogy with Sheba is central to the Middle English version's depiction of Candace, the Oriental queen who fatefully encounters Alexander.

One of the greatest disparities separating the *Roman de toute chevalerie* from *Kyng Alisaunder* is the description of Alexander's enclosure of the unclean races of Gog and Magog in the distant reaches of the north, which Smithers characterizes as "an extreme example of independent treatment."[84] The account found in *Kyng Alisaunder* is both highly condensed (*KA* 5938–6287; compare *RdTC* 5951–6637) and more coherent. The Middle English author changes the order of events found in the Anglo-Norman poem, replacing Thomas' illogical narrative (in which the sticky sealant bitumen is first described, then Alexander's prayer for inspiration, followed by the enclosure of Gog and Magog) with a more natural sequence (in which Alexander appeals to God, finds the bitumen as if in answer to his appeal, and then seals up the enemy with the bitumen). Although the account found in *Kyng Alisaunder* is almost half as long as that in the *Roman de toute chevalerie,* it includes some striking details not found in the source text. For example, Thomas' emphasis on the marvelous nature of the triumphant Alexander ("Merveillus fu Alisandre" [*RdTC* 6578]), has its counterpart in the Middle English poem's description not of the conqueror but of the bizarre, "merueillous men" (*KA* 6263) he encounters. In *Kyng Alisaunder,* marvels are located emphatically outside the explorer himself, who remains fundamentally the same man he was before he entered the hidden recesses located at the margins of the world. This view of Alexander is strikingly different from that found in the *Roman de toute chevalerie* and, especially, the *Liber Floridus,* where the greatest marvel of all is the transformation of the Macedonian warrior into an Oriental monarch.

The greatly reduced episode of the enclosure of Gog and Magog is representative of a generally weaker interest in apocalypticism in *Kyng Alisaunder* compared with the *Roman de toute chevalerie* and, especially, the *Liber Floridus.* This tendency is also manifested in the Middle English poem's treatment of Alexander's ventures to the edges of the known world, where he finds the

---

83. Smithers notes one example of the substitution of Walter of Châtillon's account at lines 3511–16 of the *Roman de toute chevalerie* (*Kyng Alisaunder* 2:26), and elsewhere notes the incorporation of proper names found in the *Alexandreis* into *Kyng Alisaunder* (2:22–23).

84. Ibid., 2:27.

monumental pillars left by Hercules during his voyages to these forbidden extremes. In the *Roman de toute chevalerie* (as in its source text, the *Letter of Alexander to Aristotle*), these moments were clearly encounters with the sacred; consequently, Alexander's transgressive behavior—breaking up the pillars as a sign of his own conquest—is necessarily followed by atonement in the form of sacrifice and prayer (*RdTC* 5400–5404). In *Kyng Alisaunder,* by contrast, Alexander's behavior at these forbidden limits is far more offhand: the poem simply describes the monumental pillars as a wonderful "merveile" (5586), with little concern about the dangers involved in the penetration of forbidden regions. Similarly, in the *Roman de toute chevalerie,* guides and companions repeatedly warn their leader not to venture too far ("Sire, avant nen irrez" [5505]); conversely, in *Kyng Alisaundre* there is little conflict regarding how far Alexander ought to go.

In the Middle English poem, the peak of Alexander's conquest seems to simply be a moment when the king has, at last, seen plenty of "wondres," though not yet enough to satisfy him completely: "Tho the kyng was hool and wel ydoughth, / Mo wondres he hath ysoughth. / Everych ydle, everych contrey, / He hath ysoughth, par ma fey" (5897–5900). In the corresponding passage in the *Roman de toute chevalerie,* however, the moment of triumph shows Alexander figuratively surmounting the entire earth:

Par tote Ynde est alez cerchant la region,
De la grant mer d'Aufruqe desques septentrion:
Qe fust en orient ou sunt li grant dragon,
Ne trovent mes merveilles; donc dient li baron:
"De aler en nos regnes est or seison,
Car tuit le mond est Alisandre a bandon;
De touz roys terriens ad il subjecion.
As treis fins del mond ad mis son pavillon,
Ses mercs e ses bondes de fin or esclavon,
Les temples e les auters de quivere e de laton.
Ore n'i ad a dire si sul occident non,
Ou meinent ly Yreis, Espaniol e Breton,
Qe la terre habitable ne seit alé environ."

He has traveled around the whole region of India,
from the great sea of Africa as far as the utter north;
no more marvels are to be found in the east,
where the great dragons are; therefore the barons say:
"It's time to go back to our own realms,

for all the world is at the will of Alexander;
he has subjected all earthly kings.
He has made his camp at the three ends of the earth,
placed his markers and his boundaries gilded with fine gold,
and temples and altars of copper and lead.
Now nothing is left except in the west,
where the Irish, Spanish, and Britons live,
for the habitable territory does not extend all around."

(5938–50)

Here, Alexander has seen everything and conquered everyone, touching even the very "ends of the earth." By contrast, the focus of *Kyng Alisaunder* is nothing more than the unquenchable thirst for wonders, a desire for the inexhaustible storehouse of curiosities and luxuries that is the Orient. "Wondres" and "marveiles" are repeatedly shown to be the explicit focus of Alexander's efforts in *Kyng Alisaunder* (e.g., 5707, 5743, 5754, 5771–72). This desire goes hand in hand with *Kyng Alisaunder*'s emphasis on the lucrative commodities to be gained in the Orient, including the abundant "golde and siluer and precious stones" of Taprobana (5650) and the remarkable Indian snake that "shitteth preciouse stones" (5661), details amplified in the Middle English adaptation far beyond their Anglo-Norman source. Such emphasis on the acquisition of wonders and commodities contrasts strongly with the coupling of desire and danger in the *Roman de toute chevalerie,* where the search is not so much for wonders or goods, but for "aventures" (5701). There, the goal is conquest, understood both militarily and intellectually, as Alexander receives tribute from all subject kings, learns all there is to know (however forbidden that knowledge might be), and expands his reach to the utter limits—or even beyond.

In general, the author of *Kyng Alisaunder* improves the coherence, reduces the digressions, and enhances the flow of the narrative found in his source text. An exception to this approach appears, however, in his treatment of the use of climate theory central to Thomas of Kent's depiction of the world. In the Anglo-Norman poem, the four extremes of north, south, east, and west are shown each to have their own diverse properties and to balance one another, thus revealing the essential unity that underlies the heterogeneity of creation. The Middle English adaptation, by contrast, omits or even misrepresents this aspect of Thomas' work. One might say that narrative coherence is primary in *Kyng Alisaunder,* while conceptual coherence is primary in the *Roman de toute chevalerie.* For example, in the course of a description of the northern reaches, the *Roman de toute chevalerie* includes an account of the large, white creatures that live there, both men and dogs (4200–14); as discussed in the previous section of this chapter, such qualities are proper to things born in the northern regions. Thomas places this account of the properties of the north in the context of a symmetrical and harmonious cosmology, in which the oppressive heat of the south ("chalur de Inde") is balanced by the paralyzing cold of the north ("septentrion al froit" [4587]).

The author of *Kyng Alisaunder* omits all this to plunge abruptly into a description of the "wondres" of India (4763–64). This cannot be due to a lacuna in his source manuscript of the *Roman de toute chevalerie,* because some of the omitted material is inserted later on in the Middle English poem where the narrative requires such details. The inserted material, however, shows that the Middle English poet is ignorant of the climate theory that underlies Thomas of Kent's original account, for he describes the men of northern Albania not as "white," but as "wiȝth" (i.e., hearty, fearless in battle; 5262). The adapter's incomprehension becomes even more evident when, in the following line, he states that "their faces are as dark as dye" ("Her visages ben blew so ynde" [5263]).[85] A similar mistranslation occurs later on, when the *Roman de toute chevalerie* refers to the remarkable and anomalous "blans Ethiopiens" (6971; cf. 4213) sent to Alexander by Candace. In terms of climate theory, Ethiopians should be dark-skinned; white Ethiopians are a marvel suitable to be delivered, together with gold and jewels, as tribute to the great conqueror. This detail of "white Ethiopians," derived from Pliny's *Historia naturalia* (see note 2), was added by Thomas to enhance the description of the Ethiopian warriors included in Candace's tribute that he found in the Julius Valerius Epitome. For the author of the Middle English poem, however, this climatic wonder goes unremarked: the marvelous white Ethiopians are simply "wiȝth" in battle (*KA* 6689). Once again in the Middle English poem, narrative coherence takes precedence over conceptual coherence.

A further departure from the *Roman de toute chevalerie* appears in *Kyng Alisaunder's* treatment of Candace. Thomas of Kent had himself departed from the depiction of Candace found in his source, the Julius Valerius Epitome, where her kingdom is said to be located in the south-eastern part of Ethiopia. Throughout the Alexander tradition, Candace's realm is located in the deepest south; for example, in the *Historia de Preliis,* Candace's realm is said to include "Meroen," the city associated with the southernmost of the seven climates that laterally divide the habitable zone. Thomas of Kent, however,

---

85. In Middle English texts, "blue" is often used to describe dark skin. See, for example, *The Sowdone of Babylone's* description of "Sarsyns felle, / Some bloo, some yolowe, some blake as More" (lines 1004–05).

introduces a variant, describing Candace's realm as having qualities of both the north and of the south. This paradox underscores her own nature, for Thomas depicts Candace as a most European lady, fair and courteous, living in an extravagantly exotic place. The exact location of her territory is unspecified in the *Roman de toute chevalerie,* adding to its mysterious nature and its dangerous quality. This is especially evident when Alexander enters its innermost space, the chamber of Candace.

Kyng Alisaunder returns to the standard depiction of Candace's realm, following the Julius Valerius Epitome in placing it in south-eastern Ethiopia. He explicitly identifies this land as "Saba" (7616) and its ruler, consequently, as heir to the alluring Queen of Sheba. Sheba is described at length in a digression inserted by the author of *Kyng Alisaunder* within his adaptation of Thomas' description of the peoples of Ethiopia. In eastern Ethiopia, he writes, there is

> a cite,
> On of the noblest in Cristiente.
> It hatte Saba in langage—
> From thennes com Sibile the sage,
> Of al the werlde the fairest quene,
> To Jerusalem, Salomon to sene.
> For hire fairhede and for hir love
> Salamon lete God above,
> And dude maumetes servyse.
> > (6376–84)

The passage goes on to recount the story of Solomon and Sheba, clearly as a cautionary preliminary to the tale of Alexander's deception by Candace.[86] The Candace of the Middle English poem is, even more emphatically than in the *Roman de toute chevalerie,* a courtly queen in the European tradition, not only listening to a song of Dido and Aeneas (*RdTC* 7650–51) but actually singing it herself (*KA* 7618–20), and having her private chamber painted with the "story" of the fall of Troy (7656–57). This is an Orient that has been domesticated and, at least in part, assimilated.

The three versions of the Alexander story found in the *Liber Floridus,* the *Roman de toute chevalerie,* and *Kyng Alisaunder* show three different faces of the

---

86. *Kyng Alisaunder* includes a number of references to Solomon and related traditions of Wisdom literature that would repay further study; see, for example, the inclusion of Solomon among his list of sources at lines 4771–72.

Macedonian ruler. They also highlight very different aspects of the Orient, ranging from the apocalyptic promise that suffuses Lambert of St. Omer's compilation to the chivalric, almost carefree celebration of the acquisition of wonders to be found in the Middle English poem. Thomas of Kent's innovative poem is perhaps the most extraordinary of these, however, for in the *Roman de toute chevalerie* we find many strands of the Alexander tradition mingled together, incorporating a wide range of writings on the "Wonders of the East" as well as the apocalyptic writings of pseudo-Methodius and Aethicus Ister. This fertile combination gives rise to a dynamic cosmology in which Alexander's path of conquest produces, almost as its mirror image, a view of the western nations that will take on the imperial mantle of Rome.

These texts illustrate the extent to which, throughout the Middle Ages, the Orient was understood as a place of mystery, danger, and (above all) multiplicity. The region of the sun was consistently defined both in terms of the east (where the sun rises) and the south (where its effects are most harshly felt). Consequently, the heart of the Orient, peculiarly enough, is located not simply in the east but in the south-eastern region. Medieval maps make it clear that Eden itself is located in the region furthest east, following the description found in Genesis 2:8, and the *regio solis* inhabited by Jonitus, the fourth son of Noah, is said by pseudo-Methodius to lie even further to the east. Related locations, however, including the eastern ocean of Eoum, the Ethiopian land of Saba, and the *insula solis* depicted on Lambert of St. Omer's world map, have less clearly defined coordinates, placed in some part of the south-eastern region. These locations, like the murky border separating India and Ethiopia, remain unmoored and ultimately indefinable, alluring yet perilous. The *regio solis* of Eocham, the distant ocean of Eoum, and the *insula solis* together mark the site of "crystallization," to use David Harvey's term, where an imagined entity comes into geographical being.[87] These regions point to (but do not delimit) the Orient, which cannot be contained in a single location. The personae associated with these regions are correspondingly elusive, related yet distinct: they include the "prestres" who attends the oracular trees of the sun and moon in the *Roman de toute chevalerie;* Jonitus, the fourth son of Noah, who inhabits the *regio solis;* and Prester John, whose kingdom lies in the furthest march of India on the shores of the eastern ocean.

---

87. David Harvey acquires this term from Adorno, using it to explain how "flows" (that is, "the relations between 'moments'") often "crystallize into 'things,' 'elements,' and isolable 'domains' or 'systems' which assume a relative permanence within the social process." Examples of such "crystallization" include both "material landscapes (such as cities)" and "even discourses which becomes so widely accepted and reified, that they themselves become part of a landscape of knowledge seemingly impermeable to change." Harvey, *Justice,* 81.

The multiplicity and variable location of the Orient stands in sharp contrast to the vision of Jerusalem as a fixed, stable center that was the focus
of the previous chapter. Nonetheless, these two terms are interdependent:
visions of the Orient certainly inform medieval imaginings of the holy city,
while Jerusalem itself is depicted as the most proximate of all eastern locations. This dialectical relationship is evident in the Alexander tradition described in this chapter, where both the *Liber Floridus* and the *Roman de toute
chevalerie* incorporate Josephus' account of Alexander's visit to Jerusalem.
This usage is entirely representative of the high medieval Alexander tradition:
as noted earlier in the chapter, the texts of the J2 recension of the *Historia de
Preliis* also incorporate passages from Josephus, while excerpts from Josephus
concerning Alexander circulated independently, sometimes within manuscript compilations of Alexander material. Though typical of the tradition,
Lambert of St. Omer's combination of the Julius Valerius Epitome with
Josephus' account of Alexander's entry into Jerusalem and obeisance to the
Jewish high priest Jaddus is quite independent, as Derolez has conclusively
demonstrated.[88] For Lambert, Alexander's journey to Jerusalem is perhaps
the most crucial moment in Alexander's path of conquest. His obeisance to
the high priest, coupled with his explanation to his puzzled soldiers that he
has done homage not to the Jewish man before him, but to the God whose
name Jaddus wears upon his breastplate (*Liber Floridus,* fol. 153'v), demonstrates that Alexander is truly an avatar of the Christian king of Jerusalem.
By placing this episode immediately after Alexander's defeat of Darius, king
of the Persians, Lambert sketches out a typological relationship between the
defeated Persians and Alexander's entry into Jerusalem, on the one hand, and
the defeated Saracens and the Frankish entry into Jerusalem, on the other.

This typology is even more pronounced in the *Roman de toute chevalerie,* where Darius' Persians are explicitly identified as "Sarazins" who adore
"Apolin" and "Tervagant," two of the three most popular deities in the medieval Saracen pantheon (1604–18). Alexander's entry into Jerusalem occurs
in exactly the same place in the Anglo-Norman text as it does in the *Liber
Floridus;* this may suggest that either Thomas of Kent himself or the redactor
of the Durham manuscript of the *Roman de toute chevalerie* was familiar with
the position of the Josephus episode found in the *Liber Floridus.* The accounts
are almost identical, with only slight variations.[89] As in the *Liber Floridus,*

---

88. Derolez, *Autograph,* 133. Derolez has also attempted, with limited success, to determine
which manuscript of Josephus was used by Lambert (127, 195).

89. These include the conditions of the Jews' relief from paying tribute (exempted for a period
of seven years in the *Roman de toute chevalerie;* paying tribute every seven years in Josephus and the

Alexander's entry into Jerusalem in the Anglo-Norman poem is intended as a prefiguration of the crusader conquest of the Holy Land; later medieval versions of the Alexander narrative, however, lack this episode because the eschatological framework that had made it meaningful to earlier generations had become obsolete. Jerusalem had not lost its importance, but it had become less of a military goal than a spiritual one.[90] Changes in Western perceptions of the Holy City, and in late medieval understandings of the relationship of Judaism, Christianity, and Islam, are the focus of the next chapter.

Liber Floridus), and Alexander's invitation to Jewish recruits to join his armies (included in Josephus and the *Roman de toute chevalerie,* absent from the *Liber Floridus*).

90. See Yeager, *Jerusalem in Medieval Narrative.*

⤺ CHAPTER 3

The Place of the Jews

Where is the place of the Jews? Although this is a difficult question with which to begin, it is crucial, for in defining the place of the Jews—not just geographically but also spiritually and epistemologically—medieval European Christians defined both themselves and the very notion of alterity. It is nothing new to suggest that Christian identity was, throughout the Middle Ages, modeled on conceptions of Jewish identity. As Daniel Boyarin has shown, the "hermeneutics of supersession" embedded in Pauline theology richly informed both the early writings of the Church Fathers and subsequent developments in Christian theology.[1] In a wide-ranging series of studies, Jeremy Cohen has illustrated the ways in which Jewish identity was used as a template to define Christianity not only directly (as its typological prefiguration) but also indirectly (in its correspondence to a series of enemies thought to threaten the Church, including heretics and Muslims).[2]

Building on Cohen's work, in this chapter I outline some of the ways in which place functions in the definition of Jewish alterity. In religious terms, Judaism is the place holder, as it were, for Christianity. It is the primitive

---

1. Boyarin, *Carnal Israel;* Boyarin, *Radical Jew.* A highly condensed (and very useful) formulation of the hermeneutics of supersession appears in Boyarin, "'This We Know,'" 474–505.

2. Cohen, "Muslim Connection," 141–62; see also Cohen, *Living Letters,* 158–65.

"type" that is fulfilled and superceded by the "antitype," as the Old Law of Moses gives way to the New Law of Christ and the so-called "Old" Testament is reinterpreted in the light of its successor, the "New" Testament.[3] In geographical terms, Jews are conceived of as at once dispersed and contained, scattered all over the world in a series of diasporas emanating from Jerusalem yet, paradoxically, contained within a variety of enclosures.[4] This spatial ambivalence, where Jews are imagined as belonging nowhere yet found everywhere, is the geographical expression of the epistemological ambivalence embedded within medieval understandings of the role of Judaism: it is both privileged, as the wellspring of Christianity, and condemned, as the "blind" Jews repeatedly refuse to recognize the Messiah among them. On the one hand, Judaism is proximate to Christianity, as its prefiguration and spiritual progenitor; on the other hand, Jews are (like heretics and Muslims) the remorseless enemy of the Church. Accordingly, medieval texts place Jews and Judaism at once at the middle of things and at the very edge of the world, ranging from the "Giudecca," the most intimate circle of Dante's *Inferno*,[5] to the *ubera aquilonis*, the mountains in the farthest north where the enclosed tribes of Gog and Magog (identified here with the tribes of Israel) were thought to have been enclosed by Alexander the Great. Jewish bodies are the site where this ambivalence is played out, as the integrity of the Church (as the mystical body of Christ) is symbolically affirmed by their dismemberment and dissolution.

In a study of European representations of Islam and the Orient, discussion of medieval depictions of Jews might seem out of place. On the contrary, however, an understanding of medieval constructions of the Jewish body is a necessary first step in the effort to comprehend medieval constructions of the Saracen body. Saracen, the most common medieval term used to describe what we would now call Muslims, is a term that defines both religious and ethnic alterity. As Norman Daniel has pointed out, the term is never used to describe Christian Arabs, although it is sometimes used generically to refer

---

3. The typological relationship of "Old" Covenant and "New" Covenant is ubiquitous in medieval culture, but is perhaps nowhere so fully apparent as in biblical glosses. For an important study of this topic in the context of thirteenth-century French culture, see Lipton, *Images of Intolerance*.

4. In this chapter, the term *diaspora* is used to refer to the historical dispersion of Jews from Jerusalem, particularly the expulsion of 70 C.E. chronicled by Josephus (who used this Greek term, and whose writings were widely disseminated throughout the Middle Ages). I do not intend to evoke the political sense of the term, which Daniel Boyarin has recently used to signal a political project in which "Diaspora" serves as "a theoretical and historical model to replace national self-determination" (*Radical Jew*, 249). Boyarin himself notes the long intellectual genealogy of this effort (333n28).

5. On the significance of Dante's "Giudecca," see Tomasch, "Judecca," 247–67.

to other kinds of non-Christian aliens.[6] (For example, the Saracens found in the Middle English *King Horn* appear to be non-Christian Danish invaders.)[7] The term Saracen thus functions in a way similar to the term Jew, in simultaneously defining both ethnic and religious difference. By ascertaining how religious and ethnic difference were intertwined in medieval European understandings of Jews, it becomes possible to understand how and to what extent these were also intertwined in understandings of Saracens. Further, by examining the ways in which Jewish humoral physiology was thought to be determined by such factors as climate and dietary habits, it becomes possible to understand how the Saracen body was constructed as the product of an Oriental climate, nourished by exotic and alien foodstuffs.

Accordingly, this chapter begins with a consideration of the geographical place of the Jews, titled "Dispersal and Enclosure." One might expect to find Jerusalem identified as the rightful place of the Jews, based on its prominent role in chronicles of Jewish history, biblical accounts, and apocrypha. Due to Jerusalem's identification as the spiritual center of Christian salvation history, however, it could be recognized as the rightful place of the Jews only in the past. Consequently, medieval Christian accounts of a Jewish Jerusalem focus relentlessly on the act of expulsion and the physical destruction of the city, constructing a narrative of triumphant Christian dominion on the razed ground of Jewish history. Paradoxically, however, such depictions of the outward flow of Jews in diaspora are mirrored by portrayals of Jews tightly contained within enclosed spaces. This section outlines the tension between centrifugal diaspora and centripetal containment in accounts of Jews found in a variety of texts, including encyclopedias, lists of nations, and historical chronicles.

The second section, "Climate and the Diasporic Body," turns to the ways in which geography intersected with emergent theories of race, with the body serving as a microcosm of the larger world. Just as medieval Orientalism defines Saracen difference both in terms of religious orientation and bodily diversity, so medieval anti-Judaic discourse defines Jewish difference in terms of both soul and body. It is precisely in this focus on bodily difference that medieval anti-Judaism shades over into antisemitism, a distinction to which I return. This chapter therefore includes a detailed discussion of the ways in which Jewish bodies—as opposed to Jewish souls—were understood to differ from those of Western Christians, laying the foundation for chapter 4's exploration of "The Saracen Body" as well as, more broadly, a deeper understanding of how climate was thought to determine the biological and behavioral characteristics of peoples.

---

6. Daniel, *Arabs and Medieval Europe,* 53–54; Beckett, *Anglo-Saxon Perceptions,* 90–115.

7. Speed, "Saracens of *King Horn,*" 564–95.

While Noachid descent, discussed at some length in chapter 1, was certainly an important component of medieval understandings of the causes of bodily diversity, climate was also thought to dictate the humoral makeup of the individual as well as the collective "natural" predispositions of nations. Within this framework, the Jews were a peculiar case: scattered from their original home within the fourth, moderate climate, they were nonetheless thought to retain essential anatomical and physiological features in spite of their itinerant nature. Conceptions of Jewish bodily diversity were intimately related to conceptions of religious diversity, so that the well-established discourse of anti-Judaism served as the substrate of an emergent discourse of antisemitism.[8] Jewish bodies were used as the medium through which anxieties regarding the integrity of the Christian community could be expressed, with anti-Judaic and antisemitic discourses operating in tandem.

↚ Dispersal and Enclosure

One might expect to find Jerusalem identified as the rightful place of the Jews, since it appears prominently in chronicles of Jewish history as well as the Bible. Such a recognition of the centrality of Jerusalem within the history of the Jews would be in keeping with more general ideas about Jerusalem, which (as we saw in chapter 1) was thought by medieval European Christians to be the symbolic center of the world, the site of mankind's spiritual rebirth at the time of the Crucifixion and the place where the Last Judgment would begin. Paradoxically, however, Jerusalem is precisely *not* the place of the Jews in the medieval imagination: they are thought to be displaced from Jerusalem by the will of God, their right to the holy city revoked by their own rejection and persecution of Jesus. Discussions of a Jewish Jerusalem, therefore, whether in historical chronicles or literary texts, reveal a profound ambiguity. Jerusalem is identified as having been the place of the Jews only in the past, not in the present or the future. Consequently, medieval depictions of

---

8. Kathleen Biddick has recently warned that the tendency to see anti-Judaism as antecedent to antisemitism reveals "an anxiety about the supersessionary fantasy at the core of the typological imaginary." Biddick, *Typological Imaginary*, 10. Nonetheless, there seems to be a consensus among historians of Jews in medieval Europe that anti-Judaism existed in the period of early Christianity while antisemitism did not, even though the definitions of these two phenomena vary widely. Among the considerable literature, see especially Langmuir, *History, Religion, and Antisemitism,* and *Toward a Definition of Antisemitism*. A useful assessment of Langmuir's efforts to define and distinguish between anti-Judaism and antisemitism appears in Stacey, "History, Religion, and Medieval Antisemitism," 95–101, esp. 98. I return to the distinction between anti-Judaism and antisemitism in the closing pages of this chapter.

a Jewish Jerusalem invariably focus not on the Jews' habitation of the city, but on their expulsion.

Other than the Bible itself, encyclopedias were the most widely distributed source of information about the geography and populations of the lands bordering the eastern Mediterranean. The account given by Isidore of Seville in his seventh-century *Etymologies* (itself based largely on Orosius and Pliny) was reproduced by later encyclopedists such as Bartholomaeus Anglicus and Vincent of Beauvais, both writing in the thirteenth century. While Vincent, in his *Speculum Naturale,* repeats Isidore almost verbatim, Bartholomaeus adds a few interesting variations. The most significant concerns the spatial relationship of the different lands of the Near East—Syria, Palestine, and Judea—to one another. Isidore simply describes each of these regions in turn, without clearly specifying their locations. Bartholomaeus, on the other hand, describes each of these regions as nested within one another. "Palestina is a prouynce of Siria," while "Iudea . . . is a cuntrey in Palestina," and Judea itself houses the central point of the entire world: "In the myddel of this Iudea is the cite of Ierusalem, as it were the nauel of alle the cuntrey and londe" (15.113, p. 792; 15.78, p. 772). (A similarly nested effect appears in the thirteenth-century *Opus maius* of Roger Bacon, which also uses Isidore's *Etymologies* for basic information on the geography of the Holy Land.)[9] The centrality of Jerusalem is thus underscored, as it were, by the borders circling around it like ripples in a pond: first the borders of Judea, then of Palestine, then of Syria.

Like Isidore and Vincent, Bartholomaeus includes Jews among the other "dyuerse naciouns" living in the region, such as "Tyries" (i.e., people of Tyre), Palestinians, "Comagines" (Carthaginians?), "Fenicis" (Phoenicians), "Nabadei" (Nabateans), and "Saraceni" (15.78, p. 772; 15.113, p. 792; 15.145, p. 809). They appear simply as one people among many, having no special claim to the territory they inhabit; no claim, that is, that the encyclopedist is willing to allow. Isidore puts it this way, in words echoed almost verbatim by Bartholomaeus and Vincent: "Therefore, because of the pleasant climate [lit., harmony of the elements], the Jews thought that [Judea] was the land promised to their forefathers, flowing with milk and honey, by means of

---

9. "Nomen enim Syriae in tempore regum Israel attribuebatur Damasco et regioni ejus. Haec igitur provincia Syriae Phoenicis habet terram Hebraeorum a meridie et terram Philistinorum; sed terra Philistinorum incipit a finibus Aconensis territorii usque ad turbidum fluvium Aegypti, et antiquitus continebat fere totam terram Judaeorum citra Jordanem" (For the name of Syria in the time of the kings of Israel was given to Damascus and its region. This province, therefore, of Phoenician Syria has the land of the Hebrews to the south and the land of the Philistines; but the land of the Philistines begins at the confines of the territory of Acon as far as the turbid stream of Egypt, and in ancient times contained nearly the whole country of the Jews this side of Jordan). Bacon, *Opus Maius,* ed. Bridges, 1:346; Bacon, *Opus Maius,* trans. Burke, 1:364.

which God promised them the privilege of the resurrection" (Unde secundum elementorum gratiam existimaverunt Iudaei eam promissam patribus terram fluentem mel et lac, cum hic illis Deus resurrectionis praerogitivam polliceretur). Implicitly, then, the Jews' claim to the territory is represented as an error of judgment grounded on coincidence: as Bartholomaeus, puts it (in Trevisa's translation), "Iewes trowede that this londe was yhote to here formefadres and that it wellid melk and hony" (15.78; pp. 772–73). The encyclopedists also emphasize that the Jews were not the original residents of the land: "This londe was first yclepede Canaan and hadde that name of Chames sone, other of tenne naciouns of Chandelos that were yput oute, and thanne Iewes hadde possessioun of that londe" (15.78; p. 772). Jewish residence in Judea is thus represented as neither original nor exclusive, for their presence is simply one stage in the habitation of the land (preceded by the Canaanites and followed by a range of other ethnic groups) and their current status is just that of one group among many. As Bartholomaeus' Middle English translator puts it, the territory of Judea itself is the "comune wonynge" of various nations (15.78, p. 772). Finally, the Jews' claim to Judea is said to be fundamentally false, grounded on the misguided belief that God had sanctioned their right to the territory: the Jews merely "believed" that the land was theirs.[10]

Bartholomaeus' account also differs from that found in Isidore's *Etymologies* in his description of the Palestinians as a kind of counterpart to the Jews, living in the same land and having many of the same faults. Bartholomaeus notes that the Palestinians were originally "yclepede Alophili that is to menynge 'aliens and straungers'; for alweye they were straunge to the children of Israel, for thei were departed fer oute of here companye and kynreden" (15.113; p. 793).[11] While Isidore had noted the earlier name "Alophili" (*Etym.* 9.2.20), it is Bartholomaeus who introduces the explanation of the name's source in the estrangement of the Palestinians from the Jews. He amplifies this observation later in the same chapter, citing as his source "Erodatus," an unidentified (probably lost) writer named elsewhere in the *De proprietatibus rerum* in connection with the characteristics of various nations.[12] Bartholomaeus states that the Palestinians "ben allweye fals and gyleful and wyly, greuous enemys

<hr />

10. Bartholomaeus' Middle English translator, John Trevisa, makes one of his rare editorial interjections in this passage, identifying Judea as "the Jewerie" (15.78, p. 772). Interestingly, this is the same term used to designate the Jewish quarter in European cities, as in Chaucer's Prioress' Tale (VII.489). On the use of this term in the Prioress' Tale, see Delany, "Chaucer's Prioress," 43–57, esp. 47.

11. "Allophili, id est, alienigenae, eo quod semper fuerunt filiiis Israel alieni, et longe ab eorum societate et genere separati." Bartholomaeus Anglicus, *De proprietatibus rerum,* 684.

12. On "Erodatus," see Greetham, "Fabulous Geography," 207–8.

to the kyngedome of Israel, bothe for they hadde enuye to the Iues, and also for they were proude of the welthe of here owne londe" (15.113, p. 793).[13] The reason for their animosity, paradoxically, is their very similarity to their enemy, for envy and pride were the faults most commonly ascribed to Jews. For example, medieval lists of nations, which encapsulate the essential characteristics of ethnic or national groups in a few memorable lines, frequently describe Jews as characterized by "invidia."[14] Their devotion to the acquisition of wealth, often through the practice of usury, is also noted in these lists. They are, in sum, a "natio nefandi generis," a nation of wicked origin.[15]

These lists of nations also describe what their writers perceive as the Jews' rightful place in the world: that is, nowhere and everywhere. They are said to be a nation scattered throughout the world as a result of their sins—that is, their supposed culpability for the crucifixion of Jesus. One of these lists of nations, appearing in a thirteenth-century manuscript and titled "De nequitia Judeorum" (On the Iniquity of the Jews), exclaims, "O gens ceca nimium vagans per inania."[16] Literally, this means "Oh blind folk, wandering wide through empty space"; "inania" can also refer to the emptiness of the "gens," however, so that the line refers not only to the wandering itself, but to the emptiness of spirit that lies behind it. Another list of nations, titled "Gentium quicumque mores" (The Habits of Every Folk) also emphasizes the scattered nature of the Jews; the order of the list, however, which follows a west-to-east geographical trajectory, reveals a curious ambiguity regarding the place of the Jews. Though they are said to be scattered ("sparsi") throughout the world, they are simultaneously located at the center of things—in terms of the sequence of the verses, at the end of the list. After ranging through western Europe, the poem moves to eastern countries such as Hungary and Poland, and then finally to ever more barbaric nations:

Tartari sunt infideles / sanguinarii crudeles, / feri et hippophagi.
Sunt Pruteni multi boni, / multi mali et coloni / variarum gentium.

---

13. "Gens, ut narrat Herodotus, astuta et callida, molesta semper regno Israelitico et infesta, tum quia prosperitati Iudaeorum invidebat, tum etiam, qui de soli sui felicitate ... nimium praesumebat" (*De prop. rerum,* 684). Trevisa's translation of "astuta et callida" as "fals and gyleful and wyly" is discussed in chapter 4 of this book, 162.

14. Meyvaert notes examples as early as the ninth century, in additions to Isidore's *History of the Goths.* See Meyvaert, "'Rainaldus est malus scriptor Francigenus,'" 743–63, esp. 747–48.

15. A useful selection of nation lists appears in Walther, "Scherz und Ernst in der Völker—und Stämme-Charakteristik mittellateinischer Verse," 263–301. In them, Jews are said to be given to usury (268, #33), envious (277, #99), hard-hearted and pitiless (274, #77), shameful ("inhonestus"; 284, #147), hard-necked and heavy-hearted (277, #99), and unstable, like whores and converts (278, #104).

16. Ibid., 269, #47a.

Marcomanni et Bohemi / sunt heretici blasphemi, / madidi Austriaci.
Turce, Mauri, et Schiite / alieque gentes mundi / hostes sunt ecclesie.
Passim sparsi sunt Judei / et quod Christi mortis rei, / his incerta
patria est.
Ergo finem faciamus / et regnum Dei queramus, / cetera non [nam?]
transeunt.

The Tartars are without faith, bloodthirsty, wild, and eaters of horses;
The Prussians are often good farmers, often bad ones—a mongrel race
of men.
Marcomanni [?] and Bohemians are heretical blasphemers, the Austrians
are sodden with drink.
The Turks, Moors, Shiites, and other races of the world are enemies of
the Church.
The Jews are scattered here and there, and because they put Christ to
death, their homeland is uncertain.
Therefore let us make an end of this, and seek the kingdom of God; all
other things will pass away.[17]

Some features of this poem mark it as a product of the late Middle Ages, especially the distinction drawn between Turks, Moors, and (unprecedented in
the earlier Middle Ages) Shiites. This line was clearly altered from an earlier
version, as the faulty rhyme indicates; other aspects, however, are very much
in keeping with the list of nations genre which, as Meyvaert notes, has its
roots as early as the ninth century.[18] The place of the Jews is, as the poem
states, "incerta": their supposed culpability is, as usual, adduced as the cause
for their dispersal. Nonetheless, in spite of their diasporic status, they remain
in the penultimate position, their "patria" foreshadowing the "regnum Dei"
to come and, inevitably, being superseded by it.

The treatment of the place of the Jews found in the encyclopedias and
lists of nations corresponds to that found in historical chronicles, especially
the accounts of Orosius and Josephus and their medieval redactors. For
Orosius, writing in the early fifth century, the physical city of Jerusalem held
little value; instead, like his mentor Augustine, Orosius urged his readers to
turn their gaze toward the spiritual Jerusalem, embarking upon the figurative
pilgrimage of the soul rather than the literal pilgrimage of the body. In his

---

17. Ibid., 273, #72. Thanks to A. G. Rigg for help with this translation.

18. Walther notes the faulty rhyme and comments that the poem is clearly much older than this
version's sixteenth-century manuscript (274). I have not been able to obtain the essay by Peiper cited
by Walther, which appeared in the *Anzeiger für Kunde der deutschen Vorzeit* 21 (1874): 103ff.

chronicle, Orosius describes the cycles of destruction and reedification of Jerusalem; his description of the Jews' habitation of Jerusalem differs, however, depending upon whether he describes the period before the time of Christ or after. Jews living after the time of Christ are portrayed as sinful, and as suffering on account of their sins: "the Jews, entirely abandoned by the grace of God after the Passion of Christ, found themselves entirely surrounded by evils" (Iudaei post passionem Christi destituti in totum gratia Dei cum omnibus undique malis circumvenirentur [7.9.2; 3: 37–38]). Jews living before the time of Christ, conversely, are described as virtuous and God-fearing. In keeping with his usual historiographical method of noting the simultaneity of events in different cultures, Orosius states that, at the same moment that the Roman republic was founded, the Jewish people returned from their captivity in Babylon to "sanctam Hierusalem" and rebuilt the "templum Domini."[19] Here, the position of the Jews in "holy Jerusalem" seems rightful and assured, as they draw together in worship at "the temple of God."

Orosius' description of the expulsion of the Jews from Jerusalem at the hands of Titus and Vespasian in 70 C.E., however, portrays them very differently. Titus lays siege to the city, breaches the walls, and approaches the Temple, where many priests and prominent citizens (multitudo sacerdotum ac principum [7.9.4; 3: 38]) had gathered to make a last stand. At that moment, Titus experiences a moment of self-doubt:

> Quod tamen postquam in potestatem redactum opere atque antiquitate suspexit, diu deliberavit utrum tamquam incitamentum hostium incenderet an in testimonium victoriae reservaret. Sed Ecclesia Dei iam per totum Orbem uberrime germinante, hoc tamquam effetum ac vacuum nullique usui bono commodum arbitrio Dei auferendum fuit. Itaque Titus... templum in Hierosolymis incendit ac diruit.

> Then, after having brought [the Temple] under his control, Titus admired the work and its noble age, asking himself whether he should burn it as an incentive toward continued hostilities, or whether he should preserve it in testimony to his victory. But, at the moment when the Church of God was already germinating in a fecund way across the whole world, this [Temple], emptied by the act of giving birth and void, and which could serve no useful purpose, must disappear by the

---

19. Orosius, *Historiarum adversum paganos* 7.2.3; 3: 17.

will of God. That is why Titus... burned and destroyed the Temple of Jerusalem. (7.9.5–6; 3: 38–39)

Though I have supplied the referent in the translation, the word *templum* is largely absent from the Latin passage, appearing only in its closing words with reference to the Temple's destruction. Such omission is appropriate to the sense of the passage, which centers on the very superfluity of the Temple, now merely an empty shell, devoid of that which once had made it holy. This description of the Temple as "vacuum," that is, empty or void, refers not just to the actual physical space of the Temple but the symbolic space of Judaism itself. The passage resonates with the words of "De nequitia Judeorum," quoted above, where the Jews are similarly characterized: they are said to be scattered through the world, "vagans per inania" (wandering through empty space), their own spiritual vacuousness precipitating their endless wandering in the void. While the destruction of the Temple is carried out by Titus, the ethnic cleansing of the city is completed only under Hadrian, as Orosius recounts: "he ordered that no Jew was to be allowed into Jerusalem, only Christians being permitted within the city" (praecepitque ne cui Iudaeo introeundi Hierosolymam esset licentia, Christianis tantum civitate permissa [7.13.5; 3: 46]). In this moment, the appropriation of Jerusalem is complete, as the Jews are driven out to make way for the Christians.

Orosius' description of the Temple as a womb emptied of its child is significant, for it imposes a gendered framework upon not only the Temple but also the city of Jerusalem, and even Judaism itself.[20] From an early date, the rending of the veil before the door of the Holy of Holies in the Temple was understood by Christian writers to be a physical manifestation of the fundamental change in the status of Judaism with the death of Jesus.[21] The moment of the sacrifice of the Lamb of God was thought to be the typological fulfillment of the sacrifice offered by Abraham, and the New Law, correspondingly, the fulfillment of the Old Law delivered to the Jews by Moses. This typological relationship was frequently signified, in both visual art and exegetical texts, in terms of the binary opposition of Ecclesia (the Church) and Synagoga.[22]

---

20. The gendered depiction found in Orosius may be derived from Augustine, who likens Jewish Jerusalem to an infertile woman. On the ninth-century afterlife of Augustine's comments, see Albert, "*Adversos Iudaeos,*" 119–42, esp. 128–35. This gendered depiction seems to be absent from earlier anti-Judaic patristic literature; see Stroumsa, "From Anti-Judaism to Antisemitism," 1–26.

21. On exegesis of Matthew 27: 51, see Schiller, *Iconography of Christian Art,* 1: 110–12.

22. On the role of gender in the personification of Synagoga and Ecclesia, see Ferrante, *Woman as Image,* 20. More generally on Synagoga and Ecclesia, see Seiferth, *Synagogue and Church,* 33–41; Schlauch, "Allegory of Church and Synagogue," 448–64.

Modern scholars often interpret Synagoga as a personification of Judaism; more accurately, it is the Jewish community that corresponds to the Christian entity of the Church, understood as a single body of believers united by their common faith. Ecclesia and Synagoga are containers, as it were, enclosing the members of their respective communities in a spiritual sense, just as the actual church or synagogue would physically enclose worshipers.

Visual depictions of Synagoga and Ecclesia during the ninth through eleventh centuries illustrate the way in which, through the fulfillment of typology, Synagoga gives way to Ecclesia. After the twelfth century, Ruth Mellinkoff has argued, depictions of Synagoga became increasingly negative, as she was seen to represent not the virtuous Jews of the period before Christ but rather those who had rejected his message, including contemporary Jews; accordingly, after the twelfth century, Synagoga came to be sometimes portrayed wearing the pointed hat or yellow clothing conventionally used to identify medieval Jews in manuscript illustrations.[23] The connotations of the gender identification of Synagoga and Ecclesia are made increasingly explicit in texts and illustrations of the later Middle Ages. For example, as Sara Lipton notes in her study of the thirteenth-century *Bibles moralisées,* the supplanting of Synagoga by Ecclesia is depicted as the rejection of a sterile, unfruitful conjugal relationship between Christ and Synagoga and Christ in favor of a new, fecund union with Ecclesia.[24] Lipton points out that the figure of Synagoga was even coupled with depictions of Haeresis (Heresy) in order to illustrate the pernicious alliance of the enemies of Christianity.[25] Orosius' metaphorical description of Jerusalem as an emptied womb can thus be seen as an early manifestation of a trend that would become prevalent in medieval Christianity: that is, the belief that Judaism was significant not in itself, but only as the preliminary phase of Christianity, the dry husk to be cast away once the seed of "true" belief had been successfully disseminated throughout the world.[26]

---

23. Mellinkoff, *Outcasts,* 1: 35–36.

24. Lipton, *Images of Intolerance,* 118. See also Lipton's study of depictions of Ecclesia and Synagoga in "Temple Is My Body," 129–64.

25. Lipton, *Images of Intolerance,* 84–86, 94–99. On the identification of heresy with Judaism in art, see Cahn, "Expulsion of the Jews," 94–109.

26. A study of the changing depiction of the Jews and Jerusalem in late medieval redactions of Orosius (including the widely disseminated vernacular adaptation, the *Histoire ancienne jusqu'à César*) would doubtless be very fruitful. For a useful survey of late medieval manuscripts of Orosius, see Olsen, *L'étude des auteurs classiques latins aux XIe et XIIe siècles,* vol. 2. On illustrations of Jerusalem in manuscripts of Old French adaptations of Orosius, see Oltrogge, *Die Illustrationszyklen zur "Histoire ancienne jusqu'à César."*

There is little doubt that the most influential strand in medieval writing about the geographical place of the Jews is made up of the many retellings of the fall of Jerusalem first chronicled by Josephus. Written in the first century, Josephus' *Bellum Judaicum* was an important source for the early fathers of the Church, accorded an authoritative status comparable at least to the Apocrypha. The *Bellum Judaicum* survives not only in numerous manuscripts of the full text, but also in innumerable quotations and excerpts in theological writings, historical chronicles, romances, and encyclopedias; during the later Middle Ages, its account of the siege of Jerusalem by Titus and Vespasian in 70 C.E. was even rendered in vernacular translations.[27] The *Bellum Judaicum* was known to medieval writers both directly, by means of a Latin translation of Josephus' Greek text, and indirectly, through the fourth-century redaction attributed to Hegesippus.[28] One of the most widely disseminated versions of Josephus' account of the siege of Jerusalem appears in Vincent of Beauvais' *Speculum Historiale,* the historical chronicle contained within Vincent's voluminous *Speculum Maius.* Vincent essentially reproduces Josephus' account of the atrocities that took place during the siege of Jerusalem: he describes the bodies of the fleeing inhabitants, eviscerated by Roman soldiers looking for the gold coins the Jews had swallowed before their flight; the terrible hunger that led to "monstrous deeds" (immunda facti) of cannibalism; the killing and burning of the priests before the Temple at the end of the siege.[29] The dismemberment of Jewish bodies, highlighted repeatedly throughout the passage, symbolically represents the fragmentary, partial nature of Judaism itself. From a medieval Christian perspective, wholeness and bodily integrity were seen as fundamental attributes of the body of the Church, mystically united by the sacrifice of the Eucharist; fragmentation and incompleteness, by contrast, were thought to be the hallmarks of Christianity's precursor, now superseded. In keeping with this view, the evisceration of Jewish bodies to find the gold coins inside is proof of the "avaritia" or avarice of the Jews themselves, not of their Roman captors; similarly, the dismemberment of bodies in preparation for cannibalistic consumption is evidence of the monstrosity of the immured Jews, not the inhuman behavior of those who laid siege to

---

27. A useful survey of the reception of Josephus can be found in Schreckenberg, *Die Flavius-Josephus-Tradition in Antike und Mittelalter.*

28. There are early printed editions (Paris: Ascensius, 1524; Cologne: Cholinus, 1559) but no modern edition of Hegesippus' *De excidio hierosolymitano.* A useful study of the text appears in Bell, "Historical Analysis."

29. Vincent of Beauvais, *Speculum Historiale* 10.4–6 (col. 370–71).

the city. In Vincent's description, as in his source text, the fragmented Jewish body is simply a visible sign of the spiritual defects intrinsic to Judaism.

Josephus' account appears once again in the *Siege of Jerusalem,* a Middle English alliterative poem written during the second half of the fourteenth century. Although it recounts the same narrative of destruction and despair, the *Siege of Jerusalem* differs from the account found in Vincent's *Speculum Historiale* in the moral valence it ascribes to the acts committed by the be-sieged occupants of the city. In the Middle English poem as in Vincent's chronicle, Jewish identity serves as the template for Christian identity, in-formed by the hermeneutics of supersession derived from Pauline theology.[30] At the same time, however, the *Siege of Jerusalem* employs tropes used in cru-sade chronicles to describe quite a different enemy of the Christian host— the Muslims who defended Jerusalem against the crusaders in the twelfth and thirteenth centuries. Such overlapping of Muslim and Jewish identity is far from uncommon; as Jeremy Cohen puts it, in the medieval "classifica-tion of the Jews together with the Muslims," both are merely "subsets in a larger genus of hermeneutically constructed *infideles* who undermined the unity of Christian faith."[31] In canon law, regulations limiting the interactions of Christians with Jews and Muslims treated the latter two as equivalents.[32] Literary texts reflect this interchangeability as well: medieval mystery plays depicting the nativity of Jesus, for example, characterize Herod using the conventions associated with Muslim sultans in the *chansons de geste* and ro-mances. He is opulently dressed, given to violent rages and, most tellingly, invokes the name of his god, Muhammad ["Mahounde"].[33] (The theological dimensions of this overlapping of Muslim and Jewish identity are discussed in more detail in chapter 5.) What makes the treatment of Jewish identity in the *Siege of Jerusalem* unique is not the identification of Muslims with Jews, but the fact that the poem uses Jewish identity as the template not only for the construction of Muslim identity, but for the construction of Christian identity as well. This complicated overlapping of categories of identity,

---

30. See Elisa Narin van Court's influential reading of the poem in terms of supersession, espe-cially as articulated by Boyarin: "*The Siege of Jerusalem* and Augustinian Historians: Writing about Jews in Fourteenth-century England," *Chaucer Review* 29 (1995): 227–48; reprinted in *Chaucer and the Jews,* ed. Sheila Delany (New York: Routledge, 2002), 165–84. On supersession in medieval English literature more broadly, see also van Court, "Hermeneutics of Supersession43–87; "Socially Mar-ginal," 293–326. On the relationship of gender and supersession, see Lampert, *Gender and Jewish Difference,* 26–35.

31. Jeremy Cohen, "Muslim Connection," 162. See also Cutler, *Jew as the Ally,* 97.

32. Simonsohn, *Apostolic See and the Jews,* passim.

33. "Mahounde full of might" (line 283; cf. 327, 406); "Vintners Playe," 156–74.

coupled with the symbolic use of space in the establishment of those categories, makes it worth examining the *Siege of Jerusalem* at some length.

Recent readers of the *Siege of Jerusalem* have tended to take one of two positions regarding the depiction of Jews in the poem. Some, recognizing the very evident resemblance of the *Siege of Jerusalem* to contemporary *chansons de geste* and crusade romances, suggest that the Jews of the poem are to be equated with Muslims, and that the poem as a whole functions as crusade propaganda.[34] Others argue that to interpret the Jews simply as coded terms for Muslims is to fail to do justice to the depiction of Jews in the poem: in spite of the fact that Jews had been expelled from England in 1290, and therefore that the poem's writer and its readers were unlikely to have met any living Jewish people, the virtual presence of Jews must be recognized.[35] The romance's treatment of Jewish bodies, ranging from the horrific cannibalism practiced by the besieged Jews to the complete immolation of the Jewish priests at the hands of the Romans, reveals some of the ways medieval Christians used Jewish identity in order to define the borders of their own community, both affirmatively (predicating Christian identity on the basis of Jewish identity) and negatively (identifying Jewish and Muslim identity as fundamentally similar, and hence excluding both).

In order to understand the strategic use of Jewish identity in the *Siege of Jerusalem*, it is helpful to examine how communities are constituted in the poem and how their borders are defined. It is certainly true that the Jews of the *Siege* are characterized, in certain respects, in terms that evoke the Muslims depicted in contemporary crusade literature. Strangely, however, the Jews are simultaneously characterized in terms that are not merely "sympathetic" (as van Court has suggested),[36] but that explicitly identify them with the Christian protagonists of the crusade chronicles—not the Muslim antagonists. This ambivalence creates a peculiar economy in the poem in which the Jews are simultaneously the object of identification for the Christian reader and that which must be abjected. The genre of the siege poem lends itself especially well to this ambivalent characterization, for siege poems in general are centrally concerned not with conversion, but with the integrity of the community.[37] They do not feature, as do the *chansons de geste* or romances, climactic scenes of conversion; the *Siege of Jerusalem* is no exception, for here the goal is not conversion, but extermination. The integrity of the Christian

34. Hamel, *"Siege of Jerusalem,"* 177–94; Lawton, "Titus Goes Hunting," 105–17, esp. 116.
35. Van Court, "Siege," 227–48; Millar, *"Siege of Jerusalem,"* 141–80.
36. Van Court, "Siege" 241.
37. Akbari, "Incorporation," 22–44, esp. 31–32.

community is affirmed, its wholeness the mirror image of the fragmented Jewish bodies in which the poem so memorably revels.

The *Siege of Jerusalem* is based on several sources, the most important one of which is Josephus' *Bellum Judaicum*. Yet it also has a curious analogue, a kind of shadow text that corresponds to it in many ways, and which also circulated under the title "The Siege of Jerusalem." The *Historia rerum in partibus transmarinis gestarum* of William of Tyre, completed in 1183, includes a history of the Holy Land from antiquity, a comprehensive account of the First Crusade, and a chronicle of the early years of the First Latin Kingdom of Jerusalem. Written originally in Latin, it was translated into Old French by 1225 and circulated widely in the vernacular (more so than in the Latin original). It was translated back into Latin in the thirteenth century, as well as into other vernacular languages.[38] In what follows, as I point out some correspondences between the *Siege of Jerusalem* and its "shadow text" of the same name, I will quote from the late fifteenth-century English translation printed by William Caxton, and will refer to it as the "Caxton *Siege of Jerusalem*" in order to distinguish it from the alliterative poem. The Caxton *Siege* differs from William of Tyre's original chronicle in many respects, most important in its overall scope and theme: it is comprised only of the first nine books of William's twenty-three, omitting the history of the Latin Kingdom following the consolidation of Christian power in Jerusalem. In this abbreviated history, the siege of Jerusalem becomes the focus of the narrative and the conquest its climax, as the crusaders, led by the heroic figure of Godfrey of Bouillon, move inexorably forward.

As Mary Hamel has noted, the scenes of violence and savage warfare depicted in the *Siege of Jerusalem* closely resemble passages found in crusade chronicles and the romances based upon them.[39] The terrible bloodshed found in the crusade histories is echoed in the alliterative poem:

Rappis rispen forth / that [rydders] an hundred
Scholde be busy to burie / that on a bent lafte.
Castels clateren doun, / cameles brosten,
Dromedaries to the deth / drowen ful swythe;
The blode fomed hem fro / in the flasches aboute
Th[at] kne-depe in the dale / dascheden stedes.

---

38. On the various versions of William of Tyre, see Riant, *Catalogue des Manuscrits de* L'Eracles; Pryor, *"Eracles,"* 293. Evidence of the early thirteenth-century Latin retranslation appears in Ralph of Coggeshall's *De Expugnatione Terrae Sanctae,* 257, in *Radulphi de Coggeshall;* noted in *Godeffroy of Boloyne,* ed. Colvin, xix.

39. Hamel *"Siege of Jerusalem,"* 183.

Guts burst forth, so that a hundred men would be needed to bury what was left on the field. Castles [containing men riding elephants] clattered down, camels burst open, dromedaries drew close to death quickly. The blood foamed forth from them into the streams nearby, so that horses galloped knee-deep in that valley. (571–76)[40]

The chronicler Raymond d'Aguiliers describes a similar scene, also set in Jerusalem, but at the time of the First Crusade: "In the Temple and porch of Solomon, men rode in blood up to their knees and bridle reins. Indeed, it was a just and splendid judgment of God that this place should be filled with the blood of the unbelievers, since it had suffered so long from their blasphemies. The city was filled with corpses and blood." Fulcher of Chartres puts it more baldly: "If you had been there, your feet would have been stained up to the ankles with the blood of the slain."[41] In the Caxton *Siege,* the blood of the vanquished enemy flows freely, as though it were water: "There was so moche blood shedde that the canellys and ruissheauls [little rivers] ronne alle of blood / and alle the stretes of the toun were couerd with dede men" (273.36–274.1).[42] Similarly, in the *Siege of Jerusalem,* the "Baches woxen ablode aboute in the vale, / And goutes fram gold wede as goteres they runne" (Streams became bloody, all through the valley, and little streams of golden clothing ran like channels of water [563–64]). The blood shed in the sacred precincts has, paradoxically, a purifying effect: as the Caxton *Siege* puts it, "It was wel couenable [suitable] thyng that . . . theyr blood sholde also be shedd, where as they had spred the ordure of mescreaunce" (274.22–26).[43]

The sheer multiplicity of faceless, nameless bodies appears in both *Siege of Jerusalem* texts as well: in the alliterative poem, "The fals Iewes in the felde fallen so thicke / As hail froward heuen, hepe ouer other. / So was the bent ouerbrad, blody byrunne, / With ded bodies aboute alle the brod vale" (The false Jews in the field fell as thickly as hail from heaven, one heap upon the other. The field was overrun with blood, and thickly spread with dead bodies around the whole wide valley [601–4]). The piles of corpses in the poem,

---

40. *Siege of Jerusalem,* ed. Hanna and Lawton; cited by line number in the text. Translations are my own; thorn and yogh are transliterated.

41. Trans. in [Fulcher of Chartes] Edward Peters, *The First Crusade,* 77, 214.

42. The Caxton *Siege of Jerusalem (Godeffroy of Boloyne)* is cited by page and line number in the text.

43. The rhetoric of pollution is discussed at greater length in the third part of chapter 5. On how the holy places were to be cleansed by bloodshed, see Cole, "Religious Pollution," 84–111.

"one heap upon the other," echo the conventions of crusade accounts found in the Caxton *Siege:* "They slewe so many in the stretes / that there were heeps of dede bodyes, and [one] myght not goo ne passe but vpon them that so laye deed" (273.7–9). The alliterative *Siege* continues similarly: "Myght no stede doun stap bot on stele wede / Or on burne, other on beste or on bright scheldes. / So myche was the multitude" (No horse could put his foot down, except on steel armor, or on men, or on animals, or on bright shields, the multitude was so great [605–7]). Yet the scenes of violence and bloodshed are not the only ones to be drawn from crusade accounts: as Christine Chism has noted, the luxurious depictions of the opulent wealth found in Jerusalem clearly come from the same source, as do the "olyfauntes" (449) used to carry groups of armed men to the battlefield.[44] The fabulous wealth of the Jewish Temple, covered "with rebies grete; / With perles and peritotes," glowing with gold and having "dores ful of dyemauntes" (1254–57), is pillaged by the Roman armies, just as the fabulous wealth of the mosques is taken by the crusaders. The treasures of Jerusalem, the poet relates, are too abundant to be described: "Telle couthe no tonge the tresours that thei ther founden: / Iewels for ioly men [and] ie[me]wes riche; / Ffloreyns of [fyne] gold [ther] no freke wanted, / [Ne r]iche pelour and pane princes to were; / Besauntes, bies of gold, broches and rynges, / Clene clothes of selke many carte fulle" (No tongue could tell all the treasures they found there: jewels for jolly men, and rich gems. No man lacked florins of fine gold, nor rich furs and cloth suited to princes, besants, gold bracelets, brooches and rings, clothes of pure silk—many cartfuls of them [1274–79]). Similarly, in the latter-day sack of Jerusalem, the crusaders "founde therin grete hauoyr [wealth], and gold, syluer, precious stones and cloth of sylk. [They] made alle to be born a way" (274.12–14). The final correspondence between the depiction of Muslims in the Caxton *Siege of Jerusalem* and that of the Jews in the alliterative *Siege* concerns the nature of the "misbelief" that earns death for the victims, whether they be slaughtered in the first century or in the eleventh. It is faith in a false "law": in the alliterative *Siege,* the Jews are said to follow "Moyses lawe" (484, 586), while in the Caxton *Siege,* the Muslims are said to follow the "lawe of machomet" (274.24, 276.38). This parallelism, central to the long tradition of polemics against Islam (discussed in chapter 5), is evoked in the alliterative poem to suggest that the Jews, like the Muslims, are a kind of perennial enemy of Christianity.

---

44. Chism, *"Siege of Jerusalem,"* 309–40, esp. 320–25.

The paradox is that, in the very same poem, the Jews are also likened to Christians—not just Christians in general, but Christians as they are portrayed in precisely the same crusade chronicles from which the parallels between Jews and Muslim were derived. In the *Siege of Jerusalem,* the suffering of the Jews is depicted in great detail; yet it is portrayed not only with malicious pleasure at their plight but, at least on occasion, with compassion. Their suffering first becomes acute when they begin to lack water after the Romans besieging them stop up the streams that flow into the city:

> The cors of the condit / that comen to toun
> Stoppen, euereche a streem / ther any str[and]e yede,
> With stockes and stones / and stynkande bestes
> That they no water myght wynne / that weren enclosed.

> They stopped the watercourse of every conduit
> that came into the town, every small stream,
> wherever any current went, using sticks, and stones, and
> rotting corpses of animals, so that
> they who were enclosed could get no water.
>
> (689–92)

Exactly the same military strategy is described in the Caxton *Siege of Jerusalem,* except that here the action is carried out by the Muslims against the Christians: "[T]hey stopped the mowthes of thyse fontaynes and of the Cysternes... ffor they thought that the pylgryms for lacke of watres sholde not mayntene theyr syege to fore the toun" (254.17.20). The Christians suffer greatly as a result, as the Caxton *Siege* recounts in detail: "Thanguysshe of thurst grewe moch of the heete that was in Iuyn, And of the trauaylle that they suffred, and for the duste that entred in theyr mowthes" (258.10–12). The suffering of the Jews in the alliterative poem becomes even greater, however, when they are subjected to the pains of hunger as well, as the Romans determine to starve them out of the city. The lack of goods causes prices to be driven up sharply, so that "Was noght for besauntes to bye that men bite myght. / For a ferthyng-worth of fode floryns an hundred / Princes profren in the toun" (There was nothing that could be eaten that could be bought with gold coins. For a penny-worth of food, princes would offer a hundred florins [1142–44]). Similar inflation is depicted in the Caxton *Siege,* where the crusaders suffer from lack of food: "a cowe was worth four marc weyght of syluer, which a man myght haue at begynnyng for echt or ten shyllyngis.

A lambe or a kyd was at sex shyllyngis, whiche to fore was worth but thre or four pens" (144.29–32).

The climax, however, of Jewish suffering in the *Siege of Jerusalem* occurs when a woman living in Jerusalem during the prolonged siege suffers terrible hunger, and is driven to commit a terrible act.[45] This is one of the most horrible scenes in the poem, but also one of the most beautifully written; in its empathetic portrayal of the mother, it differs strikingly from the parallel account found in Vincent of Beauvais' *Speculum Historiale,* described above. To convey the tone of the passage, it is necessary to quote it in full:

> On Marie, a myld wyf, / for meschef of foode,
> Hir owen barn that yo bar, / yo brad on the gledis,
> Rostyth rigge and rib / with rewful wordes,
> Sayth, "sone, vpon eche side / our sorow is a-lofte:
> Batail aboute the borwe / our bodies to quelle;
> Withyn h[u]nger so hote / that negh our herte brestyth.
> Therfor yeld that I the yaf / and ayen tourne,
> And entr ther thou [o]ut cam," / and etyth a schouldere.
> The [rich] roos of the rost / right [in]to the [strete]
> that fele fastyng folke / felde[n] the sauere.
> Doun thei daschen the dore, / dey scholde the berde
> That mete yn this meschef / hadde from men l[a]yned.
> Than saith that worthi wif / in a wode hunger,
> "Myn owen barn haue I brad / and the bones gnawen,
> Yit haue I saued you som," / and forth a side feccheth
> Of the barn that yo bare, / and alle hire blode chaungeth.
> [Forth] they went for wo / wep[ande sore]
> And sayn, "alas in this lif / how longe schul we dwelle?"

One Mary, a gentle woman, for lack of food, put on the coals her own child that she bore; she roasted the back and the ribs, with sorrowful words, saying, "Son, our sorrow is raised up upon each side: battle is all around the city to slay us, and within hunger so sharp that our heart almost bursts. Therefore, give me back what I gave you, and turn around, and go back in where you came out!" And she ate a shoulder. The smell rose up from the roast, right into the streets, so that the many starving

---

45. An analogue to the Siege's account of the cannibalistic mother can be found in a rabbinic story about the wife of Doeg ben Joseph; see Buber, *Midrasch Echa rabbati,* commentary on Lamentations 2:20. Thanks to Jeremy Cohen for this reference.

people smelled the savor. They smashed the door down, for any woman should die who had kept meat away from other people during this time of suffering. Then that worthy woman said, crazed with hunger: "I have roasted my own child, and gnawed the bones. But I saved some for you." And she went to fetch a side of the child that she had borne, and they all became pale. They went away full of sorrow, weeping, and said, "Alas, how long will we go on in this life?"

(1081–98)

The horror and sorrow experienced by those who burst in on the mother is echoed in the reader. Compassion is generated by her description as "a myld wyf" and (even after she eats her child) "that worthi wif," by the "rewful wordes" she addresses to the little body before she consumes it, and by the generosity she shows ("yit haue I saued you som"). Although the narrative has accordingly been characterized as showing "sympathy" for the besieged Jews,[46] it would be more accurate to say that it encourages the Christian reader to identify with them. The correspondence between the suffering experienced by the Jews in the alliterative *Siege of Jerusalem* and the suffering experienced by the Christians in the Caxton *Siege* encourages such identification.

In the *Siege of Jerusalem,* Judaism is presented as a parody of Christianity. This would seem, at first glance, impossible, because parody is by definition secondary, enacted subsequent to that which it imitates, and Judaism unquestionably predates Christianity.[47] Judaism after the time of Christ, then, is specifically what is identified as parodic. Accordingly, the cannibalistic mother, Mary, functions as a parody of the Virgin Mary: each mother sacrifices her son, and offers her son as food to nourish others. Even the roasting of the child in the oven is an allusion to Mary's relation to Jesus, for medieval images of the Virgin presenting her Child in the form of a baked wafer are common in the fourteenth century.[48] The purpose of such parodic identification is not so much to identify the Jews with Christians (and thus to humanize them), but rather to identify the Christians with the Jews, in order to articulate a notion of Christian identity that both takes Judaism as its model and eradicates it utterly. This act makes Judaism into the parodic ape of Christianity, and Christianity into the authentic, originary "law."

The fate of the Jews in the *Siege of Jerusalem* is therefore, paradoxically, double: on the one hand, they must be annihilated so that the superiority

---

46. Van Court, "Siege," 233.
47. On parody as repetition, see Hutcheon, *Theory of Parody.*
48. Despres, "Mary of the Eucharist," 375–401, esp. 386–87.

of Christianity can be clearly demonstrated; on the other, they must be preserved in order to maintain the authenticity of the model they offer for
Christians. Both the bodies of the captured Jewish priests and the walls and
buildings of the city are reduced to dust, so that no fragment will remain as
a locus for remembering a Jewish Jerusalem:

> [The kyng] bade "a bole-fure betyn / to brennen the corses,
> Kesten Cayphas theryn / and his clerkes [alle],
> And bren[n]en euereche bon / into the browne askes.
> Suth wen[de] to the walle / on the wynde syde
> And alle abrod on the burwe / bl[o]wen the powdere."

> The king commanded, "Kindle a great fire to
> burn up the bodies; cast Caiphas in there, and all
> of his priests, and burn up every each bone into
> brown ashes. Then go to the wall, on the windward
> side, and blow the powder all over the town."
>
> (718–22)

> Now masouns and mynours / han the molde soughte,
> With pykeyse and ponsone / persched the walles;
> Hewen throw hard ston, / h[url]ed hem to grounde
> That alle derkned the diche / for doust of the poudere. . . .
> Nas no ston in the stede / stondande alofte,
> Mortere ne m[u]de-walle / bot alle to mulle fallen;
> Nother tymbre ne tre, / temple ne other,
> Bot doun betyn and brent / into blake erthe.

> Now masons and miners dug into the earth, so
> that the walls were destroyed with picks and
> pointed tools. They hewed through hard stones,
> threw them to the ground, so that the whole trench
> was darkened with the dust from the powder. . . .
> There was no stone in the place still standing
> aloft, neither mortar nor brick wall—all was
> collapsed into dust. There was neither house nor
> tree, neither temple nor any other building; all
> was beaten down and burned into black earth.
>
> (1281–92)

Like the cannibalistic mother who is a parody of the Virgin Mary, Caiphas and his followers are a feeble imitation of Jesus and his apostles; they differ, however, in that no memorial or commemorative place remains to recall that they ever lived. The annihilation of the walls of the city, repeated in microcosm in the annihilation of the bodies of the Jewish men, is a visible manifestation of the erasure of Synagoga. Ecclesia takes her place as Christian Jerusalem—both spiritual goal and material city—is erected on the ground of its Jewish precursor.

In stark contrast to the shrines dedicated to the relics of the apostles and the Church of the Holy Sepulchre, there is no place remaining, in the economy of the *Siege of Jerusalem,* to be associated with the Jews who had lived there. What does remain, however, is portable property: not just the treasures of gold coin, jewels, and silks carried away to Rome, but also the crowning glory of Jewish learning, for the poem notes in closing that "Iosophus the gentile clerke aiorned was to Rome / Ther of this mater and mo he made fayr bokes" (Josephus, the noble cleric, journeyed to Rome, where he made great books about this topic and others [1325–26]). Here, Josephus' *Bellum Judaicum,* the primary source for the alliterative poem, appears as part of the booty of Jerusalem, both priceless treasure and authenticating document. Josephus thus functions as a witness to the victory of the Roman Christians and the destruction of the Jews; he is what Ora Limor identifies as the "knowing Jew," who "continually affirms, against his will, the truth of the Christian beliefs," and thereby acts as "the constitutor of the Christian identity."[49] However, while Limor discusses the phenomenon of the "knowing Jew" in connection with Christian sacred spaces of the Holy Land, Josephus serves as authenticator not of a specific holy place, but precisely the absence of one. He testifies to the state of Jerusalem as a *tabula rasa,* a blank slate upon which the history of Christian Jerusalem can be inscribed. The subsequent reconquest of Jerusalem by the Muslims will be characterized as a return to the "Old Law" of the Jews, a reedification of what had been cast down by the Romans in the first century; the triumphant entry of the Christians into Jerusalem, whether during the first century or the eleventh, is therefore heralded as taking place at a significant moment in salvation history. The former takes place on the "the Paske euene" (*Siege* 1215), that is, the last night before the Easter commemoration of the Resurrection;[50] the latter takes place "vpon a

---

49. Limor, "Christian Sacred Space," 55–77; quotation from 77.
50. This detail does not appear in Josephus; it does appear in the account found in Higden's *Polychronicon* (IV.10).

frydaye, aboute None...ffor on this daye and about that hour suffred [oure lord] deth on the crosse right cruel in the same place, for the Redempcion of man" (Caxton *Siege* 272.25–29). The destruction of the Muslims in Jerusalem during the First Crusade and the destruction of the Jews in the first century are equivalent, part of a cycle of destruction and reedification that will come to an end only with the Apocalypse.

Yet while the city of Jerusalem can be rebuilt and reconstituted, repopulated with "righteous" (i.e., Christian) inhabitants, the Jewish body is doomed to remain in a state of fragmentation, a symbol of the diasporic community sold into exile by the Romans. In the *Siege of Jerusalem,* Jewish bodies are repeatedly shown in the act of being torn to pieces: in the bodies that fly apart as they are struck by hurled stones (826–32), in the bodies of Jewish prisoners that are cut open by Christian soldiers eager to find the gold coins concealed in their "gottes" (1167), in the bodies of the Jewish priests flayed into "rede peces" (706). This is not only a fragmented community, but a community that is in the act of eating itself up, as is powerfully symbolized in the mother who eats the body of her child, ordering him to "turn around, and go back in where you came out" (1087–88). Steven Kruger has shown that several other late medieval English texts, including the Croxton *Play of the Sacrament* and Chaucer's *Prioress' Tale,* depict Jewish bodies as ending, inevitably, in "dismemberment and disintegration." Kruger argues that Jewish bodies are presented in this way in order to symbolize the fragmentation of the diasporic Jewish community, which functions as a mirror image of the Christian community whose integrity is reaffirmed daily in the sacrifice of the Mass.[51] Christian wholeness, then, is necessarily built on the ground of Jewish fragmentation. This is perhaps the most fundamental distinction between the depiction of Jews and Muslims in medieval literature, which otherwise correspond in many respects: the Muslim community is located outside, on the outer borders of the Christian community, and therefore is repudiated, as it were, at a distance; the Jewish community, by contrast, is located both outside and inside, within the Christian community itself, and must therefore be repudiated by being abjected from within.[52] The Jewish community is defined as internal to the Christian community based not only

---

51. Kruger, "Bodies of Jews," 301–23; quotation from 318.

52. Kruger makes a similar distinction with regard to twelfth-century perspectives: "The Muslim 'other' is conceived not, like the Jews...as a scattered presence within a Christian hegemony, but as a hegemony of its own." Kruger, "Medieval Christian (Dis)identifications," 185–203; quotation from 194. These crucial distinctions separating Jewish and Muslim alterity provide a useful corrective to Grady's reading of the pitiable Jew of the *Siege of Jerusalem* as a counterpart of the "virtuous heathen": he suggests that the *Siege* "darkly mirrors the Gregory/Trajan legend," illustrating how "the

on the actual presence of Jewish communities within the cities of western Europe (at least until the expulsions of the later Middle Ages),[53] but also on the virtual presence of Judaism as a shadowy presence prior to Christianity.

In the *Siege of Jerusalem,* as in the accounts of the events of 70 C.E. found in Orosius, Josephus, and Vincent of Beauvais, the history of Jewish presence in Jerusalem is fundamentally a narrative of dispersal. The enclosure of the Jews within the besieged city results in the self-destruction of the community, epitomized by the mother who eats up her own child. Synagoga, like Ecclesia, is a community composed of those who share a single faith; unlike Ecclesia, however, Synagoga is a self-consuming community, one which participates actively in her own destruction. Inevitably, enclosure within the besieged city results both in an eruption of goods that are carried away by the victorious Romans and in a dispersal of survivors doomed to wander the face of the earth—at least until the cycle of enclosure and dispersal begins once again. The Jews who survive the siege are, in the words of the list of nations titled "Gentium quicumque mores," a dispersed people (sparsi), whose homeland is uncertain (incerta). Thirteenth-century accounts of the "wandering Jew," condemned to linger until the second coming of Christ as punishment for his participation in the Crucifixion, can be found in a range of texts including Matthew Paris' *Chronica maiora,* affirming the fundamental importance of dispersion in medieval conceptions of Jewish identity.[54] Throughout this discourse of Jewish alterity, the centripetal movement of enclosure is immediately followed by the centrifugal motion of dispersal, generating a perennial cycle that lifts Jewish identity out of the realm of the temporal, making it into an idealized, eternal referent rather than a contemporary lived reality.

The sequence of centripetal enclosure and centrifugal dispersal is also evident in another strand in the medieval discourse of Jewish alterity: the identification of the enclosed, unclean tribes of Gog and Magog with the descendants of Israel. In chapter 2, we saw how medieval accounts of Alexander the Great highlight the conqueror's enclosure of Gog and Magog in the mountains near the Caspian Sea, drawing upon the *Revelations* of pseudo-Methodius as well as the *Cosmographia* of Aethicus Ister. In these texts, there is no question of the enclosed tribes being identified as Jews; on the contrary,

---

Middle English discourse of the righteous heathen was affiliated with the most venomous expressions" of anti-Judaism. Grady, *Representing Righteous Heathens,* 131.

53. For a useful survey of the presence of Jewish communities in England before the expulsion of 1290, see Stacey, "Jews and Christians," 340–54.

54. Matthew Paris, *Chronica majora,* 3: 161–63; 5: 340–41. On the emergence of the theme of the 'wandering Jew' during the thirteenth century, see Dahan, *Les intellectuels chrétiens et les juifs au moyen âge,* 520; Baron, *Social and Religious History,* 177–82; Glikson, "Wandering Jew."

many accounts of Alexander the Great, including the *Liber Floridus* of Lambert of St. Omer and the *Roman de toute chevalerie* of Thomas of Kent, incorporate the episode of Alexander's visit to Jerusalem found in Josephus, portraying the Jews in a strikingly positive light as worshipers of the one God. Alexander's prostration before the high priest puzzles his men until the Macedonian declares that he worships the name on the breastplate worn by the priest, not the man himself. Certainly, a hermeneutics of supersession is operational in these Alexander narratives, especially in Lambert's *Liber Floridus,* where Alexander is depicted as a typological prefiguration of the Christian king of Jerusalem in the time of the crusades. They do not, however, participate in a discourse of anti-Judaism, much less antisemitism.[55] Instead, Judaism is used as an authenticator, indicating Alexander's predisposition toward monotheism in spite of his apparent devotional promiscuity.

Other texts, however, do explicitly associate the enclosed tribes of Gog and Magog with the Jews in an expression of what both Andrew Gow and Benjamin Braude have identified as antisemitism; Braude goes so far as to describe one representative text in this tradition as "a warrant for genocide."[56] The earliest example of the association of Gog and Magog with the Jews appears in the ninth-century account of Christian of Stavelot; not until the twelfth century, however, does this tendency become more common, appearing in such widely disseminated works as the *Pantheon* of Godfrey of Viterbo and the *Historia Scholastica* of Peter Comestor.[57] The confusion—if it can be called that—of Gog and Magog with the tribes of Israel probably arose from a passage found in Orosius' fifth-century world chronicle in which he writes that, during the reign of Artaxerxes, many Jews migrated to the northern regions of Hyrcania, near the Caspian Sea: "It is thought that they still remain there today, considerably increased in number, and that they will burst out of there someday."[58] This already rather paranoid vision of exilic Jewry came to be fused with pseudo-Methodius' account of the unclean tribes of Gog and Magog, perhaps because Orosius mentions the birth of Alexander immediately prior to his description of the northern Jews.[59] Influenced by the detailed description of the northern wastes inhabited by Gog and Magog

---

55. On the distinction between anti-Judaism and antisemitism, see n. 108, below.

56. Gow, *Red Jews,* 3. Braude, "Mandeville's Jews," 133–58; quotation from 145.

57. Peter Comestor, *Historia Scholastica* (commentary on Esther), PL 198, col. 1496a–c; on the dissemination of this concept, see Gow, *Red Jews,* 37–63; Westrem, "Against Gog and Magog," 54–75, esp. 65–66. Still useful is the foundational work in Anderson, *Alexander's Gate,* along with some corrections in Westrem, "Gog and Magog," 56.

58. "[Q]uos ibi usque in hodiernum diem amplissimis generis sui incredimentis consistere atque exim quandoque erupturos opinio est." Orosius 3.7.6–7; 1: 147–48.

59. Orosius 3.7.5; 1: 147.

found in the *Cosmographia* of Aethicus Ister, later medieval writers readily coupled the Jews with the unclean tribes enclosed by Alexander behind the northern mountains, or *ubera aquilonis*. For example, in his *Opus maius,* Roger Bacon declares that the northern regions bordering the Caspian Sea include not only Gog and Magog, but "likewise, the Jews, whom Orosius and other sacred writers state will come forth."[60] Like Aethicus Ister, whom he cites explicitly, Bacon emphasizes the forbidding nature of the northern environment inhabited by these hostile tribes.

The association of the Jews with Gog and Magog became widespread during the twelfth and thirteenth centuries, mediated by such popular texts as Peter Comestor's *Historia Scholastica,* Godfrey of Viterbo's *Pantheon,* and Roger Bacon's *Opus Maius.* Its broadest dissemination, however, came by way of *The Book of John Mandeville,* a mid-fourteenth-century work which (as we saw in chapter 1) was translated into a variety of vernacular languages (and Latin) and which survives in an unusually large number of manuscripts.[61] The author of *The Book of John Mandeville* pursues several different strategies to impose order upon the heterogeneous world, ranging from the geographical (all the rivers of the world are said to flow from the four rivers of paradise) to the genealogical (all the people of the earth are said to be descended from the three sons of Noah). The genealogical schema employed in the work is rather unusual, however, as Benjamin Braude has shown in his survey of the manuscript evidence.[62] While medieval *mappaemundi* conventionally divide the world into the three continents of Asia, Africa, and Europe, assigning each of them to Shem, Ham, and Japheth, respectively,[63] *The Book of John Mandeville* reallocates the continents so that "Ham... took the largest and best part, towards the East, which is called Asia, and Shem took Africa, and Japheth took Europe" (Cham... prist la plus grande partie et la meillour partie orientele qe est appelé Asie, et Sem prist Affrique, et Japhez prist Europe [24; 378]).

More extraordinary, however, is *The Book*'s account of the extended lineal descent from Noah: the sons of Ham are the "diverses gentz" (diverse folk)

---

60. "[E]t Judaei similiter, quos Orosius et alii sanct referunt exituros." Bacon, *Opus Maius* IV; ed. 1:365, trans. 1:382 (translation modified slightly). Bacon's use of the term *similiter* to associate the Jews with Gog and Magog can be fruitfully compared with the use of the same term in thirteenth-century *Bibles moralisées* to associate Jews and Christian heretics. See Lipton, *Images of Intolerance,* passim.

61. On the dissemination of *The Book of John Mandeville,* see chapter 1 of this book.

62. Braude, "The Sons of Noah," 103–42, esp. 116–20. Braude promises a comparative edition of this section of *Mandeville's Travels,* drawing upon a variety of manuscripts and printed editions (118n35).

63. My assessment of the conventions of the *mappaemundi* differs slightly from Braude's; see Akbari, "Due East," 22.

of India, the sons of Shem are the Saracens, and the sons of Japheth include not only "nous qe demorroms en Europe" (we that dwell in Europe), but also "le poeple de Israël" (the people of Israel) (24; 379). It is entirely conventional to identify the Asiatic Saracens as the offspring of Shem and to identify the Europeans as the offspring of Japheth;[64] but to couple "the people of Israel" (that is, the descendants of Jacob, rather than the inhabitants of a certain land) with the Europeans is something quite extraordinary. One might be forgiven for optimistically believing, for a moment, that the author is suggesting that there is a kinship between the Europeans and the Jews, that they share a common birthright. Instead, however, it soon becomes clear that the purpose of the anomaly is to lay the groundwork for an alternative account of Jewish genealogical descent: that is, the identification of the Jews with the unclean, enclosed tribes of Gog and Magog, who are conventionally identified (following Genesis) as the offspring of Japheth.[65]

The author of *The Book of John Mandeville* describes the remote northern mountain pass where "the ten tribes of Jews are enclosed, that men call Gog and Magog" (les Juys de X lienés sont enclos, qe homme appelle Goth et Magoth). He retells the widely known story of how Alexander the Great shut them up there behind great mountainous gates, "so that they dwell there all locked up and entirely enclosed" (si qe ils demoerent la touz enserrez et tout enclos), and explains that "the Jews have no land of their own in all the world, except for that land between the mountains" (ly Juys n'ount point de propre terre en tout le mounde forsque celle terre entre les montaignes [29; 428–29]). So far, it would seem that the "place" of the Jews, in *The Book of John Mandeville* as in Roger Bacon's account in the *Opus Maius,* is at the margin of the known world. This placement is depicted visually on many medieval world maps that show the two enclosing mountains (or *ubera aquilonis*) at the northernmost extreme.[66] Yet in *The Book of John Mandeville*'s version of this scenario, the Jews represent a threat located both far away in the wilderness, and in one's own backyard:

[L]'em dit q'ils isseront fors en temps de Antecrist et q'ils ferront grant occisioun de christiens. Et pur ceo touz Juys qe demoerent par toutes

---

64. Among the sons of Shem: "Ismael filius Abraham, a quo Ismaelitae, qui nunc corrupto nomine Saraceni, quasi a Sarra, et Agareni ab Agar." Isidore, *Etymologiarum sive Originum* 9.2.6. With regard to Japheth: "Haec sunt gentes de stirpe Iaphet, quae a Tauro monte ad aquilonem mediam partem Asiae et omnem Europam usque ad Oceanum Brittanicum possident." Isidore, *Etymologiarum* 9.2.37.

65. Isidore, *Etymologiarum* 9.2.27; 14.3.31.

66. Andrew Gow, "Gog and Magog," 61–88. See also the examples cited in Westrem, "Gog and Magog," 61–62; von den Brincken, *Fines Terrae.*

terres apprendent toutdis a parler ebrieu, sur celle esperaunce qe, quant cils de montaygnes de Caspie isseront fors, qe ly autres Juys sachent parler a eux et les conduire en Christieneteés pur christiens destruire.

Men say that they will issue forth in the time of Antichrist, and that they will carry out great slaughter of Christian people. And for this reason, all the Jews that dwell in all lands always learn to speak Hebrew, in the hope that, when those of the Caspian mountains issue forth, the other Jews will know how to speak with them and will conduct them into Christian lands, to destroy Christian people. (29; 430)

The enclosed Jews appear almost completely alien, separated as they are by the boundaries of language: even if one of them should happen to escape, the narrator recounts, "they know no language except for Hebrew, and so they are unable to speak with the people" (ils ne scievent langage fors ebrieu si ne scievent parler as gentz [29; 430]). The Jews of the cities, by contrast, are both familiar and strange, speaking the foreign tongue of their enclosed kindred as well as the vernacular languages of Europe. They are a kind of "fifth column" located in the vulnerable heart of western power.

This "double place" of the Jews, located both within the city and at the edge of the world, is a spatial expression of their ontological status—that is, their ontological status as seen from the perspective of medieval Christians. From this point of view, Judaism itself is understood as at once the wellspring of Christianity and as the "Old Law" that must be cast off with the advent of the "New Law" of Christ; in an epistemological sense, it is both interior (in that it lies at the point of origin) and exterior (in that it must be abjected in order to accommodate that which supplants it).[67] The "double place" of the Jews—both at the center and at the margins—reflects this ambivalence. What I have tried to illustrate in these pages is the extent to which the place of the Jews is configured as being perennially in flux, always in the process of either the centripetal motion of enclosure or the centrifugal motion of dispersal. The history of Jewish Jerusalem, with its repeated cycles of destruction and reedification, illustrates this flux, as does the identification of the Jews with the unclean tribes of Gog and Magog. These two models of Jewish alterity differ, however, in that the history of Jewish Jerusalem is a repetitive narrative, made up of cycles of enclosure and dispersal: it unfolds in linear time. The identification of the Jews with Gog and Magog, by

---

67. On medieval Christian "ambivalence toward the Jew," see Jeremy Cohen, *Living Letters,* 392–94.

contrast, takes place in apocalyptic time, where the long-awaited dispersal is deferred until the Last Days, and the moment of eruption forever remains in the future.

← Climate and the Diasporic Body

The dynamics of place are fundamental to premodern articulations of Jewish difference, not only with respect to the geographical heartland of Jerusalem and the concealed nether regions of Gog and Magog, but also with respect to the role of climate in shaping the characteristics of nations. In both domains, the individual Jewish body is the vehicle for the expression of alterity, whether in the dismembered corpses of Caiphas and his fellows in the ruins of Jerusalem or in the wandering, diasporic body of the Jew, which is the focus of the following pages. It is impossible to understand the way in which medieval writers depicted Jewish bodily difference without a clear sense of the way in which they understood *all* bodily diversity to arise from the dictates of climate. It is, moreover, difficult to understand how medieval writers conceived of the relationship of climate and racial characteristics without paying special attention to the depiction of Jews within that system, for their diasporic status called into question the fundamental relationship between place and identity. Further, the diasporic body of the Jew offered a locus where Western Christians could consider how bodily diversity intersected with religious deviance, imagining how wrongly oriented devotion might be manifested in the anatomy and physiology of the individual body.

Medieval texts describe bodies in a wide variety of ways: some are tall, some short; some are fair-skinned, some dark; some are perfectly proportioned, some strangely formed, even having features like tusks or hide. Bodily diversity, in the Middle Ages, is heterogeneous and infinitely variable. In this respect, it is quite different from modern constructions of race, which posit a limited number of "races" that can be intermixed in individuals, but never ontologically blended. That is, a person can be of mixed "race," but a race itself can never be altered.[68] The strict categorization of race is often expressed in terms of binary opposition, which led Abdul JanMohamed to coin the memorable (and influential) phrase "Manichean allegory of race." However medieval the resonances of this phrase, views of bodily diversity in the Middle Ages were far from binary. The range of mankind, like the range of the whole

---

68. Malik, *Meaning of Race.*

of creation, was thought to be more like a spectrum, with normalcy lying at the middle and increasing diversity as one moved away from the center. This view of bodily diversity—or at least part of it—is visible on medieval world maps, where the margins of the ecumene, whether in the extreme north or south, are inhabited by the so-called "monstrous races," strange-looking creatures with the faces of men.[69] On such mappaemundi, of course, the region of normalcy is merely implicit, for only the anomalous creatures of the remote regions are worth portraying on the map. Medieval scientific medical and astronomical texts, however, describe in detail the variable nature of the bodies found in the seven climates of the temperate zone. In his *Speculum Naturale,* for example, the encyclopedist Vincent of Beauvais juxtaposes his description of the monstrous races with an account of how human anatomy and physiology vary in the diverse regions of the world.[70]

In spite of this disparity, modern theories of race, developed in the wake of the Enlightenment and elaborated in the colonial context, have their roots in medieval theories regarding the effects of climate in determining the humoral makeup of individuals and the anatomical, physiological, and even behavioral predispositions of nations.[71] In this section, I discuss medieval theories of how climate dictates bodily diversity and then move to a more narrowly focused discussion of how Jewish physiology was understood during the Middle Ages. There are two reasons why it is useful to combine these topics. First, it is necessary to understand humoral physiology (which lies at the basis of climate theory) in order to understand medieval discussions of Jewish physiology. Second, these discussions of Jewish physiology cast an interesting light back on climate theory itself, for the Jewish body is the anomaly that casts doubt on the validity of the theory. (This second aspect provides a useful basis for the fuller exploration of climate theory and the construction of the "Saracen" body in chapter 4.) Because Jews were conceived of as being perpetually displaced, in a state of permanent diaspora, they were thought to be not bound by the norms of climate theory in the way that other nations were. Their supposedly innate national characteristics were instead accounted for through other means: that is, through behavioral habits, especially diet.

With the reintroduction of the Aristotelian corpus during the thirteenth century, accompanied by the rich commentaries of Muslim philosophers

---

69. On monstrous races appearing on the map, see Camille, *Image on the Edge;* Strickland, *Saracens, Demons, and Jews.*

70. Vincent of Beauvais, *Speculum Naturale* 31.67–72 (on climate and humoral physiology), 31.126–32 (on monstrous races).

71. On medieval applications of climate theory, see Tooley, "Bodin and the Medieval Theory of Climate," 64–83. On early modern applications, see Chaplin, "Natural Philosophy," 229–52.

such as Avicenna and Averroës, the view of natural diversity inherited from Pliny's *Natural History* (by way of Solinus and Isidore) was substantially altered. It was no longer sufficient to describe and label the heterogeneous range of monstrous races and fabulous animals; instead, it became necessary to categorize them, to account for how their unusual features had come to be, and to explain how bodily differences such as skin color shaded off into monstrosity. Some more ambitious commentators, such as Albertus Magnus, even suggested that those bodily attributes might change within a few generations if a creature shaped by the environment of one climatic extreme were transferred to a more temperate climate. The importance of climate in determining the natural diversity of mankind is emphasized in both the astronomical and the medical tradition. In the *De Sphaera,* a popular treatise based on Ptolemy's cosmology, the astronomer Sacrobosco explains that Ethiopia must be located at the equator, that is, in the torrid zone, "for [the inhabitants] would not be so black if they were born in the temperate habitable zone."[72] His commentators, influenced by Aristotelian explanations of causation and change, elaborated on this passage with enthusiasm. One early thirteenth-century commentator launches into a digression on the physiology of the people of Ethiopia: "An example of the blackening of Ethiopians is the cooking of golden honey. First it is golden, then reddish, and finally by long cooking it becomes black and bitter, and that which was at first sweet is now salty. And it is just this way all over Ethiopia." Their blood is drawn to the surface of the skin by the great heat, where it becomes "black and bitter, and in this way it can be clearly seen why the Ethiopian is black."[73] Several other commentators and glossators include other, comparable elaborations on this same passage in the *De Sphaera.*[74]

In the medical tradition as in the astronomical, writers such as Avicenna and Haly Abbas (known in the West through the translation of Constantinus Africanus) similarly explain the blackness of the inhabitants of the southern regions in terms of natural process. In a passage frequently paraphrased by other writers, Constantinus explains that the northern regions near the pole are cold and dry, and therefore the water and air are especially clear, and the bodies of the inhabitants are healthy, of a pleasing color, the women's bodies

---

72. Sacrobosco, *Sphere,* ed. and trans. Thorndyke, 107 (Lat. text), 137 (Eng. trans.).

73. This commentary is possibly by Michael Scot; in Ibid., 334 (Lat. text); translation mine.

74. These include the thirteenth-century anonymous commentary in Cambridge, Gonville and Caius MSS 137, fol. 46b ([Sacrobosco], Thorndyke, *Sphere,* 461); another anonymous commentary preserved in two thirteenth-century manuscripts, Oxford, Bodleian Library, Canon Misc. MSS 161 and Princeton, Garrett MSS 99 (Thorndyke, *Sphere,* 439); and the fifteenth-century commentary by John de Fundis (Thorndyke, *Sphere,* 50).

soft and the men's strong. The women conceive only rarely (because they are "frigid") and give birth with difficulty, because of the dryness of the climate, which is reflected in their bodily complexion. The northerners vomit easily and have a good appetite. The southern regions are precisely opposite: being hot and humid, the bodies of the inhabitants are black in color and tend to be phlegmatic. This humor impairs their digestion, and because their natural bodily heat is dissipated through their pores, they are soft-bodied, become drunk easily, and are prone to dysentery and diarrhea. Southern women conceive more easily, but also miscarry frequently.[75]

In the thirteenth century, the encyclopedist Bartholomaeus Anglicus took up the explanations of the effects of climate on bodies found in the medical tradition and, influenced by the astronomy of Sacrobosco, integrated these views into his geographical survey of the world; in other words, he took medical theories that distinguished between northern and southern bodies in general, and applied them to a range of specific countries. Bartholomaeus' geography, found in book 15 of his *De proprietatibus rerum,* follows in rough outline the geography included by Isidore of Seville in his seventh-century *Etymologies.* By integrating medical and astronomical theories with the standard geography, Bartholomaeus differs significantly from Vincent of Beauvais, who follows Isidore quite slavishly. Though Vincent is clearly familiar with the theories of Avicenna and Constantinus Africanus, and even quotes the pertinent passages elsewhere in his vast encyclopedia,[76] he does not draw out their implications for the geographical sections. In each section of *his* geography, however, Bartholomaeus takes pains to note the correspondence of climate to the bodily nature of the inhabitants of a given land. Those of the northern countries, such as Albania and Almania, for example, are large-bodied and fair-skinned, with blond, straight hair, while those of the southern countries, such as Ethiopia and Libya, have smaller bodies, with dark skin and "crisp" hair.[77] Monstrosities—that is, bodies "wondirful and horribilche

---

75. Constantinus Africanus, *Pantegni,* book 5; quoted from Vincent of Beauvais, *Speculum Naturale* 4.110 (col. 303). For a more detailed discussion of the interrelation of climate and physiology, see chapter 4, "The Saracen Body." A deeper exploration of the relationship of climate and physiology would compare the schema found in the *Pantegni* with those appearing in Avicenna's *Canon of Medicine* (I.2.2.1 in Lyon 1498) and William of Conches' *Dragmaticon Philosophiae.*

76. Vincent of Beauvais, *Speculum Naturale* 4.110 (col. 303), quoting Constantinus Africanus; *Speculum Naturale* 6.18 (cols. 380–81), quoting Avicenna, *Liber canonis,* lib. 1, doct. 2, summa 1, cap. 11 (Venice, 1507, fol. 32r; reprint, Hildesheim: Olms, 1964).

77. Bartholomaeus Anglicus, *De proprietatibus rerum* (Frankfurt, 1601; reprint, Frankfurt: Minerva, 1964), 15.7, 15, 52, 91; 627 (15.7), 630 (15.15), 649 (15.52), 671 (15.91); also quoted in the late fourteenth-century Middle English of Trevisa, *On the Properties of Things,* 2: 728, 732, 754, 779.

yshape" (monstrosa facie horribiles [15.52; 649; 754])—are found here, in the torrid regions, where excess of heat affects conception and gestation.

Yet Bartholomaeus goes still further, for in his geography he repeatedly emphasizes not just the diversity of mankind, but its balance: each climatic extreme, each geographical location, has its opposite, or (one might say) its complement. Thus he writes of Gallia that "by the dyuersite of heuene, face and colour of men and hertes and witte and quantite of bodyes ben dyuers. Therefor Rome gendreth heuy men, Grece light men, Affrica gyleful men, and Fraunce kyndeliche fers men and sharpe of witte" (secundum enim diversitatem coeli et facies hominum et colores animorum diversitates existunt et corporum qualitates. Inde Roma graves generat. Graecia leves. Affrica versipelles. Gallia natura feroces ingenioque acres).[78] In his entry on Europe, we see the binary opposition that underlies this exuberant diversity:

> Haec mundi particula, et si sic minor quam Asia, ei tamen par est in populorum numerosa genetositate, populos enim, ut dicit Plinius alit corpore maiores, viribus fortiores, animo audaciores, forma et specie pulcriores, quam faciunt Asiae vel Affricae regiones. Nam solaris aestus adureus propter eius permanentiam super Affros, illos efficit consumendo humores corpore breviores, facie nigriores, crine crispiores, et propter evaporationem spirituum per apertos poros animo defectiores. E contrario vero est apud Septentrionales. Nam ex frigiditate poros extrinsicus opilante generantur humores in corpore, et efficiuntur homines corpulentiores, et ex ipsa frigiditate, quae mater est albedinis in exterioribus in cute scilicet et facie albiores, et ex repercussione vaporum et spirituum ad interiora efficiuntur calidiores interius, et per consequens plus audaces.

> Yif this partie of the worlde be lesse than Asia, yitte is it pere therto in nombre and noblete of men, for as Plius seithe, he fedeth men that ben more huge in bodie, more stronge in myghte and vertue, more bolde of herte, more faire and semeliche of shappe, thanne men of the cuntres and londes of Asia other of Affrica. For the sonne abideth longe ouer the Affers, men of Affrica, and brennen and wasten humours and maken ham short of body, blacke of face, with crispe here. And for

---

78. Bartholomaeus Anglicus 15.66; 657; 763. This is an elaboration of Isidore, *Etymologies* 9.2.105: "Inde Romanos graves, Graecos leves, Afros versipelles, Gallos natura feroces atque acriores ingenio pervidemus, quod natura climatum facit." This appears not in Isidore's geography, but in his book on languages and cities.

spirites passe outte atte pores that ben open, so they be more cowardes of herte.

An the cuntrarye is of men of the northe londe: for coldenes that is withoute stoppeth the pores and breedeth humours of the bodye maketh men more ful and huge; and coolde that is modir of whitnesse maketh hem the more white in face and in skynne, and vapoures and spirites ben ysmyten inwarde and maken hatter withinne and so the more bolde and hardy.[79]

Each land has its complement; but it is absolutely clear, in this binary opposition, which is the preferable climate, and which body is the beautiful and desirable norm.

These binary oppositions, curiously and paradoxically, are evidence of the fundamental harmony of the world, as Bartholomaeus describes the unity in diversity as a kind of natural music:

Mundus itaque ex rebus multis oppositis et contrariis est compositus, et tamen in se est unus. Mundus enim unus est numero, et non plures mundi.... Mundus ergo de quo hic loquimur, non est diversus in se, nequae divisus secundum substantiam, quamvis in ipsius partibus inveniatur contrarietas, quo ad aliquam qualitatis repugnantiam. Summam enim et necessariam habet mundus in suo toto convenientiam, et quasi quandam musicam harmoniam.... Ex quo patet, quod mundus ratione suae mutationis est siquidem admirandus.... Nulla enim est tam vilis, tam infima in tota mundi machina pars sive particula, in qua tam in materia, quam in virtute et forma non reluceat laus divina. Nam in materia et forma mundi quaedam est differentia, sed cum harmonia est pars [*sic*] summa.

The world is made of many thingis compowned and contrariouse, and yit in itsilf it is one. The worlde is one in noumbre and tale and nought many worldes.... The worlde of the whiche we speketh at this tyme is not diuers in itsilf nothir departid in substaunce, though contrariousnesse be founde in parties therof, touchinge contrariousnesse of the qualitees. For the worlde hath most nedeful acord [*harmonia*] al itsilf,

---

79. Bartholomaeus Anglicus, 15.50; 648; 752–53. The balanced contraries of mankind are central to Bartholomaeus' overall presentation of the natural world: see, for example, the balanced "oppositions of beast against beast" noted by Greetham, "Concept of Nature," 663–77, esp. 670. Thanks to Richard Raiswell for this reference.

and as it were acorde of musik.... Herof it folewith that the world is wondirful bicause of chaunginge therof.... Nothing in the schappe of the worlde is so vile nothir so lowe nothir partykel, in the whiche schinyth noght praysinge of God in mater and in vertu and in schap. For in the mater and schappe of the worlde is some difference, but that is with acorde and most pees. (8.1; 369–70; 443–44)

It is important to stress that, while this view of the harmonious diversity of mankind may seem ideal and even utopian, it contains within it the elements of an intellectual system, based on the relationship of climate to physiology, that could be used to justify the subjugation of peoples and would be used, eventually, as part of the justification for the institution of slavery. As early as the sixteenth century, the philosopher Jean Bodin had suggested that the principles of political administration should be tailored to match the predisposition of different national groups. That is, forms of government must vary depending upon the tractability of each national group, whose behavioral characteristics were in turn determined by their climate; here, Bodin uses Aristotelian notions concerning the role of climate in human development and applies them pragmatically to the question of how to govern most effectively.[80] By the late sixteenth and early seventeenth century, as Joyce Chaplin has shown, Aristotelian climatic theories were applied to the native populations of North America. These so-called "Indians" were, supposedly, identical to the Indians in India: they tended by virtue of their climate to be prone to disease, easily drunk (like the Ethiopians), and generally debauched. Their extermination in the wake of European settlement was thus rationalized as biological destiny.[81] Finally, climatic theory was used to explain the suitability of Africans for slavery, until climate-based explanations of their "natural" inferiority were supplanted, during the eighteenth century, by theories based primarily on the role of heredity.[82]

In *The Book of John Mandeville,* which owes much to the worldview presented in the geographical sections of Bartholomaeus' encyclopedia, bodily diversity is accounted for in terms of both heredity and climatic influence; the latter cause, however, is predominant. The bizarre features of the "monstrous races" are explained as the natural consequence of the climatic extremes found in Ethiopia and India. In each land described, climate is adduced as the cause of the physiology of the inhabitants. This is especially well illustrated in Mandeville's account of the land of the Pygmies, where the people are all

---

80. Tooley, "Bodin and the Medieval Theory of Climate," 80–81.
81. Chaplin, "Natural Philosophy," 236–38.
82. Malik, *Meaning of Race,* 79–84.

only a few spans in height; this is appropriate to their climate. Curiously, however, when men of normal stature come to live there, their offspring are also of diminutive stature, like the Pygmies. The reason for this, says Mandeville, is that "the nature of the lond is such" (la nature de la terre est tiele [22; 365; 152]).[83] Here, climate governs the physiology not only of the native inhabitants, but also of those who merely pass through. This would suggest that the effects of climate are mutable or, in other words, that the bodily diversity of mankind is not essential, but rather subject to variation.

In this, Mandeville resembles Albertus Magnus, who in his *De natura loci* suggests that if Ethiopians were removed from the first climate to the fourth or fifth climate (that is, more temperate climates), within a few generations they would be altered: their offspring would have white skin and all the other attributes of the northern climates.[84] Yet Albertus is unusual in his strict application of Aristotelian theory to the description of human physiology; more common is a composite of climatic theory and genealogical descent. This can be seen, for example, in Bartholomaeus Anglicus, who generally adheres to a climate-based theory of human diversity; in his entry on "Pictavia," however, he inserts heredity into his analysis of the inhabitants. Their qualities are a peculiar combination of what might be found in more northern and more southern climates; Bartholomaeus explains, however, that this is "no wondir" (nec mirum), for the men of Pictavia are of mixed descent, a combination of "Pictes" (Pictis) and "Frenshe men" (Gallicis). They have the qualities of each nation, qualities that were first formed by "kynde of clymes" (natura climatum) and subsequently combined through heredity (15.122; 689; 768). Here, two seemingly mutual exclusive theories of human diversity—environment and heredity—are yoked together.

Within the categories of climate theory, the Jews occupy a peculiar place. Belonging nowhere yet found everywhere, they inhabit no fixed climate that might dictate their national attributes. Their diasporic state—not only driven from their native territory but also having no permanent home elsewhere—prevents them from being definable within the norms of any single climate. As a result, texts that characterize the attributes of nations based upon their native climates face a conundrum in describing the Jews. This is particularly evident in the *De proprietatibus rerum,* where Bartholomaeus Anglicus departs

---

83. The source for the passage is Oderic of Pordenone, but the explanation of the cause (that is, the "nature of the lond") is original to Mandeville. See Odoric of Pordenone, "Relatio," 468–69 (24.2).

84. "Licet autem huiusmodi nigri aliquando nascantur etiam in aliis climatibus, sicut in quarto vel in quinto, tamen nigredinem accipiunt a primis generantibus, quae complexionata sunt in climatibus primo et secundo, et paulatim alterantur ad albedinem, quando ad alia climata transferuntur." Albertus Magnus, "De natura loci," 27 (2.3).

from his usual tendency to characterize the predispositions of each nation when he describes the Jewish inhabitants of Jerusalem and its environs. As noted in the first pages of this chapter, Bartholomaeus simply mentions the Jews as one people among several others in his description of Judea and the surrounding territories, saying nothing about how climate might have influenced their collective development.

There is one context, however, in which animated discussion of Jewish national proclivities does appear in conjunction with debates on the characteristics of inhabitants of the frigid north and torrid south: that is, the commentaries and debates occasioned by the scientific writings on climate and physiology described in the preceding pages. Some of the most revealing examples of this phenomenon appear in the records of the quodlibetal debates conducted in Paris in the years around 1300. As Peter Biller points out, several of the questions focus on the relationship between climate and physiology: these include "Are white men bold?" and "Do white women or black women have stronger sexual desire?"[85] It is easy to recognize the generalizations concerning climate made by medical writers such as Constantinus Africanus, Avicenna, and Albertus Magnus that provided the basis for these questions.[86] Those engaged in the quodlibetal debates, however, moved far beyond the medical writers' generalizations in their exploration of the relationship of climate and national predisposition as it illuminated their understanding of Jewish physiology. The relevant debates center on the cause of the flow of blood supposedly experienced by Jewish men; one version, from the quodlibets edited by Biller, states "queritur utrum iudei paciuntur fluxum" (it is asked whether the Jews suffer from a flux). The approximately contemporary *Lilium medicinae* of Bernard of Gordon addresses the same question, this time specifically identifying the bloody flux as hemorrhoidal, in keeping with the explanation of Albertus Magnus appearing in his *Quaestiones super De animalibus;* and the anonymous *Omnes homines,* a widely disseminated product of the Salernitan medical community, phrases the question similarly to the *Lilium medicinae,* but offers more elaborate explanations of the cause of the bloody flux.

While these discussions are consistent in many respects, they differ in important details. For example, while Albertus Magnus had specified that the

---

85. "Consequenter queritur utrum homines albi sint audaces"; "Alia questio fuit utrum mulier alba magis appetit virum quam nigra"; "Utrum albe mulieres magis appetant coire quam nigre." Quoted in Biller, "Views of Jews from Paris," 187–207; quotations from 200 and 200n40.

86. As Biller points out, the encyclopedist Vincent of Beauvais may well have been an intermediary for the basic outlines of humoral and climate theory (Ibid., 200–201).

flux experienced by Jewish men is not regulated by the cycles of the moon (as is women's menstruation), the *Omnes homines* states that their flux is indeed monthly.[87] Though all of the discussions indicate that the flux occurs due to the body's need to purge itself of an excess of melancholy (black humor) in the blood, they differ with regard to the causes of that excess, sometimes identifying it as the result of a cultural practice, other times attributing it to a natural predisposition. Albertus Magnus states that hemorrhoidal bleeding often appears in "those who live off gross and salted food [nutrimento grosso et salso], such as the Jews."[88] Implicitly, a change of foodstuffs would effect a restoration of humoral balance, suggesting that the flux of blood seen in Jews is the result of cultural practices rather than an innate predisposition. The corresponding passage appearing in the quodlibetal debates appears at first to be very similar to that expressed by Albertus: the Paris quodlibet, for example, specifies that Jews experience a flux of melancholic blood "because they use roast foods [alimentis assatis] . . . and these are difficult to digest. . . . Also, they have roast fat, such as oil."[89] Unlike Albertus, however, the quodlibet implies that the hemorrhoidal flux is not simply the result of cultural practices (that is, diet), but rather is innate. It states that the melancholy of the Jews is also evident in their pallor ("pallidi sunt"), their natural timidity ("timidi sunt naturaliter"), and their eagerness to keep themselves apart from the society of others ("iudei naturaliter retrahunt se a societate et coniunctione cum aliis"). The term "naturaliter," which occurs repeatedly in the quodlibet, emphasizes that the Jews' melancholy is inborn, not (as Albertus had implied) acquired. The term "naturaliter" continues to appear in texts in this tradition, including the *Omnes homines*.[90]

It is this identification of the Jewish "natural" predisposition to melancholy that reveals the limitations of the climate theory in the effort to explain the origins of bodily diversity. Because they are widely dispersed from their

---

87. Albertus Magnus: "super fluxum eius non dominatur luna sicut super menstruum," *Quaestiones super De animalibus,* 12: 205–6; reproduced in Biller, "'Scientific' View," 160. *Omnes homines:* "in eis generatur multus sanguis melanconicus qui in ipsis tempore menstruali expellitur seu expurgator," *Problemata Varia Anatomica,* 38–39; reproduced in Biller, "'Scientific' View," 164.

88. Albertus Magnus, *Quaestiones super De animalibus* 9.7, 206; reproduced in Biller, "'Scientific' View," 160.

89. Paris arts quodlibet, Paris, Bib. nat. ms. lat. 16089, f. 57ra, reproduced in Biller, "'Scientific' View," 160.

90. Another significant difference is introduced in the *Omnes homines,* where the description of the offending foodstuffs as "dense" (spissus), found in Albertus Magnus and the Paris quodlibet, is replaced by a description of the food as "phlegmatic and cold" (flegmaticis et frigidis), illustrating how Aristotelian notions of causation had given way to humoral theories derived from Hippocrates and Galen. *Omnes homines,* in *Problemata Varia Anatomica,* 38–39; reproduced in Biller, "'Scientific' View," 164.

native land, Jews should (according to climate theory) no longer have a particular physiological predisposition generated by climate. Like the hypothetical Ethiopians living in the far north discussed by Albertus Magnus, the Jews' bodily complexion should have long since altered as a result of prolonged residence in new places. Peculiarly, however, as we have seen, Jews are repeatedly described as having a "naturally" melancholy complexion, as is evident from their numerous symptoms (bloody flux, paleness, solitary nature, fearfulness, and so on). The consistency of their diet is precisely what generates their melancholy nature. To put it another way, the Jews take their climate with them. This obligation was thought to be dictated, according to another record of the Paris quodlibet, by their religious law ("lege sua"; Biller, 162). The *Omnes homines* similarly states that "many good meats are prohibited for them according to their law" (in lege eorum sunt prohibite; Biller, 164).

The association of diet with climate is widespread. In general, one's natural diet is dictated by one's climate: that is, you eat the foods native to the same climate to which you yourself are native. As a result, medieval texts frequently draw attention to the plight of travelers who find themselves obliged to eat foods unsuited to them. For example, the fifteenth-century pilgrimage itinerary of William Wey counsels the traveler to "be wel ware of dyuerse frutys, for they be not acordyng to youre complexioun, and they engender a blody fluxe."[91] Another example can be found in the late Middle English romance of *Richard Coer de Lion,* in which the king falls ill because of the unsuitability of the local foodstuffs.[92] The case of the Jews is the logical extension of this relationship between climate and food: just as the traveler must take pains to maintain a diet as close as possible to the diet he would ordinarily consume in his native climate, the Jews maintain their habitual diet. By doing so, they set themselves apart from those who are native to the lands that the Jews enter into, not just in a social or cultural sense, but physiologically as well. What they eat makes them what they are.

This connection between diet and physiology has a more sinister aspect as well, centered not on the source of Jewish melancholy and consequent hemorrhoidal flux but on the means by which this ailment might be cured.

---

91. Wey, *Itineraries of William Wey,* 6.

92. In the *Romaunce of Richard Coer de Lion,* while on campaign in the Holy Land, Richard is said to crave English food: he is "alongyd after pork." On this passage and how Richard's consumption of flesh articulates the boundaries of the English nation along the lines of the eucharistic community, see Akbari, "Hunger for National Identity." Nicola McDonald's otherwise insightful essay misidentifies Richard's desire for pork as simply an "insatiable hunger for pork" (134) rather than a longing for food appropriate to his native climate; see "Eating People," 124–50.

I refer, of course, to the Jewish "blood libel," accusations that Jews killed and consumed Christians (usually male children) as part of their religious ritual. These accusations are usually seen as part of a theological discourse of Jewish alterity, in which the act is seen as a reenactment of the Crucifixion and a hideous parody of the eucharistic sacrifice.[93] It is worth noting, however, that the scientific, "naturalistic" discourse of Jewish alterity also made reference to the practice of the Jews consuming blood in order to cure the flux caused by melancholy. One of the earliest examples of this claim appeared in the early fourteenth century, when Rudolph of Schlettstadt declared that the Jews suffer monthly from a flow of blood, along with dysentery. This ailment could be cured, Rudolph added, by drinking the blood of a baptized Christian (Sanatur autem per sanguinem honimis Cristiani, qui nomine Cristi baptisatus est).[94] Examples of this accusation became more numerous in the fifteenth century.[95]

Although Gilbert Dahan was perhaps the first to identify the importance of the quodlibetal debates and related texts in the emergence of constructions of Jewish alterity,[96] Peter Biller's work, along with that of Irven Resnick and Willis Johnson, has done much to show how widespread these notions concerning the supposed bloody flux of the Jews became during the later Middle Ages.[97] While Resnick and Johnson focus particularly on the role of gender in medieval constructions of Jewish alterity (with Resnick affirming and Johnson denying that Jewish male alterity is predicated on an identification with the feminine), they share with Biller an awareness of how constructions of alterity based on theological distinctions overlap with those based on medical or scientific distinctions.[98] In Biller's words, "in the years around 1300" these distinctions—theological and scientific—came to be like "intersecting circles in a Venn diagram."[99] Although these two strands in the discourse of Jewish alterity had different origins, they were far from mutually exclusive. For example, one commentary on the

---

93. See Rubin, *Gentile Tales,* 7–39 ("From Jewish Boy to Bleeding Host").

94. Rudolph von Schlettstadt, *Historiae Memorabiles,* 65; quoted in Johnson, "Myth of Jewish Male Menses," 290n51, and in Resnick, "On Roots of the Myth," 25.

95. Some fifteenth-century examples are cited by Resnick, "Roots of the Myth," 25–26; see also Hsia, *Myth of Ritual Murder.*

96. Dahan, *Les intellectuels chrétiens et les juifs au moyen âge,* 528–30; see also Dahan, "Juifs et judaïsme dans la littérature quodlibétique."

97. Biller, "'Scientific' View," 137–68; see also Biller, "Views of Jews from Paris." The former article represents a more mature account of the research described in the latter, and includes very useful appendices reproducing the original quodlibets and related scientific texts (154–68).

98. Resnick, "Roots of the Myth," 1–27; Johnson, "Myth of Jewish Male Menses," 273–95.

99. Biller, "'Scientific' View," 146.

pseudo-Albertus Magnus *De secretis mulierum* states that the hemorrhoidal flux experienced by Jewish men is the result of both natural causes (their melancholy nature) and the judgment of God.[100] Similarly, the *Omnes homines* makes it clear that the flux can be explained both theologically ("theologice"), as a consequence of Jewish culpability for the death of Christ, and naturally ("naturaliter") according to the medical theories of humoral physiology.[101]

It is nothing new to suggest that the supposed uncleanliness of the Jewish body can be understood in an anthropological sense: in Mary Douglas' influential formulation, that which is unclean is simply "matter out of place."[102] The bloody discharge believed to flow from the individual Jewish body reflected, on a microcosmic level, the uncleanliness of Synagoga herself, for the entire community of the Jews was believed to have become unclean (that is, "out of place," cast out, excluded) at the time of the Crucifixion. That singular event was repeated annually, as the commemoration of Holy Week was believed to herald not only the unification of the Christian community, but the exclusion of the Jewish community. This act of simultaneous unification and exclusion was made manifest in the ritual stoning of Jewish quarters carried out in various Christian cities, as David Nirenberg has shown.[103] In this context, it is significant that some of the texts describing the bloody flux experienced by the Jews specify that it regularly occurs during Holy Week.[104] In these texts, the theological discourse of Jewish alterity makes manifest the way in which the individual body was thought to mirror the status of the community as a whole. As Willis Johnson puts it, "When Christians were made clean by the shedding of blood on Good Friday, Jews were made unclean."[105] Through the rituals of Holy Week, Christ's blood could be seen to purify and unite Ecclesia even as it polluted and cast out Synagoga. A similar relationship of the individual and the community appears in texts recounting the siege of Jerusalem, where the bodies of Jewish people are shown in the act of being torn apart, cannibalistically consumed, or burned to ashes. Their individual

---

100. Commentator B, in pseudo-Albertus Magnus, *Women's Secretes,* 74; quoted in Johnson, "Myth," 294n69.

101. *Omnes homines,* in *Problemata Varia Anatomica,* 38; reproduced in Biller, "'Scientific' View," 164.

102. Douglas, *Purity and Danger.*

103. In Nirenberg's view, Holy Week riots are "repeated, controlled, and meaningful rituals" which "bind and sunder in the same motion" (229). Nirenberg, *Communities of Violence;* see especially chapter 7, "The Two Faces of Sacred Violence," 200–230.

104. Caesarius of Heisterbach, writing in the early thirteenth century, reports that Jewish males suffer from a bloody flux on the Friday before Easter (*Dialogus Miraculorum,* 1: 92). It should be noted that Willis Johnson argues that this aspect may be a fourteenth-century interpolation ("Myth," 287–88). For a useful discussion of Caesarius, see Marcus, "Images of the Jews," 247–56.

105. Johnson, "Myth," 275.

destruction and dispersal is, once again, a microcosm of the community as a whole: the walls of the city are crushed and the people are dispersed, scattered abroad like dust in the wind. Just as their individual bodies will not be reintegrated in the resurrection, so too their community will not be reconstituted after the supersession of Judaism by Christianity.

Within this dynamic, Jerusalem has two identities: as Christian Jerusalem, it is the geographical target of crusading aspirations and the eschatological goal of the individual soul. As Jewish Jerusalem, however, the city is a physical, tangible manifestation of Synagoga. Consequently, its walls are crushed and the city itself is polluted. As Paschasius Radbertus puts it in his ninth-century commentary on Lamentations 1:17 ("Jerusalem is become among them like a woman polluted by menstrual uncleanness"): "Just as a woman is an abhomination at that time when she suffers menstruation, so too even these people were an abhomination, just as are the Jews today both to us and to their enemies."[106] Like Orosius, who likened the temple at the time of the siege of Jerusalem to a womb "emptied by the act of giving birth and void" ("effetum ac vacuum" [7.9.6; 3: 39]), Paschasius describes Jewish Jerusalem as an empty vessel; both writers depict the place of the Jews as feminized and as polluted, whether by birth or by menstruation.[107]

The intersection of theological and scientific discourses described in these pages helps to illuminate the relationship between anti-Judaism and antisemitism, particularly with relationship to the role of embodiment in the discourse of Jewish alterity.[108] It would not be correct to say that antisemitism arises

---

106. "'Et facta est Hierusalem quasi polluta menstruis inter eos.' Quia sicut execrabilis est mulier eo tempore quo menstrua patitur ita et illa execrabiles erant, Iudei et sunt usque hodie tam nobis et hostibus suis." Paschasius Radbertus, *Expositio in Lamentatione Hieremiae* 1.17.

107. The book of Leviticus prescribes ritual means of purification following childbirth (Lev. 12:1–8) and contact with menstrual blood (Lev. 15:21). A brief but useful overview of ritual purity laws in Leviticus can be found in Klawans, "Ritual," 19–28, esp. 20. See also Klawans, *Impurity and Sin*.

108. A great deal has been written on the distinction between and the interrelation of anti-Judaism and antisemitism. The work of Gavin Langmuir has been particularly influential; but see Stacey's helpful assessment of the problems attendant upon Langmuir's definition of anti-Judaism as "essentially sociological," while antisemitism is "essentially psychological." For Langmuir, the former is a "nonrational response to nonrational doubts," while the latter is an "irrational reaction to repressed rational doubts" (Stacey, "History, Religion, and Medieval Antisemitism," 98). More helpful is Stacey's emphasis on the role of embodiment in the emergent discourse of antisemitism: "Ethnic or even racial antisemitism is not the creation of the modern era. It can be traced from the late thirteenth century onward in the opinion...that not even baptism could eradicate the 'Jewishness' of a convert/apostate from Judaism" (100). On the role of embodiment in antisemitism, see also Kruger, "Bodies of Jews"; Abulafia, "Bodies in the Jewish-Christian Debate," 124–37. Sara Lipton suggests that a crucial change in conceptions of Jewish alterity occurs when, during the fifteenth century, pictorial representations of Jews begin to display certain conventional, stereotyped features (*Images of Intolerance,* 20–21); Lipton bases much of her argument in this connection on the work of Eric Zafran, "Iconography of Antisemitism."

from anti-Judaism, though it is certainly true that the theological discourse of Jewish alterity exists prior to the appearance of the scientific discourse. These two discourses, however, as we have seen, do not remain separate; instead, one reinforces the other, as justifications for exclusion drawn from one discourse are used to augment the other. It is difficult to know whether to define them as distinct discourses, or as two complementary strands in a single discourse: the discourse of anti-Judaism certainly stood alone prior to the thirteenth century, but the discourse of antisemitism has never fully disentangled itself from that of anti-Judaism.[109] In this chapter, I have illustrated how, from a medieval, European, Christian perspective, the place of the Jews is by definition an unstable one, as liquid and untidy as the Jewish body itself. The centrifugal flow of diaspora reappears in microcosm in the bloody flux emanating from the individual body. In the next chapter, I show how the construction of the "Saracen" body proceeded along similar lines. Like the Jewish body, the Saracen body was defined and categorized by means of the conventions of climate theory. It differed significantly, however, in two ways, lacking the complicating factors of dispersal and expulsion and intersecting quite differently with the theological discourse of alterity.

---

109. Certain aspects of anti-Judaic and antisemitic discourse not discussed in this chapter are central to the account of medieval Western understandings of both Islam and Judaism as religions that adore the letter rather than the spirit; these include the focus on bodily circumcision (emblematic of the "Old" Covenant) and the notion of spiritual blindness (that is, willful rejection of the "New" Covenant). On the dichotomies of letter versus spirit and body versus soul in anti-Judaic and Orientalist discourse, see chapter 6 ("The Form of Heaven").

← CHAPTER 4

The Saracen Body

While modern constructions of Orientalism center on the idea of the "Arab" or the "Muslim," focusing alternatively on ethnic and religious identities, medieval constructions conflated categories of ethnicity and religion within a single term that served as a marker of both: "Saracen." This term identified its object as religiously different (not a follower of Christ, but of Muhammad), and ethnically or racially different (from Oriental regions). It is significant that the term "Saracen" is never used to identify Christian Arabs, showing that the term was understood as defining alterity in both dimensions; that is, in terms of both religion and race.[1] In this dual reference, the term "Saracen" is similar to the contemporaneous use of the term "Jew," with both groups of people thought to differ from Christians not only in religious terms, but in bodily terms as well. Unlike the diasporic body of the Jew, however, which was characterized by the qualities of leakiness and permeability that mirrored in microcosm the diasporic state of the nation, the Saracen body was understood in terms of fixed locations.

As shown in some detail in chapter 3, climate theory provided a totalizing system within which bodies of all shapes, colors, and sizes could be categorized according to their qualities and rationalized in terms of their place of

---

1. On the development of the term "Saracen," see Rotter, *Abendland und Sarazenen,* 68–77; Tolan, *Saracens,* 127–28; Beckett, *Anglo-Saxon Perceptions,* 116–39.

origin. Certain body shapes, physiological propensities, and behavioral qualities could be associated with locations, so that the disposition of a people could be understood as "naturally" arising from their land of origin. Saracen bodies—that is, the bodies of people of those nations identified as owing allegiance to the so-called "law of Muhammad"—were categorized accordingly. Although they came from different nations, ranging from the eastern realms of Persia to the more central kingdom of Egypt, all were assumed to partake in a common Saracen identity. The opposition of northern and southern bodies, taken from scientific writers among whom Albertus Magnus was perhaps the most influential, was used as the foundational principle of a system of classifying nations, as seen most strikingly in the encyclopedia of Bartholomaeus Anglicus. By the fourteenth century, the opposition of northern and southern bodies had come to be associated with a different binary opposition, that of East and West. This paradigm shift, described in more detail in chapter 1, marks a crucial moment in the development of the discourse of Orientalism. At that time, the Orient came to be characterized as a place of torrid heat and irascible, lascivious inhabitants, while the West came to be seen as a place of temperate climate and rational souls.

There is, however, a secondary dichotomy that informs the depiction of Saracens in the literary and cultural production of the Middle Ages: that is, the division of Saracens into those who are white, well proportioned, and assimilable, and those who are dark-skinned, deformed or of grotesque stature, and doomed to destruction. In medieval medical and astronomical literature, as we saw in the previous chapter, this dichotomy appears only as the bodily manifestations of climatic extremes, with white bodies found in the cold northern regions, and black bodies in the torrid south. In these texts, as in the medieval encyclopedias based upon them, bodily diversity ranges itself along the span of this broad spectrum, with a range of bodily types corresponding to the geographical range of the world. Popular medieval literature, however, ranging from the *chansons de geste* to the Middle English romances inspired by them, regularly features attractive, European-looking Saracens side by side with dark-skinned, grotesque Saracens having the bodies of giants and the bodily features of animals. Perhaps the most famous example of this first category is the Saracen emir Baligant, in the *Chanson de Roland*. At the sight of this tall, imposing knight, with fair skin and white flowing hair, the poem's admiring narrator exclaims, "God, what a baron; if only he were made a Christian!" The comment makes explicit a longing for assimilation, the integration of the pagan other in the Christian community: the term "christentet" is a transitive verb, so that the whole phrase might be more accurately translated, "If only he were 'christianized,'" suggesting the potential of complete change of the individual and full assimilation into the community. Baligant's appearance thus suggests that the spiritual transformation of conversion would simply be the completion of a transformation that is already evident on the level of the flesh.

The suggestion that a spiritual reorientation might simultaneously be a kind of bodily metamorphosis, which remains only implicit in the description of Baligant, appears explicitly in other narratives of Saracen conversion, ranging from the *chanson de geste* of *Fierabras* to the Middle English romance of the *King of Tars* and Wolfram of Eschenbach's *Parzival*. In each of these texts, the Saracen body is the site of transformation not only of soul but of body, the place where the discourse of religious alterity and the discourse of ethnic alterity are aligned with one another. In these scenes of conversion, the individual body of the Saracen in the act of transformation marks the moment where the border separating the communities of Christian and pagan becomes porous. Just as the diasporic body of the Jew represents, in microcosm, the scattered state of his people, so the transforming body of the Saracen is a microcosm of the wished-for assimilation and integration of the Islamic world by Christendom. This desired assimilation comprehends within itself not only military conquest but also the appropriation of the rich intellectual and cultural trappings of the Islamic world, the luxurious commodities and the immense learning revered by Western intellectuals.

Such use of the Saracen body as a microcosm that would epitomize the integration of the Islamic world into Christendom is in keeping with wider currents in late medieval thought. As I have argued elsewhere, the late medieval discourse of nationalism is frequently deployed using theological forms, with the symbolic structure of the Eucharist serving as a especially powerful model for the community. While the Eucharist, as the body of Christ, is readily recognized as a synecdoche for the 'other' body of Christ—that is, the community of the faithful united within the Church—it has only recently become widely recognized that eucharistic symbolism also lay beneath many early formulations of national identity.[2] During the fourteenth and fifteenth centuries, the template of religious community proved to be readily adaptable to the definition of the community of the nation. In romances such as the *Siege of Melayne* and the *Romance of Richard Coer de Lion,* for example, eucharistic symbolism is used to delineate the contours of the imagined community of the English nation. In each of these texts, one single figure—in *Melayne,* Bishop Turpin; in *Richard Coer de Lion,* the king himself—is the

---

2. On the Eucharist as the preeminent medieval symbol of community, see Rubin, *Corpus Christi;* Beckwith, *Christ's Body.*

focus for the eucharistic symbolism, so that his bodily experiences (suffering wounds, or eating flesh) stand for the experience of the whole community. Through his body, which is representative of the body of Christ (in the case of Turpin) or of the body of the priest in the Mass (in the case of Richard), the incorporate community of the nation is united.[3]

A wide range of other medieval texts participate in a similar tendency to use the body of the individual as a synecdoche for the body of the community, among which the narratives featuring Saracen bodies described in this chapter must be included. Accordingly, the first section of this chapter, "The Male Saracen," focuses on *Fierabras,* one of the earliest surviving *chansons de geste* that survives in numerous versions in a range of vernacular languages. In *Fierabras,* the assimilability of the Islamic world is acted out twice: once in the figure of the eponymous hero who, badly wounded, is persuaded on the battlefield of the right of the Christian cause, and goes on to join the Christian community out of a heart-felt devotion to their God; and once in the figure of Fierabras' sister, Floripas, who becomes a Christian not out of pious faith but out of a desire to be united with one of Charlemagne's knights, Guy of Boulogne. Floripas' variable portrayal throughout the *Fierabras* tradition is the focus of the second portion of this chapter, "The Female Saracen." The very differently motivated—but equally willing—conversions of Fierabras and Floripas are countered by the utterly unwilling, forced conversion of their father, the emir Laban, who fights his way out of the baptismal font and physically assaults the bishop until he is mortally wounded. While the elder generation resists assimilation, the younger generation embraces it, and the changes experienced by them bear witness to the transformative power of the Christian community.

The third section of this chapter, "The Hybrid," turns to the Middle English *King of Tars,* in which the transformative power of the Christian community (as in *Fierabras*) is made manifest in not just one but two scenes of transformation. The first of these is the transformation of the formless "flesche" born as a result of the union of a Christian princess and a Saracen sultan which, upon baptism, receives the form of a perfect male infant. The second is that of the Sultan himself, whose flesh changes from "black and loathly" to shining white once he is immersed in the baptismal font. Here, two generations, both young and old, participate in the assimilation of Saracen identity within the Christian community. This narrative has a fascinating counterpart in the Middle High German *Parzival,* in which Wolfram von Eschenbach

---

3. Akbari, "Incorporation," 22–44; Akbari, "Hunger for National Identity," 198–227.

expands upon Chrétien de Troyes' romance of *Percival* to integrate the exotic matter of the Orient, including the legend of Prester John and the Wonders of the East. For Wolfram, the offspring of the union of Saracen and Christian is not a formless lump but rather the chivalric hero Feirefiz, whose parti-colored skin, checkered like the breast of a magpie, reflects both of the disparate parts of his heritage. In this pair of narratives, each of which features the hybrid offspring engendered by the union of Saracen and Christian bodies, the struggle to completely assimilate the Saracen "Other" is shown to be protracted, complex, and ultimately incomplete.

↞ The Male Saracen

Modern efforts to make sense of medieval depictions of Saracens have tended to draw upon anachronistic categories, especially that of "race." Some of these efforts are quite nuanced and produce rich insights regarding how medieval efforts to distinguish between populations on the basis of skin color might be related to early modern constructions of race produced in the colonial context. Exemplary in this respect is Thomas Hahn's introduction to a special issue of the *Journal of Medieval and Early Modern Studies* on "Color and Race before the Modern World." Hahn intelligently negotiates the dilemma of whether we can refer to a medieval idea of "race" at all, making it clear that there is a profound disjunction between medieval perceptions of bodily diversity and post-Enlightenment constructions of racial difference. Nonetheless, Hahn suggests, it can be helpful to interpret medieval representations of bodily diversity in terms of race as formulated in the early modern period, if only to note the continuities between medieval and modern modes of discrimination and alienation.[4] Others have been somewhat less subtle in their use of "race" as a defining term for medieval depictions of Saracen alterity, and have even argued that the Middle Ages gave rise to racism itself: for example, Jacqueline de Weever states that depictions of black Saracens in the *chansons de geste* are "racist portraits. When skin color is linked to ideas of inferiority... racism is born."[5]

It is beyond doubt that there is a value in recognizing the foundations of modern racism in medieval texts. It is vitally important, however, to first

---

4. Jeffrey Cohen similarly attempts to trace the genealogy of the "racialized bodily otherness" that gives rise to "medieval constructions of race"; Cohen, "On Saracen Enjoyment," 113–46. See also Heng, *Empire of Magic.*

5. De Weever, *Sheba's Daughters,* 100.

develop a clear understanding of how categories of bodily diversity function within specifically medieval systems of knowledge. Only by doing so is it possible to perceive how ethnic and national categories were shifted and their borders redefined in order to produce the distinctly early modern systems of racial knowledge generated during the earliest periods of colonial expansion. Once the medieval system of knowledge is well mapped out, it becomes possible to assess with some accuracy what kind of paradigm shifts took place to make it possible, in the early modern period, to perceive race as inherited, immutable, and polluting. In order to carry out this essential first step, it is necessary to examine closely works focused on producing methodical systems of knowledge, especially encyclopedias and scientific writings. In them, a very elaborate system can be found that maps out the bodily diversity of mankind, classifying the heterogeneous range of humanity within the natural order, dominated by climate, astrological influence, and physiological complexion.

Within the medieval discourse of bodily diversity—in sharp opposition to modern racial discourse—corporeal difference is not an either/or, black/white dichotomy. Rather, it is a continuum, with the monstrous races found at the fringes of the ecumene located on one end, and the normative European body on the other. Saracen bodies are located along this continuum, which is precisely why the Saracen body is so variable in the literature. This point cannot be stressed too much, for a number of readers have tended to assimilate medieval depictions of bodily diversity to modern racial dichotomies, suggesting that Saracen bodies are in some way singular, or of only two kinds. In an influential article, for example, Jeffrey Cohen describes "the Saracen body" as being fundamentally black, sometimes having monstrous qualities like tusks or fur.[6]

For others, the modern racial dichotomy is even more fully foregrounded, with explicit reliance on the paradigm of the "Manichean allegory" of race as formulated by Abdul JanMohamed. Thus de Weever, describing the nature of Muslim women in the *chansons de geste,* writes that there are "two aspects of the Saracen woman—one white, one black.... The white Saracen represents [the] wealth and beauty [of the East]; the black Saracen its strangeness and horror."[7] Lynn Ramey similarly refers to the "split view of the Saracen" and the "dual nature of the Infidel": "The enemy is at once an exotic beast and a lovely woman.... The Infidel is both things at once."[8] Ramey's reference to

---

6. Cohen, "On Saracen Enjoyment."

7. De Weever, *Sheba's Daughters,* 96.

8. Lynn Tarte Ramey, *Christian, Saracen, and Genre,* 35; on the "Manichean allegory" of race, see 11–12.

"the Infidel" suggests the reason for this binarism, which is also hinted at in Andrew Fleck's interpretation of Muslim and Christian difference in *The Book of John Mandeville* in terms of the "Manichean allegory" of race.[9] The discourse of religious difference is indeed predicated on binarism—that is, right belief and wrong belief. The discourse of racial difference, conversely, is not predicated on binarism: there is a norm, and there is greater or lesser deviation from that norm. The discourses of religion and race intersect, however, in the scene of conversion, where bodily transformation is concomitant with the reorientation of spiritual devotion. Because "Saracen" identity, like "Jewish" identity, is depicted in medieval texts as being the product simultaneously of religious and ethnic difference, it partakes in both the binarism of religious alterity and the spectrum of bodily diversity.

Within that spectrum of bodily diversity, Saracen bodies are influenced by the torrid climate within which they are born and nourished. As we saw illustrated in some detail in chapter 3, medieval encyclopedias such as the thirteenth-century *De proprietatibus rerum* of Bartholomaeus Anglicus were instrumental in the wide dissemination of learned conceptions regarding bodily diversity into wider reading communities. As we saw, Bartholomaeus Anglicus took up the explanations of the effects of climate on bodies found in the medical tradition and, influenced by the astronomy of Sacrobosco, integrated these views into his geographical survey of the world. In other words, Bartholomaeus took medical theories that distinguished between northern and southern bodies in general and applied them to a range of specific countries. It is crucial to note that skin color was just one in a whole range of corporeal features that were used to distinguish between peoples of various nations, engendered in diverse climates.[10] These sophisticated explanations of the nature and the genesis of bodily diversity were widely disseminated through Bartholomaeus' encyclopedia, which was extremely popular both in its Latin original and in vernacular translations. Many copies survive, and the late fourteenth-century English translation by John Trevisa was among the first titles produced by William Caxton on his printing press. While one might object that the arcane learning of Albertus Magnus and Avicenna could not possibly have exerted an influence on the depictions of Saracens in medieval romance, no such argument can be made with regard to

---

9. Fleck, "Here, There, and In Between," 379–401, esp. 390, 398.

10. On medieval medical views of skin color, see the essays gathered in Agostino Paravicini Bagliani, ed., *La pelle umana / The Human Skin,* Micrologus 13 (Florence: SISMEL edizioni del Galluzzo, 2005), especially van der Lugt, "La peau noire dans la science médiévale" (439–75), and Biller, "Black Women in Medieval Scientific Thought" (477–92).

the encyclopedia of Bartholomaeus Anglicus. His geographical section was particularly popular, circulating independently from the encyclopedia as a whole in many witnesses. In each section of that geography, Bartholomaeus takes pains to note the correspondence of climate to the bodily nature of the inhabitants of each land. Those of the northern countries are large-bodied and fair-skinned, with blond, straight hair; those of the southern countries have smaller bodies, with dark skin and "crisp" hair. Monstrosities—that is, bodies that are "horrible, with different faces and monstrous appearance" (gentes diverso vultu et monstruosa specie horribiles [15.52]) are found here, where excess of heat affects conception and gestation.[11]

Bartholomaeus also characterizes the various peoples of the world in terms of their "natural" qualities: these include not only their physical features, but their behavioral predispositions as well. The Asturians of Spain, for example, are "of elegant stature and beautiful shape, according to the location of the country and of the hot region" (elegantis stature et pulcre forme, secundum situm patrie et calide regionis [15.20]). The land also dictates their behavior, however: because of the climate, "they are light of tongue, for speaking and perhaps for mocking" (ad loquendum et forsan deridendum alios lingua levis [15.20]). In Brabant, the "land [is] fertile in grain, populous, a race of elegant height and beautiful form, warlike, bold toward enemies, but peaceful and quiet among themselves" (terra fertilis in frugibus, populosa, gens elegantis stature et venuste forme, bellicosa, animosa contra hostes, inter se autem placita et quieta [15.25]). The Palestinians, conversely, live in a climate that makes them "astute and hot-tempered" (astuta and callida [15.114]).[12] These characterizations of the behavioral predispositions of nations is entirely keeping with the humoral theory prevalent in medieval medical discourse, which Bartholomaeus himself summarizes in book IV of his encyclopedia, basing his comments largely on the medical writings of Constantinus Africanus.

Bartholomaeus explains that the ideal body, like the ideal climate, is medium; it is equally balanced between the extremes, inhabiting the golden mean. Ideally, none of the four humors (blood, cholera, phlegm, and melancholy)

---

11. Quotations from book 15 only of Bartholomaeus Anglicus, *De proprietatibus rerum,* are taken from the edition and translation (in preparation for the Pontifical Institute for Mediaeval Studies Press) *The Parts of the World,* and are cited in the text by book and chapter number.

12. Note the Middle English translation by John Trevisa, which renders "astuta and callida" as "fals and gyleful and wyly": The Palestinians "ben allweye fals and gyleful and wyly, greuous enemys to the kyngedome of Israel, bothe for they hadde enuye to the Iues, and also for they were proude of the welthe of here owne londe" (*On the Properties of Things,* 15.113, 763). The original reads in full: "Gens, ut narrat Herodotus, astuta et callida, molesta semper regno Israelitico et infesta, tum quia prosperitati Judeorum invidebat, tum etiam quia de soli sui felicitate...nimium praesumebat" (15.114; note the slight discrepancy in the chapter numbering between the Latin and Middle English texts).

should predominate; in practice, of course, one or more does, at least to some degree, as a result of the individual person's qualities (sometimes called their "root complexion," by Roger Bacon, for example)[13] coupled with outside stimuli. Chief among these stimuli is climate, although other factors such as food and drink, gender, age, and astrological influences are also significantly influential. For example, Bartholomaeus outlines the qualities of a "fleumatik man," who is naturally "lustles, heuy, and slowgh; dul of wit and of thought, foryeteful; neissche of fleissche." Such men, he adds, often suffer badly in wintertime, "for thanne the qualitees of fleume, coolde and moist, beth istrengthid."[14] A similar effect of climate is evident in "colerik men," who are "generalliche wratheful, hardy, vnmeke, light, vnstable, inpetuous; in body long, sklendre, and lene; in colour broun; in eer blak and crips, hard and stif; in touche hoot; in puls strong and swifte." Just as phlegmatic people suffer more acute symptoms in winter, the choleric nature is exacerbated in the heat of summer—or by dwelling in hotter climates. Bodies in places dominated by the heat of the sun, therefore, can be expected to display qualities of the choleric temperament: irascible, impetuous, and (in the words of Bartholomaeus' Middle English translator) governed by the "appetite . . . of the werkes of Venus."[15]

It is in this context that we can productively interpret the depiction of Saracens in medieval popular literature, such as *chansons de geste,* romances, and drama. The wild impetuosity and fury of the followers of "Mahon," or Muhammad, must be understood as the product of not only religious deviance, but also bodily diversity. These qualities are crucial to the Saracens of medieval literature, whether they appear in the attractive, European-looking bodies of Baligant, in the *Chanson de Roland,* or Guiborc, in the Guillaume d'Orange

---

13. Bacon, *Opus Maius,* trans. Burke, 1:159.

14. "[A] verray fleumatik man is in the body lustles, heuy, and slowgh; dul of wit and of thought, foryeteful; neissche of fleissche and quauy, b[l]oo in colour, whitliche of face, ferdeful of herte . . . neissche, yelowh and streit [of here]; neissche, grete and slough of puls. . . . Men of that complexioun hath often coolde yueles and beth itrauayled therwith and nameliche in wintir, for thanne the qualitees of fleume, coolde and moist, beth istrengthid" (quoting Constantinus Africanus; 4.9; 157). Quotations from Bartholomaeus Anglicus, *De proprietatibus rerum* (with the exception of book 15, on geography, cited separately), are taken from the Middle English translation of John Trevisa, ed. M. C. Seymour et al., owing to the current lack of a modern edition of the Latin text. An edition of the full text is in preparation under the general editorship of B. van den Abeele (Brepols, forthcoming).

15. "[C]olera . . . bredith boldenes and hardynes and meuynge and lightnes and wreththe and appetite of wreche and also of the werkes of Venus. . . . And so colerik men beth generalliche wratheful, hardy, vnmeke, light, vnstable, inpetuous; in body long, sklendre, and lene; in colour broun; in eer blak and crips, hard and stif; in touche hoot; in puls strong and swifte" (Trevisa, *On the Properties of Things,* 4.10; 159). For a more detailed account of the medieval association of choleric temperament with the dry and hot regions of the east and south-east, see Tooley, "Bodin and the Mediaeval Theory," 64–83, esp. 73.

cycle. While the categories of bodily diversity as laid out in encyclopedic texts such as Bartholomaeus Anglicus only became available to medieval readers and writers in the thirteenth century, the spectrum of bodily diversity—and the role of climate in dictating the nature and scope of that diversity—was already adumbrated in texts drawing upon the geography and ethnography of Pliny's *Historia naturalis,* such as Isidore of Seville's *Etymologiae* and the *Imago mundi* of Honorius of Autun.[16] In these encyclopedic works, composed well before the thirteenth-century flourishing of scholasticism, the heterogeneous range of mankind was already coming to be ordered within a system of knowledge.

While a wide range of *chansons de geste* and the medieval romances they inspired could be used to survey the depiction of Saracens in popular literature, *Fierabras* (originally composed early in the twelfth century or late in the eleventh) offers a particularly useful textual resource. It can best be described not as a "text" but as "texts," for *Fierabras* was extraordinarily popular, surviving in a large number of Old and Middle French manuscripts as well as a wealth of translations and adaptations. These include texts written in Middle English, Provençal, Italian, Spanish, Latin, and Old Irish; oral versions of the romance survived into the twentieth century in South America and, in the nineteenth century, yet another version was adapted as an opera by Schubert.[17] On the one hand, the widespread popularity of the *Fierabras* romance reveals what cultures have in common, extending over a long period of time and including a wide geographical range: they share an interest in the matter of chivalric romance—that is, the competition of knights, the alluring pagan princess, defiant and hideous giants, and so on.[18] At the same time, however, the numerous redactions of *Fierabras* reveal how cultures differ from one another, for several of the versions vary in ways that reveal how the narrative was adapted to fit the needs, concerns, and interests of the culture in which it appeared. Some versions, for example, depict the Saracen knight Fierabras as a giant, others merely as a magnificently built knight; some versions minimize the descriptions of the relics of the Passion sought by the Christian knights, while others expand those sections, transforming courtly romance into devotional literature.[19] The narrative of *Fierabras* centers on the victory of the

---

16. On early medieval dissemination and adaptation of Pliny's *Historia naturalis,* see Beckett, *Anglo-Saxon Perceptions,* 84–88.

17. On the versions of *Fierabras,* see de Mandach, *La Geste de Fierabras,* 165–86.

18. On the general appeal of the *Fierabras* romance during the Middle Ages and the insights it offers into the cultural history of the period, see Gourlay, "'Faire Maide.'"

19. An overview of the versions of the romance can be found in Ailes, "Comparative Study." On the Fillingham *Firumbras* as "devotional romance," see Akbari, "Hunger for National Identity," 218; and "Incorporation in the *Sege of Melayne.*"

Christian host against the Saracen armies, a victory that is reflected in microcosm in not one but two narratives of individual conversion. The first of these, that of the Saracen prince Fierabras, is the focus of the remainder of this section of chapter 4; the second conversion, that of Fierabras' sister, Floripas, is the focus of the following section. Borrowing a term coined by Iain Higgins to describe the many versions of *The Book of John Mandeville,* the textual "isotopes" of *Fierabras* discussed in this chapter include four French versions and three Middle English versions. One of these French versions, an Anglo-Norman redaction that is among the earliest surviving witnesses of the *chanson de geste* of *Fierabras,* is the main text cited in this section of the chapter. In the following section, the development of the Saracen princess Floripas is surveyed in more detail as it evolves throughout several of the French "isotopes" of *Fierabras.* By exploring the depiction of Fierabras through a single version of the narrative, and the depiction of Floripas through a collection of related versions, I hope to be able to foreground the basic narrative of Saracen conversion while also demonstrating the variability of its presentation throughout the broad range of *Fierabras* "isotopes."

Although three baptisms are staged in *Fierabras,* only two of them are completed. The third of these, the planned baptism of the father of the eponymous hero Fierabras (that is, the Sultan "Laban d'Espaigne") does not take place after all. After the Christian military victory, the Sultan is to be baptized in a font, watched over by Charlemagne and his peers. Instead, he violently resists, striking the bishop who stands ready to preside; the Sultan responds harshly to the appeal of his children, who call on him to be baptized, by cursing his son Fierabras and by calling his daughter Floripas a "pute" (whore [1709]).[20] The Sultan's irascible nature expresses itself unchecked until finally, at Charlemagne's order, one of the Christian lords strikes off the Saracen ruler's head. However, the baptisms of the Sultan's two children, Fierabras and Floripas, are more successful. Both of the Sultan's children share his irascible nature: Fierabras is, precisely, "fier," distinguished by the ferocity with which he wages war. Though Floripas is outwardly a model of feminine beauty and graceful deportment, consistently identified as "Floripas la curteis" (Floripas the courteous) [541]), her outer beauty covers a nature as fiery and irascible as that of her father. Until her baptism, which takes place only in the last lines of the narrative, Floripas behaves with extreme aggression. She speaks out forcefully; she laughs openly, often in response to violent behaviors of

---

20. Quotations from the Anglo-Norman *Fierabras* are taken from the edition of Louis Brandin and cited in the text by line number; translations are my own. [*Fierabras*], Brandin, "*La Destruction de Rome et Fierabras,*" 18–100.

which she approves; she even kills with her own hands, twice. Her behavior, however outrageous, is acceptable simply because it is directed toward a good end: Floripas is not only the exquisite object of men's admiration, but also the dominant mastermind who supervises the Christian victory over the Saracen forces led by her father. Her brother Fierabras displays similar ferocity; his violent behavior, however, falls within the norms of chivalric deportment as defined within the framework of the *chansons de geste*. His violent nature is abruptly attenuated when, following his defeat in battle at the hand of one of Charlemagne's men, Fierabras chooses to convert to Christianity. After his baptism, which takes place relatively early in the text, Fierabras ceases to make war entirely and takes up a life of holy devotion, with the new name "Florien" (496).

Yet behavioral qualities such as irascibility are not the only factors that are changed in the scenes of baptism found in the romance of *Fierabras*. Saracen bodies, too, undergo change as they are assimilated into the Christian community. These changes are not made visible in the strikingly explicit way that we see in the *King of Tars*, where the Saracen Sultan, as soon as he is dipped into the baptismal font, becomes white. Instead, they are evident in the way in which the romance characterizes the two types of Saracen bodies: those that are assimilable, like that of Fierabras and his sister Floripas; and those that are unassimilable, that is, the giants both male and female who populate the text. The scene of conversion, in other words, is anticipated in the initial depiction of the Saracen body. This form of teleological portrayal, where the rebirth of baptism is imaginatively anticipated, appears not only in *Fierabras* but also in other *chansons de geste*, such as in the case of Baligant in the *Chanson de Roland*, noted above in the introduction to this chapter.

In the romance of *Fierabras*, this binary distinction is most pronounced in the depiction of female Saracens: the beautiful, fair-skinned, blonde pagan princess is desirable and assimilable in a way that her counterpart, the hideous, black-skinned giantess Barac, is not. Both female figures, the dainty princess and the deformed giant, are characterized in terms of aggressive, dangerous behavior; both are irascible and violent. Floripas' ability to be assimilated is expressed through her appearance, a precursor of the normative behavior that she will embrace following her full incorporation into the Christian community upon being baptized. Conversely, the unassimilable nature of the giantess Barac is expressed in her physical form; from her first appearance in the text, it is clear that Barac's fate can only be a violent death in battle. A similar binary opposition informs the depiction of male Saracens in the text. We have, on the one hand, two male giants, Agolafre and Astregot, and on the other the Saracen prince Fierabras. It might seem that the situation here closely parallels that of Barac and Floripas, where both are Saracen females, but one is a hideous giantess and one an alluring princess. Interestingly, however, Fierabras' male gender causes the dynamic to function quite differently, mainly because the qualities of aggression and even violence are valued highly within the chivalric system where warfare is the natural state of affairs.

Fierabras is characterized, therefore, as a man both "orgoilouse et fier" (proud and fierce [168]) and "de mult grant fierté" (of great fierceness [183]). His name tells us who he is, highlighting the qualities that make him a typical Saracen, on the one hand, and a marvelous knight on the other. The narrator states, "Ne fu tiel chivaler jusc'al la Rouge mer" (there was never such a knight as far as the Red Sea [171]), suggesting both his exotic origins (this is, after all, "Fierembras d'Alisandre") and his desirability as a chivalric recruit to the Christian armies of Charlemagne. In subsequent redactions of the romance, however, Fierabras' Saracen qualities become more exaggerated. In the late fifteenth-century French prose version of Jean Bagnyon, quickly translated into English by William Caxton and published in 1485, Fierabras is actually described as a "geaunt," a man "hugely membred."[21] This characterization of Fierabras as a giant is not an alteration introduced by Bagnyon, but is rather an emphasis introduced simultaneously, in parallel, in a number of the later textual isotopes of *Fierbras*. As early as the fourteenth-century Ashmole version, a Middle English adaptation of the Anglo-Norman text, the corresponding passage amplifies the giant-like qualities of the Saracen prince:

> Fyrumbras of Alysaundre was a man of gret stature,
> And ful brod in the scholdres was and long man in forchure. . . .
> And the Sarsyn thanne a drow ys brond that was so gret of strengthe,
> And wan it was nakede on his hond vij fet it had of lengthe.
> (*Sir Ferumbras* 550–51; 580–81)

In the Ashmole version, the body of Fierabras is virtually the body of a giant. He is of huge stature, said to exceed fifteen feet in height. His long "forchure"—that is, the length of his stride—echoes the descriptions of other Saracen knights in the *chansons de geste,* such as Baligant in the *Roland*. In keeping with his great scale, Fierabras wields an enormous sword, seven feet in length. In spite of his evident physical prowess, Fierabras is defeated in

---

21. Bagnyon, *Histoire de Charlemagne.* Quotation from Caxton translation, 85, line 1.

battle by the Christian knight Oliver; seeing the futility of his pagan gods, Fierabras asks to be baptized. Unlike his sister, Floripas, who is explicitly motivated to convert only by her love for the Christian knight Guy, Fierabras explicitly declares that his conversion is motivated by religious conviction: "My gods," he says, "may do no more than a stone" (757). Fierabras declares that he will "scatheye hem night & day that bileueth on Mahounde; / Cristendom by me schal encressed be" (759–60). Fierabras is so devout that he goes on to become known as "Saint Florens."

In being converted, however, Fierabras is unmanned. Before his baptism, his military prowess and chivalric behavior are constantly on display;[22] after his baptism, Fierabras virtually disappears from the plot, even though one might expect him to be recruited to fight on the side of the Christians. Fierabras does not reappear until the very end of the poem, at the scene of baptism where his father, the Sultan Laban, refuses to convert to Christianity. Fierabras' behavior in this scene goes beyond conventional displays of filial piety, as he begs his father, on his knees, to accept Charlemagne's order to convert. After Laban refuses, Fierabras "wep & wyghte sore" (5832), renewing his pleas to his father. He stays on his knees, weeping and sighing, for almost a hundred lines of the poem (5776–5857). This extended plea is in sharp contrast to the corresponding passage in the Anglo-Norman text, where Fierabras' appeal to his father appears in a brisk four lines. The feminine quality of Fierabras' behavior in the Ashmole text is heightened by the aggressive behavior of his sister. Floripas, who in the Anglo-Norman text displays demure daughterly emotion, simply says to Charlemagne: "Wy tariest thou so longe wyth that man?... / Al ys for noght...ye ne bringeth him neuere to youre purpos" (5820–21). The violent, impulsive behavior shown by Floripas throughout the poem is a manifestation of her Saracen identity, the irascibility natural to Saracen bodies. The warlike nature of Fierabras is similarly founded on that Saracen identity; consequently, after conversion, he does not appear as a warrior on the Christian side of the conflict. As long he belongs to the Saracen religion, he exhibits Saracen behavior: he is violent and aggressive. Once he becomes a Christian, his acts are governed by compassion rather than aggression, and his body is shown bowed in supplication, his face covered with tears. Fierabras undergoes a bodily change—not anatomical, but

---

22. "Fierabras' character is shown from the beginning to [be] a noble and chivalrous one: he offers the balm to the wounded Oliver...; when he kills Oliver's horse he himself dismounts.... this after Oliver has refused the offer of his own horse; when Oliver loses his sword he offers to let him retrieve it.... Truly Fierabras is too good to remain a pagan by the standards of his time." Ailes, "Faith in *Fierabras*," 125–133, quotation from 132.

physiological—in the course of his religious conversion. In terms of humoral physiology, he becomes cold and wet, a combination of qualities not normally found in males, but typical of females. No longer hot-tempered, warlike, and irascible, Fierabras exhibits the humility and emotional nature of a woman, passive and weepy.[23] His new, Christian name, "Florien" or "Florens," echoes the name of his sister, "Floripas," perhaps underlining the demasculinization that is concomitant with Fierabras' assimilation into the Christian host.

The bodily change experienced by Fierabras, in which his humoral disposition appears to have been altered, is explicitly manifested in the poem in the form of a wound. Following his defeat at the hands of Oliver, Fierabras is laid out before the assembled Christian knights in a tableau that anticipates the climactic scene at the end of the poem, where Floripas' naked body is paraded before the Christian knights prior to baptism:

> Le roi ad duc Neimes et Ogier apellé:
> "Fetes tant q'il seit as pavilons amené...."
> Charl, li roi de France, s'ad son tent entré.
> Ces mires en aveit hastivement maundé:
> "Cerchés moi cest paiem li flanc et li cousté."
> Les mires l'en cerchierent, qant fu defublé.
> Les boweles troverent qe nuls fu atamé.
> Cils sunt venu al roi, si l'ont nuncié:
> "Sire, nous vous le rendroms seine ainz qinze jours passé."
> Kant Charl les entent, grant joi s'ad demenee.

> The king called upon Duke Neimes and Ogier:
> "Have him brought to the encampment...."
> His physicians he had summoned hastily:
> "Examine for me this pagan, his thighs and sides."
> The physicians examined him, when he was unarmed.
> They searched his guts, to be sure that nothing had been pierced.
> They then came to the king, and announced to him:
> "Sire, we will render him to you before fifteen days have passed."
> When Charles heard them, he expressed great joy.
>
> (*Fierabras* 473–85)

---

23. For a useful overview of premodern perspectives on the humoral qualities of coldness and wetness and their association with women, see Paster, "Unbearable Coldness of Female Being," 416–40; an expanded version focused on Shakespeare appears in Paster, *Humoring the Body*, 77–134 (chapter 2, "Love Will Have Heat").

In the fourteenth-century Middle English adaptation, the passage has become embellished, both more detailed and more alluring in its description of the unclothed body of Fierabras.

> Charlis hemself & sire Oger, ounarmede him tho anon,
> & wan he was sengle amoung hem, ther hy auysed is schap echon.
> Brode scholdres had he with-alle, & brustes ful quarree [well-developed chest],
> Wyth longe sydes & middel smalle, a wel schape man was hee.
> With Browes bente & eyen stoute, and lokede so the facoun:
> To seche the worlde al aboute, ne was man of fairer fasoun.
> Al that him be-hulde than, among hem that saide there,
> That Olyuer was a doghty man, wan hym he might conquere.
> A wel faire knight was Firumbras, ounarmid wan he lay....
> At is [Charlis] heste they wente ther-to and softe gonne taste is wounde,
> His lyure, ys lunge & is guttes al-so, & found hem hol & sounde.
>   (Ashmole *Sir Ferumbras* 1070–78; 1094–95)

Stripped of its armor, Fierabras' body appears attractive and desirable. His visual appeal magnifies the stature of his opponent in battle, the knight Oliver, who was able to conquer such a magnificent specimen of manhood. In this scene, Fierabras appears as a passive object, an effect that is heightened in the closing lines describing the doctors who attend to his wounds. Immediately following his baptism, "on a bed than was he laid, / that with riche clothes was y-sprad, and ful faire araid" (1090–91). The doctors approach his bed, "& softe gonne taste is wounde, / His lyure, ys lunge & is guttes al-so, & found hem hol & sounde" (1094–95). Fierabras' body is "whole and sound," his anatomy undamaged; his physiology, however, *is* altered, and his behavior permanently affected.[24]

There are a variety of Saracen bodies in the *Fierabras* texts, ranging from the repellent, animalistic bodies of the giants to the dainty white body of the Sultan's daughter Floripas. The body of Fierabras falls somewhere in between, for its beautiful form is at odds with its overwhelmingly large size. His great stature, amplified (as we have seen) in the later, Middle English redaction of the Anglo-Norman text, marks him as related to the Saracen giants of the poem; the beauty of his form, however, marks Fierabras as an appropriate addition to the European Christian community. In his assimilability, Fierabras

---

24. Later versions of *Fierabras* shorten this scene considerably; compare Bagnyon, 68; prose *Fierabras,* paragraph 57.

is much like his sister; the nature of their assimilation, however, differs significantly. The woman is assimilated not just by baptism but by marriage to a Christian knight to whom, presumably, she will bear Christian heirs who will rule over both Christian and pagan territory. The man, however, is assimilated by baptism alone: Fierabras is said to take on the name "Florien" and to live a saintly, chaste life after his adventures on the battlefield come to an end. Both his name and his body are changed by the act of conversion, unlike his sister who is specifically said to be not renamed in the course of baptism, and whose aggressive behavior remains unchanged up until the poem's last lines. Saracen assimilability is thus clearly articulated in different terms across gender lines.

The more general limitations of Saracen assimilability are highlighted in a final passage from *Fierabras,* which illustrates both the nature of European Christian desire to assimilate its Saracen Other, and the nature of the boundaries that limit that assimilation. Immediately after the defeat in battle of the giantess Barrok, the Christian knights make an extraordinary discovery:

> En un cave troverent deus enfanz de valour.
> Fiz esteient Barac, qi occis fu en l'estour;
> N'i furent qe uit mois de aage li vavasour;
> Cinc piéz furent de lee et qatorze de longour. . . .
> Danz Richard les amena l'emperer devant;
> Charls fist faire apparailler un fonce de maintenant.
> L'un appellent Oliver et l'autre Rollant.
> Grant joi aveit le roi de les deus enfant.
> Amener les quidout en France et les faire poiant;
> Mais cils en moergent ainz sun returnant,
> Car lour mer lour failli, qi lour voit alaitant.
> Charls fu dolent, qant l'em le voit disant.

> In a cave they found two mighty infants.
> They were the sons of Barrok, who had been killed with a great blow;
> They were no more than eight months of age.
> They were five feet in breadth and fourteen feet in length. . .
> Lord Richard brought them before the emperor;
> Charles had a font brought forth at once.
> They called one of them "Oliver" and the other "Roland."
> The king had great joy from the two infants.
> They believed they would take them to France and make them into warriors;

But these ones died before they could go there,
For their mother was lacking to them, who had been nursing them.
Charles was sorrowful, when he was told of it.

(*Fierabras* 1588–1601)

Charlemagne's joy at the discovery of the twins is matched by his sorrow
at their loss. The twins are of monstrous size, five feet broad and fourteen
feet tall; far from making them repellent, however, their stature makes them
potential heroes to be included within the Christian host, a little Oliver and
Roland who will one day be mighty heroes facing the Saracen hordes. Charlemagne's hope is that he will have giants of his own to match against his enemies; this hope is disappointed, however, by the twins being cut off from the
nourishing milk that had sustained them. In a poem dedicated to "la glorious
virgine qe Marie est nomé" (the Glorious Virgin called Mary [282]), which
praises the "douce mamelles enlattastes al virgine honoré" (sweet milk-bearing
breasts of the Blessed Virgin [283]), the milk of the giantess represents a
material—not spiritual—connection to Saracen identity. Precisely because
it is material and not spiritual, this milk is aptly associated with the faith of
the Saracens, which was thought by medieval Christians to be grounded in
a literal, fleshly, even idolatrous theology. Nonetheless, without this support,
the Saracen Other remains unable to be assimilated, although it remains the
object of desire. Instead of becoming full-grown Christian heroes, the giant
infants die; instead of leading the Christian armies, Fierabras retires into a life
of seclusion and prayer.

In order to understand the symbolic function of giant stature in the work,
both in the infant twins and in the hero Fierabras, it is helpful to look more
closely at the various contexts used during the Middle Ages to interpret
gigantism. The nature of giants was explained both in terms of their biblical lineage and scientific reasoning. According to Genesis, giants walked the
earth as a result of the unnatural mingling of fallen angels and the "daughters
of men" (Gen. 6:1–4), an account richly elaborated in the textual history
surrounding the apocryphal Book of Enoch.[25] As early as the seventh century, however, in the encyclopedia of Isidore of Seville, we find alternative
explanations that counter the biblical account. Isidore affirms that races of
giants do exist, but states that they are in fact not the offspring of the fallen
angels, as commonly thought, for the angels' descendants all perished in the
Flood. Isidore adds that their name comes from the Greek *gegéneis,* "id est

---

25. On the elaboration of the Genesis account in the "Book of the Watchers," recounted in
Enoch 1:1–36, see Reed, *Fallen Angels.*

terrigenas." "Ge" denotes *terra,* or earth, and "genos" is *genus;* therefore, he says, the giants are born of the earth (*Etym.* 11.3.13–14).

This link of giants to materiality is ubiquitous. It appears in Aristotle's explanation, in the *Generation of Animals,* of how giants come to exist: when the quantity of matter exceeds the dimensions of the form, he states, a giant results. Great size, therefore, can be good and beautiful, but only if the form corresponds to the matter.[26] In other words, when both the form and the matter are large, you get a great, handsome specimen of manhood. This is what the body of Fierabras represents, and what Charlemagne must have eagerly looked forward to when he first saw the twin giant infants of Barrok. In Aristotle's formulation, when the form and matter are inconsistent, the product is a monstrous giant; the giant's great size is neither good nor beautiful, because the matter contained within the body does not correspond to its form. Such giants are typical of the Saracen giants found in *Fierabras.* Here, giant stature is sometimes monstrous, but sometimes not; in the case of Fierabras, as with the twins, it is instead a sign of the alluring might of the Saracen, a source of power that Christian Europe seeks to assimilate.[27] Such assimilation is impossible for the twins, and possible only to a limited extent for the male Saracen. Instead, assimilation is most readily possible for the female Saracen.

⇐ The Female Saracen

The figure of the "Saracen princess" or the "Saracen queen" has received considerable attention during the last several years, most astutely in the fine work of Sharon Kinoshita.[28] This attention is likely due to the intersection of the dynamic field of women's studies with the steadily increasing scholarly interest in religious and cultural difference as depicted in literature of the Middle Ages, intensified by recent work on intersection of postcolonial theory with medieval culture.[29] While some treatments of "the Saracen princess" convention are rather limited due to their focus on a single, paradigmatic

---

26. For a brief overview of Aristotle's presentation of monstrosity, see Daston and Park, *Wonders and the Order of Nature,* 192. Aristotle's *Generation of Animals* (4.4 on monstrosity) was translated twice in the Middle Ages, by Michael Scot (from Arabic) and William of Moerbeke (from Greek). For the earlier version, see Aristotle, *De animalibus.*

27. For a provocative reading of gigantism in medieval culture that tends to assimilate giant stature to monstrosity, see Jeffrey Cohen, *Of Giants.*

28. See the brilliant discussions of Orable and Bramimonde in Kinoshita, "Politics of Courtly Love," 265–87, and "'Pagans Are Wrong,'" 79–111. See also the revised versions of these arguments in chapters 1 and 2 of Kinoshita, *Medieval Boundaries,* 15–73.

29. On the usefulness of such approaches, see the seminal collection of Jeffrey Cohen, *Postcolonial Middle Ages.* A provocative survey of the relationship of medieval studies and postcolonial theory

exemplar, others provide a broader, more nuanced account of the variations.[30] This section of chapter 4 also focuses on a single exemplar of the convention, the Saracen princess Floripas, not because her character is originary or foundational to the tradition (although *Fierabras* is certainly among the earliest *chansons de geste*—some have argued, the earliest), but rather because the multiple textual "isotopes" of the *Fierabras* narrative make it especially well suited to an effort to track the mutability of the figure of the "Saracen princess."

Yet the widespread diffusion of *Fierabras* is just one reason that the figure of Floripas merits special attention. She differs significantly from other figures seen as representative of the Saracen princess convention in being the daughter of a Saracen emir, rather than the wife of one, like Bramimonde, in the *Chanson de Roland,* or Orable, in the Guillaume d'Orange cycle.[31] While all of these Saracen women traverse the gap separating pagan and Christian cultures, delivering their Saracen kinfolk into the hands of the Frankish knights, they differ with regard to the nature of the obligations they disavow, and consequently differ both in the nature of their disobedience and in the nature of what they bring to their new environment. Moreover, Floripas also differs in two significant ways from the Saracen princesses sometimes considered in connection with her, such as Nubie in the *Prise de Cordres et de Sebille,* Malatrie in the *Siège de Barbastre,* or Josiane in *Boeve de Haumtone.*[32] The baptism of the Saracen in *chansons de geste* and romances is conventionally accompanied by a change of name in recognition of the person's spiritual rebirth and renewal: Bramimonde becomes Juliane, Orable becomes Guiborc, and so on. Floripas, however, retains her name even after baptism, a fact to which the text ostentatiously draws attention.[33] The omission is rendered all the more

---

appears in Holsinger, "Medieval Studies," 1195–1227. See also Heng, *Empire of Magic;* Ingham and Warren, *Postcolonial Moves;* Kabir and Williams, *Postcolonial Approaches.*

30. Ramey, for example, fixes on Orable/Guiborc as "probably the most remarkable Saracen princess of them all" (41); Ramey, *Christian, Saracen and Genre.* De Weever discusses several examples of the Saracen princess convention, but assimilates them all into a singular manifestation of the "white" Saracen woman; de Weever, *Sheba's Daughters.* A useful overview of the convention appears in Metlitzki, *Matter of Araby,* 160–77, and a more detailed summary in Bancourt, *Les Musulmans dans les chansons de geste du cycle du roi,* 571–665; neither Metlitzki nor Bancourt, however, discusses the significance of the variations.

31. On this distinction, see Kinoshita, *Medieval Boundaries,* 61–64.

32. In an unusual oversight, Kinoshita dismisses Floripas as a typical example of minor female characters whose "roles in the overall plot remain fairly minor" (*Medieval Boundaries,* 55).

33. This anomaly is found elsewhere only in *Gaufrey,* where Flordespine's baptism similarly results in no change of name. The passage corresponds very closely to the account of Floripas' baptism (verse *Fierabras,* line 6013; compare *Gaufrey,* lines 9163–64); perhaps the redactor of *Gaufrey* (which survives in a single manuscript, Montpellier Faculté de médecine MS H.242) based his depiction of

remarkable by the fact that the conversion of her brother, Fierabras, is accompanied by a change in name: after baptism, as we have seen, he is renamed Florien.

The second, even more striking difference between Floripas and other Saracen princesses pertains to her status and behavior during the period between her avowal of the desire to become Christian and her actual baptism at the close of the narrative. During this time, Floripas exhibits apparently paradoxical behavior: she is beautiful and delicate, but also aggressive and violent. Floripas is both the exquisite object of men's admiration and the dominant mastermind supervising the Christian victory over the pagan forces led by her father. She speaks out forcefully; she laughs openly, often in response to violent behaviors of which she approves; she even kills with her own hands. In some versions of *Fierabras,* Floripas' behavior is explicitly characterized as unfeminine, and she herself is described as a dangerous combination of masculine and feminine qualities. In others, Floripas' behavior is not characterized as unfeminine, because her Saracen identity is dominant in the determination of what constitutes normative behavior. In each case, however, the extended period during which Floripas is neither wholly Saracen nor wholly Christian repays examination, for it constitutes a liminal phase during which Floripas' identity is in flux. She is in the process of assimilation to Western Christian normative modes of behavior, which intersect with normative modes of feminine behavior. Floripas thus offers insight not only into the medieval characterization of Saracens, but also into the complex ways that categories of gender alterity intersect with categories of religious and ethnic alterity. Moreover, because of the unusual existence of the text of *Fierabras* in numerous versions, it is possible to use the depiction of Floripas as a way to chart this interaction of categories over a long period, and to use this example of the "Saracen princess" convention to chart the development of at least one strand of medieval Orientalism.

As Hans-Erich Keller has shown, a comparison of the different versions of the medieval *Fierabras* reveals discontinuities indicative of the changing tastes of reading communities all around Europe, from the twelfth century to the fifteenth.[34] Keller's work focuses mainly on Floripas' physical beauty. Other aspects of her character, however, also vary significantly; for example, some versions accentuate her violence, while others subdue it. In addition, other discontinuities cast an indirect light on the variable role of Floripas. These

---

Flordespine on that of Floripas in the ubiquitous *Fierabras. Gaufrey,* ed. Guessard and Chabaille, *Les Anciens Poètes de la France.*

34. Keller, "La belle Sarrasine dans *Fierabras* et ses dérivés," 299–307.

include (as we have seen) the characterization of her brother, Fierabras, and the changing illustration of pagan idolatry in the text. The conversions of Fierabras and Floripas are, in a sense, mirror images of one another. While both siblings convert to Christianity, they do so independently: one is persuaded to believe devoutly as the result of a military confrontation visibly influenced by the hand of God, while the other is led to Christianity more pragmatically, as the only means to achieve marriage with the Christian knight she has come to adore. The emotional softness of Fierabras displayed in the closing scenes of the narrative contrasts sharply with the harsh dismissiveness expressed by his sister as they witness the death of their father the sultan. Changes in the depiction of pagan idolatry in *Fierabras* illuminate the figure of Floripas in a different way. Their increasing luxuriousness illustrates a growing interest in the sensuous abundance of the Orient, an interest that extends to the body of the Saracen princess herself. Some fifteenth-century versions of *Fierabras* thus amplify both the opulence of the pagan images and the erotic potential of the scene of Floripas' baptism recounted in the last lines of the narrative. Both the jewel-studded image and the shining white body of Floripas are foci of desire, each of them a bridge between two worlds: the image links the material and the spiritual, while the pagan woman links the Christian and the pagan. Both, however, also entail danger, for the pagan image leads to idolatry, while the pagan woman even after conversion may pollute the Christian world she enters.[35]

The following pages in this chapter illustrate the variable depiction of Floripas using three Continental French versions of the text. One of these, the verse *Fierabras,* represents a very early version of the work, though the earliest manuscript of the complete text dates from the fourteenth century; the other two, selected for the insights they offer into the evolution of the narrative in accord with late medieval reading tastes, include the anonymous prose *Fierabras,* which survives in two early fifteenth-century manuscripts, and the prose version completed in 1478 by Jean Bagnyon.[36] This last version enjoyed immediate popularity, being published in an English version by Caxton

---

35. On the residue of Saracen identity remaining even after the woman's conversion, and the danger it poses, see Kahf, *Western Representations,* 53–54.

36. Quotations from the verse *Fierabras* originally edited by Kroeber and Servois and recently reedited by Marc Le Person are noted in the text as "verse F." followed by line number; those from the anonymous prose version edited by Miquet are noted as "prose F." followed by line number, with paragraph number in parentheses; those from the version edited by Keller are noted as "Bagnyon" followed by page number, along with part and chapter number in parentheses. *Fierabras,* ed. Kroeber and Servois in *Les Anciens Poètes de la France;* re-edited as *Fierabras: Chanson de geste du XIIe siècle* by Person. *Fierabras: Roman en prose de la fin du XIVe siècle,* ed. Miquet. Bagnyon, *Histoire de Charlemagne.*

just seven years later and a Spanish version in 1521.[37] A comparison of the versions reveals great variety with regard to both the depiction of Floripas' body (that is, her status as the passive object of desire) and her depiction as an active subject, who directs the actions of the Christian knights and displays violent aggression. After outlining these variations, I illustrate the alterations in the manifestation of masculine desire for Floripas, giving attention to the ways in which the impurity of the Saracen woman's body is gradually erased in the various texts. The depiction of Floripas' body closely parallels the depiction of the relics stolen by the pagans and eagerly sought by Charlemagne. Like the body of Floripas, the relics are guarded by prohibitions regarding who may touch them and when they may be touched.

In terms of the narrative, the late fifteenth-century version by Bagnyon corresponds closely to the Old French verse text; it differs remarkably, however, in the extent to which Bagnyon lingers on the image of Floripas' body, both in her initial description and in the concluding description of her nude body at the baptismal font. The verse *Fierabras* itself includes an elaborate description of Floripas, her "flesh as tender and white as summer flowers, her face pink as the rose in spring, her tiny mouth, with teeth straight and as white as polished ivory" (car... tenre et blance comme flours en esté, / La face vermellete comme rose de pré, / La bouce petitete, et li dent sont seré, / Ki plus estoient blanc k'ivoire replané [verse F. 2008–11]). Although this long blazon includes a detailed account of Floripas' luxurious and opulent garments, its last lines seem to see right through her clothes: "The young girl was very wise and of great beauty, with small little breasts, a body well made and moulded, hard as little apples, white as flowers in springtime" (Moult estoit la pucele sage et de grant biauté; / Petites mameletes, cor bien fait et molé, / Dures comme pumetes, blankes com flours de pré [2037–39]). Bagnyon amplifies this account even more. His detailed description of her face, body, and clothing concludes by telling how the sight of Floripas would affect any man who saw her: "Floripas was so beautiful that if a person had fasted three or four days and saw this beautiful girl, he would be filled up and sated" (Et estoit Florippes si belle atout ses abillemens que, se une personne eust jeusné trois ou quatre jours sans mengier et il veoit celle belle fille, il estoit remplis et saoullez [Bagnyon 74 (2.2.2)]). Floripas' beauty satisfies physical needs, even hunger, and appeals not just to the sense of sight, but to the sense of smell: "She had such a great sweet smell that it was a marvel; everyone

---

37. [Bagnyon], Caxton, *Hystory and Lyf of the Noble and Chrysten Prynce Charles the Grete*. Nicolas de Piemonte, *Hystoria del Emperador Carlo Magno y de los doze pares de Francia*. Other early editions are cited in de Mandach 178.

marveled at the beauty of this noble girl" (Et avoit si grande oudeur que c'estoit merveille. Pour quoy de la beaulté d'icelle dame pucelle chescun se merveilloit [Bagnyon 74 (2.2.2)]). For Bagnyon, the effect of Floripas' beauty on those who witness it is as significant as that beauty itself.

This is apparent in the scene of Floripas' baptism that comes at the climax of the *Fierabras* narrative, where Bagnyon seizes the opportunity to give a second elaborate anatomy of Floripas, corresponding closely to the initial one. Even in the verse *Fierabras,* the response of the men to Floripas' beauty is emphasized. She disrobes "while all the barons watch" (voiant tout le barné [5999]), and at the sight of her "small breasts" (petites mameletes [6000]), shapely body, and golden hair, nearly all of the barons have their desire stirred, and even Charlemagne himself is moved to smile with pleasure. In Bagnyon's version, however, the description both of Floripas' body and of the response of the men is more elaborate. He adds a detailed anatomy of Floripas which corresponds to that given in her initial description, down to the "two small and round breasts, lifted up on the body like two small mountainettes" (deux mamelles petites et rondettes, / eslevees sur le corps comme deux petites montaignetes): "she was so well made with regard to every part of her body, conveying such beauty and also such amorous pleasure, that she struck the hearts of many with the desire to possess her love, because she was so pleasing and beautiful—especially Charles the emperor, even though he was broken down and old" (Et si bien fut faite a l'aventaige de ses membres, procedans en toute beaulté et pareillement en toute plaisance amoreuse qu'elle frappa le cuer de pluseurs en desir d'avoir son amour, tant estoit plaisant et belle, et par especial Charles l'empereur, combien qu'il fut cassé et ancien [Bagnyon 171 (2.3.15)]). For Bagnyon, the spectacular nature of Floripas is foremost. Even though he preserves the integrity of the romance's narrative, in which Floripas plots, threatens, and even kills, her agency and aggressiveness are overshadowed by the spectacle of her body, which exerts a powerful effect on those who see it.

The anonymous prose *Fierabras* handles the sight of Floripas very differently. In this version, Floripas is made more conventionally feminine: she does not physically attack the jailer or her governess (both of whom she kills in the other versions), nor does she verbally abuse either the Christian knights or her father, the sultan. Yet this feminization of Floripas, interestingly, does not include an increased emphasis on the spectacle of her body. On the contrary, in the anonymous prose *Fierabras,* Floripas is introduced simply as "the most beautiful woman that was in the world at that time, very richly attired" (la plus belle dame qui fust en monde en ce temps, et tante richement ordonnee et vestue [prose F. 743–44 (69)]). The concluding scene of her baptism merely states that she "was the most beautiful creature that any man had ever seen; that day, she was desired by many" (estoit la plus belle creature a regarder que oncques homme e[u]st veue. A ce jour elle fut moult dessiree de plusseurs [3133–34 (287)]). The redactor even adds a detail, unique among the different versions: Floripas' body is not seen by "all the barons," as in the verse *Fierabras* (5999). Instead, Charles "throws out the young men" (fit ouster les jeunes), keeping with him only the two oldest barons; "even though the three were quite old, they smiled and had great pleasure to see her naked, she was so beautiful" (non obstant que lé troit fussent bien vieulx, sy rioient ilz et avoient grant plaisir de la voyr ainxi toute nue, tant estoit belle [prose F. 3136–39 (287)]). Here, the overwhelming effect of the sight of Floripas' body is acknowledged; but while Bagnyon takes this opportunity to indulge in an extended description of the contours of Floripas' body, the writer of the anonymous prose text (as it were) censors the scene, keeping out of the chamber those men who would be most vulnerable to the effect of the spectacle. The magnitude of that effect can be gauged by the reactions of the men who, though old and gray-haired, cannot keep from smiling with pleasure.

The depiction of Floripas as an active subject also varies significantly in the various versions. The anonymous prose *Fierabras* presents a neutralized Floripas: in the other versions of the text, Floripas initially saves the Christian knights by striking their jailer with a club so hard that "his eyes flew out of his head, and he fell dead at her feet" (les ex li fist de la teste voler; / Devant lui à ses piés le fist mort craventer [verse F. 2090–91]). In the anonymous prose version, however, she merely asks her seneschal to "punish [the jailer] right away so that he will be an example to others" (l'en pugnissez presentement et tellement que ce soit exemple es autres [prose F. 732–33 (68)]). In a subsequent episode, both in the verse text and in Bagnyon's prose, when Floripas' governess threatens to reveal that the princess is hiding the Christian knights from her father, Floripas lures the governess to the window and pushes her out; the author of the anonymous prose version simply omits the episode entirely. Again, when the Christian knight Guy is initially reluctant to reciprocate Floripas' love, Floripas "swears by Muhammad, 'If you don't take me, I will have you all hanged and left to blow in the wind'" (jure Mahomet: "Se vois ne me prenés, / Je vous ferai tous pendre et au vent encruer" [verse F. 2812–13]).[38] In the anonymous prose version, on the other hand, Guy responds to Floripas' avowal of love by saying, "Madame, I am entirely yours, you can know that for certain" (Madame, et je suis tout voustre, tenez vous en sceure [prose F. 1026 (91)]). While in the verse text and Bagnyon's prose, Guy has to be forced by his companions to accept Floripas, in the anonymous prose text the knights all desire Floripas, and all envy Guy. Roland states, "Now I see very well, Guy, that he who is good-looking is not poor: because of your beauty and your youth, you are the best beloved, and you should praise God, because you have got a beautiful woman" (Or voi je bien,...Guy, qu'il n'est pas pauvre qui est bel; pour voustre beaulté et voustre jeunesse este le mielx amé et vous devez bien louer Dieu, car vous avez belle dame). Duke Naymes adds, "She is the most beautiful one I have ever seen. Whoever could sleep with her for a single night would never need any other paradise" (C'est la plus belle que je veisse oncques mes. Qui pourroit coucher une seulle nuyt avecques elle, il ne luy fauldroit james aultre paradis [prose F. 1028–34 (92)]). Throughout the anonymous prose *Fierabras,* Floripas is presented as a model of feminine deportment: restrained, demure, and courteous. Nonetheless, her physical allure remains: to partake in the joys of her body is to inhabit paradise.

Yet while the anonymous prose *Fierabras* stands apart from the other two versions in its normative treatment of women's deportment, it shares with Bagnyon's prose text a tendency to generalize about women's behavior based on the behavior of Floripas. This can be seen in two episodes in which one of the sultan's councilors advises him not to trust his daughter, based on the fact that the nature of woman is essentially changeable. In the verse *Fierabras,* the councilor simply asks, "Sire, now I see you're crazy. Do you want to test the heart of a woman?" ("Sire...or vois voi assoté; / Veus tu donc cuer de fame essaier n'esprouver?" [verse F. 2733–34]). In both later prose versions, however, this moment serves as the springboard for misogynistic generalizations. In the anonymous prose text, the councilor states, "Sire, you are unwise to believe your daughter. You know that the heart of a woman is easily changed and, by my faith, if you trust her with [the prisoners], you will repent of it. And you should believe that a man who puts his trust in a woman is out of his mind or mad—I know this very well because of my own [wife], who has made a fool of me many times" (Sire, vous n'estes pas sage de croire vostre fille. Vous savez que cueur de fame est toust changé et par ma foy, si vous les ly baillés, vous vous en repentirez. Et croiez que homme qui se fie en famme est hors du sens ou enragez, je le sçay bien pour la moye, qui maintez foiz m'a moqué [prose F. 969–73 (87)]). Similarly, in Bagnyon's text, the councilor states, "Sire, it is not appropriate that you should rely on a woman in this matter, because of their mutability. You have heard many examples illustrating this, and know the truth about how many men have been deceived by

women" (Sire admiral, ce n'est chose convenable que sur ce fait vous doyés
fier en femme a cause de leur mutabilité. Et vous en avez beaucoup ouÿ dire
d'exemples et congneu la verité comme pluseurs ont estés deceuz par femmes
[Bagnyon 93 (2.2.8)]).

In each of the prose texts, outside experience—whether the personal experience of the councilor or the examples written down in "books of wicked
women"—is used to support the claim that Floripas, like all women, is at
best changeable and at worst a liar. The mutability of women is the central
theme of several misogynistic *dits* produced in the fourteenth century: as "La
Contenance des fames" puts it, "A woman's heart is mutable.... A woman's
heart is just not able / To chart a course that's firm or stable" (Moult a feme
le cuer muable.... Feme a un cuer par heritage / Qui ne puet estre en un
estage [Fiero *et al.* 1989, lines 20, 27–28]). The appearance of misogynistic
truisms in the two later prose versions of *Fierabras* marks a dramatic shift
from the earlier verse text, in which Floripas' deceit and erratic behavior were
evidently motivated by her pagan identity; the two later prose versions, even
though they differ from one another in many respects, share the tendency
to interpret Floripas' behavior as stereotypically feminine.[39] The anonymous
prose *Fierabras* even includes additional reminders designed to remind the
reader of women's "true" nature. For example, after the sultan has become
aware of his daughter's disloyalty, his councilor states, "Sire, we told you before that you did not do well to give [the knights] to your daughter to guard;
a wise man never trusts in a woman, because she is too mutable!" (Sire, nous
vous disoions bien que vous fasoiez que foul de les bailler a voustre fille en
garde; onc sage homme ne se fia en fame, car elle est trop muable [prose F.
1196–99 (110)]).

The allusions to misogynistic tradition found in both prose versions of
Fierabras are significant not just because they illustrate the extent to which
the story of Floripas came to be assimilated to prescriptive norms of women's
behavior, but also because they highlight the paradox at the center of her
depiction. What precisely is Floripas? Is she pagan or Christian? Is she a
passive object of desire or an aggressive agent? Is she feminine or is she masculine? In his prose adaptation, Bagnyon highlights this split at the center of
Floripas' character, formulating it in terms of Floripas' gender identity. He
interjects the following comment immediately after Floripas avows her love

---

39. As Kay observes, actions that a modern reader reflexively interprets as masculine may have
quite a different value in a medieval text: "The *chansons de geste* are less committed to a categorical
view of gender than their critics. On the one hand they can take sexual difference as fundamental; on
the other, they may subordinate it to the category of the person" (*Chansons,* 35).

for Guy: "All in all, considering the whole of this chapter, there is a great work contained within it: for at the beginning, Floripas the courteous, who was pagan, had the desire to speak with the Frenchmen, and this touches very well on the desire of women to always know new things. But that part which touches on the work that she did against the jailer at the prison, and how [the knights] were brought out of there, that was the very capable work of a man" (Touteffois, bien consideré cestuy chappitre, grande euvre y fut comprise, quant premierement Florippes la courtoyse, qui estoit payenne, eut le desir de parler és Françoys, et cecy touche bien la voulenté des femmes pour sçavoir nouveaulx. Mais tant qu'il tousche l'euvre qu'elle fit contre le maistre et garde de la prison et comment ilz furent mis dehors, ce fut euvre d'omme bien approuv[é]e [Bagnyon 79 (2.2.3)]). The author of the prose text simply erases this paradox, omitting the "capable work of a man" within Floripas, while continuing to interpret her behavior as stereotypically feminine. Bagnyon, conversely, emphasizes the contradiction, heightening it by providing elaborate, erotic portraits of Floripas that awaken the desire of the Christian men who see her.

Carnal desire for Floripas is central to all three versions of *Fierabras* discussed here. They differ, however, with regard to how that desire is constituted, and the freedom with which it is expressed. In all three versions, a pivotal scene takes place in which an evil enchanter is sent out at night by the sultan to steal from Floripas the *ceinture* or magical belt that keeps hunger away from those who touch it. By having it stolen, the sultan hopes to force the Christian knights out of the tower they have been occupying. Once in Floripas' chamber, however, the enchanter is overcome by the sight of her naked body: "He came to the bed of Floripas and searched until he found the belt, and wrapped it around himself. Having done that, he looked at the girl, all naked, who was so white and pretty, and became inclined to sleep with her, so that he began to embrace her thighs, all naked" (Et puis vint au lit de Florippes et sercha secretement tant qu'il trouva la centure, et la ceint autour de luy. Cecy estre fait, il regarde la fille toute nue, qui estoit moult blanche et belle, et fut incliné a dormir avec elle, tellement qu'il la va accoller toute nue par les flancs [Bagnyon 102 (2.2.10)]). She wakes up and screams; this awakens Guy, who rushes in and kills the thief. In this episode, the beauty of Floripas' body awakens the desire of the man who sees it, just as in the baptism scene described above; yet it also awakens the desire of the man who intervenes, that is, Guy. It is necessary to recall that until this point in the narrative, in both the verse *Fierabras* and Bagnyon's text, Guy has accepted Floripas' love reluctantly and only because Roland has commanded it. This scene, then, marks the first time that Guy responds to Floripas and acts on her behalf. Bagnyon's version of this scene differs subtly from the verse *Fierabras* with regard to both the basis of the thief's desire for Floripas' body and the basis of Guy's newly awakened desire. In the earlier version, the thief "looks at Floripas, who was so beautifully colored" (Floripas resgarda, qui tant fu coulourée [verse F. 3078]), while in Bagnyon's version, her nude body is "white and beautiful" (moult blanche et belle [102 (2.2.10)]). Her body contrasts dramatically with that of the thief, who is (in the words of the verse *Fierabras*) "more black than a peppercorn" (plus noir d'une pevrée [3085]); in Bagnyon's words, "black as a Moor" (ainssy noir comme meure [102 (2.2.10)]).[40] His blackness makes her look more white; that is, both more beautiful and less alien. In both versions, but more emphatically in Bagnyon's text, the desire of the black pagan man for the white pagan woman awakens the desire of the white Christian man.

This scene is pivotal because it marks a shift in Floripas' status, making her more accessible to the Christian knights, less clearly marked off as alien. Her initially forbidden status is evident in her early encounters with the knights. When she first discovers Guy, for whom she has long cherished a passion, "she did not dare to kiss him on the mouth, because she was a pagan and he was a Christian" (en la bouce ne l'osa adeser, / Pour ce k'ele est paiene, il est crestiennés [2822–23]). Here, their mutual difference causes the prohibition on physical contact. In the later text, her status alone is the cause: "she did not dare to kiss him on the mouth, nor on the cheeks or chin, because she was a pagan" (ne l'ose baisier en la bouche sy non és joues et out menton pour la cause qu'elle estoit payenne [Bagnyon 96 (2.2.8)]). Even though the pleasures of Floripas' body are forbidden, she does possess something precious that the knights can kiss freely. Both texts immediately go on to describe how (in the words of Bagnyon) "Floripas joyfully and because of great love brought out a chest and opened it before the barons, and displayed a beautiful silk drapery, and then unwrapped the relics... and said to Roland, 'Look at the treasure which you have so much desired.' When the French came before the relics, they cried tenderly with joy, and then one after the other came and kissed them, on their knees" (Florippes joyeusement et par grant amour s'en vint un

---

40. "Meure" literally means "blackberry"; by the fourteenth century, however, wordplay on "meure" and "more" was very common. See, for example, usages of the expression, "noirs come mores mëures" (black as blackberry-dyed Moors) cited in the *Tobler-Lommatzsch Altfranzösisches Wörterbuch,* 11 vols. (Wiesbaden: Franz Steiner, 1925–89), vol. 6, p. 267, s.v. "more, meure." The pun appears to be based on the same logic displayed in Brunetto Latini's explanation of the origin of the name Ethiopia: "Ethiopia... where the people are black as blackberries [*meure*], and this is why they are called 'Moors'" (Etyope... ou sont les gens noires come meure, et por ce sont il apelé mors [Latini, 120; book 1, chap. 124]).

ung escrin et l'a ouvert devant les barons et fait estendre ung beau drap de soye, puis desvelloppe les reliques. . . . Et puis dist a Roland: "Veez cy le tresor que vous avés tant desiré." Quant les François furent ainssy devant les reliques, de joye ilz vont tous plourer moult tendrement, et l'un après l'autre les vont baiser a genoulx moult humblement (Bagnyon 96 (2.2.8)]). The kisses that cannot be received by Floripas' body, because she is still marked off as pagan and therefore forbidden, can instead be received by the relics that are in her possession, wrapped in the same luxurious silks that the princess herself wears.[41] The desire for Floripas' body is thus deflected onto the relics.

In the anonymous prose *Fierabras,* this scene is simply omitted; it is not necessary, because Floripas' body is not forbidden. On the contrary, Floripas freely kisses Roland himself on the lips and goes on to say to Guy, "You can kiss me if you wish. You will never have any sin from it, because I shall believe in God; because of my love for you I will be a Christian. . . . For God's sake, my love, kiss me, for no woman was ever more joyous than I am at your arrival" (Si vous plaist, vous me baiserez. Ja vous n'y aurez pechié, car je croyroy en Dieu; pour l'amour de vous je seray crestienne. . . . Pour Dieu, mon amy, baisez moi, car oncques fame ne fut joyeuse que je suys de voustre venue [prose F. 1013–15, 1024–25 (91)]). Conversely, in the verse *Fierabras* and in Bagnyon's text, Floripas' body only gradually becomes licit. With the attack of the enchanter, Floripas becomes more appealing to the Christian knight Guy, so that he comes to kiss her "most amorously" (moult amoureusement [Bagnyon 120 (2.2.16)]). With her subsequent second display of the relics of the Passion, which takes place on the battlements of the castle, Floripas moves still farther away from her earlier state of impurity. When the Christian knights become demoralized by the prospect of defeat in battle, Floripas restores their spirits by promising to bring out the "relics which you've desired so much" (reliques c'avés tant desiré [verse F. 5222]). She touches the relics both when she removes them from their casket and when she returns them, in Bagnyon's words, "reverently" (reveramment [156 (2.3.10)]). Only with her baptism at the climax of the narrative, however, does Floripas become wholly accessible. By becoming spiritually "clean," dipped in the purifying waters of the baptismal font, the Saracen princess at last ceases to be a potential source of pollution to the Christian knights.

Significantly, even as she becomes available to the Christian men upon exiting her former liminal state (neither wholly Christian nor wholly Saracen), Floripas comes to be affected by conventional prohibitions on women's

---

41. Floripas is wrapped in "paile galacien" (verse F. 2016), as are the relics (5243). On silk as an Oriental luxury commodity, see Burns, *Courtly Love Undressed;* Kinoshita, "Almería Silk," 165–76.

behavior. In both the prose *Fierabras* and Bagnyon's text, Floripas does not touch the relics she presents to Charlemagne after her baptism, even though she had earlier handled them freely. Instead, the archbishop is summoned to unwrap and display the relics (Bagnyon 172 [2.3.16]; prose F. 3196–3203 [293]). This marks a significant change from the verse text, in which Floripas continues to be able to touch the relics even after her full assimilation into the Christian community (verse F. 6048–57). This change may indicate the extent to which gender roles dictate the norms of feminine behavior in the late medieval texts, in contradistinction to the earlier verse *Fierabras;* alternatively, it may reflect prohibitions on laypeople touching sacred objects. Similar reinforcement of religious orthodoxy can be found in the digressions on the right use of images in worship found elsewhere in Bagnyon's text (153 [2.3.9]; 168–69 [2.3.15]).

To summarize, then, the three French versions of *Fierabras* described here make very different use of Floripas in her role as mediator between Christian and Saracen worlds. The earliest version, the verse *Fierabras,* presents a Floripas who must be understood within the terms of the ideology of crusade. Like Orable/Guiborc in the Guillaume d'Orange cycle, she is moved by love to betray not only her countrymen but her family.[42] Her desire for the Christian man magnifies his image, revealing how potent and desirable he himself is, and the righteousness of his cause. Her beautiful exterior belies the irascible, naturally "Saracen" impulses that lie beneath, impulses that lead her to threaten, lie, and kill. Gradually, however, Floripas' Saracen impulses are tamed: the two murders take place very early in her encounters with the Christian knights, and after her initial threat to "hang them all" if Guy does not reciprocate her love, Floripas confines her insults to her Saracen father and his henchmen. Correspondingly, Floripas' body, initially untouchable due to her pagan identity, becomes an appropriate object of desire, even (in the final scene) to the emperor Charles himself. Like the relics of the Passion, like Jerusalem itself, Floripas is a beautiful prize that—in keeping with the ideology of crusade—is rightfully reclaimed from the dirty hands of the Saracens.[43]

The anonymous prose *Fierabras* is quite another matter. Here, Floripas' paradoxical nature is erased, and she behaves according to the finest standards

---

42. On Guiborc's behavior, see Joan M. Ferrante's Introduction to her translation *Guillaume d'Orange: Four Twelfth-Century Epics,* 1–61, esp. 43–44. On the interrelated development of the characters of Floripas and Guiborc, see Bennett, "Storming of the Other World," 1–14.

43. On the rhetoric of pollution in crusade documents, see Cole, "Religious Pollution," 84–111. See also the discussion of the rhetoric of pollution in connection with Islamic "idolatry" in chapter 5 of this book.

of women's behavior. The death of the jailer is not even explicitly ordered by Floripas, much less committed, and the murder of the governess is omitted entirely. She never threatens the Christian knights, because such rebuke is unnecessary: her kisses are accepted by Guy from the outset, eliciting the envy of the other Christian knights who adore her as well. A particularly striking contrast can be seen in Bagnyon's rendition of the scene in which the sultan's councilor reminds him how foolish it is to trust women. Floripas exclaims: "Son of a whore! Disloyal traitor! Liar! If I didn't think I would be blamed for doing it, I would give you such a blow from my fist on the nose that the blood would flow right down to your mouth" (Filz de putain! Traitre desloial! Parjure! Se je ne penssoye plus oultre estre blasmee de moy prandre a toy, je te donneroye tel coup sur le vaisaige que le sang aval en viendroit habondamment [Bagnyon 93 (2.2.8)]). The anonymous prose text, however, simply relates that, "when Floripas heard Bruillant speak this way, she was filled with contempt, even though she didn't let it appear, and begged God to make him pay for it later" (quant Floripez ouÿt Bruillant ainsi parler, elle en eut grant despit en son cueur, combien qu'elle n'en fist nul semblant et jura Dieu qu'il ly en souviendroit [prose F. 978–80 (88)]). Similarly, when a second councilor of the sultan comes to Floripas' chamber to investigate the presence of the knights, and is attacked by one of them, Floripas responds with enthusiasm. When the Saracen lands in the fireplace, Floripas says, "Sire, now let him cook! He loves the fire, he doesn't care to lift himself up" (Sire . . . or le laisiés caufer; / Moult aime le foier, il n'a soing de lever [verse F. 2941–42]). In the anonymous prose text, she simply thanks the knight, saying "you've given me a very great pleasure" (vous m'avez fait un tres grant plaisir [1128 (102)]), and comes over to kiss and embrace him.

The Floripas of the anonymous prose *Fierabras* is an exemplary woman, given to devout expressions, displaying modesty and restraint. In the scene where she is attacked by the thief, for example, the writer of the anonymous prose text specifies that she was "all covered up" (couchee toute vestue [1254 (115)]) as she lay on the bed. Perhaps the most dramatic illustration of how neutralized Floripas is, in the anonymous prose version, appears in the closing baptismal scene, when her father has just refused to be christened (and just before Floripas herself disrobes). Floripas' brother is moved and appeals to their father to convert; not so Floripas. In the verse text, she turns to the emperor and says "Charles! Why are you waiting? This is a living devil; why don't you kill him? I don't care if he dies, as long as you give me Guy. I won't cry much for him, if I have my way about it" (Karles, que demourés? Ce est .I. vis diables; pou coi ne l'ociés? / Moi ne caut se il meurt, mais que Gui me donnés; / Je ne plourai moult peu, se j'ai mes volentés [5955–58]). In

Bagnyon's prose, Floripas is only slightly more polite: "Sire emperor, why do you wait so long to have this disloyal devil put to death? It doesn't disturb me if he dies, as long as Guy of Burgundy be my spouse" (Sire empereur, pour quoy mettés vous tant a fayre mourir celluy deable tant desloyal? Il ne m'en chault s'il meurt, seullement que Guy de Bourgoigne soit mon espoux [169 (2.3.15)]). In the anonymous prose text, however, Floripas falls to her knees to intercede alongside her brother: "My lord and father, for God's sake, have pity on yourself and don't make yourself die because of your folly; for God's sake, do the pleasure of King Charlemagne" (Monseigneur mon pere, pour Dieu, aiez pitié de vous et ne vous faictez pas mourir par voustre follie; pour Dieu, faictez le plaisir au roy Charlemaigne [3091–93 (283)]).[44] Here, Floripas is a dutiful daughter and a dutiful subject, appealing humbly to her father to submit himself to the will of their common ruler, which is (in turn) the will of God. While little is known about the circumstances under which the anonymous prose *Fierabras* was commissioned, it is tempting to speculate that it may have been intended for women readers, as a romance narrative with didactic intent embedded both in the misogynistic allusions to women's "true" nature, and the exemplary submissiveness of Floripas.[45]

The prose text of Bagnyon closely follows its verse model with regard to the progress of the narrative. Unlike the verse *Fierabras*, however, Bagnyon's text no longer partakes fully in the ideology of crusade that governs the role of Floripas in the earlier work. Instead, the rhetoric of the misogynistic texts popular in the fourteenth and fifteenth centuries is brought to bear, explicating the capricious and unrestrained behavior of Floripas in terms of woman's essential nature, rather than in terms of Saracen identity. The spectacle of the woman's body, in Bagnyon's text, is accentuated dramatically, highlighting both the appeal of the desired object and its effect on those who look at it: it fills them up. Recall how, in his opening description of Floripas, Bagnyon inserts a curious phrase into the blazon: "if a person had fasted three or four days, without eating, and he saw this beautiful girl, he would be filled up and sated." This notion of fullness produced through the sight of the woman's body reappears in the scene where the thief pauses in the act of stealing the magical belt, arrested by the sight of Floripas. Like the belt itself, which takes

---

44. The Provençal version of *Fierabras* also includes this variation; see Bekker, "Der Roman vom Fierabras provenzalisch," 111ff. Floripas also intervenes in the Anglo-Norman *Fierabras* (ed. Brandin, lines 1704–07), but Ailes argues persuasively that this is due to the scribe's misreading of the abbreviation "F" in his exemplar (Ailes, "Comparative Study," 46–47).

45. For an overview of women readers of vernacular romances, see Krueger, *Woman Readers,* 17–30. On women as readers and patrons, see also Ferrante, *To the Glory of Her Sex;* McCash, *Cultural Patronage of Medieval Women.*

away the hunger of those who touch it, the sight of Floripas fills up the man who looks at her, paradoxically both satisfying and awakening the hunger for more. This satisfaction and fullness is experienced once again in the closing scene of baptism, quoted above: "she was so well made with regard to every part of her body, conveying such beauty and also such amorous pleasure, that she struck the hearts of many with the desire to possess her love" (Bagnyon 171 [2.3.15]). At this moment, Floripas is the passive and delightful object of desire, a beautiful package of Oriental abundance, sensuous pleasures, and wealth.

Sarah Kay suggests that women, in the *chansons de geste,* function as a kind of "colle sexuelle," a sexual glue that brings men together into various kinds of relationships.[46] In the romance of *Fierabras,* Floripas does indeed bring men together, not just across the boundary separating Saracen from Christian but within the Christian community itself, as they bask in the sight of her beautiful body. Her essential nature, however, is defined very differently in the various versions. In the verse *Fierabras,* her verbal aggression and physical violence are attributed not to her feminine nature but to her eastern origins. In the late medieval prose versions, however, her feminine nature, mutable and unstable, is repeatedly identified as her dominant quality. When Bagnyon states that her "capable work" is that of a "man," he implies that Floripas is a kind of virago, an unnatural woman who exists at the very border of gender norms. The open display of her nude body at the baptismal font and her subsequent surrender of the relics to Charlemagne mark her full entry into the sphere of normative patriarchal culture—reached, paradoxically, through the repudiation of her "natural" filial obligations to her Saracen father. The multiple redactions of *Fierabras* are striking testimony to the flexibility of the narrative in which Floripas plays such a crucial role: one can readily imagine how her position within the ideology of crusade, found in the early *chansons de geste,* could be adapted for use within the ideology of conquest in the versions of the romance propagated in Central and South America as described by de Mandach.

The narrative of *Fierabras,* throughout its many textual "isotopes," is unique in that it anatomizes a paired model of conversion that features both male and female Saracens, that is, Fierabras and his sister Floripas. In comparable texts that feature Saracen conversion, such as the poems of the Guillaume d'Orange cycle, only female conversion is highlighted, in the figure of Orable, who converts out of love for Guillaume and takes the name "Guiborc." A rather special case of female conversion appears in the *Chanson de Roland,* where the Saracen queen also converts out of love ("pur amur"); in the case of

---

46. Kay, "La représentation de la fémininité dans les chansons de geste," 223–40; quotation from 223.

Bramimonde, however, her love is said to be devoted to God rather than to a Christian knight. The affirmation of the rightful focus of love on the divine rather than on the human being found in the Oxford *Roland* is typical of the devotional focus common to Anglo-Norman *chansons de geste* and romances; it is significant that other versions of the *Roland* are less emphatic in their description of Bramimonde's devotion.[47]

In the double narrative of conversion featured in *Fierabras,* the female convert continues to inhabit a special role, for it is through Floripas that cultural assimilation takes place by means of the production of a lineage, offspring who (half-Saracen and half-Frankish) will rule the territories formerly under the sway of the Sultan Laban. While the giant twins "Roland" and "Oliver," like their fellow convert Fierabras, are fated to produce no line of descent, Floripas' offspring, fathered by her beloved Guy of Boulogne, will command the now-Christian lands of Spain. In taking his leave of Floripas, Charlemagne makes this explicit: "'Fair One,' so said the king, 'I have crowned you and you have been, thank God, baptized and raised up; I have married you to the best knight to be found as far as the land of Africa, beyond the salt sea, and he and Fierabras now hold this land'" (Bele, ce dist li rois, je vous ai couronnee, / Si estes, Dieu merci, bautizie et levee; / Au milleur chevalier estes vous espousee / Ki soit jusques Aufrique, outre la mer salee. / Et il et Fierabras tenront mais la contree [Verse F. 6225–29]). Since Fierabras is said explicitly to take up a life of monastic devotion (1944–49), the ruling lineage of Christian Spain can arise only from the union of Floripas and Guy. The case of Floripas illustrates how, in medieval narratives of Muslim-Christian interaction, the Saracen woman is the conduit through whom that interaction is realized. Through the fulfillment of Floripas' desire for the Christian knight Guy, the Saracen world is at once conquered (through military defeat) and assimilated (through the lineage produced by Floripas and Guy). She is both the frontier of cultural conflict and the fertile ground that gives rise to a Christian Self that incorporates the Muslim Other.

↞ The Hybrid

The offspring of Floripas and Guy remain merely hypothetical in the closing lines of *Fierabras.* Other medieval texts, however, imagine what the progeny

---

47. Of the growing literature on the place of romance within Anglo-Norman devotional literature, see Wogan-Browne, "'Our Steward, St Jerome'"; Watson and Wogan-Browne, "French of England," 31–58. For comparison of Bramimonde's conversion, see other French versions of the *Roland,* edited by Duggan in *La Chanson de Roland / The Song of Roland.*

of the union of Christian and Saracen might look like, and how such off-spring might be properly assimilated within the Christian community: these include the Middle English *King of Tars* and the Middle High German *Parzival* of Wolfram von Eschenbach. The *King of Tars,* a late thirteenth-century Middle English romance that survives in two fourteenth-century manuscripts, relates the story of the union of a Christian princess, daughter of the King of Tars, and the Saracen Sultan of Damascus.[48] The Christian princess, who remains unnamed throughout the narrative, is repeatedly said to be "white as fether of swan" (12); her mate, the Sultan of Damascus, who also remains unnamed (at least up until his eventual baptism), is correspondingly identified as "blac and lothely" (928). The Princess' physical whiteness mirrors her spiritual purity, which is amply demonstrated in the humility with which she willingly offers herself in marriage in order to bring about peace between her own people and the forces of the Sultan of Damascus. By the end of the poem, predictably, the Sultan has been persuaded to accept baptism: "The soudan, with gode wille anon, / Dede of his clothes euerichon / To reseyue his baptize" (922–24). The priest, Cleophas, christens the Sultan with his "owhen name" (927). The Sultan's willing acceptance of baptism causes an extraordinary miracle: "His hide, that blac and lothely was, / Al white bicom, thurth Godes gras, / and clere withouten blame. / And when the soudan seye that sight / than leved he wele on God almight" (928–32). The miracle is not the cause of the Sultan's conversion, but rather the confirmation of its efficacy. "That sight"—that is, the sight of the Sultan's own newly whitened flesh—strengthens his belief and affirms the "gode wille" that initially impelled his conversion. The Sultan's renaming is concomitant with the transformation: his soul is converted from false belief to true belief (in Christ), a change that is mirrored in the physical metamorphosis his body undergoes.

On one level, this moment fits in very well with the "Manichean allegory" that is sometimes applied to depictions of bodily diversity in medieval texts: white and black correspond clearly to the dichotomy of good and bad, Christian and Saracen. On another level, however, this text engages with contemporary discourse regarding the nature of skin color, and the ways that geographical origin dictates its nature and even its potential for change. Here, the bodily diversity that arises from geographical distance appears in the white body of the Christian princess and the black body of the Saracen sultan. Bodily diversity seamlessly reflects religious orientation, so that the

---

48. On the manuscripts and sources, see Judith Perryman's introduction to her edition of *The King of Tars*. Quotations from *The King of Tars* are cited in the text by line number.

sultan's corporeal metamorphosis is the inevitable by-product of his spiritual conversion: formerly "blac & lothely," his flesh becomes "al white" (928–29) following his immersion in the baptismal font. The seemingly unproblematic alignment of bodily diversity and religious orientation that appears in the case of the Sultan's conversion, however, is called into question by the other scene of baptism staged in the *King of Tars:* that of the infant born to the Sultan and his Christian spouse.

The union of Saracen and Christian results in the birth of a "flesche," a shapeless lump without life or form: "lim no hadde it non. / Bot as a rond of flesche yschore / In chaumber it lay hem bifore / Withouten blod and bon" (579–81). The "sorwe" of the "sori" attendants (583, 578) is interwoven with a protracted description of the inert "flesche," which has "noither nose no eye, / Bot lay ded as the ston" (584–85). After its baptism, however, the "flesche" is transformed into a "wele schapen" child, with "liif & lim & fas" (783, 776). The princess has brought to her a Christian priest whom she has found in her husband's prison, and begs him to do for her "a wel gret priuete" (747):

> Her is a child selcouthe discriif.
> It hath noither lim, no liif,
> No eyghen forto se.
> Hali water thou most make,
> and this ich flesche thou take,
> Al for the loue of me.
> And cristen it, withouten blame,
> In the worthschipe of the Faders name,
> That sitt in Trinitee.
>
> (748–56)

The "soudans wiif" (745) knows very well what this baptism will accomplish, affirming that "Yif it were cristned aright / It schuld haue fourme to se bi sight / With lim and liif to wake" (760–62). The priest "toke the flesche anon," and, giving the "flesche" the "name of Ion [John]" after the Baptist, patron saint of that day, baptizes it. A miracle occurs: after baptism, the "It hadde liif and lim and fas, / and crid with gret deray. / And hadde hide and flesche and fel" (776–78). As Jane Gilbert points out, what the child lacks, and subsequently acquires at the time of baptism, is form.[49] While medieval physicians

---

49. Gilbert, "Putting the Pulp into Fiction," 102–23, esp. 105–06. See also the perceptive readings of *The King of Tars* in Lampert, "Race, Periodicity, and the (Neo-) Middle Ages," 391–421, esp. 405–09; and Calkin, "Marking Religion on the Body," 219–38.

and scientific writers usually invoked Galenic theory in their accounts of conception, the Aristotelian theory—where the father's seed imposes form on the shapeless matter provided by the mother—was more commonly drawn upon in literary texts. The *King of Tars* is no exception, for the hybrid child is precisely the failure, in Aristotelian terms, of conception. The birth results only in unformed matter, because it lacks the necessary masculine imprint owing to the spiritual defects of the father. In other words, the father's spiritual incompleteness manifests itself on the level of the child's body, in his inability to provide form that can be imposed on the matter provided by the body of the Christian princess. The subsequent baptism confers on the child not just spiritual renewal but also bodily conception, as the matter provided by the mother is—at last—imprinted with the necessary form. The perfection of the form provided is attested by the male sex of the child.[50]

In the *King of Tars,* then, as in *Fierabras,* conversion entails bodily change. While that change is made dramatically visible in the *King of Tars,* in *Fierabras* the change is more subtle, perceptible not through physical appearance but through changes in bodily physiology. The scene of conversion, whether that of Floripas or Fierabras, or that of the black Sultan or his formless offspring, is a pivotal scene of spectacle within the romance. At the moment of immersion, the deviant body is assimilated to the physical and spiritual norm, where it has a white body and a Christian soul. In baptism, spiritual orientation and bodily origin come to a point of intersection, where corporeal transformation is simultaneous with the reorientation of spiritual devotion. Conversion (literally, turning toward God) entails metamorphosis, in which bodily change is necessarily concomitant with spiritual change. It is precisely this moment when Saracen identity—an identity that, it must be recalled, is always defined in terms of both religious affiliation and ethnicity—is transmuted.

The themes of spiritual conversion and bodily metamorphosis appearing in texts such as *Fierabras* and the *King of Tars* can be productively examined in the light of a third medieval literary text, the Middle High German romance of *Parzival,* composed by Wolfram von Eschenbach in the first decade of the thirteenth century. Like *Fierabras* and related romances and *chansons de geste* that feature the clash of Saracen and Christian armies, *Parzival* includes a striking scene of combat between a Christian knight and his

---

50. Baptism is often described in terms of birth in medieval texts, based on scriptural sources such as John 3:5: "Unless a man be born again of water and the Holy Ghost, he cannot enter into the kingdom of God." Cf. John 1:12–13; Titus 3:3–7. On baptism as birth, see Neunheuser, *Baptism and Confirmation,* 31–37, 78–80; Bedard, *Symbolism of the Baptismal Font,* 17–36. For an interesting twelfth-century iconographic representation of baptism as birth on a font, see Patton, "'Ex partu fontis exceptum,'" 79–92.

"heathen" counterpart. Like the battle of Oliver and Fierabras, the battle of Parzival and Feirefiz ends in peaceful reconciliation and, ultimately, the baptism of the Saracen knight. Unlike Oliver and Fierabras, however, Parzival and Feirefiz turn out to be parts of a single whole, "both but one person" (bêde niht wan ein [740.28]),[51] brothers begotten by a single father. Like the giant twins of *Fierabras,* Parzival and Feirefiz represent the military potential and regenerative capacity of the Christian assimilation of Saracen might; unlike the twins, however, this pair of brothers go on to reap victories at once military and spiritual. The lineage produced by the Saracen Feirefiz, after he is spiritually cleansed by baptism and united with the Grail maiden in marriage, gives rise to Prester John, the imagined Oriental savior of Christendom (822.21–30).

Like *The Book of John Mandeville,* Wolfram's *Parzival* is often characterized as a remarkable, exemplary narrative of medieval tolerance and cultural understanding.[52] While it is undeniable that these two literary works stand apart from the great majority of medieval writings in their generous view of cultural and religious alterity, it is necessary to survey the macrocosmic, encyclopedic nature of their enterprise in order to understand what role Saracen alterity plays within it. The Middle High German *Parzival* is based upon the Old French *Perceval* of Chrétien de Troyes, which provides the greater part of the narrative material related in the middle twelve books of Wolfram's poem (books 3–14). The first two and last two books, however, are independently conceived, and form a kind of frame narrative to the Grail quest narrated in the central poem. These four books are the cosmographical matrix in which the Perceval-story is embedded, and in which the quest of Parzival appears at once as personal journey and universal history.[53] In terms of this universalizing tendency, Wolfram's *Parzival* can productively be read in the light of a range of other twelfth-century encyclopedic texts, including the Alexander romances, Lambert of St. Omer's *Liber Floridus,* and the legends of Prester John discussed above in chapter 2.[54] The apostolic mission of

---

51. Quotations from *Parzival* are cited by section and line number within the text and are taken from Wolfram von Eschenbach, *Parzival,* ed. Lachmann; Wolfram von Eschenbach, *Parzival with Titurel and the Love-Lyrics.* I have occasionally altered Edwards' translation in order to render the text more literally.

52. On racial tolerance in *Parzival,* see Frakes, "Race, Representation, and Metamorphosis," 119–33.

53. On the "Oriental" background to *Parzival,* especially prominent in the first book of the poem, see Groos, "Orientalizing the Medieval Orient," 61–86; Noltze, *Gahmurets Orientfahrt.*

54. On the integration of Alexander source-texts with the narrative of *Parzival* in the late thirteenth-century Alexander romance of Ulrich von Etzenbach (which recounts Alexander's travels through the land of Parzival's mother, Belacane), see Stock, "Vielfache Erinnerung," 407–48, and "Alexander in der Echokammer," 113–33.

Pentecost narrated in the book of Acts, when the apostles were sent out to the four corners of the earth to convert the peoples of the world to Christianity, finds its counterpart in the journey back to the spiritual center enacted by the Saracen brother of Perceval. Like the three Magi, Feirefiz emblematizes the Christian fantasy of the peoples of the world journeying westward to bear tribute to their rightful ruler, the figure identified in *Parzival* as "the highest hand" (die hoehsten hant [13.13; cf. 744.23]) whose guidance many knights, both Christian and Saracen, seek endlessly.

Feirefiz is the hybrid product of the union of a Christian father, Gahmuret of Anjou, and Belacane, the black-skinned queen of Zazamanc, whom he meets when he is in the service of the "Baruc," ruler of Baghdad. Belacane's skin is "nâch swarzer varwe" (black in color [24.11]), contrasting with the "light color" (liehte varwe [29.3]) of her beloved Gahmuret. Unlike the *King of Tars,* however, *Parzival* does not feature a dichotomous world where Saracens are dark-skinned and Christians are white; on the contrary, Belacane states, her first husband, Isenhart, was "of black color, like myself, a Moor" (in swarzer varwe als ich ein Môr [26.22]). Other Saracens, however, are clearly not dark; for example, when Belacane first sees Gahmuret, she is able to compare his fair good looks in comparison to other fair-skinned Saracens: "her eyes at once informed her heart that he was handsome. She knew how to judge light-colored complexions, for she had seen many a light-skinned heathen before" ("ir ougen dem herzen sân / daz er waere wol getân. / si kunde ouch liehte varwe spehen: / wan si het och ê gesehen / manegen liehten heiden" [29.1–5]). Some Saracens are clearly dark-skinned, such as Belacane herself and her husband Isenhart, while others are fair-skinned, such as the Saracen from Seville who "was not like a Moor in color" (was niht als ein Môr gevar [55.2]). Aided by the fair-skinned Saracen from Seville, Gahmuret, longing for "deeds of knighthood" (rîterschefte" [54.19]), abandons Belacane (who is pregnant with their child) and returns to Europe, where he fathers a second son, the eponymous Perceval. In spite of the apparent openness of the text to what might be (albeit anachronistically) called a racially multicultural society, black skin color continues to be at least occasionally interpreted as a marker of danger and duplicity. For example, the light-skinned mariner who assists Gahmuret to leave Seville urges secrecy: "You must quietly conceal this from all those who have black skins" (ir sulz heln lîse / vor den die tragent daz swarze vel [55.4–5]).

In some ways, Belacane is representative of the figure of the "Saracen queen" so well described by Sharon Kinoshita: beloved by a Christian knight, the Saracen queen expresses a loving devotion to her chosen partner so profound that she is willing to betray her nearest and dearest for his sake.[55] Belacane departs from this model, however, in that conversion and baptism are never presented to her as an option. (This peculiarity is even more striking in view of the fact that Wolfram does include the figure of "Gyburc," Guillaume d'Orange's Saracen queen, in his own romance of *Willehalm*.) When the restless Gahmuret abandons Belacane, he leaves behind a letter that makes explicit the grounds for his desertion, which are, precisely, the religious difference that intractably separates them: "The lady found in her purse a letter in her husband's writing, in French—which she knew. The writing told her: 'Here one sweetheart sends a message to another sweetheart....Lady, I cannot conceal from you that if your religion were within my law, then I would always long for you....Lady, if you'll be baptised, you may yet win me for your own.' She wished for no other outcome" (diu frouwe in ir biutel vant / einen brief, den schreib ir mannes hant. / en franzoys, daz si kunde, / diu schrift ir sagen begunde / "Hie entbiutet liep ein ander liep....frouwe, in mac dich niht verheln, / waer dîn ordn in mîner ê, / sô waer mir immer nâch dir wê....frouwe, wiltu toufen dich, / du maht ouch noch erwerben mich." / Des engerte se keinen wandel niht [55.17–21, 24–26; 56.25–27]). Belacane immediately expresses her willingness to convert, motivated by the compelling power of love: "For the honor of his god...I would gladly be baptised and live as he would wish" (sîme gote ze êren.../ ich mich gerne tougen solte / unde leben swie er wolte [57.6–8]). This option, however, remains foreclosed. Conversion and assimilation into the Christian community is not presented as an option for Belacane as it is for Floripas and Guiborc. Instead, Belacane will die a martyr to her passionate love. Her child, however, will return to his father's people, becoming a member of the Christian community that remains inaccessible to his mother.

This child bears the marks of his disparate origins, Saracen and Christian, upon the surface of his body: "When her time was due the lady gave birth to a son, who was of two colors. By him God devised a miracle—both black and white was his appearance. The queen kissed him incessantly, very often on his white marks. The mother called her baby Feirefiz Angevin....His hair and his entire skin, too, became, in hue, like that of a magpie" (diu frouwe an rehter zît genas / eins suns, der zweier varwe was, / an dem got wunders wart enein: / wîz und swarzer varwe er schein. / diu küngîn kust in sunder twâl / vil dicke an sîniu blanken mâl. diu muoter hiez ir kindelîn /

---

55. Kinoshita, *Medieval Boundaries*, 55.

Feirefîz Anschevîn.... als ein agelster wart gevar / sîn hâr und och sîn vel vil gar [57.15–22, 27–28]). Later on in the narrative, at the moment when Parzival recognizes Feirefiz as his brother, Feirefiz's skin is likened to parchment that has been written on, making his body a counterpart of the letter written to Belacane by Gahmuret. When questioned regarding the reputed appearance of his Saracen brother, Parzival states, "like a written-on leaf of parchment, black and white here and there" (als ein geschriben permint, / swarz und blanc her unde dâ [747.26–27]). What follows is a striking moment of mutual recognition and sudden collapse of the boundaries that normally separate Christian and Saracen: "The Heathen said, 'I am he!' Then both hesitated little, but each quickly bared his head of helmet and coif, simultaneously.... The heathen was soon recognized, for he bore the magpie's marks. Feirefiz and Parzival put an end to enmity by a kiss" (der heiden sprach "der bin ich." / si bêde wênc dô sûmten sich, / Ieweder sîn houbet schier / von helme unt von hersenier / enblôzte an der selben stunt.... der heiden schiere wart erkant: / wander truoc agelstern mâl / Feirefiz unt Parzival / mit kusse understuonden haz [747.29–30, 748.1–3, 6–9]). With their embrace, the brief union of Gahmuret and Belacane is fulfilled at last, in an embrace of brothers who make up a single whole. In Feirefiz's words, "It is with your own self that you have fought here. It was to do battle against myself that I came riding here" (mit dir selben hâstu hie gestritn. / gein mir selbn ich kom ûf strît geritn [752.15–16]). In recognizing himself in the face of his brother, Feirefiz's Saracen identity begins to become subsumed into the Christian community, as his tears prefigure the baptism that is his destiny: "His heathen eyes started to shed water, all in accordance with baptism's honours" (sîn heidenschiu ougen / begunden wazzer rêren / al nâch des toufes êren [752.24–26]). These tears initiate a liminal period in Feirefiz's process of conversion, a process that will be complete only with his immersion in the baptismal font and concomitant spiritual rebirth. In this respect, his process of conversion resembles that of Floripas, who similarly experiences a long liminal period initiated by her declaration of her love for Guy and statement of willingness to convert, and completed only at the end of the romance in the climactic scene of baptism.

Parzival's embrace of his brother is reiterated by the other members of the Grail community, one after another, as Feirefiz is welcomed into their midst and becomes one of them. They are able to see beyond his speckled appearance to the "true heart" that lies beneath, except for the child Loherangrin, who is repelled by Feirefiz's "black and white" (swarz unde wîz [805.30]) appearance. This childish failure of perception is perceived not as a social slight, but as simply comic: "At that, the heathen laughed" (des lachte der heiden

[806.3]). Feirefiz's arrival at the castle marks the completion of the circle, the fulfillment of the journey of his father, Gahmuret, to the Orient. The letter left behind by Gahmuret, enfolded in Belacane's "purse" (biutel [55.17]) is the eerie double of the unborn child she carries within her womb. Both letter and flesh are "like a written-on leaf of parchment, black and white here and there" (747.26–27). However, while the letter signified the apparent impossibility of Saracen assimilation, the "parchment" of Feirefiz's flesh signifies the union of Saracen and Christian. This union, however, remains resolutely on the level of the spirit and not of the flesh, for Feirefiz's pied flesh also signifies the simultaneous difference and sameness of the assimilated Saracen. His skin remains both black and white, marked by its ethnically double nature, even as his newly Christian soul is washed clean of every spot.[56]

The "miracle" (wunder [57.17]) of the newborn Feirefiz's speckled body is, at first sight, a perfect counterpart to the "miracle" enacted on the shapeless "flesche" born from the union of Saracen and Christian in the *King of Tars*. In the Middle English poem, however, not the birth of the hybrid offspring but rather its transformation during baptism entails the miracle; by contrast, in the Middle High German poem, the varigated, black-and-white nature of the body is itself the miracle, marking the beginning of a process of reintegration that will be complete only with Feirefiz's conversion at the end of the narrative. To put it another way, the initial "wunder" of the parti-colored child is the first stage in a process that is fulfilled in the greater wonder of Feirefiz's integration into the Christian community, mediated by the power of love.[57] Though, as a "heathen," Feirefiz is unable to see the Grail, he is able to see the maiden who carries it. The love he should rightly direct toward the Grail is therefore redirected toward its bearer, Repanse de Schoye, for whose sake Feirefiz willingly accepts baptism: "If it helps me against distress, I'll believe all that you command. If her love rewards me, then I'll gladly carry out his command. Brother, if your aunt [Repanse de Schoye] has a god, I believe in him and in her.... All my gods are renounced.... For the sake of your aunt's god have me be baptised!" (ist ez mir guot für ungemach, / ich gloub swes ir gebietet. / op mich ir minne mietet, / sô leist

---

56. It is striking that, while the late thirteenth-century *Alexander* of Ulrich von Etzenbach features a giant named "Geon" who is clearly modeled on Wolfram's Feirefiz, the allegorical significance of Feirefiz's pied skin is completely erased: as Marcus Stock puts it, "Die Tatsache, dass Feirefiz' Hautfarbe als Bild für genealogische und ethische Problemstellungen dient, spielt im *Alexander* keine Rolle." Stock, "Alexander in der Echokammer," 124–25.

57. On the increasingly careful distinction between "wonder" and "miracle" in late medieval theology and ecclesiastical practice, see Goodich, *Miracles and Wonders,* esp. chap. 2, "'Signa data infidelibus non fidelibus': The Theology of Miracle."

ich gerne sîn gebot. / bruoder, hât dîn muome got, / an den geloube ich unt an sie. . . . al mîne gote sint verkorn. . . . durh dîner muomen got heiz toufen mich [818.2–7, 9, 12]). While Feirefiz's martial combat with Parzival follows the template of other battles of Saracen and Christian knights, such as that of Fierabras and Oliver, his acceptance of baptism follows the "feminine" model of conversion exemplified by figures such as Floripas and Guiborc, and which was not available to his mother, Belacane. Feirefiz's conversion is initiated in the act of martial combat, but, following a protracted period of liminality, is completed through the power of love.

The emphasis on sight as the nexus of transformation from Saracen to Christian is ubiquitous in the romances studied in this chapter. In the *King of Tars,* the black Sultan experiences spiritual renewal in the moment that he "sees" his newly white flesh (928–32), just as Feirefiz does in his miraculous glimpse of the Grail: "He had been blind when it came to seeing the Grail, until baptism had covered him. Thereafter the Grail was revealed to his vision" (an den grâl was er ze sehen blint, / ê der touf het in bedecket: / sît wart im vor enblecket / der grâl mit gesihte [818.20–23]). The transcendent experience of spiritual vision at the heart of conversion is underlined, in the *King of Tars,* in the name given to the Sultan by the priest who baptizes him: Cleopas, after the witness of Christ's resurrection on the road to Emmaus. The Sultan's moment of spiritual rebirth, mirrored in physical transformation from black to white, is preeminently a triumph of sight. While the physical transformation of the Sultan has no counterpart in the persistently pied flesh of Feirefiz, the emphasis on vision remains, as the father of Prester John glimpses his redemption in the form of the Grail. Universal salvation, mediated through the imagined apocalyptic might of Prester John, is mirrored in the unique salvation of the individual soul.

The Saracens of medieval *chansons de geste* and romance seen in this chapter differ from their European Christian counterparts in two respects: outward physical appearance, dictated by ethnic diversity, and inward spiritual orientation, determined by the ability to perceive the presence of the divine. Saracen alterity is consistently defined along these two vectors, categories of difference that overlap but are articulated in terms of very different systems of thought. By reading the different ways that conversion and assimilation are described in medieval narratives, especially where the existence of multiple textual "isotopes" as in the case of *Fierabras* makes possible a richly comparative reading, we can understand more fully the flexible yet highly overdetermined way that medieval European Christians understood their place in the world. Through the Saracen Other, they were able to define their own boundaries, both physical and spiritual. The next chapter turns to the ways in which boundaries were defined in theological terms in the medieval Western view of Islam, focusing on the ways that perceptions of Oriental difference served to reinforce depictions of Islamic theology as fundamentally superficial, and as oriented away from rather than toward God. In the discursive formations of medieval Orientalism, spatial relationships served as a conceptual template not only for the geographical description of the parts of the world, but also for the relationship of Judaism, Christianity, and Islam to spiritual truths.

CHAPTER 5

Empty Idols and a False Prophet

It is generally assumed that, from the twelfth to the fifteenth centuries, there were two fundamentally different ways that European Christians viewed Islam. On the one hand, a series of *chansons de geste* and romances showed Muslims as polytheistic idolaters; on the other, Latin and vernacular biographies of Muhammad chronicled the Prophet's life in detail, illustrating his career as trickster, deceiver, pseudo-prophet, and representative of the power of Antichrist. Modern readers have tended to distinguish sharply between these two modes of representation. In his influential study of *Western Views of Islam in the Middle Ages,* Richard Southern posited a metanarrative of Christian attitudes toward Islam, one of progress from an "age of ignorance" to an "age of enlightenment," from a simple lack of "real" knowledge to a more generous understanding of religious differences.[1] In a series of works on Western attitudes toward Islam, Norman Daniel reinforced this binary, both in the divergent foci of his books and in several explicit statements: in his *Heroes and Saracens,* he focused exclusively on "popular" ideas of Islam as seen in the *chansons de geste,* while in his *Islam and the West,* he analyzed "learned" historical and clerical assessments of Muslims and Islamic culture.[2] It would be hard to overstate the

---

1. Southern, *Western Views of Islam.*
2. Daniel, *Heroes and Saracens;* Daniel, *Islam and the West.*

extent of Daniel's influence on the orientation of subsequent work in this area, as Blanks and Frassetto have articulately shown.[3] This binary opposition continues to this day to inform the parameters of current research, as can be seen even in John Tolan's superbly detailed book on medieval views of *Saracens:* in keeping with the precedent set by Daniel, Tolan titles one chapter "Saracens as Pagans" and the next chapter "Muhammad, Heresiarch." Tolan even echoes Southern's teleological description of an increasingly accurate knowledge of Islam, in stating that "Western writers ... increasingly portray it as a variant, heretical version of Christianity."[4]

One might agree that it is worth separating learned discourse from un-learned, written texts from those designed primarily for oral enjoyment, and Latin texts from those composed in the vernacular. Yet this distinction breaks down almost immediately, as can be seen in Daniel's own use of Latin historical chronicles as sources and analogues for the *chansons de geste* he de-scribes. He is undoubtedly right to analyze these texts in tandem, but just as certainly wrong to claim (as he does repeatedly) that the treatment of Islam in the *chansons de geste* and related texts is "wholly distinct from that of the academic and journalistic ... attitudes" found in more explicitly historical or theological texts.[5] Daniel argues that there are "two entirely separate con-ventions within which the mediaevals expressed themselves," and that these two traditions differ not only in their different circumstances of composi-tion but in the nature of their reception. While the learned texts were used in order to construct persuasive theological counter-arguments based on a relatively accurate representation of Islam, says Daniel, the *chansons de geste* are "entertaining." Of the depiction of Muslims as polytheistic idolaters and the elaborate descriptions of their many gods, Daniel goes on, "It is hard to see that these are intended other than as fun."[6]

It is important to make clear that Daniel is not being used here as a straw man to denigrate earlier efforts to take stock of medieval representations of Islam. On the contrary, it is precisely because of the quality and breadth of Daniel's work that his influence has been so profound and has set the terms for subsequent research, particularly the ubiquitous view that there are

---

3. Blanks, "Western Views of Islam," 11–53, esp. 24–29.

4. Tolan, *Saracens,* 134. Elsewhere, Tolan again seems to rely upon Daniel's paradigm of two tradi-tions (as well as Southern's description of increasing accuracy in Western views of Islam) in declaring that, in the early twelfth-century *Vita Mahumeti* of Embrico of Mainz, "Muhammad the heresiarch begins to replace Muhammad the golden idol in the European imagination." "Anti-Hagiography," 25–41; quotation at 30.

5. Daniel, *Islam,* 26.

6. Daniel, *Islam,* 341–42; 338.

two fundamentally distinct modes of medieval representations of Islam, one rooted in imaginative projection, the other in historical truth. Though Tolan, as noted above, does continue to use the binary model established by Daniel in his own treatment of Western representations of Islam, he observes that, *contra* Daniel, "the situation is far from being so simple.... When one examines the texts closely, the distinction between 'learned' and 'popular' blurs."[7] In the following pages, I build upon Tolan's observation, showing precisely how that distinction proves to be more apparent than real, and illustrating the extraordinary intersection of the two traditions that Daniel takes such pains to separate one from the other. This demonstration reveals the extent to which the same audience might appreciate an exaggerated caricature of Muslim practice on the one hand, and a more "realistic" depiction of the theological depravity of Islam on the other.

It is worth noting, first of all, that even Daniel himself sometimes signals an awareness of the difficulty in maintaining such a rigid distinction. He notes that the "audiences... must have overlapped a little,"[8] and even acknowledges the likelihood that a single person might embrace both ideas simultaneously: "It is always possible for a man to hold mutually exclusive views simultaneously... or... to repeat mutually exclusive views without giving both—or either—credence."[9] It is not simply "possible" for one person to have two ideas concerning Islam and Muslims; it is highly desirable, because the two conventions are mutually reinforcing and nourish one another. This chapter begins by offering a view of what Norman Daniel calls the "fanciful" mode of representation: that is, the depiction of Muslims as polytheistic idolaters, dedicated to a collection of gods (usually three) including Tervagant, Apollo, and Muhammad. The first section, titled "The Broken Idol," shows how depictions of Muslims as idolaters reflect contemporary Western views concerning the use of images in Christian worship at least as much as they express a sense of Islam as a religion devoted to the superficial and the literal. This portion of the chapter uses four literary texts, drawn from different genres, periods, and national literatures, in order to give a representative overview of this "fanciful" view of Muslims as idolaters. The emptiness of the idol is located not only in its conspicuous lack of any real, potent god lying beyond the image, but in the repeated enactment of the idol's fragmentation and dissolution.

The following section, "The Place of Muhammad," turns to what Daniel calls the "realistic" mode of representation, focusing particularly on the

---

7. Tolan, *Saracens,* 136–37.
8. Daniel, *Islam,* 26.
9. Ibid., 410n7.

polemical Western biographies of the Prophet Muhammad and arguing that the "fanciful" rhetoric of idolatry thoroughly permeates this "realistic" mode. A close reading of the depiction of Muhammad and Ali in Dante's *Inferno,* in conjunction with the medieval commentary tradition on the *Commedia,* anchors this portion of the chapter. The chapter's final portion, titled "The Filthy Idol," focuses on the depiction of sacred spaces in non-literary anti-Islamic texts, especially the preaching of the Crusades and crusade chronicles. It points out the ways in which sacred spaces, their sanctification and desecration, have been central to the discourse of religious alterity that underlies Western Christian understandings of Islam, and which (in a more subtle form) persists today. The chapter then closes with a brief comparative overview of how sacred spaces are presented in theological and cartographical frameworks.

← The Broken Idol

The so-called "fanciful" mode of representation is ubiquitous in the *chansons de geste* as well as late medieval romances. Muslims are characterized as fierce, belligerent idol worshipers, devoted to a pagan pantheon often made up of three gods—"Mahom" (Muhammad), "Apolin" (Apollo), and "Tervagan" (Tervagant)—but sometimes including a much larger number. Modern readers frequently comment on the absurdity of suggesting that Muslims worship idols in view of Islam's absolute condemnation of any veneration of images, suggesting that such depictions of Muslims are based on the identification of Islam with ancient Greek and Roman polytheism.[10] In this view, the ignorance of Islamic theology on the part of western European writers is supplemented, as it were, by recourse to the familiar traditions of late antiquity, while the persecution of the early Church martyrs at the hands of Roman imperial authorities is conflated with the medieval conflict of Christianity and Islam enacted in the crusades.

Interestingly, however, the accusation of idolatry has played a major part in polemics against Islam written as early as the eighth and ninth centuries, soon after the penetration of Muslim armies into regions formerly under the sway of the Byzantine Empire. Although these texts predate the time period

---

10. On Saracen polytheism as a manifestation of antique or classical polytheism, see Zink, "Apollin," 1: 503–9. Useful references and general discussion can be found in Camille, "Idols of the Saracens," chap. 3 of *The Gothic Idol,* 129–64. For an overview of medieval perspectives on pagan idolatry, see Minnis, *Chaucer and Pagan Antiquity,* 32–60.

which is the focus of this study (approximately from the First Crusade to the fall of Constantinople), it is imperative to point out, at least briefly, the continuities that link depictions of Islam after 1100 with the characterizations found in earlier polemics. In the Byzantine context, it is clear that accusations of idolatry are not the product of ignorance; on the contrary, several of the Eastern Christian apologists who condemned Muslims as polytheistic idolaters were in a position to be familiar not only with the Arabic language but with Islamic theology. The most famous of these, John of Damascus, even served as an administrator in the court of the caliph in Damascus. Evidence of Byzantine views of Muslims as idolaters appears in a variety of sources, including not just theological writings but pictorial programs as well. As Kathleen Corrigan has shown, ninth-century Byzantine psalters produced in the wake of the Iconoclastic Controversy explicitly associated Islam with idolatry. They did so, Corrigan argues, in order to defend their Christian belief in the efficacy of images in worship against the accusations of idolatry leveled at them by Muslims and Jews. Christians thus turned the accusation of idolatry back upon their accusers.[11] It is striking that even the qur'anic description of God as "al-Samad" (singular, self-contained) is distorted, in certain Byzantine polemics, into an assertion of the material nature of the divine within Islamic theology. The ninth-century apologist Nicetas of Byzantium renders the term "al-Samad" as "holosphyros," that is, "a material sphere... unable to act unless someone else moves him." As Daniel Sahas puts it, in Nicetas' interpretation, Islam appears to be simply "a gross idolatry."[12]

Perhaps the most elaborate Byzantine effort to characterize Muslim devotion as idolatry appears in the *De haeresibus,* composed in the eighth century by John of Damascus, famous for his defense of the use of images in worship during the Iconoclastic Controversy.[13] The refutation of Islam, which appears near the close of the *Liber de haeresibus* ("Book of Heresies"), centers on the accusation of idolatry. The author rhetorically asks of Muslims, "Why then do you rub yourselves against that stone at your Ka'aba, and love that stone to the point of embracing it?" He suggests not only that the veneration

---

11. Corrigan, *Visual Polemics,* 35–37, 91–94.

12. Nicetas of Byzantium, Patrologia Graeca 105: 705D–708A; translated in Sahas, "'Holosphyros'?" 109–27; quotation from 112.

13. It is not certain whether the refutation of Islam contained in the *De haeresibus* was composed by John of Damascus himself or interpolated a few decades later by a member of his circle. See Sahas, *John of Damascus on Islam,* 51–58. The text's most recent editor, Le Coz, argues that the work is not by John himself, but by a member of his circle or student; in this, he disagrees with Sahas, who argues that at least the last three chapters were authored by the Damascene himself. A summary of the work and overview of John's cultural background can be found in Tolan, *Saracens,* 50–55. Tolan subscribes to Sahas' view regarding the work's authorship (*Saracens,* 297n48).

of the Black Stone at Mecca is idolatrous, but that it is a remnant of pagan antiquity: "It is said that this stone is the head of Aphrodite, before which they
prostrate themselves.... And to this day, the traces of the carving appear to
those who stare at it intently."[14] This passage is striking not only in its identification of Islam as a form of ancient pagan worship, but in its implication
that the pagan worship indulged in by worshipers at the Ka'aba is the same
as the worship indulged in by those inhabitants of the Roman Empire who
had become Christian: in this view, both cultures, Muslim and Christian,
share a history of devotion to Aphrodite.[15] While the Christians, however,
have turned their backs on the goddess, the Muslims continue to cling to the
remnants of this pagan past, disguising their attachment to Aphrodite under
the thin covering of monotheism. Idolatry, in the view of the author of the
De haeresibus, remains at the center of Muslim devotion—an idolatry which
is, in the end, a fragmentary relic of the spiritual blindness of antiquity. The
Muslims' attachment to Aphrodite manifests itself not only in the form of
the image they adore, but in their manner of devotion, as the worshipers sug-
gestively "rub" themselves against the Black Stone.

The *De haeresibus* did not exert a formative influence on Western Christian views of Islam, although Latin translations of the work were produced by
Eriugena and Robert Grosseteste.[16] It is, however, a very early manifestation
of a set of conventions regarding Muslim worship that permeate medieval
Christian depictions of Islam, whether produced in the sphere of Byzantine
influence, in Christian Spain, or elsewhere in Europe. Islam is consistently
portrayed as a stubborn turning back to pre-Christian worship, whether in
the form of a return to classical paganism (as seen in the *De haeresibus*) or
in the form of a return to Judaism—that is, the "Old Law" of Moses. It is
associated with a devotion to the pleasures of the body rather than the care
of the soul, here in the form of physical prostration before the image of
the goddess of carnal love. The brittle foundation of this devotion, founded
on the body which is doomed to decay and dissolution rather than on the
eternal soul, manifests itself in the repeated scenes of the destruction of the
idols, whether at the hands of the Muslims themselves or at the hands of their

---

14. John of Damascus, *De haeresibus,* chap. 100, para. 5, 218–21. My English translation is based
on Le Coz's French translation, with emendations to render the text more literally. See also Sahas,
John of Damascus on Islam.

15. On Saracen worship of Aphrodite in Byzantine polemics, see Khoury, *Polémique Byzantine
contre l'Islam,* 162–63, 240–41, 275–78.

16. On Grosseteste's translations, see Thomson, *Writings of Robert Grosseteste;* Holland, "Robert
Grosseteste's Translations," 138–54. Grosseteste's translation of the *De haeresibus* can be found in Holland, "Edition of Three Unpublished Translations."

Christian conquerors. The fragmented shards of the idols mirror the disintegration of the community of misguided believers who obstinately refuse to recognize the Christian God.

In order to illustrate the function of idolatry within the discourse of Islamic alterity, this section of the chapter focuses on four literary works drawn from the twelfth through the fifteenth centuries, composed in a range of genres including epic, drama, and romance. These include the *Chanson de Roland,* one of the earliest surviving *chansons de geste;* the *Jeu de saint Nicolas,* a play produced at the very beginning of the thirteenth century, which partakes both in the conventions of the epic poem and in the emerging form of the medieval drama; the *Sowdone of Babylone,* an early fifteenth-century romance based on the epic poems of battle contemporary with the *Roland;* and the late medieval Digby *Mary Magdalen* play which, like the *Jeu de saint Nicolas,* is a drama devoted to the life of a saint that dramatizes the conflict of Christendom and the realm of Islam in terms of the competing claims of good and bad images. Four texts are certainly not enough to offer a comprehensive picture of Western views of Islam as a form of idolatry, let alone to illustrate precisely how the contours of that perception altered over four centuries. These four texts do, however, offer some reference points on which to base an overview of how idolatry came to be seen, by the Western Christian, as emblematic of the superficial nature of Muslim devotion.

Beginning in the late eleventh century, the *chansons de geste* emerged in France and quickly began to be exported into the other literary traditions of medieval Europe. In these epics glorifying war and chivalric heroism, Muslims are depicted as similar to Christians: the structure of their armies, their kings, and their martial techniques are essentially the same. The main thing that sets them apart is their religion. While the Christian knights appeal to their God and their saints verbally, without recourse to the veneration of images, the Muslims of the *chansons de geste* are polytheistic idolaters who worship graven images of "Mahum," "Apolin," and "Tervagan." These idols are frequently mentioned in the *chansons de geste* as well as in the numerous romance texts based upon them. Their presence serves as a signal of the waning power of the Muslims, who turn upon their gods whenever they suffer a military defeat. Perhaps the most famous example of this behavior appears in the *Chanson de Roland* where, following a disastrous battle, the Muslims attack their own image of Apolin:

> Tencent a lui, laidement le despersunent:
> "E! Malvais deus, por quei nus fais tel hunte?
> Cest nostre rei por quei lessas cunfundre?

Ki mult te sert, malvais luër l'en dunes!"
Pui si li tolent ses ceptre e sa curune.
Par mains le pendent sur une culumbe,
Entre lur piez a tere le tresturnent,
A granz bastuns le batent e defruisent.
E Tervagan tolent sun escarbuncle
E Mahumet enz en un fosset butent
E porc e chen le mordent e defulent.

They rail at it, they abuse it in vile fashion:
"Oh, evil god, why do you cover us with such shame?
Why have you allowed this king of ours to be brought to ruin?
You pay out poor wages to anyone who serves you well!"
They tie it by the hands to a column.
Then they tear away the idol's sceptre and its crown.
They topple it to the ground at their feet.
They beat it and smash it to pieces with big sticks.
They snatch Tervagant's carbuncle,
Throw the idol of Muhammad into a ditch,
And pigs and dogs bite and trample it.

(2581–91)[17]

It is important to note that this is not simply a scene of idolatry, but of icono-clasm: the Muslims' idols are seen not when they are being worshiped, but precisely when their impotence is revealed, as their disappointed followers smash their idols in anger. This has the effect of simultaneously condemning the Muslims for their idolatry and pointing out the futility of their wrongly directed worship. Interestingly, the Muslims' abuse of their own images re-sembles the punishment of images practiced by medieval Christians, when an image of a saint or of the Virgin Mary would be displaced from its usual position and verbally abused until the saint once more displayed the efficacy expected by the supplicant.[18] This parallelism suggests the extent to which medieval Christians used their own theology to imagine Islam.

---

17. Quotations of the *Chanson de Roland* are from Brault, ed. and trans., *Song of Roland: An Analytical Edition,* and are cited in the text by line number.

18. Geary, "Humiliation of Saints," 123–40, esp. 135–38. A literary example of the humiliation of the Virgin Mary appears in the *Siege of Melayne;* discussed in Akbari, "Incorporation in the *Siege of Melayne,*" 22–44, esp. 26–27.

Nowhere is this phenomenon more evident than in the *Chanson de Roland,* in which the Christian Trinity is mirrored by a corresponding pagan anti-trinity of Apolin, Mahum, and Tervagan. In almost all respects, the Christian force led by Charlemagne resembles the pagan force led by Marsilie: each has an elite corps of twelve knights, each king is depicted surrounded by retainers and seated on a sumptuous throne, each side includes warriors distinguished by their bravery. The two sides differ, it seems, only with regard to their leadership: Charlemagne's men owe allegiance to "God" (Deus), while Marsilie's men follow "Mahum" (e.g., 3641). The deities, both Christian and pagan, are seen as military leaders, whose success or failure is measured on the battlefield. Marsilie's queen, Bramimonde, laments the Muslims' losses, saying, "Those gods of ours have given up the fight.... They allowed our knights to get killed. They failed my lord in battle" (Cist nostre deu sunt en recreantise. / ... / Noz chevalers i unt lesset ocire. / Cest mien seignur en bataille faillirent [2715–18]). Conversely, when Charlemagne weakens in the midst of battle, God sends the angel Gabriel to encourage him (3608–11; cf. 2526–68 and 2458–59). Gods participate actively on both sides of this holy war.

In the *Chanson de Roland,* Muslims resemble Christians every way except in the gods they follow: as the redactor of the poem puts it, "Pagans are wrong and Christians are right" (Paien unt tort e chrestïens unt dreit [1015]). Pagans are "wrong" because they are a "gent averse" (2630, 3295), that is, a people who have "turned away" from the right. The battle of Christian and pagan can only end, says the redactor, when "one of them admits he is in the wrong" (li uns sun tort i reconuiset [3588]). Since it is the "pagans" who are "wrong," only they can come to recognize their own error.[19] Therefore when the pagan emir Baligant sees the standard of Muhammad brought low in battle, signifying the god's military defeat, he "begins to realize that he is wrong and Charles is right" (s'en aperceit / Que il ad tort e Carlemagnes dreit [3553–54]). Baligant's realization, however, does not move him to convert and join his righteous enemy: unlike other *chansons de geste* such as *Fierabras,* the *Chanson de Roland* does not include valiant pagan heroes who willingly convert when they observe the superior power of the God of the Christian knights. Instead, conversion takes place by the sword. After the conquest of Saragossa, Charlemagne orders that baptismal water be prepared, and that any who wish to remain Muslim "be taken prisoner, burned, or put to death" (fait prendre o ardeir ou ocire). In order to escape this fate, writes the redactor, "Well over a hundred thousand are baptized" (Baptizet sunt asez plus

---

19. See Kinoshita's thoughtful exploration of how the religious dichotomy of "right" and "wrong" in the *Roland* intersects with national and feudal affiliations (*Medieval Boundaries,* 25–31).

de.C. milie [3670–71]). Only the queen, Bramimonde, is taken to France, because Charlemagne wishes her conversion to be "par amur" (3674), that is, motivated by true conviction rather than by force.[20]

The conversion of "over a hundred thousand" Muslims at Saragossa is simultaneously accompanied by the destruction of idols. Unlike the abasement of Mahum, Apolin, and Tervagan by the disappointed Muslims themselves that takes place earlier in the poem, this episode of iconoclasm has as its purpose the erasure of any memory of image-worship at Saragossa:

> A mil Franceis funt ben cercer la vile,
> Les sinagoges e les mahumeries.
> A mailz de fer e a cuignees qu'il tindrent
> Fruissent les ymagenes e trestutes les ydeles,
> N'i remeindrat ne sorz ne falserie.

> Orders are given for a thousand Frenchmen to search the city,
> The synagogues and the mosques.
> Holding iron hammers and axes,
> They smash the statues and all the idols.
> No sorcery or false cult will remain there.
>
> (3661–65)

This passage differs significantly from the earlier episode of iconoclasm practiced by the Muslims themselves. There, the redactor emphasizes the humiliation of the gods at the hands of their former worshipers rather than the physical destruction of the graven image. This is more evident in the original Old French text rather than in modern translations, where (as in Brault's widely used text) the word "idol" is repeatedly inserted to describe what is being abused. The original text simply refers to the god himself as the object of abuse. Thus a more literal translation of the text would read: "They run to Apollo. . . . They rail at him, they abuse him in a vile fashion. . . . Then they tear away his sceptre and his crown. They hang him by the hands on a column. . . . From Tervagan they wrench his jewel, And throw Muhammad into a ditch, And pigs and dogs bite and trample him" (2580–91). The punishments enacted on the gods sound less like the smashing of stone, metal, or wood than like the torture and humiliation that might be enacted on a living

---

20. For a perceptive analysis of Bramimonde's place in the *Roland,* see Kinoshita, *Medieval Boundaries,* 36–45. See also the extended discussion of the conversion process of female Saracens in chapter 4 of this book.

prisoner, hung up by the hands, his body gnawed by animals. In fact, this last fate is one which Charlemagne's men fear that they themselves will suffer if the Christian army does not come to their aid in time: Bishop Turpin hopes that their bodies will be retrieved and buried in hallowed ground, where "Neither wolves, nor pigs, nor dogs will devour us" (N'en mangerunt ne lu ne porc ne chen [1751]). In this scene, the gods worshiped by the Muslims are conceived of as more than just idols. They have an independent existence, although they are ultimately impotent and "wrong."

Conversely, the scene of iconoclasm practiced by the Christians, which is recounted near the end of the *Chanson de Roland,* emphasizes not the independent existence of the Muslim gods but their status as material objects that must be destroyed in order to wipe out any memory of what they once represented. What this act accomplishes is not only the extermination of the rival religion, but also the destruction of any evidence that idolatry was practiced. To put it another way, the fact that there are no pagan images at Saragossa, no evidence of Muslim idol worship, is perfectly understandable: they were all systematically destroyed by Charlemagne's victorious army. Charlemagne's victory is thus completed in an erasure of the Islamic culture that previously ruled Saragossa. Thousands of Muslims are compelled to convert; those who decline to do so are burned, and the images that might otherwise remain as mute testimony to earlier practice are reduced to dust. In the *Roland,* then, the broken idols function in two very different ways. When damaged and denigrated by the Muslims themselves, they make visible the impotence of the Muslims' gods, but remain present as reminders of the fundamentally "wrong" nature of the pagan host. When smashed by the victorious Christians, however, the idols are reduced to nothingness, so that their absence becomes—paradoxically—proof of the Christians' success in eradicating the false practice of image-worship.

Jehan Bodel's *Jeu de saint Nicolas* maintains many of the conventions regarding Muslims found in the *Chanson de Roland.* It is one of the earliest surviving mystery plays written in the French vernacular, composed about 1200 at the time when vigorous efforts were being made to mount the Fourth Crusade: Bodel himself took up the cross but fell ill before he could actually embark upon the Crusade.[21] It is therefore unsurprising that the Saint Nicholas play reproduces so much of the crusade rhetoric found in texts such as the *Chanson de Roland.* While the narrator of the *Roland* declares that "Pagans are wrong and Christians are right" (Paiens unt tort e crestiens unt dreit),

---

21. See the biographical note on Jehan Bodel in Albert Henry's introduction to his edition of [Bodel], *Le Jeu de saint Nicolas,* 21–26.

the *Jeu de saint Nicolas* includes a character who states flatly that "Paradise will be ours and hell will be theirs" (Paradys sera nostres et eus sera ynfers [406]).[22] As in the *Chanson de Roland,* the Muslims in the play worship a kind of pagan anti-trinity made up of Apollo, Muhammad, and Tervagant. They swear by the names of these deities and, like the Muslim knights of the *Roland,* express their allegiance to the gods in terms of fealty or military command, declaring, "Let us be commanded by Muhammad" (a Mahommet soiions nous commandé [395]). When the Muslim king decides to convert to Christianity, he makes what amounts to an oath of fealty, offering himself up to Saint Nicholas "with hands and heart" (de mains et de cuer [1451]) and telling the saint, "Sire, here and now I become your man" (Sire, chi devieng jou vostre hom [1459]).

While the Saint Nicholas play resembles the great poems of crusade in its depiction of a pagan anti-Trinity made up of Apollo, Muhammad, and Tervagant, it differs from them in the elaborateness with which it works out the parallelism and symmetry of Christianity and Islam. In the *Jeu de saint Nicolas,* the central deity in the Muslim pantheon is not Muhammad but Tervagant, who appears in the play as a large golden statue in a "mahomerie" or mosque adjoining the palace of the king. Like the Muslims of the *Roland,* the king abuses his idol, rebuking it for his men's lack of military success and mocking the statue's "ugly face and ugly body" (lait visage et...lait cors [137]). Tervagant is not the only statue in the play, however; his power is countered by that transmitted through a simple "man of wood" (home de fust [1200; cf. 31]), a simple wooden statue of Saint Nicholas.[23] Efforts to reconstruct medieval stagings of the play suggest that the symmetry of these two figures would have been heightened by the placement of the golden statue of Tervagant opposite to the wooden image of Saint Nicholas.[24] The symmetry is also underlined by the Muslims' repeated reference to the image of Nicholas as a "horned mahommet" (mahommet cornu [458]); to them, apparently, an image of Nicholas is fundamentally like an image of Muhammad.

---

22. Bodel, *Le Jeu de saint Nicolas,* ed. Albert Henry. Quotations are cited in the text by line number; translations are my own. A somewhat idiomatic English translation can be found in [Bodel, *Le Jeu de saint Nicolas*] *Medieval French Plays.*

23. In *Gothic Idol,* Michael Camille argues that the image of Saint Nicholas used in stagings of the play would have been "a two-dimensional picture...an icon rather than an idol" (127; cf. 133). He is able to argue this point only by focusing on the identification of the saint's representation as an "ymage" and disregarding the numerous times that the representation of Nicholas is referred to as a "mahommet" (458; cf. 465, 513, 585, 779), a term that in Old French texts invariably refers to a free-standing statue. Camille himself notes this fact with reference to Middle English texts (135).

24. Rey-Flaud, *Pour une dramaturgie du Moyen Age,* 44. See also Rey-Flaud, "Le sentiment religieux dans *Le Jeu de saint Nicolas,*" 571–77, esp. 572–73.

As one might expect, the image of Saint Nicholas proves to be the more efficacious. The saint performs miracles wherever his image is present; conversely, the image of Tervagant repeatedly fails the Muslims. Finally, at the end of the play, persuaded by the power of Saint Nicholas and repelled by the impotence of his own god, the Muslim king converts to Christianity and has the golden statue of Tervagant thrown down from its place. In some ways, this episode resembles the abuse of idols at the hands of their former worshipers seen in the *Chanson de Roland:* in both texts, the Muslims throw down their statues, distraught by their obvious defeat at the hands of the Christians. In other ways, however, the *Jeu de saint Nicolas* differs significantly from the *Chanson de Roland,* for in the earlier work the gods clearly survive after being thrown down into the ditch. The Muslims continue to swear by Muhammad, and idols of the gods clearly continue to exist, for they are explicitly said, at the end of the poem, to be utterly destroyed by the victorious Christians. In the Saint Nicholas play, conversely, the destruction of Tervagant by the Muslims is final: when the king goes beyond merely denigrating and humiliating his idol and actually destroys it, the two separate episodes of iconoclasm in the Roland—one carried out by the pagans, one by the Christians—are conflated. The credit for the destruction of the pagan idol, moreover, is attributed not to the Christian forces for military conquest (as in the *Roland*), but to the saint who achieves a more far-reaching spiritual conquest.

It is striking that even though Tervagant is ultimately rejected by his followers as an ineffectual deity, he is not simply an inanimate golden statue. When his former worshipers are on the verge of converting to Christianity, Tervagant comes alive and speaks several lines in an incomprehensible tongue. The words that appear to be gibberish, however, prove to be intelligible to the Muslim king. When the Christian man present asks what Tervagant is saying, the king replies, "He is dying from sorrow and anger because God has converted me. But I don't care anymore what he says" (il muert de duel et d'ire / De che c'a Dieu me sui turkiés; / Mais n'ai mais soing de son prologe [517–19]). Tervagant's "language" is bizarre, creating an effect that appears to be at once comic and frightening.[25] It also serves, however, to reiterate the correspondence of Christian and Muslim religions, for Tervagant's dying words are almost immediately followed by words from the Christian liturgy, spoken in a language only imperfectly understood by

---

25. A comparable passage of pagan gibberish (with "Englys" translation) appears in the account of Richard I's military victories in the Holy Land that concludes the *Romaunce of Richard Coer de Lion.* See [*Richard Coer de Lion*], *Der mittelenglische Versroman über Richard Löwenherz,* lines 6929–34.

the majority of those who used it in worship: the "Te Deum laudamus" concludes the play, supplanting Tervagant's now obsolete foreign tongue with the language of the Church.

Like the great *chansons de geste,* such as the *Chanson de Roland, Fierabras,* and the poems of the Guillaume d'Orange cycle, the *Jeu de saint Nicolas* was written for a French-speaking audience during a time when the impulse toward crusade was at a high point. The earliest surviving redaction of the *Roland* was composed around the time of the First Crusade, preached at Clermont in 1095.[26] Jehan Bodel wrote the *Jeu de saint Nicolas* in or around 1200, at just the time when he himself prepared to join those embarking upon the Fourth Crusade.[27] In each case, the enemy portrayed in the literary work, whether it be those who oppose Charlemagne in Spain or those who persecute the followers of Saint Nicholas, is colored by the contemporary war between European Christians and the Muslims of the Middle East. Both the conquest of Saragossa and the conversion of the king by Saint Nicholas are expressions of the desire, long cherished by Western Christians, to regain the sacred spaces of the Holy Land.[28] The switch in genre, however, from the *chanson de geste,* where Christian victory can be achieved through martial means, to the mystery play, where the saint's miraculous intervention alone enables the Christian triumph, may reflect the decreased hopefulness regarding the enterprise of crusade. As John Tolan puts it, in describing the cultural context of the *Jeu de saint Nicolas,* after the failures of the Third Crusade, "perhaps conversion miracles seem[ed] more plausible than crusader victories."[29]

It is fruitful to juxtapose these two early medieval texts, different in genre yet similar in language and historical context, with a complementary pair of texts drawn from a very different place and time. The *Sowdone of Babylone* and the Digby *Mary Magdalen* play were both written in Middle English during the fifteenth century.[30] Each has something in common with the

---

26. See "Date et manuscrits de la chanson" in *La Chanson de Roland: Edition établie d'après le manuscrit d'Oxford,* 142–46, esp. 144.

27. Bodel became ill before he could embark upon the Crusade. See the biographical note in [Bodel], *Le Jeu de saint Nicolas,* ed. Albert Henry, 21–26. As Rey-Flaud puts it, "Le *Jeu de saint Nicolas* est d'abord l'histoire d'une croisade" (*Dramaturgie,* 139).

28. This is not to minimize the dramatic differences, both in motivation and execution, that distinguish the Fourth Crusade from the First. On literary and cultural manifestations of the Fourth Crusade, see Kinoshita, Medieval Boundaries, 139–75.

29. Tolan, *Saracens,* 129.

30. The *Sowdone of Babylone* is dated to the very end of the fourteenth century or the early fifteenth century on the basis of some echoes of Chaucer's *Canterbury Tales.* See Alan Lupack's introduction to *The Sowdone of Babylone,* 1; quotations from *Sowdone of Babylone* appear in the text, cited by line number. The *Digby Mary Magdalen* play is dated at the end of the fifteenth century by Donald C. Baker, John L. Murphy, and Louis B. Hall, Jr., in [*Digby Mary Magdalen*], *Late Medieval*

Old French texts described above: like the *Chanson de Roland,* the *Sowdone of Babylone* concerns the deeds of Charlemagne and his men and centers on the martial conflict of Muslim and Christian; like the Saint Nicholas play, the Digby *Mary Magdalen* focuses on the efficacy of saints in the lives of believers and on their ability to convert the unbeliever and to destroy the idols he worshiped before. By surveying how these very different yet comparable texts represent the function of images in worship, it is possible to get a broad sense of how the depiction of Muslims as idolaters developed during the years from 1100 to 1500.

The *Sowdone of Babylone,* like the *Chanson de Roland,* concerns the deeds of Charlemagne and his men as they attempt to beat back the advance of the Muslim armies in Spain. It follows the *chanson de geste Fierabras,* however, in extending its narrative beyond the events at Saragossa, telling the story of the sultan's son, Ferumbras, who converts to Christianity and becomes a powerful force against Muslim might. The *Sowdone of Babylone* is the most creative of the Middle English adaptations of the Old French *Fierabras,* fully incorporating the related *Destruction de Rome* and introducing a number of changes to the narrative. In keeping with a general tendency in Middle English romance adaptations of *chansons de geste,* the *Sowdone of Babylone* elaborates on motifs found in the Old French epic. For example, the *Roland* alludes only briefly to the dark skin of the Muslims: "Roland sees the accursed people, who are blacker than ink and whose teeth alone are white" (Rollant veit la contredite gent / Ki plus sunt neirs que nen est arrement, / Ne n'unt de blanc ne mais que sul les denz).[31] By contrast, in the *Sowdone of Babylone,* the Muslims are repeatedly described as being not only black but deformed and even chimerical, having leopard's heads and boar's tusks.[32] The anti-Trinity of Mahum, Apolin, and Tervagan worshiped by the Muslims of the *Roland* is expanded, in the *Sowdone of Babylone,* into a wider pantheon, including not just Mahounde, Apolyne, and Termagaunte but "Jubiter, Ascarot and Alcaron also" (2762).[33] As in the *Jeu de saint Nicolas,* the Muslim idols are said to be made of gold; but in the *Sowdone of Babylone,* the luxuriousness both of the idols and of the sacrificial materials offered up to them is emphasized

---

Religious Plays, xl. Quotations from the *Mary Magdalen* play are from this edition and are cited in the text by line number.

31. *Chanson de Roland,* lines 1932–34; cf. 1917–18, 1631–35.

32. *Sowdone of Babylone,* lines 2191–98; 346–57; 1005–06. On racial identity in the French and English versions of *Fierabras,* and on Fierabras' depiction in particular, see chapter 4 in this book, 159–73.

33. Interestingly, this identification of "Alcaron" as a god does not preclude the more accurate identification of the Qur'an as a holy book earlier in the poem: after a funeral, the Muslim mourners "songe the Dirige of Alkaron, / That Bibill is of here laye" (2271–72).

still more. The Sultan orders his men to burn frankincense before the idols, to blow brass horns in their honor, and to offer them milk, honey, oil, gold, and silver.[34] The abuse of the Muslim gods by their worshipers, occurring once in the *Chanson de Roland* and twice in the Saint Nicholas play, appears no less than four times in the *Sowdone of Babylone*.[35] But what in the *Roland* was tragedy appears in the *Sowdone of Babylone* as farce. The Sultan never goes through with his threat to burn his idols, but instead becomes remorseful and renews his sacrificial offerings. The repeated deferral of the act of iconoclasm heightens the comic effect, as the same reaction of fury followed by repentance appears again and again after each defeat in battle.[36]

One aspect that remains constant in the Middle English adaptations of the *chansons de geste,* however, is the fundamental reality of the gods represented by the images, their continuing presence. In the *Chanson de Roland,* the gods are still invoked even after their images are thrown into a ditch while, in the *Jeu de saint Nicolas,* the statue of Tervagan weeps in sorrow and speaks aloud even as the Muslim king renounces him. Similarly, in the *Sowdone of Babylone,* the gods preserve an independent existence beyond the images that embody them. When the Muslim giant Estragot is killed in battle, "Mahounde toke his soule to him / And broght it to his blis" (447–48; cf. 2017). The pagan gods, like the Christian God, take part in the battle, though sometimes, as the poem puts it, they "come to late" (410) or "holpe us not todaye" (898; cf. 913–17). They are, as in the epic, still martial leaders, which is why the vow to convert is also a vow of fealty. The Muslim Ferumbras tells the victorious Oliver, "I yelde me to the, / And here I become thy man. / ... / To Jhesu Crist I wole me take / ... / And all my goddes forsake" (1353–54, 1360–62). When Ferumbras takes Oliver as his lord, he becomes the vassal of Oliver's divine Lord as well. The king in the Saint Nicholas play takes this vow of fealty even more explicitly, telling the saint, "here I become your man / And leave Apollo and Muhammad / And that bastard [pautonnier] Tervagant" (1459–61). The failure of Islam, in these texts, is a failure of orientation, the choosing (in the words of the *Roland*) of "tort" rather than "dreit," the rejection (in the words of the Saint Nicholas play) of "paradys" in favor of "ynfers." Conversion—literally, a turning away from the wrong object of

---

34. *Sowdone of Babylone,* lines 677–86, 2449; cf. 1020–30, 2519–22, 2787–89.

35. The sultan's abuse of his images is greatly elaborated in the *Sowdone of Babylone,* compared with the French and Middle English precursors and analogues of the romance. For a detailed comparison of the depiction of idols in the Middle English versions of *Ferumbras* (including the *Sowdone of Babylone*), see Akbari, "Responses to Lollardy" (in preparation; presented at the International Congress on Medieval Studies, Western Michigan University, Kalamazoo, MI, May 3–6, 2001).

36. *Sowdone of Babylone,* lines 2431–56, 2495–2526, 2761–90; cf. 276–77.

worship toward the right object—is the means toward assimilation, the sub-suming of religious deviance within the sphere of Christendom.

These texts, however, are not designed to persuade Muslims to convert, to bring about actual transformations of the soul in imitation of the conversions repeatedly dramatized in the literature. On the contrary, the depiction of Muslims in western European literature holds up a mirror to medieval Christian practice, showing the readers of those texts what they are *not* so that they may understand what they *are.* It is a startling inversion: Muslims, whose devotion is based on the fundamental unity and oneness of God, are seen as polytheists, while Christians, who venerate a triune God, are represented as monotheists. Muslims, who utterly reject the use of images in worship, are seen as idolaters, while Christians, who do use images in worship, are thought to communicate with the divine more directly. It is striking that, in works that depict Muslims as idolaters, Christians are almost always shown appealing to God and his saints directly, without the intervening medium of any image. The one exception to this appears in the *Jeu de saint Nicolas,* in which Jehan Bodel directly confronts the distinction between idolatry and the rightful use of images in worship. He counters the golden statue of Tervagant with the simple wooden statue of Nicholas, and shows how greatly the saint's power outweighs that of his pagan rival. Jehan Bodel's careful distinction between idolatry and image veneration, however, is unusual. More frequently, texts depicting the clash of Christianity and Islam heighten the religious contrast by showing the Christian protagonists using an alternative mediator between the spiritual and material worlds, one that functions like the image of the saint but that more readily evades the charge of idolatry.

This alternative mediator is, of course, the relic, which plays a crucial role in both the *Sowdone of Babylone* and the Digby *Mary Magdalen* play. Interestingly, however, while relics are featured in the devotion of Christians in the former text, in the latter they appear in a more peculiar setting: in the Digby *Mary Magdalen,* relics are the object of pagan devotion, in the form of the broken fragments of "Mahowndys" body. Although relics are more common in later medieval depictions of the conflict of Christians and Muslims, they appear in earlier works as well. For example, in the *Chanson de Roland,* Durendal, the sword wielded by Roland in battle against the pagans, has embedded in its handle "Saint Peter's tooth, some of Saint Basil's blood, some of my lord Saint Denis' hair, some of Saint Mary's clothing" (La dent seint Perre e del sanc seint Basilie / E des chevels mun seignor seint Denise, / Del vestement i ad seint Marie [2346–48]). Charlemagne's sword, Joyeuse, is similarly endowed: its pommel contains "The lance . . . with which Our Lord was wounded on the cross" (la lance . . . / Dunt Nostre Sire fut en la cruiz

nasfret [2503–4]). Here, the weapon used to persecute Christ is, paradoxically, turned upon those who attack His followers. Through the use of such
weapons, national and religious goals are made coterminous, as a military
victory comprises conquest both by France and by Christ.

In later medieval depictions of Islam, however, the depiction of relics
serves a slightly different purpose, perhaps due to the changing status of the
relic in religious practice during the thirteenth and fourteenth centuries.[37]
Relics were increasingly depicted as central not only to Christian devotion,
but to Muslim worship as well. In the *Chanson de Roland,* the Muslims' interest in acquiring Durendal was based solely on its status as the sword wielded
by Roland (2281–82); conversely, in the *Sowdone of Babylone,* the Muslims
seize "alle the relekes… / The Crosse, the Crown, the Nailes bente" even before they "dispoile al the cite / Both of tresoure and of golde" (664–68). The
theft of the relics is referred to repeatedly (716, 748), highlighting their fundamental importance and building anticipation of their return to their proper
place following the Christians' victory in war. Muslim desire for Christian
relics serves as testimony to the essential power and desirability of these rare
and treasured objects.

While the recovery of the relics is indeed an important part of the climax
of the narrative of the *Sowdone of Babylone,* they are, significantly, not replaced
in "Seinte Petris" (663), whence they came. Instead, Charlemagne donates
the Cross to Notre Dame de Paris, the Crown to Saint Denis, and the Nails
to Boulogne.[38] Charlemagne redistributes these relics in order to make their
spiritual power available not in their traditional home at the seat of clerical
authority—Rome—but rather in a range of locations distributed throughout his newly formed empire. Charlemagne's donation is a manifestation of
translatio imperii, in this case, the transfer of imperial authority from ancient
Rome to the medieval Holy Roman Empire. A similar transfer is enacted
through a different means in the *Chanson de Roland,* where Charlemagne's
army is said to bear a marvelous battle standard: "It once belonged to Saint
Peter and its name was 'Romaine,' but it had taken the new name Monjoie
there" (Seint Piere fut, si aveit num Romaine, / Mais de Munjoie iloec out
pris eschange [3094–95]).[39] In the *Roland,* what formerly belonged to Peter

---

37. Geary suggests that, during the ninth through eleventh centuries, relics "assumed their
broadest and most essential roles.… After this period, they faced increasingly stiff competition from
other sources of mundane and celestial power." Geary, *Furta Sacra,* 17.

38. See *Sowdone of Babylone,* lines 3137–50, 3235–38. On relics in the *Fierabras* romances (including the *Sowdone of Babylone*), see Ailes, "Faith in *Fierabras,*" 125–33.

39. See Brault's discussion of this passage in connection with *translatio imperii* in [*La Chanson de
Roland*], *The Song of Roland: An Analytical Edition. I. Introduction and Commentary,* 289–90.

now belongs to Charlemagne, and the name evoking Rome has been replaced by the battle cry of the emperor's men. The physical movement of
the relics described in the *Sowdone of Babylone* is also a transfer of authority
from Peter to Charlemagne, from Rome to the Holy Roman Empire. Here,
however, the transfer is expressed not through a symbol or an emblem, but
through a tangible remnant of the presence of the divine on earth. More
powerfully than in the *Roland,* the movement of the relics in the *Sowdone
of Babylone* displaces the center of the empire (Rome) to what was formerly
the periphery (France). The clearly pivotal role of the relics in the *Sowdone
of Babylone* is made all the more striking by the fact that, of all of the Middle
English romances based upon the Old French *Fierabras,* the *Sowdone of Babylone* focuses the least on Christian devotion to relics. By contrast, one of the
other Middle English versions, the Fillingham *Ferumbras,* not only reproduces
every reference to relics found in the Old French original virtually word for
word, but actually augments the descriptions substantially.

In the Fillingham *Ferumbras,* the description of the relics (relatively brief in
the other versions) is used as an opportunity to name a whole range of holy
items, their historical background, and their devotional function. The first
display of relics in the text is followed by a sequence of elaborate showings.
In the second display of relics, for example, the Muslim princess Floripas exclaims "here hys the croune of goddys passyoun; / Lo, here ys the spere and
the nayles also / That longes pyt in hys hert, the blod ran there-fro" (594–96).
In the third display, we see not only the crown, nails, and spear, but also the
"voluper" and "sudary" (that is, Veronica's veil and the cloth used to wipe
Jesus' sweat). In the fourth display, Floripas brings "the crowne and the nayles
of goddys passioun, / And hys spere also that was in hys syde, / ther-with lon-
gens made hym a wounde wyde, / And othyr Relykys mo" (1769–73). This
final scene centers on the validation of the relics, which are shown beyond
any doubt to be worthy of adoration: when the crown floats miraculously in
the air, the bishop states "Nowe we haue preuyd, the sothe wete we mown,
/ that thys ys the Crown of goddys passyoun, / That was on hys heued there
that the blode out ran" (1795–97). The devotional function of this unusual
depiction of the relics in Fillingham is made explicit in the closing lines of
the manuscript, which asks God to bless those "that hauen herd thys gest
with gode deuocyoun / of the spere & the naylys and of the crovn! / Schul-
len [thay] haue an.C. dayes vnto pardoun!" (1836–38). The relics are adored,
wept over, and clearly demonstrate their efficacy. Just hearing about them
with "deuocyoun" assures the faithful reader time credited in purgatory.

Like the Fillingham *Ferumbras,* the Digby *Mary Magdalen* play emphasizes
the role of relics in religious devotion. Startlingly, however, they are used not

in Christian worship but in the pagan worship carried out by the king of Marseilles. One might argue that the Digby *Mary Magdalen* play is not a typical case of the representation of Muslims in medieval literature, since it would clearly be anachronistic to find Muslims in the life of a saint contemporary with Christ. Yet the king of Marseilles, whom Mary visits in an effort to convert him and his people, sounds very much like the Muslim rulers found in the *Sowdone of Babylone* and other Middle English romances. Like them, he makes sacrifices to his god "Mahownd" (1210; cf. 1140) and, like the Muslim king in the *Jeu de saint Nicolas,* he is in the end persuaded to convert by the miracles performed by the Christian saint.

The scene of sacrifice is richly expanded, however, in the Digby *Mary Magdalen,* as the religious offerings are accompanied by song and an elaborate liturgy performed by the king's "Prysbytyr" and his young altar boy. The climax of this religious ritual is the display of sacred relics: the Muslim presbyter displays "relykys brygth," including "Mahowndys own nekke bon" (1232–33). He allows the worshipers to kiss the bone, along with another relic of "Mahowndys own yeelyd" (1237). The eyelid is a particularly appropriate relic for the Muslims of the Digby *Mary Magdalen,* because the closed eye symbolizes the pagans' inability to perceive the divine light of God. They have eyes, but do not see; as the Muslim presbyter observes, the relic of Muhammad's eyelid "woll make yow blynd for ewyrmore" (1240). The centrality of relics in Muslim worship, as depicted in the play, is further emphasized by such repeated ejaculations as "be Mahondys bonys" (142) and "Mahowndys blod" (1175).

It goes without saying that the literary texts described above misrepresent Islam, for they suggest that Muslims practice polytheism and idolatry, that they have an established clergy, and so on. Yet the Digby *Mary Magdalen* is unusual in also suggesting that Muslims use relics in worship, thus showing how closely the author modeled his notion of Muslim religious practice on his experience of Christian ritual. The pagan worship enacted in the Digby *Mary Magdalen* is a detailed parody of Christian worship, employing images, song, liturgy, and ritual sacrifice in the veneration of "Seyntt Mahownde" (1205). This parody is most pronounced in the reading of the Muslim holy scripture, called the "leccyo mahowndys," performed by the presbyter's altar boy (1186–1201). This "lesson" is gibberish, like the sounds uttered by the dying Tervagan at the end of the Saint Nicholas play. Unlike Tervagan's words, however, which sound imposing and rather frightening, the words uttered by the altar boy have a comic effect. The Latinate endings of "cownthtys fulcatum" and "fartum cardiculorum" (1189, 1191) thinly conceal scatological language that could only have titillated the play's audience.

In the Digby *Mary Magdalen,* as in the *Sowdone of Babylone,* comic parody is evident in the depiction of Muslims to an extent not seen in the *Chanson de Roland* or the *Jeu de saint Nicolas.* In both of these early works, the depictions of Muslims can be described as parodic in a very general sense. Etymologically, the parody is "para odê," beside the song or a parallel to it.[40] Accordingly, the Muslim of the *Chanson de Roland* is "fiers" (897) as any Christian knight, while in the *Jeu de saint Nicolas,* Christians and Muslims both venerate a "mahommet." But the aspect of ridicule often associated with parody is not in evidence in these earlier depictions of Islam; conversely, in the *Sowdone of Babylone* and the Digby *Mary Magdalen,* comic parody is clearly at the fore. The increasingly exotic depictions of Muslims in the Middle English romances as giants having the faces of animals, "some bloo, some yolowe, some blake,"[41] suggest that the elements of comedy and fantasy had become increasingly important in representations of the Islamic Orient produced during the fourteenth and fifteenth centuries.[42]

In addition, however, the use of relics by the pagans of the Digby *Mary Magdalen* play fulfills more than a merely comic function. The repeated references to the different parts of the body of "Seyntt Mahownde"—the "nekke bon," the "yeelyd," "bonys," and "blod"—invites the reader to see Muslim worship as characterized by fragmentation, as being of an essentially partial and decaying nature. The degenerate language of the "leccyo mahowndys" reinforces this message, reminding the hearer of the medieval identification of Babylon, home of the great sultan, with Babel, the place where pride caused the confusion of tongues. Appropriately, this false etymology is placed in the closing lines of the polemical *Roman de Mahomet,* after a scathing indictment of the false prophet of the Muslims:

> Babylon, c'est confusïons:
> Pour chou li fu donnés li nons
> Que on i fist la tour jadis
> Pour monter haut em paradys,
> Par grant orgueil et par grant rage,
> Mais dex lor mua lor langage.
>
> Babylon, that is, "confusion";
> it was given the name because

---

40. On definitions of parody, see Hutcheon, *Theory of Parody,* 30–49.

41. *Sowdone of Babylone,* line 1005.

42. On the irrecoverable element of comedy that surely existed for medieval audiences of these texts, see Gourlay, "'Faire maide' or 'Venomous serpente.'"

the tower was built there long ago
in order to climb up as high as paradise,
out of great pride and great passion;
but God then transformed their language.

(1978–83)

Caroline Bynum has eloquently described how central the complementary notions of fragmentation and wholeness were to medieval conceptions of the self. She points out how thirteenth-century hagiography reveals the "tendency to assert wholeness," a triumph of the saint (and of the saint's community) over the decay and degeneration endemic in a post-lapsarian world: "What is underlined repeatedly is either a reassembling of body parts for burial or... the victory of intactness over division."[43] The scattered parts of "Seyntt Mahownde" are thus more than parody, for they illustrate the degenerate nature of the religious practice he represents.[44] The body of Muhammad in the Digby *Mary Magdalen* play manifests the lack of unity that, for the medieval Christian, lay at the heart of Islam. The relics in the hilts of Durendal and Joyeuse unify the community of the *Chanson de Roland,* while the rallying cry "Monjoie," derived from the name of Charlemagne's sword Joyeuse, continually renews the solidarity of the group and guarantees their ultimate victory (2503–11). Conversely, "Mahowndys own yeelyd" secures for his people only spiritual blindness and failure.

← The Place of Muhammad

So far, this chapter has focused on the "fanciful" mode of medieval depictions of Islam, where the notion of Muslims as polytheistic idolaters is paramount. From this point of view, Islam appears to be a continuation of pre-Islamic idolatry, the primitive, retrogressive belief of an ignorant people.[45] The following pages turn to the "realistic" mode of medieval depictions of Islam, where the prophet Muhammad appears as the charismatic leader of a deviant, heretical sect, characterized by a superficial attractiveness and a repellent kind

---

43. Bynum, *Resurrection of the Body,* 309, 312. See also Bynum, *Fragmentation and Redemption.*

44. In her description of the *Legenda Aurea* of Jacques de Voragine, Bynum notes that, paradoxically, "the good are intact when divided, while the evil fragment or decay even without violence" (*Resurrection,* 313).

45. On the continuity of Islamic "idolatry" with Greek and Roman use of images in worship, see Camille, *Gothic Idol,* 129–64. On Saracen devotion to Venus, see Beckett, *Anglo-Saxon Perceptions,* 212–16. In his *Dialogi contra Iudaeos,* Petrus Alfonsi describes Saracen worship of Saturn and Mars; see Tolan, *Saracens,* 150–51, and *Petrus Alfonsi,* 30–31.

of slippery cleverness. My contention in this chapter is that these two modes are far from being mutually exclusive; on the contrary, they are complementary and mutually reinforcing. Perhaps readers have been led to think of them as two separate modes in the hope that a more realistic view of Islam coexisted with those views that, to a modern eye, seem bizarre and disturbingly prejudiced. By identifying the more obviously prejudiced view as "fanciful," the reader automatically makes the alternative view seem "realistic," at least by comparison, and therefore marginally acceptable, if only within a medieval frame of reference.

As described in the first section of this chapter, anthropomorphism of the Islamic idols is a common feature in literary texts of the Middle Ages. The idol is at once an inanimate object and a quasi-person: its material content (stone, metal, or wood) makes it an object, but its bodily form makes it a semblance of a person. This ambiguity is repeatedly invoked, both in texts of the "fanciful" mode and the "realistic" mode. For example (to cite what is probably the most commonly cited representative of this phenomenon), the *Chanson de Roland* includes a scene in which the Muslims, disappointed by the weakness of their king, Marsilie, run out and smash the images of those gods that both he and they have served. They strip the image of "Apolin," tie it up by the hands, and beat it with sticks; this image, however, is described in terms more befitting a human body:

Ad Apolin en curent en une crute,
Tencent a lui, laidement le despersunent:
"E! malvais deus, por quei nus fais tel hunte?"
. . .
Puis si li tolent ses ceptre e sa curune.
Par mains le pendent sur une culumbe.

They run to Apollo, in a crypt,
They rail at him, they abuse him in vile fashion:
"Oh, evil god, why do you cover us with such shame?"
. . .
Then they tear away from him his sceptre and his crown.
[and] hang him by his hands upon a column.
                                        (laisse 187, lines 2580–86)

Comparable scenes featuring anthropomorphized idols appear in many other *chansons de geste* as well. For example, in the thirteenth-century *Enfances Guillaume*, an epic poem of the *Guillaume d'Orange* cycle, the pagan army led by

Thiebaus marches out bearing at their head a great image of "Mahon" covered with a green canopy and surrounded by many glowing lamps. Outraged by the sight, the Christians attack:

> Lancent li lances et gitent pelz agus,
> Pieres reondes et grans caillos cornus.
> Ainz ke paien se fussent perceü
> Ot Mahomet cent plaies voire plus;
> Li colz li froise et li piz et li buis,
> Celui tuerent ki enz el cors li fui,
> Et Mahon est a la terre abatu.

> They launch their lances and throw sharp stakes,
> Round rocks and great rough stones.
> As soon as the pagans became aware
> Muhammad already had a hundred wounds or more;
> The neck is shattered, and the feet and the trunk,
> They kill him who is in front of the body,
> And Muhammad is struck down onto the ground.
>   (laisse 37, lines 1564–70)[46]

As in the *Chanson de Roland,* this scene dramatically illustrates both the practice of idolatry and the impotence of the gods revered in the act of worship. The figure of Muhammad is, on a material level, stuff that can be shattered into fragments; on a formal level, it is a body with "neck" and "feet" and able to suffer "wounds." This passage, in *Les Enfances Guillaume,* also includes emphasis on the luxurious exoticism of the image, which appears covered by a rich canopy, surrounded by lanterns set with gemstones that exude a "light...like the sun that shines" (claret...comme solois ke raie [laisse 36, line 1537]).

The characterization of Muslims as idolaters illustrated here seems at first sight dramatically different from the views of Islam found in historical chronicles and theological writings, which focus on the life of Muhammad and stress his advocacy and practice of deviant behaviors, his eloquent powers of persuasion, his ability to work apparent miracles by ingenious means, and his disgraceful death. As John Tolan has rightly observed, however, these apparently distinct modes share common ground: of the sophisticated

---

46. *Les Enfances Guillaume, chanson de geste du XIIIe siècle.*

twelfth-century polemics against Islam, Tolan states that, "when one examines the text closely, the distinction between 'learned' and 'popular' blurs." While Tolan focuses particularly on such "popular" elements as the "trickster Muhammad,"[47] it is also fruitful to explore the common ground of idolatry shared by these two modes of representing Islam, and to examine more closely the symbolic system that underlies both of them. The embodiment of the prophet Muhammad in the image or "mahum" encapsulates the range of deceitful qualities attributed to Islam by medieval Christians: the devotion to fleshly pleasures rather than spiritual fulfillment, the duplicity and deception carried out by the Simon Magus-like figure of Muhammad,[48] and the wrongly directed worship of the "foolish people" (as the *Roman de Mahomet* repeatedly calls the Muslims).

Western biographies of the Prophet appeared in many forms, ranging from the short epitomes found in the *Legenda Aurea* (*Golden Legend*) of Jacques de Voragine and the *Speculum Historiale* of Vincent of Beauvais to the full-length treatments found in the eleventh-century *Vita Mahumeti* of Embrico de Mainz, the twelfth-century *Otia de Machomete* of Gautier de Compiègne, and its thirteenth-century adaptation in the *Roman de Mahomet* of Alexandre du Pont. In spite of their brevity (or perhaps because of it), the short accounts in the *Golden Legend* and in the *Speculum Historiale* were among the most widely distributed and best known. The longer accounts, however, are worth examining for the intricacy with which they develop an image of the Prophet designed to taint any real knowledge of Islamic theology. These texts tell of a pseudo-prophet who represents himself as what he is not. He is an antichrist in two senses: first, in that he represents himself as a messiah, and is therefore an inadequate copy or simulacrum of the real savior of humanity; second, in that he represents a manifestation of *the* Antichrist, the enemy of humanity whose coming was foretold in the book of Revelation.[49]

The eleventh-century *Vita Mahumeti* differs from the twelfth- and thirteenth-century biographies by Gautier de Compiègne and Alexandre du Pont in certain respects, most notably in featuring a kind of bifurcated Muhammad: the figure of the Prophet appears both as a devious, manipulative magician and as an upstart slave who, due to a successful marriage, rises to power.[50] It resembles those later texts, however, in its focus on the licentious and deceptive nature

---

47. Tolan, *Saracens,* 137.

48. On the Simon Magus tradition underlying the depiction of Muhammad in the *Vita Mahumeti* and related texts, see Ferreiro, *Simon Magus,* 20–23.

49. See Akbari, "Rhetoric of Antichrist," 297–307.

50. *Embricon de Mayence, La vie de Mahomet.* For a detailed discussion of the text, see Tolan, "Anti-Hagiography," 25–41; for a more general account, see Tolan, *Saracens* 137–47, passim.

of its subject. In the latest and most elaborate of these related texts, the *Roman de Mahomet,* the Prophet's love of sensuous pleasures is evident not only in his own personal behavior but in the behavior he advocates for his followers: not content with ordaining that "each man should have ten wives" (.X. femmes ait uns hons), he further ordains that "each woman should have ten husbands" (.X. maris ait une femme [lines 1390–91; cf. 1529–30]).[51] (So scandalous is this point that du Pont feels the need to mention it twice.) This licentious behavior is just one feature of a broader deviance, one that manifests itself both physically, in unorthodox behaviors such as polygamy and polyandry, and spiritually, in the practice of worship which proves to be idolatrous. It centers not on a pantheon of images as in the *chansons de geste,* but on a single figure: that of Muhammad. Yet this "realistic" mode of depicting Islam, as Norman Daniel influentially called it, is just as unrelenting as the more "fanciful" *chansons de geste* in characterizing Islam in terms of idolatry.

In spite of their apparent differences, these two modes (the "realistic" and the "fanciful") overlap in startling ways. While the *chansons de geste* lack any detailed account of Islamic theology or practice, they preserve from the biographical tradition the central role of Muhammad both in the presence of "Mahum" as one of the members of the pagan pantheon and in the usual name for any pagan image: that is, "mahum," "mahummet," or "mahon." Such biographical texts as the *Vita Mahumeti* and Guibert de Nogent's *Gesta Dei per Francos* recount the disgraceful death of Muhammad, stating that he fell, drunk, into a ditch where his body was devoured by pigs and dogs.[52] This scene is reflected in the act of iconoclasm recounted in the *Chanson de Roland,* where the image of Muhammad is thrown into a "ditch" (fosset) where "pigs and dogs bite and befoul him" (e porc e chen le mordent et defulent" (laisse 187, lines 2590–91]). The idol is anthropomorphized, even embodied, by its identification with the Prophet himself, violating the apparently distinct separation of the two modes of representation of Muslims. Similar overlap can be located elsewhere: for example, the early twelfth-century *Gesta Tancredi* of Raoul de Caen includes a description of a monumental statue adored by the Muslims at Jerusalem that Raoul identifies, with a frisson of recognition, as the "ancient Antichrist, / Mahummet the depraved, Mahummet the pernicious."[53] In these passages, the image appears as both a

51. Alexandre du Pont, *Le Roman de Mahomet.*

52. On the representation of the fragmented and destroyed body of Muhammad in Western anti-Islamic polemic, see Tolan, "Un cadavre mutilé," 53–72.

53. Raoul de Caen, *Gesta Tancredi,* c. 129 (RHC occ. 3:695–96); cited and quoted in Tolan, "Muslims as Pagan Idolaters," 97–117; citation from 108.

generic "mahummet" or idol and, in some sense, Muhammad himself. They thus suggest that the relationship between the two traditions is sequential: that is, as time passes, the depraved religion preached by the pseudo-prophet Muhammad degenerates further into idolatry centered on a collection of stone gods that includes "Mahum" among their number.

Such a teleological interpretation, however, obscures the profound extent to which the two traditions continuously reinforce each other, and the extent to which in both traditions idolatry is presented as the focus of Saracen worship. Like its precursors, the thirteenth-century *Roman de Mahomet* includes a scene in which Muhammad, apparently miraculously, causes a white bull to appear on a hillside bearing the Qur'an suspended between its horns.[54] (He has actually trained it to come at his call from the time that it was a young calf.) On one level, this scene illustrates the conventional role of Muhammad as trickster and pseudo-prophet; on another, it evokes the prototypical scene of idolatry that the Israelites performed with the golden calf during their journey through the desert led by Moses. This biblical allusion is reinforced in the text by a series of comparisons between the "old law" of Moses and the "new law" of Muhammad (1385–88, 1397–1403, 1492–98). By mounting the book of this "new law" (loi nouviele [1484]) between the horns of the apparently miraculous animal, the sacred scripture itself, which could readily have been seen as a point of similarity and convergence between Abrahamic religions, is instead characterized in terms of idolatry. This displacement serves to widen the gulf between Christian and Muslim and to reinforce the centrality of the image in Western understandings of Islam.

Idolatry is also the focus of attention in the closing pages of the *Roman de Mahomet,* where the death and entombment of the Prophet is recounted. Like the magnificently adorned images of Muhammad seen in the *Gesta Tancredi* of Raoul de Caen and in the *Enfances Guillaume,* the tomb of the Prophet is said to be surrounded with "a lamp of shining crystal" (une lampe de cristal cler) and "other stones... garnet and pure carbuncles" (auchune piere... pirope u escarboucle fine [1935, 1941–42]). Even more remarkable, however, is the position of the sarcophagus: it hangs, unsupported, "in the midair, without any support" (en l'air sans nul loier [1908]).[55] The light cast by the lamp and the shining stones surrounding the tomb is a parody or false simulacrum of the real illumination offered by the true God, just as the floating sarcophagus of this false messiah parodies the ascent into heaven of the resurrected Christ.

---

54. On the comparable scene in Gautier de Compiègne's *Otia de Machomete,* see Tolan, *Saracens,* 140–41.

55. On the comparable scene in Gautier de Compiègne's *Otia de Machomete,* see ibid., 143.

The tomb is suspended, apparently by a miracle; actually, du Pont reveals, the tomb is made of metal and is held aloft by magnets embedded in the walls of the surrounding structure. The apparent miracle, once again, proves to be simply the product of human ingenuity.

A similar scene appears in the *Chanson d'Antioche*. There, however, the form of Muhammad suspended in mid-air is not the entombed body, but a graven image: "Muhammad was in mid-air by the power of the magnet, and the pagans adored him and paid him worship, they offered him gold and silver" (Mahomés fu en l'air par l'aïmant vertus / Et paien l'aorerent et rendent lor salus, / Or et argent li offrent [laisse 202, lines 4891–93]).[56] These scenes in the *Roman de Mahomet* and the *Chanson d'Antioche* are fundamentally the same: the only difference is that, in the former, pagans make offerings to the suspended *body* of Muhammad, while in the latter, they make offerings to the suspended *image* of Muhammad.[57] In both cases, idolatry is the heart of the pagans' error: their worship is misdirected, whether toward an inefficacious idol or toward a false messiah. The sensuous pleasures ordained by the Prophet, too, prove to be a form of idolatry: the writer of the *Roman de Mahomet* states that the "new law" of Muhammad preaches not only polygamy but also a return to "fleshly circumcision" (charneus circoncisïons [1389; cf. 1527]). Turning from the circumcision of the heart enjoined by the Apostle Paul to the circumcision of the flesh, from the renunciation of sensuous satisfaction to the embrace of the pleasures of the body, from the unsullied worship of God to the deviant adoration of the image, this new faith can offer only damnation and death. Idolatry itself is a kind of sensuous pleasure, reaching only as far as the luxurious surface of the image.

It is significant that both strands of the medieval depiction of Islam—one focused on Islam as idolatry, the other focused on Islam as Christian heresy—insist on the fundamentally retrogressive nature of the religion. The identification of Islam as a polytheistic, idol-worshipping continuation of pagan idolatry is clearly regressive, suggesting that all such worship is, in some sense, the same, collectively and universally anterior to the advent of Christianity. In a more subtle way, the identification of Islam as a Christian heresy is similarly retrogressive. While one might expect that such an identification might make Islam appear to be a dangerous novelty built upon the foundations of Christianity, texts such as the *Roman de Mahomet* instead take pains to insist that this apparent "new law" of Islam is, in fact, a return to the "old law" of Moses—that is, Judaism. Such identification of Islam with the Judaic "law of

---

56. *La Chanson d'Antioche.*
57. See Eckhardt, "Le cercueil flottant de Mahomet," 77–88.

the letter" is explored in more detail in the following chapter, which focuses on the competing claims of literal and spiritual, flesh and soul, in medieval visions of heaven. For the present, however, it is necessary to continue this chapter's survey of the intertwined strands of idolatry and heresy that make up the premodern Western view of Islam, turning to what is arguably the most sophisticated and nuanced treatment of Islam in medieval literature: Dante's *Commedia*. This chapter explores Dante's depiction of Islam in the *Inferno*, while the next chapter ("The Form of Heaven") considers the *Paradiso*'s characterization of the Christian heaven in terms of the Islamic *mi'raj*.

Dante's view of Islam is ambivalent. This tremendously overused term is, in Dante's case, highly appropriate for, as Maria Rosa Menocal has eloquently shown, Dante at once uses Islamic theology as a template for transcendent truths in his *Paradiso* and denigrates it in the strongest terms in his *Inferno*.[58] At first glance, the depiction of Muhammad in Dante's *Inferno* is a typical example of the "realistic" mode of representing Islam. Muhammad is placed deep in hell, in the ninth pouch (or *bolge*) of the eighth circle. He appears in the circle of the schismatics, in keeping with the view that Islam is a form of Christian heresy. While Dante's Muhammad is a schismatic, the instigator of a split in the body of the community of Christian believers, his followers are individually guilty not of schism but of heresy (that is, false faith), a sin punished in a separate, less onerous circle of hell. They are led into this sin by Muhammad's preaching of a "new law" (nuova legge) based on Christianity, which is at the same time "the contrary" (il contrario), as early commentators on the *Commedia* such as Jacopo Alighieri and the *Ottimo* put it.[59] The phrase "nuova legge" clearly recalls the formulation found in writers such as Vincent of Beauvais in the *Speculum Historiale*, or Alexandre du Pont in the *Roman de Mahomet*: in this view, Islam is a theological innovation, a schismatic departure from Christian truth. Because of the crucial distinction between schism and heresy, Ali alone appears not in the circle of the heretics, but together with Muhammad in the circle of the schismatics. Ali is present among the schismatics not on account of his belief in Islam, which would place him among the heretics, but because of his role in the development of the Shi'a movement within Islam which, from an orthodox perspective, is schismatic. Dante's identification of Ali as a schismatic is all the more remarkable in that it implies that, in spite of all that separates them, Islam remains a form of Christianity, albeit a perverted form of it. Only if Islam is, in some sense, still a form of Christianity can Ali's transgression be seen as schism.

---

58. Menocal, *Arabic Role in Medieval Literary History*.
59. Jacopo Alighieri, *Chiose all'*Inferno; *L'Ottimo commento della* Divina Commedia.

Early commentators on the *Commedia* display ignorance regarding the sophisticated theological perspective underlying Dante's treatment of Islam. Several, including Jacopo Alighieri (1322), Jacopo della Lana (1324), the *Ottimo* commentator (1333), and (most elaborately) the *Anonimo Fiorentino* commentator (1400), repeat the popular story that Muhammad was a Christian cleric who, when frustrated in his effort to achieve the papacy, satisfied his lust for power by founding his own religious sect.[60] Unaware of the position of Ali in the development of Islam, they ignore him or, at best, like Jacopo Alighieri, refer to him as "one of [Muhammad's] companions named Ali." Not until the nineteenth century do commentators show knowledge of Ali's specific role in the early history of the Islamic community.

The importance of Dante's treatment of Ali has also been largely overlooked by modern commentators on the *Inferno,* who state (following the influential nineteenth-century study by d'Ancona) that Dante's representation of the Prophet is in keeping with the popular legend of Muhammad as an apostate Christian cardinal. The entry under "Mäometto" in the *Enciclopedia dantesca,* for example, refers to "the western legend, which was the only source used by Dante."[61] It is certainly true that the "western legend" was the only source used by the early commentators, who used it to expound their understanding of Muhammad's placement in the *Inferno.* Dante's own treatment of Ali, however, an enigma to the early commentators, illustrates the poet's remarkably subtle view of the theological relationship between Christianity and Islam. This is evident not only in the care with which Dante distinguishes between heresy and schism, but also in the specific nature of the punishment assigned to Muhammad and Ali. The "contrapasso" (Inf. 28.142) experienced by Muhammad embodies the split in the Christian community caused by schism. His mutilated torso is "cleft from the chin to the part that breaks wind; his entrails were hanging between his legs, and the vitals could be seen and the foul sack that makes shit of what is swallowed" (rotto dal mento infin dove si trulla. / Tra le gambe pendevan le minugia; / la corata pareva e 'l tristo sacco / che merda fa di quel che si trangugia [Inf. 28: 24–27]). Here, the fractured community of the faithful is mirrored in the fragmented body of Muhammad, in a microcosmic representation of the group within the individual similar to that which we saw in the Jewish bodies

---

60. A detailed account of this tradition can be found in d'Ancona, "La leggenda di Maometto in Occidente," 199–281. See also Daniel, *Islam and the West,* 19–20; Tolan describes the refutation of the tradition by Peter of Cluny (*Saracens,* 157).

61. "[L]a leggenda occidentale, a cui esclusivamente Dante s'ispirò." *Enciclopedia dantesca,* s.v. "Mäometto."

described in chapter 3. Ali's body is similarly a microcosm of the community: his body, "cleft in the face from chin to forelock" (fesso nel volto dal mento al ciuffetto [Inf. 28.33]), illustrates the split in the caliphate, or headship of the Muslim community, which resulted from his rule.

It is worth looking more closely at the precise nature of the corresponding punishment (or "contrapasso") experienced by Muhammad and Ali, because this canto is the sole location, in all of the *Commedia*, that Dante explicitly uses the term that has come to be universally applied to the system of punishments in the *Inferno*. The term *contrapasso* is derived from the Latin *contrapassum,* which appears in the medieval translation of Aristotle's *Nicomachean Ethics* as a rendering of the Greek term for "reciprocation" (to antipeponthos).[62] Medieval commentators including Thomas Aquinas used the discussion of *contrapassum* in the *Nicomachean Ethics* as an opportunity to point out the limitations of the "lex talionis" of the so-called Old Law of the Jews, which simply elicited a punishment ("an eye for an eye") corresponding to the crime committed. This appears not only in Aquinas' commentary on the *Nicomachean Ethics* but also in the *Summa Theologica,* where Aquinas' discussion of the "lex talionis" of the Old Testament incorporates the Aristotelian *contrapassum:* "Retaliation [*contrapassum*] denotes equal passion repaid for previous action.... This kind of justice is laid down in the Law (Exod. 21: 23–24): 'He shall render life for life, eye for eye,' etc."[63]

Dante's use of the term "contrapasso" to denote the nature of the bodily punishments in the *Inferno* can profitably be understood in the context of Aquinas' discussion of the "lex talionis" and the Aristotelian "contrapassum," as has long been noted.[64] Just as the Old Law of the Jews, in the view of medieval Christians, carried out the administration of justice on the literal level of the flesh rather than the spiritual level of the immortal soul, so too the bodily phenomenon of the "contrapasso" in the *Inferno* makes visible to the bodily eye the nature of the invisible punishment of the soul. This relationship is made clear in the closing lines of the canto, in which the Provençal poet Bertran de Born describes how his own "contrapasso" reflects both the sin he committed on earth and the eternal fate of his own damned soul: "Because I parted persons thus united, I carry my brain parted from

---

62. *Nicomachean Ethics,* 5.5.1132b, in Aquinas, *In decem libros Ethicorum Aristotelis ad Nicomachum expositio,* 266.

63. "[H]oc quod dicitur 'contrapassum' importat aequalem recompensationem passionis ad actionem praecedentem.... Et hoc quidem iustum determinatur in lege, Exod. 21, 23: 'Reddet animam pro anima, oculum pro oculo,' etc." Aquinas, *Summa Theologica* 2.2, quaest. 61.a.4, resp.

64. See, for example, the seminal study of d'Ovidio, "Sette chiose alla *Commedia,*" 5–82, esp. 27–34.

its source, alas, which is in this trunk. Thus is the retribution [contrapasso] observed in me" (Perch' io parti' così giunte persone, / partito porto il mio cerebro, lasso!, / dal suo principio ch'è in questo troncone. / Così s'osserva in me lo contrapasso [Inf. 28.139–42]). The crime committed on earth—in this case, setting Henry, the young king, against his father, the Angevin Henry II—is mirrored in the split body of the poet, a division of the individual body that is a microcosm of the divided family and the divided kingdom resulting from Bertran's transgression.

Although the term "contrapasso" appears only once in the *Commedia,* in this description of Bertran's punishment, the phenomenon is equally visible in the riven bodies of Muhammad and Ali, who similarly represent in microcosm the communities they sinfully divided. Muhammad's body, split from chin to anus, is a dramatic split whose scope corresponds to the magnitude of the schism created (in Dante's view) by the splitting off of Islam from Christianity. Ali's riven face, from chin to forelock, represents a narrower social division, a split in the headship of the community rather than of the community as a whole. In addition, there is a further aspect of Dante's depiction of Muhammad's body that bears on the broader topic of his presentation of Islam, and which draws specifically on the rhetoric of idolatry we already saw illustrated both in the "fanciful" *chansons de geste* and the "realistic" biographies of Muhammad. This aspect concerns the phenomenon of suspension.

Dante's narrator engages in conversation with Muhammad, eliciting a prophecy from the damned soul concerning another schismatic living in Dante's own time, Fra Dolcino. Following his prophetic utterance, Muhammad sets his foot to the ground and resumes his pacing through the circle of the schismatics: "After he had raised one foot to go on, Muhammad said this to me, then set it on the ground to depart" (Poi che l'un piè per girsene sospese, / Mäometto mi disse esta parola; / indi a partirsi in terra lo distese [Inf. 28.61–63]). This peculiar detail has drawn some rather strained explication by modern commentators, as it is not evident why Muhammad should stand with one foot "suspended" [sospese] during his prophetic utterance.[65] I would suggest that the notion of suspension here draws upon the rich tradition of the suspended tomb of Muhammad, which in a series of medieval Western biographies of the prophet is said to be held aloft by cleverly positioned magnets, a perpetual focus of veneration in Mecca. The

---

65. See, for example, the rather unsatisfactory explanation of d'Ovidio, who suggests that Muhammad's foot is partially on the ground, but not yet extended fully ("Sette chiose," 26). It is still not clear why the position of the foot should be emphasized by the poet.

Vita Mahumeti, the *Otia de Machomete,* the *Roman de Mahomet,* and a variety of other versions all describe the floating tomb of Muhammad, suspended in a parodic imitation of the true bodily ascent of Christ. This tomb, filled with the bones of the pseudo-prophet, is a carnal imitation of the divinely empty Holy Sepulchre; its apparently miraculous weightlessness is no manifestation of divinity, but simply a deceptive trick.

In a seminal article, Alexandre Eckhardt delineated the evolution of the floating tomb narrative, from its earliest applications to pre-Islamic paganism to its rich elaboration within the context of medieval Western biographies of Muhammad.[66] Eckhardt points out a particularly interesting example found in the *Liber Nycholay,* a late thirteenth-century anti-Islamic polemic that describes Muhammad as a schismatic Christian.[67] In this text, the tomb is said to contain fragments of Muhammad's body, contained in a metal tomb miraculously suspended by magnets: "a disciple of his named Chanila prayed over the right foot of this [Muhammad], addressing God and all the angels, that they would raise him up into the heavens, asking them to mercifully place the foot into their hands as a relic. They then made a tomb [arcam] covered in gold and placed the foot into it.... All Saracens make their pilgrimage to Mecca and adore the foot in the tomb there, the foot of Muhammad. Truly, the arc rests suspended in the air, drawn in each direction by three great magnetic stones."[68] Of the various texts describing the contents of the floating tomb of Muhammad, the *Liber Nycholay* alone focuses specifically on the foot of Muhammad. Like the description of the heels of Muhammad supposedly venerated by his followers described by Guibert de Nogent in the short anti-Islamic polemic included in his *Gesta Dei per Francos,* the foot signifies baseness, lowness, and filth.[69] The biblical account of Jezebel, thrown from a window for her sins and devoured by hungry dogs who leave

---

66. Eckhardt, "Le cercueil flottant de Mahomet," 77–88.

67. While d'Ancona dated the *Liber Nycholay* to the fourteenth century, in his recent edition, Muñoz redates the work to the second half of the thirteenth century, and demonstrates its Italian origin: Muñoz, "*Liber nycholay,*" 5–43.

68. "[Q]uaedam discipula eius nomine Chanila incantavit pedem extrum ipsius ad Deum et ad omnes angelos, qui ipsum elevaverunt et ferebant in celum misericordiam invocando quod pes pro reliquiis in manibus ejus remisit. Quare fecerunt arcam deauratam et in ea posuerunt pedem.... Omnes Sarraceni peregrinationem faciunt ad Mecham et adorabant ibi pedem in archa, pedem Machumeti. Archa vero in aëre detinetur suspensa et trahitur a tribus magnis lapidibus." Quoted from the transcription of Eckhardt from MS Bib. Nat. f. lat. 14,503, f.353v (Eckhardt 85); see also the edition of Muñoz, "*Liber nycholay.*"

69. Guibert writes: Muhammad "left his heels fittingly, since he had wretchedly fixed the traces of false belief and the foulness in deceived souls." Guibert de Nogent, *Dei gesta per Francos,* 1.99, trans. Robert Levine, *The Deeds of God through the Franks,* 33. See the discussion of this passage in Tolan, *Saracens,* 142–43.

behind only the "palms and soles of her feet," provides a resonant analogue for the mutilated body of the prophet. The account in the *Liber Nycholay* goes beyond this context, however, in describing the foot as the focus of worship, richly enshrined and the central site in the practice of pilgrimage by the Saracens. It may not be too far-fetched to suggest that crusader accounts concerning the Dome of the Rock, so named for the rock containing Muhammad's footprint made at the time of his miraculous night journey (or *mi'raj*), may lie behind the description of Saracen worship of the "foot of Muhammad."[70] As we will see in the next chapter, the *mi'raj* account was known to Western Christians through various intermediaries, and was even appropriated into a Christian framework by Dante himself.

My purpose in identifying the motif of the suspended tomb and, more particularly, the placement of the foot of Muhammad in the suspended tomb is not simply to identify possible sources for Dante's depiction of the prophet in the *Inferno*. Rather, I would suggest that the context laid out here makes it possible to appreciate more fully the sophisticated and nuanced character of Dante's engagement with Islam, including his understanding of Islam as being at once a Christian schism *and* a retrogressive return to the Old Law of the Jews. Again, this identification is expressed in Dante's work through the theme of suspension. The motif of Muhammad's floating tomb appears most clearly in the *Inferno* not in the circle of the schismatics, but in the frozen heart of Dis itself. As Sylvia Tomasch has eloquently pointed out, the depiction of alternative religions in the *Inferno* coalesces the "two great religious foes" of Christianity into a single misguided whole: "Although heretics appear in various guises, at bottom, it is implied, they are all the same. In this way, the profane temple of the Jews is suggested, repressed, and superseded by the appearance of the mosques."[71] In this reading, the "meschite" of the upper circles of Dis are prefigurations of the central profane space located in the depths of the Inferno; significantly, that space is, precisely, a "tomb" (tomba [Inf. 34.128]).

In the final canto of the *Inferno,* Dante's narrator and his guide, Virgil, observe the hideous figure of Satan, frozen in the icy center of hell. As Virgil helps the narrator to ascend one of Satan's legs as they depart from the final circle, the narrator expresses confusion: "Where is the ice? And he there, how is it that he is fixed upside down?" (ov' è la ghiaccia? E questi

---

70. Enrico Cerulli has suggested that the popular notion of the relic of Muhammad's foot was adored at Mecca played a role in Western receptions of the *mi'raj* account. See Cerulli, *Nuove ricerche sul "Libro della Scala" e la conoscenza dell'Islam in Occidente,* 250–54.

71. Tomasch, "Judecca," 247–67, quotation from 253–54.

com' è fitto / sì sottosopra? [Inf. 34.103–4]). Virgil explains that, like the worm within the core of the ripe apple, Satan is an "evil worm that pierces the world" (vermo reo che 'l mondo fóra [Inf. 34.108]), located at the very center of the earth: "As long as I descended, you were on that side; when I turned myself, you passed the point to which all weights are drawn from every part" (Di là fosti cotanto quant' io scesi; / quand' io mi volsi, tu passasti 'l punto / al qual si traggon d'ogne parte i pesi [Inf. 34.109–11]). The center of the earth is a point of suspension, the place where (according to medieval understandings of physical laws) all matter is inexorably drawn. In his *Dragmaticon,* the twelfth-century philosopher William of Conches explains this physical law with reference to the tomb of Muhammad: "a similar antagonism of forces draws [the earth] to the front and the back, to the right and the left, as we have heard of the tomb of Mahomet [*sic*], which, being of iron, is sustained on every side by a magnet."[72] Like the suspended tomb of Muhammad described in the *Liber Nycholay,* which is "suspended [suspensa] in the air, drawn [trahitur] in each direction,"[73] the body of Satan is at "the point to which all weights are drawn [traggon]" (Inf. 34.111). The physics, in each case, are opposite: the magnetic weights pull on the suspended tomb, while the heavy matter pushes on the suspended figure of Satan.[74] In both cases, however, the result is suspension, an in-between state mirrored in the narrator's own state of being: at the sight of Satan, he says, "I did not die and I did not remain alive...deprived alike of death and life" (Io non mori' e non rimasi vivo...d'uno e d'altro privo [Inf. 34.25, 27]).

For Dante, this suspended point is a "tomb" (tomba [Inf. 34.128]), a typological fulfillment of the suspended tomb of Muhammad venerated by the Saracen pilgrims who stream to Mecca. At the same time, the point is also described as a "ladder" (scala [Inf. 34.119]), in a parodic allusion to the heavenly ascent of the prophet Muhammad recounted in the *Libro della scala* ("Book of the Ladder"), a text that Dante draws upon later in the *Commedia* in order to describe the layers of the heavenly paradise. The heavenly ascent or *mi'raj* of the prophet, marked on earth by the footprint miraculously impressed in the stone located within the Dome of the Rock, is placed by Dante within the very foundations of hell, in an inverted image of Saracen sacrality. Both sites of false worship—the floating tomb at Mecca, and the

---

72. William of Conches, *Dragmaticon* book 2, paragraph 9; trans. Ronca and Curr, *A Dialogue on Natural Philosophy,* 35.

73. Quoted from the transcription of Eckhardt from MS Bib. Nat. f. lat. 14,503, f.353v (Eckhardt 85); see also the edition of Muñoz, "*Liber nycholay.*"

74. On the medieval physics of magnetism, see Stecher, *Magnetismus im Mittelalter.*

footprint in the stone at Jerusalem—find their ultimate telos in the worm at the center of the apple, the forbidden fruit of Eden perpetually remembered in the body of Satan.

✦ The Filthy Idol

As we have seen, the distinction between the "fanciful" and "realistic" modes of depicting Islam, so carefully distinguished by Norman Daniel and those who have followed him, is more apparent than real. The two modes are mutually reinforcing, both rooted in the symbolic system of idolatry; consequently, both reiterate consistently that Islam is wrongly oriented in terms of its object of devotion, and that it is a faith focused on the superficial level of the flesh rather than the exalted level of the spirit. This notion of Islam as a wrongly directed and fundamentally superficial religion is pervasive in the literature of the Christian medieval West. Whether manifested in the convention of Muslims as polytheistic idolaters, or in the depiction of Muhammad as the heretical leader of a Christian schism, Islam is consistently described as a religion of surfaces: it is said to privilege the fleshly body above the eternal soul, the letter above the spirit, and the physical image above its referent. This insight regarding the pivotal role of space in the construction of the alterity of the Muslim—that is, the characterization of Islam as a religion of the outside, of the exterior—provides a valuable tool in examining a third, separate aspect of medieval representations of Islam: namely, the depiction of Islam as a source of contamination or pollution, and the description of Muslims as filthy and abject. As we will see, the rhetoric of pollution, ubiquitous in crusade preaching and chronicles, proves to be, once again, grounded in the symbolic system of idolatry.

In a wide range of texts written in connection with the Crusades, the city of Jerusalem is described as being contaminated. Pope Urban's original sermon calling for a crusade to the Holy Land, delivered at the Council of Clermont in 1095, survives in several different forms, recorded by different chroniclers. The chroniclers all agree, however, in their rendering of the language used to describe the current state of Jerusalem and the urgent need for intervention on the part of Western Christians. One chronicler writes that Urban declared that Jerusalem is "possessed by unclean nations. . . . The holy places . . . are . . . irreverently polluted with their filthiness."[75] Another records

---

75. Robert of Reims (Robert the Monk), RHC Occ 3; trans. Peters, 3.

Urban's statement that "the sanctuary of God...is everywhere profaned" and that Jerusalem "has been reduced to the pollution of paganism." As Penny Cole has shown, the rhetoric of pollution was essential not only to the preaching of the First Crusade, but also to subsequent chronicles of the Crusade and even the preaching of the Second and Third Crusades, later in the twelfth century. More remains to be said, however, both about the nature of that pollution as it is expressed in Western accounts, and about the language used to explain how the contamination might be wiped away, how the holy places might once again be made clean.

Crusade chronicles and sermons often represent the pollution of Muslim presence in physical, corporeal terms. Muslims are characterized as "filthy" or "unclean," likened to "pigs" and "dogs." Their bodily presence, whether alive or dead, was thought to be enough to pollute a sacred place. For example, the Council of Nogano of 1303 stated that a church could be "polluted...by the burial within it of those under interdict, heretics, schismatics, pagans, or Jews."[76] Other texts specify that the filth produced by Muslims comes from bodily fluids, particularly blood. Blood, of course, is not necessarily unclean in itself: in the right place, as in the sacrifice of the Mass, it can even be viewed as sacred or precious. Yet, when it is out of place, blood can be seen as contaminating filth or pollution. As the cultural anthropologist Mary Douglas suggested almost forty years ago, pollution signifies nothing more than the violation of boundaries: "dirt," as she puts it, is precisely "matter out of place."[77]

It is paradoxical but true that the same substances that can pollute a sacred space can also be employed to make it sacred. As Douglas writes, "To talk about a confused blending of the Sacred and the Unclean is outright nonsense. But it still remains true that religions often sacralize the very unclean things which have been rejected with abhorrence."[78] This ability of blood both to consecrate and to desecrate is illustrated in two letters written by Bernard of Clairvaux in support of the abortive Second Crusade. In them, he describes the contemporary state of Jerusalem, emphasizing the sacred nature

---

76. Grayzel, *Church and the Jews,* 263.

77. Douglas, *Purity and Danger,* 35. Douglas goes on to observe: "Uncleanness or dirt is that which must not be included if a pattern is to be maintained. To recognize this is the first step towards insight into pollution" (40). See also her remarks on "pollution by blood" (60): "Injunctions, which in their origin may have been concerned with removing pollution of blood, are interpreted as carrying only a symbolic spiritual significance. For example, it is usual to reconsecrate a church if blood has been shed in its precincts, but Saint Thomas Aquinas explains that 'bloodshed' refers to voluntary injury leading to bloodshed, which implies sin, and that it is sin in a holy place which desecrates it, not defilement by bloodshed" (61).

78. Douglas, *Purity and Danger,* 159.

of the Holy Land and harshly condemning the contamination of the Muslims who, he says, "pollute the sacred places" (polluant loca sancta). Bernard refers to the "filth of the pagans" (spurcitia paganorum) and likens the Muslims to pigs and dogs whose presence, he says, "profanes the holy of holies, the place where the... immaculate Lamb was purpled with blood."[79] What is remarkable in these letters is not only their harshness, but also their emphasis on the sanctity of place, and on the relationship between holiness and cleanliness, profanation and filth. Bernard indicates clearly that blood has the power to make things holy as well as to pollute: after all, it is the shedding of the blood of the Lamb, as he puts it, that made the holy places sacred to begin with.

Just as Jerusalem was made sacred through the shedding of blood, so it was polluted through the shedding of blood. This act of pollution is recounted in Robert of Reims' version of Pope Urban's sermon at Clermont:

> They destroy the altars, having defiled them with their uncleanness. They circumcise the Christians, and the blood of the circumcision they either spread upon the altars or pour into the vases of the baptismal font.[80]

It is interesting to note that the same accusation of forced circumcision of Christians was used in the thirteenth century in England and France not against Muslims, but against Jews, who were perceived as an enemy within Christendom allied with the Muslim enemy outside. In this passage, blood both sacralizes and profanes: Jerusalem is made holy by the sacrificial blood spilled at the Crucifixion, often associated in devotional literature with the drops of blood produced during the circumcision of the infant Jesus.[81] Conversely, however, the blood of the Christians forcibly circumcised by the Muslims pollutes the sacred places. The consecrated wine, transubstantiated into blood, is sacred and clean upon the altar, being in its rightful place; this other blood, however, can be seen only as filth.

Since blood was believed to have the power both to consecrate and to desecrate, it is unsurprising that medieval Christians thought that Jerusalem could be made pure again only through the spilling of blood. This is made amply evident in the chronicles of the First Crusade, where the climax of the

---

79. "[P]rofanare sancta sanctorum, loca dico Agni immaculati purpurata cruore" (287, lines 35–36). Texts of the two letters appear in Leclercq, "L'Encyclique de Saint Bernard en faveur de la croisade," 282–308; quotations from 287, 295–96.

80. Robert of Reims, RHC 3: 727; trans. Peters, 2.

81. Bynum, "The Body of Christ," 79–117, esp. 86–87.

siege of Jerusalem is the slaughter of the Muslims who had taken sanctuary at the Temple of Solomon (that is, the al-Aksa mosque). For example, Fulcher of Chartres writes, "Within this Temple about ten thousand were beheaded. If you had been there, your feet would have been stained up to the ankles with the blood of the slain. What more should I tell?"[82] Another chronicler, Raymond d'Aguiliers, similarly relates what he calls "wonderful sights":

> Piles of heads, hands, and feet were to be seen in the streets of the city. It was necessary to pick one's way over the bodies of men and horses. But these were small matters compared with what happened at the Temple of Solomon. . . . What happened there? . . . Men rode in blood up to their knees and bridle reins. Indeed, it was a just and splendid judgement of God that this place should be filled with the blood of the unbelievers, since it had suffered so long from their blasphemies. The city was filled with corpses and blood.[83]

In what appears to be an eyewitness account of the First Crusade, the anonymous chronicler of the *Gesta Francorum* describes the scene at the Temple of Solomon where, he says, "there was such a massacre that our men were wading up to their ankles in enemy blood." He goes on, however, to explain the motivations of the Christians who carried out the slaughter:

> Our men entered the city, chasing the Saracens and killing them up to Solomon's Temple, where they took refuge and fought hard against our men for the whole day, so that all the temple was streaming with their blood. . . . On the roof of the Temple of Solomon were crowded great numbers of pagans of both sexes. . . . After this our men . . . came rejoicing and weeping from excess of gladness to worship at the Sepulchre of our Saviour Jesus, and there they fulfilled their vows to him. Next morning they went cautiously up on to the Temple roof and attacked the Saracens, both men and women, cutting off their heads with drawn swords.[84]

The juxtaposition of slaughter and worship in this passage is significant. The phrase used to describe the Christians' act of worship, "reddiderunt ei capitale debitum," can be translated "they fulfilled their vows to him"; literally,

---

82. Fulcher of Chartres, chap. 27.13; trans. Peters, 77.

83. Raimundi de Aguilers, RHC 3: 300; trans. Peters, 214.

84. *Gesta Francorum et aliorum Hierosolymitanorum,* in *Deeds of the Franks,* 89–92 (facing-page Latin text and English translation).

however, it means, "they paid him [Jesus] what they owed him." The chronicler seems to imply that this debt is paid both spiritually, though the act of worship, and physically, through the use of the sword. This notion of slaughter as a pious act is made explicit in Peter the Venerable's sermon "In Praise of the Holy Sepulchre," in which, referring to the violent acts in Jerusalem, Peter tells his audience "with pious swords you cleansed this place and habitation of heavenly purity from the defilements of the wicked."[85] Here, the sword itself is "pious." Physical violence is itself worship, as Odo of Deuil affirms: the purpose of crusade is "to visit the Holy Sepulchre and to wipe out our sins with the blood or the conversion of the infidels."[86]

The reconsecration of Jerusalem by the crusaders involved more than the ritual cleansing of the Temple Mount with the blood of the captive Muslims. It also entailed restoring sacred places to their former state, removing reminders of the pagan past and restoring the Christian treasures that had been hidden away. In his chronicle, Fulcher of Chartres describes how in the newly Christian Jerusalem, "a small piece of the Lord's Cross was found in a hidden place. From ancient times until now it had been concealed by religious men, and now, God being willing, it was revealed.... This particle... was first carried to the Lord's Sepulchre and then to the Temple joyfully."[87] This making visible of what had previously been hidden is echoed in Fulcher's account of the Church of the Holy Sepulchre. He emphasizes the circular structure of the church, an emblem of its spiritual perfection, and the hole cunningly built into its roof: he states that "through a wide opening which was skillfully devised by a wise architect, the Sepulchre can always be seen from above."[88] In other words, the emptiness of the tomb is always visible, always on display. For the Christian believer, the sight of the empty tomb is a testament to the miracle that took place there and a reminder of the heavenly assumption of the glorified body of Christ. It is a pointer to the divine rather than an object of worship in itself for, paradoxically, what makes it holy is not Christ's presence but his absence. This spot—often said to be, as in *The Book of John Mandeville* and other pilgrim itineraries, the geographical center of the world—marks the threshold between the human and the divine.[89]

---

85. "[P]iius gladiis ab impiorum sordibus caelestis munditiae locum et habitaculum expurgastis...." Constable, "Petri venerabilis sermones tres," 232–54; quotation from 247. Trans. in Berry, "Peter the Venerable and the Crusades," 141–62, quotation from 154; trans. also in Cole, "Religious Pollution," 85–111, citation at 103.

86. Odo of Deuil, quoted in Berry, "Peter the Venerable," 146.

87. Fulcher of Chartres, chap. 30.4; trans. Peters, 80.

88. Fulcher of Chartres, chap. 26.6; trans. Peters, 73–74.

89. On Jerusalem as the center of the earth, see Higgins, "Defining the Earth's Center," 29–53; Akbari, "From Due East to True North," 19–34, esp. 20–21; chapter 1 in this book, 50–66.

I have discussed the depiction of Jerusalem in these crusade accounts at some length because it is necessary, I think, to have a clear sense of the nature of Christian beliefs concerning the sacred space of the Holy Sepulchre in order to try to understand precisely what these writers meant when they described the Muslim presence in Jerusalem as pollution. Several crusade accounts specify the precise nature of the pollution of Islam: they say that the Muslims practice idolatry. While this may appear to be a bizarre accusation to modern readers, who are aware of the extreme iconoclasm of Islamic theology, medieval chroniclers repeatedly make this accusation; in this respect, they are quite similar to the romances and *chansons de geste* discussed earlier, which also describe Islam in terms of idolatry. References to Muslim idolatry appear in many chronicle accounts, including both those written by people who appear to have been eyewitnesses to the crusade and those based upon earlier accounts.[90] The most suggestive version appears in the *Gesta Tancredi* written by Raoul de Caen during the early twelfth century. Raoul recounts how Christians entering Jerusalem found a giant silver statue of "the pristine Antichrist, Depraved Muhammad, Pernicious Muhammad." Like the preachers of the crusades described above, Raoul emphasizes the role of place or location in the contest between good and evil in the Holy Land. He states, "God's house is possessed by the inhabitant of the abyss. Pluto's slave parades as God in Solomon's house!"[91] Raoul seems to suggest that the discovery of the statue came as a shock to the crusaders: at first, he writes, they were not even sure whether the statue was of Christ or Muhammad. Other crusade texts, however, suggest that Muslim idolatry is not something the Christians discover, to their surprise, upon entering the holy places in Jerusalem. In his account of Pope Urban's sermon at Clermont, Baudri de Dol quotes the pope as asking, "Why do we pass over the Temple of Solomon, or that of the Lord, in which the barbarous nations placed their idols contrary to law, both human and divine?"[92] Urban's statement reveals that Muslim idolatry is precisely what the crusaders anticipated they would find—or, to put it another way, what they planned to discover.

---

90. First-generation sources include Fulcher of Chartres, who says that the Muslims have an "idolo in nomine Mahumet" (RHC p. 357, chap. 26), and that they practice "idolatriae superstitioso ritu" (RHC p. 359–60, chap. 28). Robert of Reims also refers to an image of Muhammad, "pulchrisque de te imaginibus decoratis" (RHC p. 878). Second-generation sources include Jacques de Vitry, who refers to "ymaginem Machometi ponentes in templo, nullum Christianum permittunt intrare" (Jacques de Vitry, *Historia Hierosolymitana,* chap. 63, PPTS XI-2).

91. "Pristinus Antichristus, Mahummet pravus, Muhammet perniciosus.... [A]rce Dei potitur conviva baratri; Vernaque Plutonis Deus est operi Salomonis!" (RHC 3: 695, chap. 129; trans. in Muratova, "Western Chronicles of the First Crusade," 47–69; quotation from 48.

92. Baudri de Dol, RHC; trans. Peters, 7.

The accusation of Muslim idolatry found in the crusade documents described here is perpetuated in a variety of medieval texts, ranging from universal chronicles like the *Speculum Historiale* of Vincent of Beauvais[93] and the
Polychronicon of Ranulf Higden[94] to epic poems, romances, and drama. As
we have seen, moreover, medieval romances and *chansons de geste* commonly
feature a kind of pagan anti-Trinity made up of Muhammad, Tervagant, and
Apollo. In these texts, the presence of Muslim idolatry serves to emphasize
the sanctity, and the violation, of sacred spaces; predictably, the destruction of
the idols worshiped by the Muslims is presented as the single most essential
feature of the purification of those sacred spaces. For example, in the *Jeu de
saint Nicolas,* the Christian Trinity and the pagan anti-Trinity are explicitly
set up in opposition to one another, while the effectiveness of the simple
wooden statue of Saint Nicolas is contrasted to the impotence of the golden
idol of Tervagant, housed in the Muslim kings "mahommerie" or mosque.
This house of pagan worship, like the city of Jerusalem as it is described
in the crusader chronicles and sermons, must be cleansed, the pollution of
idolatry removed. This is exactly why the *Jeu de saint Nicolas,* like the *Roland,*
concludes with the physical destruction of the idol in the "mahommerie" so
that the Muslim holy place, like the Muslims themselves, can be made ready
to accept Christianity. The cleansing of Jerusalem is thus the model for the
cleansing of all polluted holy places in literary texts.

A peculiar logic underlies the claim that Muslims are idolaters: Christians
know that Muslims are idolaters, so the fact that no idols exist currently does
not prove that Muslims are not idolaters, but is simply the consequence of
the fact that the Christians have utterly destroyed their idols during the act
of conquest. To put it another way, the absence of proof is simply proof that
the evidence was destroyed. Accordingly, the *Chanson de Roland* concludes
by recounting the erasure of any memory of Muslim presence in Saragossa:
the Christians are ordered

> to search the city
> The synagogues, and the mosques.
> Holding iron hammers and axes,

---

93. Vincent of Beauvais, *Speculum Historiale,* chaps. 39–67, pp. 912–22. Vincent states that Muhammad removed only the name of idolatry, but that the practice actually continues (cum tamen
caetera idolatrie[m] praestigia removisset [chap. 20, p. 920]). On the transmission of anti-Islamic
polemic (ultimately derived from al-Kindi) by way of Vincent's *Speculum Historiale* and its Dutch
translation by Jacob von Maerlant, see Platti, "Bagdad-Beauvais-Bruges," 31–44.

94. Higden relates that "in margine maris Hispaniae" is a monumental "idolum Machometi."
Polychronicon Ranulphi Higden monachi Cestrensis, 6: 40.

> They smash the statues and all the idols,
> No sorcery or false cult will remain there.[95]

The belief in Muslim idolatry absolutely requires that the charge be unprovable. This is precisely why chroniclers including Fulcher of Chartres, Jacques de Vitry, and William of Malmesbury immediately follow claims of Muslim idolatry with the remark that Christians were never allowed to see the idols.[96] Fulcher, for example, when he refers to the "holy place" of the Temple of Solomon, cautions the reader that "I say 'holy,' although nothing divine was practiced there at the time when the Saracens exercised their form of idolatry in religious ritual. They never allowed a single Christian to enter."[97] These kinds of justification reveal that the idols supposedly worshiped at Jerusalem were imagined, not discovered.[98]

The chronicle accounts that report Muslim idolatry, unsurprisingly, vary with regard to precisely where the idol was said to be located. One says that the statue of Muhammad was in the "Temple of Solomon" (the al-Aqsa Mosque); another places the idol in the "Temple of the Lord" (the Dome of the Rock); a third says that there were images both in al-Aqsa and the Dome of the Rock. The instability of the charge is due to the fact that each of these chroniclers bases it on Fulcher of Chartres' statement that there was in Jerusalem "an idol in the name of Muhammad" (idolo in nomine Mahumet). A closer look at Fulcher's words, however, suggests that his statement is based not on the presence of an actual monumental statue, but rather on the Muslim veneration of the rock that gives its name to the Dome of the Rock. Fulcher states:

> Since that rock disfigures [deturpebat; lit., "makes filthy"] the Temple of the Lord, afterwards it was entirely covered and encased in marble. Its present position is under the altar where the priest performs the rituals. All the Saracens had greatly revered this Temple of the Lord. Here they made their prayers more gladly than elsewhere, although they wasted them, since they erected an idol in the name of Muhammad. They permitted no Christian to enter there.[99]

---

95. *Chanson de Roland,* ed. and trans. Brault, lines 3661–65, laisse 266.

96. On William of Malmesbury, see Cole, "Pollution," 88 and n. 12. See also the other sources cited in Muratova, "Western Chronicles of the First Crusade," 49, and on Jacques de Vitry, see Muratova, n. 32.

97. Fulcher of Chartres, chap. 26, and cf. 28.2; trans. Peters, 78.

98. For a contrary view, see Xenia Muratova's attempt to reconstruct the historical background of the image described by Raoul de Caen in "Western Chronicles of the First Crusade," 47–69.

99. Fulcher of Chartres, chap. 26.9, trans. Peters, 74: "idolo in nomine Mahumet" in the Templum Domini, but "in quod etiam nullum ingredi Christianum permittebant" (RHC 3: 357). See the discussion of this passage in Cole, "Pollution," 90–91.

The rock concealed beneath slabs of marble represents a focus of Muslim de-votion that could not be recognized as legitimate by the Christians entering Jerusalem. It could only be seen as a focus of wrongly directed worship, as an object that leads the supplicant away from and not toward God; in short, it could be seen only as idolatry. The reason for this, of course, is because the rock at Jerusalem stands in precisely the same liminal position as the Holy Sepulchre. As the place where the Prophet began his *mi'raj* or miraculous night journey into the heavens, like the empty Sepulchre, it marks the thresh-old between the human and the divine.

Clearly, the Muslim veneration of Jerusalem as the third holiest city in Islam was seen by Western Christians as nothing more than contaminat-ing presumptuousness; but presumably their veneration of their "own" holy place, at Mecca, would be respected somewhat more. Yet Mecca, too, is seen as polluted and polluting, a focus of pagan worship. Like the holy places of Jerusalem, the Ka'aba is described as a "house of God" (domus Dei); but Vincent of Beauvais qualifies this term by calling it an "unlawful house of God" (domum Dei illicitam). He goes on to state that the circumambula-tion of the Ka'aba at the time of the annual pilgrimage is done in honor of Venus.[100] In his *Polychronicon,* Higden confirms that Muhammad told his followers to "worschippe Venue, and therfore it is that Saracens holdeth the Fridy holy."[101]

In some ways, the rhetoric of pollution applied to the Ka'aba is very like that applied to the sacred places of Jerusalem: both are said to be tainted by idolatry, and in both constructions of an imaginary idol are based on the presence of a rock that marks the threshold between heaven and earth and serves as a pointer to the divine.[102] In other ways, however, the rhetoric of pollution differs with respect to how the idolatry in each place is character-ized. The idolatry at Jerusalem can be assimilated by the Christian crusaders: Raoul de Caen recounts how the statue of Muhammad was torn to pieces and melted down, so that "the metal, when its shape is lost, is changed back from vile to precious."[103] Raoul's account is echoed by the continuator of Tudebodus, who elaborates on how the metal of the statue actually became

100. Vincent of Beauvais, *Speculum Historiale,* chap. 64, p. 921; chap. 60, pp. 919–20.

101. Ranulf Higden, *Polychronicon,* ed. Lumby (vols. 3–9), 6: 28–29 (quoting the Middle English translation of Trevisa).

102. Interestingly, the act commemorated by the veneration of the black stone at the Ka'aba is blood sacrifice: that is, Abraham's willingness to sacrifice his son in accord with the will of God. For Christians, Abraham's act is a prefiguration of the sacrifice of the Crucifixion, where Christ's blood washes away the taint of Original Sin. For Muslims, however, the act commemorated at the Ka'aba does not signify a washing away of sin but rather, as M. E. Combs-Schilling puts it, "intercourse with the divine." *Sacred Performances,* 238; cf. 242–43.

103. Raoul de Caen, RHC 695, chap. 129; trans. Muratova, 48.

currency with which the crusaders "clothed the naked, cared for the needy, armed the defenseless, and"—most important—"added to the numbers of the army."[104] Similarly, in the last lines of the *Jeu de saint Nicolas,* the golden image of Tervagant is thrown to the ground and the newly converted pagan king fulfills his threat to melt down the image and divide the gold among his men.[105] The idol found in the polluted sacred space proves to be an unexpected source of wealth.

The idolatry at the Ka'aba, however, is characterized quite differently, for it is not assimilable and cannot become currency to be appropriated by the West. Instead, it is repeatedly associated with sexuality, femininity, and blackness. As early as the beginning of the ninth century, polemics against Islam identified the Ka'aba with the practice of idolatry in precisely this way. In the final chapter of his *De haeresibus,* John of Damascus discusses the status of Islam and refutes the charge leveled by Muslims that Christians, in venerating the images of saints, practice idolatry. John turns this charge back upon the Muslims themselves: "Why then do you rub yourselves against that stone at your Ka'aba, and love that stone to the point of embracing it?...It is said that this stone is the head of Aphrodite, before which they prostrate themselves.... And to this day, the traces of the carving appear to those who stare at it intently." This Byzantine text is far removed from the Western European writings that are the focus of this chapter. Nonetheless, it too displays the relentless focus on idolatry that is fundamental to a very wide range of writings on Islam, not just in the Middle Ages, but in the present day as well.

The existence of this focus on idolatry well before the First Crusade, and well after the Middle Ages, may make it worthwhile to very briefly point out its persistence in both scholarly and political discourses in the modern world. The first example appears in an art historical study of the function of the *mihrab* in mosque architecture. (The *mihrab* is the pointer, often an indentation in a wall, to direct worshipers toward Mecca.) However, the study's author, Alexandre Papadopoulos, states that the *mihrab* actually represents the continued presence of Muhammad in every congregation: it is "a certain absence that suggests a presence." In Papadopoulos' view, the mediating function of the *mihrab* is converted into a kind of idolatry, with the Prophet placed (so to speak) in the line of worship. The second example appeared in media reports concerning a senior military official in the U.S. government, General Boykin, who described his battles against a Muslim warlord in Somalia this

---

104. *Tudebodus continuatus* 222; trans. Muratova, 49.

105. "Je vous ferai ardoir et fondre / Et departir entre me gent. / Car ous avés passe argent: / S'estes du plus fin or d'Arrabe." *Jeu de saint Nicolas,* lines 140–43.

way: "I knew that my God was bigger than his god. I knew that my God *was* God and that his god was an idol."[106]

As we have seen, the accusation that Islam is actually idolatry is fundamental to both strands in the depiction of Islam in the medieval West, whether the "fanciful" convention that Muslims are polytheistic idolaters or the "realistic" view that Muhammad was a Christian schismatic. Moreover, the rhetoric of pollution deployed in connection with the preaching and the historiography of the crusades is similarly grounded on the accusation of idolatry. The holiness of sacred spaces is based on their transcendence of the site itself: the absence of Christ's body is, paradoxically, visible proof of the presence of God. The right use of images in worship is, ideally, intended to imitate this scene of absent-presence: in worship, the image ought to (so to speak) disappear as it is replaced by the wholly spiritual referent to which it alludes. All this, for the medieval Western Christian, is precisely what Islam is not. As the foolish followers of a false religion, Muslims were thought to adore the image rather than the referent, the Black Stone rather than the divine reality toward which it gestures.

Clearly, the "realistic" and "fanciful" strands in the medieval depiction of Islam were far from being "two entirely separate conventions," as Norman Daniel puts it.[107] On the contrary, the two nourished and supported one another. A reader who doubted the verity of the ludicrous depiction of Muslims as polytheistic idolaters in the *chansons de geste* need only look at the historical and sober biographical accounts of the life of the Prophet: here, the reader could be certain, was the real truth. No matter what angle you viewed it from, whether it be paganism or heresy, Islam was always idolatry. It is difficult to understand, therefore, why modern scholars have been so willing to follow Daniel in regarding these traditions as wholly distinct. In his insightful analysis of modern scholarship on medieval depictions of Islam, David Blanks suggests that Norman Daniel's work, like Richard Southern's, suffers from a tendency to "forc[e] viewpoints into preestablished categories" (19). For Daniel, Blanks writes, "the true value of gaining a better understanding of Islam" is not simply to acquire knowledge, but to facilitate conversion. He quotes Daniel's own words: "Conversion may not follow, but it cannot possibly precede, the day when prejudice and hatred on both sides have been dispelled."[108] While the breadth of Daniel's work remains breathtaking, the

---

106. Associated Press report, October 23, 2003; reprinted and discussed in Rajiva, *Language of Empire,* 171–73.

107. Daniel, *Islam and the West,* 341.

108. Blanks, "Western Views of Islam," 11–53, esp. 24–29; quotation from 26–27.

hope he holds out for a future characterized by mutual understanding and theological exchange—as well as, perhaps, conversion—exerts a subtle yet formative influence on his approach to the topic, and on the ways in which he treats certain key issues such as idolatry. Daniel could afford to recognize the imputation of idolatry in the *chansons de geste;* he remained blind to it, however, in the biographical polemics, perhaps because they serve as a kind of model (albeit a distorted one) for the new, clearer depiction of Islam and Muslims he sought to present.

Such blindness to the nature of medieval representations of Islam is also to be attributed to the gap that separates medieval and modern perspectives on identity, especially with respect to how collective identity is constituted through religious forms—preeminently, the Eucharist. As David Lawton has shown in his brilliant reading of the late medieval Croxton *Play of the Sacrament,* medieval cartography was predicated on the symbolic system of the Eucharist: "Christ's body is the wafer. It is also the whole world, as in the Ebstorf Map, where Christ's head, hands, and feet protrude as compass points beyond the world itself."[109] The Croxton play incorporates a prose geography that, Lawton argues, frames in spatial terms a fundamental question posed by the conflict between the claims of Christian theology and the extent of the geographical spread of Christians in the world: "If the religion is so right, and its one true God so omnipotent, how does it come about that Christendom itself is so circumscribed?"[110] In theological terms, the whole community, symbolically represented by the wafer, should be coterminous with the extent of the world itself. The fact that this is not the case is not evidence of the falseness of the imperative, but rather the deferred nature of this imperative: in theological terms, the eucharistic community will be co-terminous with the world in the fullness of time, at the end of days. The existence of rival religious laws, then, is simply a distraction, a series of parodic simulacra that multiply from the primary referent, which is located in the truth of the Incarnation.

The consequent need to represent Islam as an inferior copy of Christianity results in the generation of a whole range of parodic texts, some depicting Muslims as polytheistic idolaters, others depicting the prophet of Islam as a deceptive Antichrist. As Michael Uebel has provocatively suggested, such representations participate in the "simultaneous recognition and denial of alterity," so that "to affirm the radical alterity of Muslims, Christians turn them into endlessly repeatable simulacra of themselves, and in the process

---

109. Lawton, "Sacrilege and Theatricality," 281–309, quotation from 281.
110. Lawton, "Sacrilege," 286.

create themselves retroactively."[111] This process can be fittingly epitomized in the figure of the footprint, which has appeared earlier in this chapter in connection with Muslim worship at the Dome of the Rock in Jerusalem. As we have seen, for Muslims, the footprint of the prophet in the stone at the Dome of the Rock is a marker of the liminal space separating earth from heaven, the place where Muhammad's ascent through the heavens began. Such veneration is similar to the Christian regard for the miraculously preserved footprints of Jesus and Mary, or veneration of the footsteps of the gods (and of past pilgrims) at shrines dedicated to Isis.[112] In a sense, the footprint, hovering between materiality and immateriality, is a ladder that links contraries of matter and form, flesh and spirit, earth and heaven. It is a pointer, like the *mihrab* itself, that orients the worshiper toward God.

For medieval Christians, however, the footprint of the prophet marked in stone at the Dome of the Rock was simply a sign of misguided, wrongly oriented worship. The stone itself was an idol, a material object that directs the worshiper toward the fleshly world of creation rather than the heavenly realm of spirit. It is not a sign marking the orientation of the divine, but rather a pollution of the sacred space. The footprint epitomizes the medieval view of Islam as idolatry: if the footprint is understood as form, it is a pointer to the divine. If it is understood as matter, it is nothing more than the repulsive "foot" of Muhammad that, in the *Liber Nycholay,* lies within the suspended tomb at Mecca, recalled in the "suspended" foot of the prophet who suffers endlessly in the depths of Dante's hell. This ambivalence of matter and form, surface and interior, in medieval representations of Islam are the focus of the next chapter, which turns to the depiction of paradise.

---

111. Uebel, "Pathogenesis of Medieval History," 47–65, quotations from 58–59.
112. Takács, "Divine and Human Feet," 353–69.

✦ CHAPTER 6

The Form of Heaven

The Islamic paradise is far from dead in the Western imagination. Hardly a day goes by that a news article on Islamist terrorism does not allude to the "seventy-two virgins" that await the successful suicide bomber upon his arrival in the heaven of the Muslims. This formulation has long since been parodied, as in the well-known *Doonesbury* comic in which a female would-be suicide bomber is asked what on earth she will do with her seventy-two virgins once she gets them. She replies, "I'm saving them for my little brother." Such examples in the current media—whether comic or all too tragic—remind us that the Islamic paradise, in the Western imagination, has a long genealogy. Conceived both as fantastically alluring and repellently fleshly, it was at once a focus for Western desire and a summation of all that was thought to be disturbing and deviant in Islam. The Islamic paradise was both enormously attractive and profoundly dangerous, a place of luxury and sensuous stimulation that must be rejected on the basis of its devotion to the body above the spirit, and its elevation of the literal word above the meaning embedded within. For European Christians, this false felicity was a microcosm of all that was wrong with Islam, its fetishization of the beautiful surface making it the epitome of what must be rejected.

In order to approach the subject of Western views of the Islamic paradise, it is useful to begin by placing it in comparative perspective by considering Western views of the Christian paradise. For the medieval Christian, paradise

is always, of course, in two places at once. It is both the earthly paradise of
Eden, inhabited by Adam and Eve until their transgression, Fall, and ultimate expulsion; and the heavenly paradise above, inhabited only by God, His
angels, and those sufficiently blessed to taste the joys of the Beatific Vision
even before the Last Judgment that would come at the end of time. While
the first paradise was thought to be located on earth, the other in heaven,
they shared the quality of inaccessibility: after the Fall, it was believed, no one
could enter Eden, whose gates were perpetually guarded by an angel armed
with a fiery sword. The divine heaven, of course, was equally remote, barred to
all but those most closely touched by God. As we have seen demonstrated
in chapter 1, it is no exaggeration to say that paradise was the single most
important reference point for medieval westerners: it was both the omphalos
or point of origin that marked mankind's place of birth, and the destination
of all Christian souls. In order to observe the centrality of paradise to the
Western imagination, we have only to look at medieval world maps. These
invariably place Eden at the top of the map, in the furthest East. This spot
marks the temporal and spatial point of origin, the birthplace of mankind
and the fountainhead of the rivers of Eden, which water the earth both literally and spiritually. On diagrams of the cosmos, which depict the tiny round
orb of the Earth at the center of nine concentric circles representing the
celestial spheres, paradise is located both at the middle of things—as Eden—
and at the top of the diagram, at the outermost circumference that marks the
hem of the divine. It is located at both spatial and temporal extremes, placed
simultaneously at the center and at the circumference of space, and at the
beginning and the end of time.

It is necessary to have a sense of this binary, double view of the Christian
paradise in order to take stock of Western views of the Islamic paradise. Medieval Christians believed that the Earthly Paradise of Eden was supplanted
and typologically fulfilled in the Heavenly Paradise above; Muslims, they
believed, could conceive of paradise only in earthly, fleshly terms, with pleasures experienced in the present moment rather than in the fullness of apocalyptic time. Medieval Europeans learned about the Islamic view of paradise
through a number of written sources, including the Latin translations of the
Qur'an that began to be produced in the twelfth century. The chapters of
the Qur'an that offered descriptions of paradise were read with avid interest, generating particularly detailed marginal glosses.[1] Such passages—along
with their salacious commentaries—soon found their way into anti-Islamic

---

1. On the Latin translations of Robert of Ketton and Mark of Toledo, see Burman, *Reading
the Qur'an.*

polemical writings, such as the *Summa totius haeresis Sarracenorum* (*Summation of all Saracen Heresies*) composed by Peter the Venerable, and the treatise *Contra legem Sarracenorum* (Against the Law of the Saracens) written by Riccoldo of Monte di Croce.[2] Some writers, like Peter, suggest that the fleshly excesses of the Islamic paradise prove that Islam is actually a form of Christian heresy.[3] Others, like Riccoldo, argue that this carnal element is, on the contrary, evidence of Islam's nearness to Judaism.[4] In both cases, however, the sensuous nature of the Islamic paradise is repeatedly presented as proof of what, for these writers, is the fundamental error of Islam: that is, its privileging of the letter above the spirit, and of the body above the soul.

Additional sources for Western views of the Islamic paradise were available in the lives of Muhammad that, from the eleventh century, began to circulate in both Latin and vernacular versions. The *Roman de Mahomet,* discussed in chapter 5 in connection with its use of the rhetoric of idolatry in its polemical biography, like its Latin precursors focuses particularly on the salacious nature of the paradise that Muhammad promised to his faithful followers. The fullest and most detailed source, however, for Western imaginings of the paradise of the Muslims was to be found in the several Latin and vernacular translations of the *Kitab al-mi'raj;* that is, the Islamic narrative recounting the Prophet Muhammad's miraculous night journey and ascent (or "mi'raj") into the heavens. There are many versions of the *Kitab al-mi'raj,* some in Arabic, others in Persian; one Arabic version was translated in the thirteenth century into Castilian, Latin, and Old French, and survives today under the title of the *Libro della scala,* or *Livre de l'eschelle* (Book of the Ladder). The first part of this chapter includes an account of the Western assimilation of the *Kitab al-mi'raj* in the *Book of the Ladder,* and then briefly turns to some of the Western adaptations of this place of sensuous luxury that identify a paradise-like location called "Cockaigne." In this fantastical land, bodily hungers are fully and richly satisfied. In Cockaigne, however, as in the Islamic paradise depicted in the *Book of the Ladder,* the satisfaction of bodily pleasures is revealed to be limited, transitory, and—ultimately—as leading to damnation rather than redemption. This fleshly view of the Islamic paradise also appears in *The Book*

---

2. On polemics concerning Saracen lasciviousness, see Daniel, *Islam and the West,* 158–85, 351–53; Tolan, *Saracens* 135–69.

3. On Peter the Venerable's view of Islam as heresy, see Tolan, *Saracens,* 155–65. On the relationship of the depiction of Islam as heresy to Cluniac self-definitions, see Iogna-Prat, *Order and Exclusion.*

4. On Riccoldo's view of Islam as comparable to Judaism, see Burman, *Religious Polemic;* Tolan, *Saracens,* 245–54.

of John Mandeville, where the generally positive, tolerant view of Islam also includes a detailed depiction of the Saracen heaven, as well as a dark imitation of it in the manufactured paradise of the Assassins.

Following this account of the mi'raj narrative and related texts, the chapter turns to its reflection in Dante's *Paradiso,* a text that reveals the strong influence of Islamic views of heaven on the Western Christian perspective. Throughout the literary tradition, Islam is depicted as a religion that satisfies only carnal impulses, a view that is based on the Western understanding of Islam as a return to the "Old Law" of Moses. From the Christian perspective, Islam was thought to be (like Judaism) a religion in which the letter is privileged over the spirit, and earthly joys are prized more than heavenly joys. To illustrate this view, we return to the *Roman de Mahomet* and its use of the hermeneutics of supersession in order to define Islam as being at once a heretical "new law" and an obstinate return to the "old law" of the Jews. The false prophet's promise of a paradise that satisfies every bodily urge reveals the superficiality and fleshliness imputed to Islam. In chapter 5, we saw the ascent of Muhammad parodically reflected in the floating tomb at Mecca, an ingenious deception that lures the gullible Saracens into wrongly directed pilgrimage. In Dante's *Paradiso,* Muhammad's mi'raj is again the object of parody, but in this case the parody is a subtle reinscription of the evocative ascent through multiple heavens found in the *Book of the Ladder* into a Christian theological framework.

The final section of this chapter turns to the presentation of Islam found in Roger Bacon's *Opus Maius,* in which Bacon attempts to at once assert the preeminence of Islamic philosophy and the absolute authority of Christian theology. In order to reconcile these competing views, Bacon chronicles the pursuit of wisdom through the ages, arguing that the highest achievements of non-Christian philosophers are in fact a return to the primordial, perfect wisdom available to man through divine gift at the Creation. For Bacon, the hermeneutics of supersession in which the old covenant of Judaism is supplanted by the new covenant of Christ is complicated by the place of Islamic philosophy at the top of the ladder of intellectual ascent. His solution necessarily takes refuge in apocalypse and revelation, with reason and philosophy ultimately cast aside with the assertion of divine omnipotence. Like Dante, Bacon at once praises Muslim philosophers in the highest terms, but condemns Islamic theology with corresponding harshness. The exercise of the rational mind thus appears as mankind's highest achievement and the source of his damnation: the effort to know the divine results, paradoxically, in the embrace of the image rather than of the Creator.

← The Beautiful Surface

The *Book of the Ladder* (*Il Libro della scala, Le Livre de l'eschelle*) is, as noted above, the title of one family of Western medieval translations of the Arabic *Kitab al-mi'raj*.[5] (For the purposes of this discussion, I will quote from the Old French text which, like the Latin version, descends from the lost Castilian translation of the unknown Arabic original.)[6] While in its original form, the *Book of the Ladder* was a devotional text, in translation it came to be read within the context of anti-Islamic polemic.[7] There are two striking features of the depiction of paradise in the *Book of the Ladder* that are worth pointing out: first, the extreme luxuriousness and sensuousness of the experience; second, the hierarchical structure of the spiritual ascent. Both luxuriousness and sensuousness are qualities that can be seen as degenerate and dangerous, and were certainly seen that way in Christian dogma of the Middle Ages. The sensuous beauty of paradise described in the mi'raj (as in the Qur'an itself and the prophetic traditions, or Hadith) was often understood as metaphorical, especially by Muslim writers influenced by neoplatonic philosophy.[8] The most sublime physical pleasures experienced by the senses figuratively represent those spiritual pleasures that cannot be expressed in words, those heavenly joys to which no earthly experience can compare. Only an obstinate literalist—modern or medieval—could interpret the "spouses" of the Qur'an as legions of enfleshed naked women.

The second significant aspect of the depiction of paradise in the *Book of the Ladder* is its hierarchical nature. The hierarchical structure of paradise found in the mi'raj account is important for the way in which it synthesizes what we might call scientific, mathematical views of the cosmos with theological notions of heaven. Medieval illustrated manuscripts of the Arabic mi'raj make

---

5. One manuscript of a French version and two manuscripts of a Latin version of the *Book of the Ladder* currently survive. Both versions were made by Bonaventura da Siena, based on a translation from Arabic into Castilian made (according to Bonaventura) by "Abraham the Jew" at the behest of Alfonso the Wise. For a useful study of the manuscript tradition of the Latin version, see the introduction to *Liber Scale Machometi, ed.* Werner. On the manuscript of the French version (of English provenance), see the introduction to *Le Livre de l'Eschiele Mahomet, ed.* Wunderli, as well as the updated bibliography to be found in the introduction to *Prophet of Islam in Old French,* trans. Hyatte.

6. All quotations from the *Book of the Ladder* are from the French text *Le Livre de l'Eschiele Mahomet,* edited by Wunderli. Quotations are identified in the text by chapter and page number. Translations are my own, but a less literal translation can be found in *Prophet of Islam,* trans. Hyatte.

7. Maria Subtelny has recently argued that the text may be not merely devotional, but a conversion text: "'Holy, Holy, Holy.'" On the multiplicity of religious movements in the Maghreb generally and al-Andalus in particular, see Garcia-Arenal, *Messianism and Puritanical Reform.*

8. On Islamic views of paradise, see Smith and Haddad, *Islamic Understanding of Death;* Gardet, *Dieu et la destinée de l'homme.*

clear that the seven heavens traversed by the Prophet on his journey to God are precisely the seven spheres of the known planets.[9] While some versions of the Arabic text explicitly point out the correspondence of the seven heavens with the seven planetary spheres of the planets, others leave the analogy implicit. One such Arabic version may have been the source for the *Book of the Ladder,* in which just the first sphere is explicitly identified as that of the moon (chap. 12; 48). Presumably the reader could be counted on to know the order of celestial bodies, and to associate them with the subsequent heavens; this is especially likely because the ruler who commissioned the mi'raj translation, Alfonso the Wise, is best known for his patronage of astronomical works (especially the so-called Alfonsine Tables).[10] This amalgamation of the scientific and the theological structures of heaven is among the most significant aspects of the transmission of the mi'raj account into the Western tradition. It appears, as we will see, in Dante's *Commedia,* and may have played a role in other Western medieval and early modern conceptualizations of the nature of paradise.

The *Book of the Ladder* begins by accompanying the Prophet through the various levels of heaven, each of which includes marvelous angels, extraordinary wonders, and prophets who speak to Muhammad, including John the Baptist, Joseph and Jacob, Moses, Abraham, and Jesus—who, for Muslims, is among the most revered messengers of God. Following his ascent through these seven heavens and his prayers at the foot of the divine Throne, Muhammad goes on to explore the joys of heaven that await the faithful. These include a series of gardens abundant in wonderful pleasures: beautiful women who are present merely to satisfy the sexual desires of the virtuous souls rewarded in heaven; walls and houses constructed of brightly colored jewels flashing with light, which delight the eye; and rivers flowing with delicious liquids, including milk, honey, and wine. These elements work together to create an environment that, for the medieval Christian, was at once an imitation of their notion of the heavenly paradise and a parodic travesty of it. The Islamic paradise was seen as a place of sensuous pleasures, where material things satisfy corporeal urges and appetites.

In this paradise, each of the senses is stimulated. The sense of sight, for example, is almost overwhelmed by the vision of many paradises, individual gardens ("les autres paradis") made up "wholly of light, and...many cities

---

9. On the equivalence of the seven heavens to the seven planetary spheres, see the illustrations reproduced in Gruber, "Prophet Muhammad's Ascension."

10. On Alfonso as a sponsor of astrological translations, and of the *Book of the Ladder* in particular, see Cerulli, *Nuove ricerche sul "Libro della Scala" e la conoscenza dell'Islam in Occidente,* 11–18.

and castles entirely of light" (toz de clarté, et... mout de cités et de chasteux qui toz de clarté sunt [34; 67]). The sense of hearing is stimulated by the songs of the beautiful women found there, who "sing so well and clearly and sweetly that every voice or instrument one might name is of no account compared with their song" (chantent si tresbien et tant de cler et tant doucement que tottes autres voiz et toz estrumenz que hom poust conter ne valent rien ver le chaunt qu'elles font [35; 68]), while musical instruments produce sounds that are "more sweet and delightful to hear than anyone could imagine" (tant doulz et tant delictables ad oir que nul cueor d'ome penser ne le porroit [36; 69]). The fruits found in the gardens "are sweeter and more savory than anything else" (plus doulz et plus savoreus que nule chose [36; 69]), and the very bricks of the buildings are composed "entirely of ambergris and musk, which smell marvellously good" (tot d'ambre et de musc qe fleroit ad merveille bien [36; 70]). The sense of touch is an exception in this sensuous paradise, for the narrator of the *Book of the Ladder* (the Prophet Muhammad himself) does not describe the satisfaction of the sense of touch as he does the senses of sight, hearing, smell, and taste. Its satisfaction remains implicit, in the description of the numbers of wives who wait to satisfy the needs of deserving men in the afterlife. The narrator recounts that even the lowest person in paradise receives

> .V. cent fammes en mariage, et quatre mil virges dom il il fera ses fammes quant li plerra; et.VIII. mile des autres que ne sunt vierges por lui servir en tottes ces choses. Et celle cui il plus aimera, quant il la voudra acoller, si vendra elle tot por soi meisme ad lui por ce faire. Et li accoller sera en itel maniere que tant com il l'aimera, si se ne porra elle de lui partir, ne il de lui ausinc. Et il avront une table mise devant soi que jameis ne lor faudra nulle chose qu'il vuoillient mangier ne boivre.

> five hundred women as wives, and four thousand virgins whom he will take as wives when it pleases him; and eight thousand others who are not virgins to serve him in everything. And that one whom he loves the most, when he wishes to embrace her, she will come to him entirely on her own in order to do so. And the embrace will be in such a way that, as long as he loves her, she will not be able to part herself from him, nor he from her, just the same. And they will have a table set before them that never will fail to bear whatever they wish to eat or drink. (37; 70)

The essential aspect of this paradise is, precisely, satisfaction, as all appetites are satisfied fully and abundantly.

The fleshly pleasures central to the Western misunderstanding of the mi'raj accounts were rapidly disseminated into a much wider literary tradition. Depictions of the so-called land of "Cockaigne" found in poems written in a variety of languages, including Old French, Middle Dutch, and Middle English, incorporate many of the same sensuous pleasures featured in the mi'raj accounts.[11] This is especially evident in the Middle English version, which emphasizes the sexual satisfaction experienced in this all-too-earthly paradise more than the Old French and Middle Dutch versions do.[12] The poem makes it clear from the outset that the Land of Cockaigne is a kind of paradise; it begins:

> Fur in see bi west Spayngne
> Is a lond ihote Cokaygne.
>
> . . .
>
> Thogh Paradis be miri and bright,
> Cokaygn is of fairer sight.
> What is ther in Paradis
> Bot grasse and flur and grene ris?
>
> $(1–8)$[13]

The land of Cockaigne is said to be located at the point furthest west, and is thus a kind of parody or inversion of the earthly paradise of Eden, which invariably appears as the easternmost point of medieval world maps, and is always introduced first in the geographical portions of encyclopedias as the easternmost location in the ecumene. Correspondences between the earthly paradise of Eden and the parodic paradise of Cockaigne appear throughout the poem. The four rivers of Eden appear in the land of Cockaigne in the form of "rivers gret and fine / Of oile, melk, honi, and wine" (45–46). Instead of the tree of life found in Eden, the land of Cockaigne contains a marvelous tree made up of a variety of exotic spices: the root is ginger and

---

11. Pleij, *Dreaming of Cockaigne,* 208. The connection between this literature and the mi'raj was noted by Manzalaoui, "English Analogues," 21–35, esp. 30–31; see also Metlitzki, *Matter of Araby,* 211–13.

12. Compare the Old French version ("De Cocaingne") edited by Väänänen, "Le 'fabliau' de Cocagne," 3–36 (text at 20–29).

13. "The Land of Cockaygne," 138–44; cited in the text by line number.

galingale, the flowers of mace, the fruit of cloves (73–77). The whole place is characterized in terms of overwhelming abundance and plenitude: fruits literally fall from the trees into your mouth, while "the gees irostid on the spitte / Fleeth . . . / And gredith [cry out]: 'Gees, al hote, al hot!'" (102–4).

Each of the aspects that makes the land of Cockaigne into a sensuous and satisfying paradise has a counterpart in the mi'raj tradition. The rivers of paradise are present, just in the form that they appear in the land of Cockaigne: the *Book of the Ladder* describes a paradise where the Edenic rivers Phison, Euphrates, Gihon, and Tigris run deliciously with honey, milk, wine, and sweet water (33; 66–67). In the *Book of the Ladder,* the counterpart to Eden's tree of life is made not of spices, but of exquisite jewels: the magnificent "tube tree" (un arbre qui a nom en sarrazinois "Tube") has a trunk of ruby, branches of emerald, flowers made of cloth of gold, and fruits of pearl (39; 72). The abundant food of Cockaigne, where fresh fruit and cooked fowl offer themselves up to be eaten, finds its counterpart in the heavens of the mi'raj account, where "if somebody . . . desires to eat a certain one of the fruits in paradise, the tree which bears this fruit appears immediately before him" (47; 78–79). The trees even bear "bowls of meats" (esquelles de viands) that are "neither boiled in water nor roasted in fire. And they are as delicious to eat as butter and honey mixed together, and they smell of musk and ambergris" (ne sunt cuiz ne en aive ne ad feu rostiz. Et sunt aucinc savoreus ad mangier com bur et miel mesleez ensemble. Et si flerent ad musc et ad ambre [37; 70]).

The luxurious abundance of the land of Cockaigne as described in the Middle English poem extends, unsurprisingly, to the erotic pleasures of the flesh. The rivers running through this land include one "of swet milke" (149) in which nuns from the local convent bathe. When the nearby monks see them swimming naked, they "committh to the nunnes anon, / And euch monde him taketh on" (161–62). As a result, each monk has "withoute danger /.xii. wiues euch yere" (169–70). While this does not exactly match up to the five hundred wives and four thousand virgins enjoyed in the Islamic paradise of the mi'raj account, the difference is of degree rather than of kind. Although in the Middle English Cockaigne poem, the emphasis on materiality and corporeality is not connected with Islam, it is still connected to religious deviance, for the sensuous pleasures of this land are identified as the fleshly excesses of contemporary monks and nuns. Spiritual corruption, in both cases, inevitably leads to the indulgence of bodily appetites and sexual license.

While there are many striking resemblances between the *Book of the Ladder* and the poems on the land of Cockaigne, there are significant differences as well. These differences help us to identify what qualities of the Islamic paradise were seen, by Western Christians, as being specific to Islam, rather than representative of worldliness and corporeality in general. While food is abundant in the mi'raj account—rivers flowing with delicious drinks, food falling down from the trees—beautiful jewels are even more predominant. Buildings, houses, and trees appear that are made up of assorted jewels, or even of a single perfect gem. While in the mi'raj account all the senses are stimulated, the Cockaigne poems focus more particularly on the sense of taste: the satisfaction of the belly is paramount, rather than the overwhelming splendor and beauty of the sight. We might conclude that the Cockaigne poems appealed particularly to a class of people accustomed to feeling, at least sometimes, the pangs of hunger and want. In the *Book of the Ladder,* by contrast, the sense that is emphasized the most is not taste, but sight; and the quality most prized is not satiety (or fullness), but rather novelty.

In the mi'raj accounts, the newness and excitement of the various tastes is emphasized, not the satiation of hunger, as in the Cockaigne poems. For example, in the *Book of the Ladder,* certain trees found on one of the many levels of heaven are said to bear fruits that have "the flavors of all the other fruits that are known to be good in this world" (les savours de toz les autres fruiz qui sachent bien en ce monde [44; 76]). On another level of heaven, when someone "has in his mouth one of the fruits which are there and he wants a different one, the fruit he has immediately changes its taste into that of the other one he wanted" (47; 78–79). The sense of taste is perpetually stimulated by the satisfaction of every new desire—with the added promise that every subsequent new, new desire, will be satisfied in its turn. It is therefore completely unsurprising that the bliss of paradise prominently features women who are virgins, and who remain virgins in spite of having intercourse: "every time the husbands lie down with them, they find them to be virgins, just as they were before" (tottes foiz que les maris gisent avec elles, si les truevent ausinc pulcelles com devant [35; 68]). Like the fruits of the garden of paradise, these women are always "new."

This quality of novelty is enormously significant, for it is central to Western Christian views of Islam, not just in their understanding of the Islamic paradise but also in their perception of Islamic theology as a "New Law" that—paradoxically—represented a regression to the "Old Law" of the Jews. This aspect of Western views of Islam can be most profitably studied by way of medieval accounts of the life of Muhammad that formed an important aspect of the polemical tradition against Islam. These accounts range from brief biographical summaries incorporated into universal histories like those of Vincent of Beauvais and Ranulf Higden, to free-standing texts like the Old French *Roman de Mahomet.* Regardless of their length, however, these sources consistently foreground a devotion to sensuous pleasures in the life of the

Prophet, both sexual lasciviousness and gluttony. For example, in Vincent of Beauvais' *Speculum Historiale* (Historical Mirror), the extended description of Muhammad's ministry and the early history of the Muslim community emphasizes his sexual license. Muhammad is said to have had fourteen wives and additional concubines, to have wrongly appropriated the wife of one of his followers, and to have advocated polygamy, incest, and adultery for his followers.[14] In Vincent's encyclopedia, the description of the sensuous pleasures of the Islamic paradise immediately follows these allegations of sexual depravity on the part of the Prophet, acting as a kind of doctrinal counterpart to the filthy biographical details recounted earlier. These two aspects—the licentiousness of Muhammad himself and the sensuous nature of the Islamic paradise—are closely linked, for both of them are presented as manifestations of the essential nature of the so-called "law of Muhammad."

This "law of Muhammad" is depicted, paradoxically, as both a "new law" (lex nova) and a return to the "old law" of Moses. This formulation appears frequently in Western polemics against Islam, gaining perhaps its widest currency in the thirteenth-century encyclopedia of Vincent of Beauvais. Vincent initially identifies the "law of Muhammad" as a "new law" (lex nova), but he soon goes on to exclude it from consideration as a legitimate theological development atop the foundations of Judaism and Christianity. (It is important to recognize that, from the Muslim perspective, Islam is thought to supersede Christianity just as, from the Christian perspective, Christianity supersedes Judaism; hence, for Muslims, Islam is the third and final revelation in religious history, and Jews and Christians are consequently, as it were, spiritual "older brothers" of Muslims.) Vincent explicitly refutes precisely this Islamic view. He asserts that there are truly only two laws—the law of Moses and the law of Christ—and that this "third law" (tertia lex) of Muhammad can only be the work of the devil.[15]

An even fuller exposition of the place of the "law of Muhammad" relative to the "old law" of Moses and the "new law" of Christ can be found in the *Roman de Mahomet* written by Alexandre du Pont in the thirteenth century. While Muhammad is said to invent a theology based in part on the teachings of Nestorian Christians, his law is explicitly said to be, not a "new law," but rather a return to the "old law" of Judaism. He declares to his followers:

Que la loys de Moisy revaigne,
Et toute la gens se raaingne;

---

14. Vincent of Beauvais, *Speculum Historiale,* chap. 53 (taking wife of his follower), chap. 43, p. 914 (polygamy, incest, and adultery).

15. Ibid., chap. 39–40, p. 913 (*lex nova*); chap. 50, p. 916 (*tertia lex*).

Que la nouviele soit quassee
Et la vielle soit restoree,
Et charneus circoncisions.

Let the law of Moses return,
And everyone be redeemed;
Let the new law be quashed,
And the old one, restored,
Along with circumcision of the flesh.
                    (1585–89)[16]

The correspondence between Islam and Judaism is reinforced, in the *Roman de Mahomet,* by the false miracles performed by Muhammad in his effort to win over the "foolish people" (as they are repeatedly called). He prepares channels in the ground filled with milk and honey and covers them with brush, so that he can miraculously "discover" them. He trains a white bull from the time that it is a calf to come at his call; he then gathers the people on a hillside and calls out, which summons the white bull to kneel before him, presenting the Qur'an (which Muhammad has prepared previously) attached to its horns (1397–1584). The first episode is intended to evoke the land of milk and honey, the long-sought goal of the Israelites. The second recalls the presentation of the tablets of the law to Moses at Sinai, with this new Moses, as it were, conflating the "law" itself with the very act of idolatry.

The law of Muhammad is thus presented as a revival of the "old law" of Moses, entailing a return to circumcision of the flesh rather than the figurative "circumcision of the heart" advocated by the Apostle Paul (Rom. 2:28–29). The false miracles of milk and honey identify the apparently innovative, recently revealed "law" of Muhammad as being actually a return to the "old law" of the Jews; simultaneously, however, the rivers of milk and honey also highlight the sensuous nature of the appeal of Islam. The delicious pleasures of the Islamic paradise are presented as fundamental to the deception of Muhammad's followers, while a devotion to materiality and sensuality is thought to pervade the faith. Food remains central to the allure of the Orient—not its nutritive, satiating qualities, but its ability to appeal to the senses, and—ultimately—its power to seduce the soul.

Sensuous delight is also the focus of the depiction of the Islamic paradise found in *The Book of John Mandeville,* which was—as noted in chapter

---

16. Alexandre du Pont, *Le Roman de Mahomet,* ed. Yvan Lepage; *Prophet of Islam,* trans. Reginald Hyatte. Cited by line number in the text.

1—among the most popular and widely disseminated texts of the premodern period: composed in the mid-fourteenth century, it rapidly became a medieval best seller. Mandeville's *Book* includes many distinctive features, the most striking of which may be its remarkably inclusive depiction of religious diversity. In a sharp departure from the anti-Islamic polemic common in medieval literature, the narrator of *The Book of John Mandeville* enjoys a private audience with the Sultan of Babylon in which the comparative merits of Islam and Christianity are debated. Immediately prior to that debate, however, the narrator offers an account of Islamic theology in which the paradise of the Muslims features prominently, presented as at once a common ground of Islam and Christianity and a point of stark contrast. This view of the Islamic paradise is clearly drawn from the mi'raj tradition: it is "a place of delights" (un lieu de delices), having "beautiful and stately houses...made of precious stones and of gold and silver" (maisouns beles et nobles...faites des pieres preciouses et d'or et d'argent). These delights extend beyond the beautiful exteriors of the houses, for in this place, "every man will have twenty-four wives, all virgins, and he will have intercourse every day with them, and nonetheless he will always find them still virgins" (chescun avera IIIIxx femmes toutes pucelles, et avera touz les jours affaire a elle, et toutdis les trovera pucelles [chap. 15; 272–73]). (Fearing perhaps to have tempted his reader too much with this description, the redactor of the Egerton manuscript of the Middle English Mandeville quickly adds, "this is against our creed.")

This relentlessly literal reading of the Qur'anic account of heaven is clearly an image of a false Paradise. The rivers of this Eden transmit not spiritual blessings but sensuous pleasures, "running with milk and honey and wine and sweet water" (corantz de lait et de mel et de vin et de douce eawe [chap. 15; 273]). It contrasts strongly with the Christian Earthly Paradise, the rivers of which water the earth both literally and spiritually, and recalls instead the false, man-made false paradise of the Assassins. This sect of Muslims, Mandeville recounts, was led by a man who had a very special way of preparing his warriors. He built magnificent walled gardens, stocked them with beautiful and exotic birds and beasts, and peopled them with "the most beautiful young women under the age of fifteen years that he could find, and the most handsome young men of similar age, and he dressed them all in clothes of gold" (les plus [belles] damoyselles souz l'age de XV aunz q'il poait troever, et les plus beaulx jeovenceaux de autiel age et touz estoient vestuz des draps d'or). To complete the illusion, he had underground wells built so that "one would run with milk, another with wine, another with honey, and this place he called 'Paradise'" (l'un courre de lait, l'autre de vin, l'autre de meel, et cel lieu appelloit il Paradis [chap. 30; 441]). He would bring one of his novice Assassins into this false paradise, and convince him that he had experienced a foretaste of the joys of the eternal paradise to be enjoyed after death. With this motivation, the leader of the Assassins could persuade his men to carry out any mission, promising that "after his death, he would put them into another paradise a hundred times more beautiful than the first, and there they would remain with even more beautiful young women than before" (il les metteroit après la mort en un autre paradiz, cent tant plus beal, et la demorient ovesqes plus belles damoyselles a toutdis mais). There, he assures them, they will perpetually enjoy these maidens, who "forever remain virgins" (toutdis demoroient pucelles [chap. 30; 442]).

This elaborate description of the false paradise of the Assassins is clearly constructed on the basis of the depiction of the heavenly paradise found in the Qur'an and in mi'raj accounts, which is retold in *The Book of John Mandeville* as part of the summary of Islamic theology that precedes the narrator's private interview with the Sultan. There, we will remember, the narrator describes the Islamic notion of paradise:

> Et si homme lor demaunde quel paradis ils entendent, ils dient qe ceo est un lieu de delices ou homme trovera toutes manerres des fruitz en toutes saisons, et riveres corantz de lait et de vin et de douce eawe. Et qe il y avera maisons beles et nobles... faites des pieres preciouses et d'or et d'argent, et qe chescun avera IIII xx X femmes toutes pucelles, et avera touz les jours affaire a elle, et toutdis les trovera pucelles.

> And if one asks them what they mean by Paradise, they say that it is a place of delights, where a man will find all manner of fruit in every season, and rivers flowing with milk and with honey and with sweet water. And that they have there beautiful and stately houses... made of precious stones and of gold and silver, and that every man will have twenty-four wives, all virgins, and he will have intercourse every day with them, and nonetheless he will always find them still virgins. (chap. 15; 272–73)

Both paradises—the false paradise of the Assassins, and the heavenly paradise anticipated by the Muslims—run with rivers of milk and honey, wine and sweet water; both are replete with jewels, gold, and alluring partners. Most importantly, at least from the perspective of the medieval Western Christian, both are false paradises: whether experienced in the garden of the deceptive trickster who leads the Assassins or in the imaginative anticipation of the delights of the Islamic heaven, these carnal paradises are believed to be, in the end, devoid of merit or substance.

The precise nature of the limitations and the ultimate emptiness of the Islamic paradise is made explicit in *The Book of John Mandeville* in a passage that follows the description of heaven I just quoted. The narrator explains the nature of Islamic theology in a way that reveals what lies (in his view) at the basis of their sensuous understanding of the afterlife. He writes: "They know much of Holy Scripture. But they understand it only according to the letter, just as the Jews do, for they do not understand the letter at all spiritually, but only bodily. And for this reason St. Paul says, 'The letter kills, but the spirit gives life'" ([ils] scievent moult de Seint Escripture. Mes ne la entendent fors qe selonc la lettre. Et / auxi ne font les Juys, qar ils n'entendent mie la lettre espiritalment, mes corporelment, et et pur ceo dit seint Paul: "Littera enim occidit, spiritus autem vivicat" [chap. 15; 277–78]). The word he uses to describe this resolutely literal understanding of scripture is "corporelment"; that is, not just literally, but "bodily." From the point of view of medieval Christians, then, Muslims (like Jews) understand the letter rather than the spirit. The result, for the Muslims at least, is a superficial and fleshly understanding of the joys of heaven. Unable to grasp the true nature of spiritual bliss, they can imagine only the fleeting pleasures of the body and the limited surface of the word.

↰ The Paradise Inside

Paradoxically, the *Book of the Ladder* gave rise not just to parodic mimicry of the Islamic paradise, such as that found in the Cockaigne poems discussed earlier, but also to imitation in what is unquestionably the most famous depiction of heavenly bliss found in Western medieval literature—Dante's *Commedia*. As Miguel Asín Palacios argued early in the twentieth century, and as Maria Corti has conclusively demonstrated over the last two decades, Dante drew upon the *Book of the Ladder* not only for his structure of heaven, organized into a series of concentric levels, each of which rewards virtuous souls with heavenly pleasures appropriate to their merits, but for a number of other features as well.[17] These include the hierarchical structuring of the heavens,

---

17. Asín Palacios, *La escatología musulmana en la* Divina Comedia. On the tangled reception of Asín's work, see Cantarino, "Dante and Islam," 172–92; Menocal, "Andalusianist's Last Sigh," 179–89. Seminal studies on the transmission of the mi'raj narrative into Western tradition are Cerulli, *Il "Libro della Scala" e la questione delle fonti arabo-spagnole della "Divina Commedia"* and *Nuove ricerche sul "Libro*

in which scientific cosmology is coterminous with the celestial ranks of the heavenly paradise; the emblematic figure of the great bird—a rooster, in the mir'aj account, an eagle in the *Paradiso*—that anchors the concentric circles of heaven; and the golden ladder that surmounts the last heavenly spheres. Finally, and most important for our purposes here, Dante makes use of the extraordinarily sensuous nature of the Islamic paradise—its begemmed beauty, its overmastering luminescence—in his own depiction of the Christian heaven.[18]

In the second canto of the *Paradiso*, Dante and Beatrice discuss the optical properties of the light of the moon. Dante likens the vast form of the celestial body not just to a "shining... cloud," but also to a "diamond struck by the sun" and "the eternal pearl" (nube... lucida... quasi adamante che lo sol ferisse; l'etterna margarita [Pa. 2.31–34]). In doing so, he evokes the language of the *Book of the Ladder*, in which the moon is also likened to a precious stone. At each step of the ascent through the celestial spheres, heavenly bodies are named, each in turn, dazzling with gems such as the sparkling stones that make up the sphere of Jupiter (18.114–17), and radiating light that flows outward from each planet.[19] Emblems central to the *Book of the Ladder* are echoed in Dante's paradise: for example, the rooster that holds up the heavens in the Islamic paradise is supplanted, in Dante's vision, by the majestic eagle who dominates the great sphere of Jupiter (19–20). The eponymous ladder of the *Book of the Ladder* marks the starting point of ascent into the heavenly regions in the narrative of Muhammad's journey; in Dante's *Paradiso*, however, the ladder appears instead surmounting the seven celestial spheres (21.29), marking the point of the pilgrim's ascent from the planetary circles to the ranks of angels surrounding the heavenly rose at the pinnacle of paradise.[20]

Perhaps the most striking echo of the mi'raj appears in the emphasis, in Dante's *Paradiso*, on the satiation of hunger and quenching of thirst. Dante's appropriation of the form of heaven found in the mi'raj is, in this respect, particularly delicate and subtle. In the *Book of the Ladder*, as we have seen, the rivers flow with milk and honey, deliciously satisfying the cravings of those

della Scala" e la conoscenza dell'Islam in Occidente; Corti, "La 'Commedia' di Dante e l'oltretomba islamico," 301–14.

18. See the excellent article on gems in the *Paradiso* by Schildgen, "Wonders on the Border," 110–34.

19. On the metaphysics of light in the *Paradiso*, see Cantarino, "Dante and Islam," 3–35; Akbari, *Seeing through the Veil*, 164–77.

20. On the ladder motif in the *Book of the Ladder* and Dante's *Commedia*, see Morgan, *Dante and the Medieval Other World*, 38–46.

who inhabit paradise. In the *Paradiso,* the hunger that is sated is the hunger for knowledge; and the flowing liquid that satisfies such yearnings is the spiritual milk of the divine. For example, when Beatrice answers Dante's question but awakens curiosity on another point, the continued seeking after knowledge is described in familiar terms. Following Beatrice's response, Dante writes, "Then it was clear to me how everywhere in Heaven is Paradise. . . . But as it happens when of one food we have enough and the appetite for another still remains, that this one is asked for while thanks are returned for that other one, so I did" (Chiaro mi fu allor come ogne dove / in cielo è paradiso. . . . Ma sì com' elli avvien, s'un cibo sazia / e d'un altro rimane ancor la gola / che quel si chere e di quel si ringrazia / così fec' io [3.88–93]). Finally, the rivers flowing with milk, honey, and wine in the mi'raj account are transmuted by Dante into a flowing light that is experienced by the narrator as the sweet milk taken in by a new-born baby at the breast:

> Non è fantin . . .
> Col volto verso il latte, se si svegli
> Molto tardato da l'usanza sua,
> Come fec' io, per far migliori spegli
> Ancor de li occhi, chinandomi a l'onda
> Che si deriva.

> No infant . . . so suddenly rushes with face toward the milk, as then did
> I, to make yet better mirrors of my eyes, stooping to the wave which
> flows there.
>
> (Pa. 30.82–87)

It is through this experience that Dante comes to see—to drink in, with his eyes—what he calls "the general form of paradise" (la forma general di paradiso [31.52]), a vision that gives way to a still higher vision, that of "the universal form" (la forma universal [33.91]). With this vision, the power of language finally fails, and Dante's narrator is left in the position of the word-less infant, who can communicate only through his yearning for milk.

In these highest reaches of the *Paradiso,* the maternal manifestation of divine beatitude in the Christian framework is in sharp contrast to the representation of the divine in the Islamic framework of the mi'raj account, where God's fundamental unity, majesty, and power are embodied in the image of the divine throne. The throne of God is surrounded by seventy thousand veils, each of which the Prophet has to penetrate in order to come—entirely alone—to the sight of God. This throne, emblematic of the utterly aloof

God of the Islamic tradition, is dramatically at odds with the Marian Theo-tokos so well known in Christian iconography, in which the body of the Virgin Mary is itself the throne of the Infant Christ. In dramatic contrast to the role of the image central to Christian conceptualizations of the divine, in the mi'raj account, it is utterly imperative that the image is transcended in the experience of God. In Dante's "form of heaven," conversely, the image is retained even as the self is subsumed into the divine vision. Further, the body—hungry flesh, nourishing milk—is retained as well, assimilated into the transformative experience of the journey to God. To note the inter-textual relationship of the *Book of the Ladder* and Dante's *Commedia,* then, is not to diminish the latter work by illustrating its dependence on a literary precursor. On the contrary, the strikingly distinctive features of Dante's vi-sion of heaven stand out in even fuller relief when juxtaposed with its source in the *Book of the Ladder.*

The retention of bodily imagery at the very summit of heaven, in Dante's *Paradiso,* casts an indirect light on Dante's ultimate rejection of intellectual vision as a poor simulacrum of the Beatific Vision. For Dante, the light of the mind alone is limited: in the *Inferno,* even the most brilliant philosophers and poets of antiquity remain merely half-illuminated by the dim light of rea-son.[21] Their privation is expressed both in terms of the hermeneutics of light and in terms of space, as figures such as Averroës and Aristotle remain at the edge of hell, unworthy alike of condemnation or salvation. The narrator and his guide, Virgil, enter the portal of the city of Dis, and immediately come upon an intermediate territory that is neither fully part of hell nor separate from it, housing those who belong neither in the realm of the damned nor of the saved. This territory, Limbo, is not only marginal (literally, the "margin" or "hem") but also temporary, for the medieval theology of Limbo dictates that it will come to an end with the Second Coming and Last Judgment.[22] The inhabitants of the place are "suspended" (sospesi [Inf. 4.45]), cut off from spiritual ascent and descent alike. Divided into three groups of poets, philosophers, and warriors, the residents of Limbo are within the "porta" or gate of hell (3.11), but outside of the "porta" of baptism (4.36). They are inside and outside at once.

Virgil explains to the narrator that those in Limbo did not sin, but are excluded from salvation by being unbaptized. Those who were not baptized due to having lived before the Incarnation remain in Limbo owing to their fail-ure to "worship God aright" (non adorar debitamente a Dio [Inf. 4.38]); Virgil

---

21. On the dim light of reason in the *Inferno,* see Akbari, *Seeing through the Veil,* 147–53.
22. On the temporary nature of Limbo (as of Purgatory), see Le Goff, *The Birth of Purgatory.*

includes himself among this group. The inclusion of figures such as Averroës, Avicenna, and Saladin, however, is peculiar, because their lack of baptism is clearly volitional: all three lived after the Incarnation, and all three knew of the existence of Christ and the Christian Church. Dante's inclusion of these figures in Limbo is therefore provocative, and prompting the question of why Dante wished to retain these figures in the marginal space of Limbo rather than condemn them to the lower levels of the Inferno, nearer to their prophet Muhammad and his companion Ali.

A number of efforts have been made to explain Dante's position regarding the fate to be experienced after death by those who, in life, were not members of the Church. In her survey of theological treatments of the virtuous pagan, Marcia Colish acknowledges that Dante's inclusion of Muslims in Limbo is "peculiar," while Amilcare Iannucci simply suggests that Limbo is populated by those pagans who were "born too early or too far away" to be included in the redemption by Christ.[23] While Dante's inclusion of Aristotle and other philosophers born before the Incarnation of Christ may seem an appropriate recognition of the almost divine quality of philosophical truth, it is more difficult to rationalize his inclusion of Muslims who must have actively rejected Christ, such as Avicenna and Averroës, both of whom refer explicitly to Christianity and Christians in their writings. Averroës, moreover, was a product of the multicultural environment of medieval al-Andalus, hardly insulated from the "truth" of Christian revelation. Nonetheless, for Dante these men's common allegiance to the pursuit of truth through means of the intellect makes them members of a single "philosophical family" (filosofica famiglia [Inf. 4.132]), a family whose bonds continue into the afterworld. The treatment of Saladin, however, remains stubbornly difficult to explain: far from being "too far away" from Christians (as Iannucci puts it), he was continually at war with them. Saladin—Sultan Yusuf ibn Ayyub (1138–93), surnamed Salah ad-Din—could not easily be conceived of as a friend to Christendom, having reclaimed Jerusalem for the Muslims in 1187 and defended the city against European assaults during the Third Crusade. In spite of this seemingly inauspicious relationship to Christianity, popular literature including the *Decameron* depicts Saladin as a model of munificence and generosity, a noble knight whose frequent and often friendly contacts with Christians are widely attested. Some accounts even go so far as to claim that Saladin had a Christian mother.[24]

---

23. Colish, "Virtuous Pagan," 43–77; Iannucci, "Limbo," 69–128. See also Schildgen, "Dante and the Indus," 177–93; updated version in Schildgen, *Dante and the Orient*, 92–109.

24. On medieval French depictions of Saladin, see McCracken, *Romance of Adultery,* esp. chap. 4 ("Adultery, Illegitimacy, and Royal Maternity").

In chapter 5, in connection with Dante's depiction of Muhammad and Ali in the circle of the schismatics in the *Inferno,* we noted that medieval commentators on the *Commedia* were largely oblivious to the nature of Dante's relatively subtle view of Islam as a schism within Christianity, and Shi'a Islam as a further schism. The commentators display a similar uncertainty in their exegesis of the presentation of Saladin in the *Inferno.* Dante's commentators recognize that Saladin was a Muslim, or, as the *Anonimo Fiorentino* commentator puts it, "of the law of Muhammad" (delle legge di Macometto). They also fix on Saladin's physical position as an indicator of his status within the afterworld. Noting that Saladin is said to be "by himself apart" (solo, in parte [Inf. 4.129]), the *Ottimo* commentator explains that this reflects Saladin's special position among the Muslims: "Among Muslims he was unique" (Intra Saraceni fu singulare). Benvenuto glosses the phrase similarly, stating that Saladin "was unique in virtue among those of his time" (fuit singularissimus in virtute temporibus suis). Jacopo della Lana, however, interprets the reference in the context of the many popular legends of Saladin, in which the Muslim ruler travels throughout the West in disguise. Jacopo states that Saladin, dressed as a pilgrim, "came alone to Paris, and went his way alone" (venne a Parigi solo e passando per una via solo). Here, the commentator draws upon a popular tradition that saw Saladin not only as a model of generosity (as Dante also portrays him in the *Convivio*),[25] but as a man of the East who could pass unnoticed throughout the West, his identity concealed by his clothing and by his mastery of the local language. Such portraits of Saladin appear in Boccaccio's *Decameron* and the *Novellino,* as well as many other vernacular accounts.[26] In this view, Saladin is a man who can circulate almost invisibly among disparate cultures, not only a figure of exile but a kind of trickster figure whose identity is both provisional and temporary.

Throughout the *Inferno,* spatial metaphors are crucial to Dante's representation of Muslims, ranging from the riven body and "suspended" foot of Muhammad to the figure of Satan fixed in the icy hell that is at once central (to Dis) and peripheral (to the wellspring of divine creation). As we saw in chapter 5, the suspended body of Satan and foot of Muhammad serve as markers of wrongly directed belief, both recalling the legend of the suspended tomb of Muhammad and the ability of this false miracle to deceive the credulous Saracens who make pilgrimage to it at Mecca.[27] The "suspended" souls

25. Dante Alighieri, *Convivio* 4.11.14.

26. Paris, "La Légende de Saladin," 284–99, 354–64, 428–38, 486–98; Castro, "Presence of the Sultan Saladin," 241–69; Kirkham and Menocal, "Reflections on the 'Arabic' World," 95–110.

27. On the relationship between the popular notion of the relic of Muhammad's foot contained in the suspended tomb at Mecca, and the rock in Jerusalem displaying the imprint of Muhammad's foot at the point of departure narrated in mi'raj accounts, see Cerulli, *Nuove ricerche,* 250–54.

of Limbo (sospesi [Inf. 4.45]) are similarly marked off, consigned to a liminal space that is neither fully central nor fully peripheral. Saladin's location, however, stands at cross-purposes to this general approach: he is, in a sense, located at his own center, standing "solo in parte." This evocative phrase, noted by the commentators, identifies Saladin as a figure of exile, as an individual, and as a figure (however ambivalent) for the poet himself.

Dante's *Commedia* repeatedly expresses ambivalence toward the Saracen Other—admirable on the one hand, reprehensible on the other—and expresses that ambiguity in spatial terms.[28] Saladin's position among the virtuous pagans in Limbo is liminal in a double sense. Like his companions, he is both within Hell and outside it; simultaneously, however, he is separated from his companions, "solo, in parte" (by himself, apart). In this sense, he is a figure of exile, the heroic equivalent of the narrator himself at the outset of his journey to God. For this reason, perhaps, Saladin's physical position parallels that of the narrator himself as he momentarily joins the souls in Limbo. Saladin is named last among the political figures, just as Averroës appears last among the philosophers (Inf. 4.144) and Dante himself brings up the rear among the poets (4.102). This symmetrical arrangement magnifies the narrator, implicitly comparing him to "Averroës, who made the great commentary" (Averoìs che 'l gran comento feo [4.144]) and Saladin, unique in his munificence. The coupling of Dante with exemplary Muslims also supports Maria Rosa Menocal's argument that Dante's position with regard to Islamic culture is one not just of ambivalence, but of "anxiety."[29] She suggests that Dante's treatment of Muhammad and Ali, his depiction of the pit of Hell as a city full of "meschite" or "mosques" (Inf. 8.70), and his condemnation of Averroism collectively represent a rejection of Islam, seen by Dante as a religion that elevates the intellect above all else, placing the individual on a level with God. The positioning of the narrator alongside Averroës and Saladin emphasizes the immediacy of the world of Islam, representing it not as a threat located far away on the other side of the world, but rather (in the form of Latin Averroism) as a danger appallingly close to home. The danger conveyed by Averroës and Saladin, however, is coupled with an undeniable admiration for these men, set apart from their peers by their intellectual, ethical, and personal virtue: this virtue becomes itself an object of desire, expressed in the poet's unwillingness to consign them to the inferno. Through their liminal status, Averroës and Saladin are figured as what we might call

---

28. On Dante's ambivalence toward Muslims, see Toorawa, "Muhammad, Muslims, and Islamophiles"; Mallette, "Dante e l'Islam," 39–62.

29. Menocal, *Arabic Role.*

"companions of the poet," compassionately saved by him from the punishment of hell, but necessarily excluded from the spiritual exodus upward, through purgatory, to the gates of heaven.

The dangerous allure of Islam, for Dante, lay precisely in its elevation of the intellect, and its promise of transcendent experience mediated through the mind. The philosopher Roger Bacon, writing in the thirteenth century, was susceptible to the same allure. In his *Opus Maius*, to which we now turn, Bacon struggles with the same ambivalence toward the Muslim world that Dante does. Like the poet, Bacon attempts to reconcile reason and faith, intellectual ascent and mystical revelation; unlike Dante, however, he does so not within a narrative of ascent of the individual soul but in a chronicle of the ages of world history. Bacon fixes on the relentlessly literal Islamic paradise and its focus on sensuous, bodily pleasures as the key to simultaneously denigrating Islamic theology while elevating Muslim philosophers. Spatial metaphors and the hermeneutics of supersession are central to Bacon's effort to integrate both Islamic theology and Muslim philosophers into a coherent universal history that ultimately acknowledges the indisputable truth of Christian revelation.

↢ The Place of Philosophy

In his *Opus Maius*, Roger Bacon repeats a dictum that he attributes to the neo-platonic philosopher Porphyry: "place is the beginning of the generation of things, as Porphyry says; because in accordance with the diversity of places is the diversity of things; and not only is this true in the things of nature, but in those of morals and the sciences, as we see in the case of men that they have different manners according to the diversity of regions, and busy themselves in different arts and sciences."[30] This quotation, which characterizes location as the crucial determinant of the nature of all things, offers useful insights into what we might call Bacon's "theory of everything"; that is, his capacious, encyclopaedic approach to philosophy in all its many forms, ranging from speculative and moral philosophy to natural philosophy. For Bacon, natural philosophy also extends to the quadrivial fields of astronomy and geometry, with mathematics acting as the foundation of these. Within Bacon's comprehensive "system of knowledge," Islamic philosophy—in all its many forms—plays a crucial role. In Bacon's presentation, Islamic philosophy at

---

30. Roger Bacon, *Opus Maius*, book 4, trans. Burke, 320. Subsequent citations are cited in the text by page number in Burke's translation.

once emerges from a local Arab, non-Christian context and transcends that context, forming a vital element in the collective, general quest for knowledge in which all "lovers of wisdom" participate.

The following pages offer a very brief summary of the structure of the *Opus Maius* before turning to the two foci of this section of the chapter. These foci are, first, the role of "philosophers" in Bacon's system of knowledge, be they Muslim or members of another non-Christian community; second, the place of Islam (or, as Bacon calls it, the Saracen "law of Muhammad") within world geography and universal history. These two foci illuminate what can only be described as ambivalence in Bacon's depiction of Islam, one which is found in a number of medieval texts that reflect both admiration of Islamic learning and contempt for the religious belief of Muhammad's community. This ambivalence is strikingly similar to that which we have just seen demonstrated in Dante's *Inferno,* which damns Muhammad and Ali to the circle of schismatics while carefully preserving Saladin and Averroës in the relative comfort of Limbo. Bacon's system of knowledge, which is based on an understanding of place that extends beyond the dimensions of physical space to encompass the virtual space of universal history, makes room for Islam within world chronologies. His assignation of that place, however, varies in interesting ways ranging through the *Opus Maius,* offering fascinating insights not only into Bacon's own view of the place of Islam and Islamic philosophy within world culture, but also into the intellectual context in which he expected his writings to be received. Since Bacon's efforts were not warmly met (it seems likely that he spent several of his last years in prison), we may expect that his judgment of how his work would be received was not as accurate as it might have been.[31]

The story of the composition of Roger Bacon's great work is well known. In 1266, Bacon received a letter from Pope Clement IV in response to a message he had sent earlier that year. In his letter, the pope commanded Bacon to send him his promised volume of "writings and remedies for current conditions." The volume Bacon had promised, however, existed only in the philosopher's mind, not on manuscript pages; a doubtless somewhat panicked Bacon immediately embarked upon a prospectus of the major work he hoped the pope would commission him to write. This prospectus—in seven books, two fat volumes in the Latin critical edition—is the *Opus Maius.* An understanding of the haste in which the *Opus Maius* was composed and its status as a prospectus or abstract of a future, lengthier work helps us to understand

---

31. For an overview of Bacon's life and work, see the introduction to Bacon, *Roger Bacon's Philosophy of Nature,* ed. Lindberg.

more clearly its variable nature; in particular, it helps us to understand the changing role of Islam within Bacon's universal history and the role of Muslim writers within his core narrative, the history of philosophical thought from its earliest origins to the present day. The *Opus Maius* is composed of seven books: book 1, on the causes of error; 2, on the place of philosophy relative to theology; 3, on the study of foreign languages; 4, on mathematics (which includes astronomy and geography); 5, on optics; 6, on experimental science; and, finally, book 7, on moral philosophy. It is in book 7 that Bacon engages most fully with the place of Islamic philosophy within the wider quest for knowledge, demonstrating how the work of Muslim philosophers (especially Avicenna) can serve the ends of Christian revelation.

The backbone of the *Opus Maius,* as I have already suggested, is a powerful argument for the central place of philosophy (in all its various forms) in the understanding of human history and in contemporary efforts to solve the problems of the world—that is, in Bacon's worldview, to prepare for the calamitous advent of Antichrist. In Bacon's presentation, philosophy is not the product of an individual thinker, or even the product of an individual culture. It is, instead, the product of "a succession of men" (23), with the quest for wisdom making its way from Aristotle to Avicenna to Averroës. This model of intellectual "succession" in some ways recalls the progress of *translatio imperii,* the movement of imperial power from one great kingdom to the next, from the glories of Babylon to the puissance of Rome. Bacon makes repeated reference to the fifth-century chronicler Orosius, whose universal history was the primary source for this formulation throughout the Middle Ages. Bacon's philosophical analogue to *translatio imperii,* however, differs from Orosius' formulation in having one specific point of origin, one original "translation" of wisdom that subsequently went on to make its way, over thousands of years, through a range of cultures. Bacon explains that the transmission of wisdom—specifically, philosophical learning—took place from the earliest stages of the history of mankind, beginning with Noah, Abraham, Joseph, and Moses, and flowering in King Solomon who, "wiser than all preceding or following him... possessed the full power of philosophy" (52). In his careful, detailed justification of the place of philosophy as the handmaid of theology rather than her competitor, Bacon makes it absolutely clear that, while philosophy may play a subservient role, she has a vital role nonetheless: he acknowledges that "philosophy is merely the unfolding of the divine wisdom by learning and art.... There is one perfect wisdom which is contained in the Scriptures, and was given to the saints by God; [it is] to be unfolded, however, by philosophy as well as by canon law" (65). In Bacon's view, "there is one complete wisdom, which suffices the human race" (68); it is therefore unsurprising that (according to Bacon) Avicenna quotes the Hebrew prophet Isaiah, while Plato quotes Exodus. The "one complete wisdom" that Bacon describes is thus reflected not only in the teachings of Christian theology, but in the writings of philosophers, be they Christian or non-Christian.[32] Among the latter, the pre-Christian Seneca and the Muslim Avicenna are perhaps most dear to Bacon, quoted at length and named with respect and what can only be termed affection.

Avicenna figures prominently not just in the final book of the *Opus Maius,* which is devoted to moral philosophy, but also in the first two books, in which Bacon lays out the proper relationship of philosophy to theology and provides an overview of the history of philosophy throughout universal history. While Bacon identifies Aristotle as being, among philosophers, "the greatest of them all" (63), he honors Avicenna almost as highly, describing him as "the man who completed philosophy as far as it was possible for him to do so" (63–64). In stating that Avicenna came close to "completing philosophy," Bacon reaffirms his belief, asserted in the second book of the *Opus Maius,* that philosophy was initially provided as a gift, whole and complete, to mankind by God. Since then it was lost, and the efforts of philosophers throughout history, as in Bacon's present day, are simply to recover the "complete" philosophy, the original divine gift. In this narrative, the multiplicity of philosophical approaches and divergences of opinion are inevitably destined to merge into a single stream of truth, leading to a full confirmation, Bacon asserts, of the truth of Christian doctrine. Islamic philosophy, like other forms of non-Christian thought, is thus subsumed into a single trajectory within Bacon's intellectual history.

Such assimilation came at a price. Bacon was only one among a number of Latin Christian writers of the Middle Ages who sought to make use of the riches of Islamic learning, while simultaneously avoiding the taint of Islamic doctrine. Bacon, however, goes further than most, arguing that certain Muslim philosophers actually refuted the teachings of Muhammad in their own writings. As John Tolan has shown, Bacon distorts Avicenna's denial of bodily resurrection, suggesting that Avicenna's claim that bodily pleasures do not exist in the afterlife is actually a refutation of the Qur'an's description of the nature of the heavenly paradise. As Bacon puts it, "Avicenna . . . proves Muhammad in error because he has set forth only physical delights and not

---

32. While Bacon praises Avicenna in the highest terms, he exhibits significant reservations about Averroës, probably reflecting contemporary controversy surrounding Latin Averroism (*Opus Maius* books 1–2, passim). Considering that Bacon was writing to the pope, some circumspection may have been prudent.

spiritual ones" (808; cf. 649, 801). In fact, Avicenna's argument against bodily pleasures in the afterlife is far from an endorsement of Christian doctrine; he also denies the existence of the torments of hell and the existence of any bodily resurrection at all. For Bacon's purposes, however, it is enough that Avicenna's argument can be used as a weapon against one of the central features of Islamic belief. Avicenna thus becomes, in Tolan's memorable phrase, "not part of the Muslim team, but... rather a sort of intellectual free agent ready to sign on to Christianity."[33] As a result of the holistic view of philosophy outlined in the first books of the *Opus Maius*, Avicenna (like other non-Christian philosophers featured in the text) inevitably works toward what Bacon calls the "complet[ion of] philosophy," which, when complete, is coterminous with Christian theology. Although he "finds fault with his own lawgiver" (that is, Muhammad [649]), Avicenna does not go so far as to seek out one who more properly serves the ends of that wisdom beloved by the philosopher—that is, for Bacon, Christ.

As we have seen, the place of Islamic philosophy is in the middle, its great thinkers part of a "succession" or sequence of learned men who all strive to reach the "complet[ion of] philosophy." It is no coincidence, I would suggest, that this structure of philosophical "succession" resembles the multiplication of species fundamental to Bacon's natural philosophy; as Bacon puts it, the "species causes every action in this world; for it acts on sense, on intellect, and all the matter in the world for the production of things" (130).[34] The multiplication of species accounts for all perception, all action, all reproduction; it is therefore not surprising that the history of philosophy, in Bacon's view, follows a similar conceptual model. On the one hand, therefore, we can say that the place of Islamic philosophy is in the middle; on the other hand, however, the place of Islam and of the Saracen "nation," in Bacon's account, is much more variable. I refer to "place" because of the emphatic role of location in Bacon's universal history and world geography: he schematizes and categorizes the religious sects and people of the world, placing Islam sometimes in a medial position, one of a range of non-Christian beliefs; sometimes in a privileged position alongside Judaism, one of three possible "laws," only one of which is truly valid (810–11); and sometimes in a potentially climactic

---

33. Tolan, "Saracen Philosophers," 184–208; quotation from 199.

34. For a brief account of Bacon's theory of the multiplication of species, see Akbari, *Seeing through the Veil,* 37, 92–94. For a more detailed account, see the introduction to Bacon, *Roger Bacon's Philosophy of Nature,* ed. Lindberg, and Bacon, *Roger Bacon and the Origins of Perspectiva,* ed. Lindberg.

position, as a contender for the status of the pernicious "law of Antichrist," which will reign supreme during the last days of salvation history.

In the fourth book of the *Opus Maius,* Bacon explains how mathematics enables a fuller understanding not only of the natural world, but also of universal history. By means of mathematics, Bacon writes, "we are fortified in advance against the sect of Antichrist," enabled to measure its progress relative to the other sects that have preceded it: "A very excellent examination of this kind is made by considering all the principal sects from the beginning of the world, which are six in number, nor can there be more, namely, Jews, Chaldeans, Egyptians, Agaren[es] or Saracens..., the Church of Christ, and the sect of Antichrist" (276). In the following pages, Bacon discusses this sequence of "sects" in chronological order, with the rise to power of Muhammad coming twenty revolutions of Saturn after the appearance of "Jesus, son of Mary,"[35] which in turn took place ten revolutions of Saturn after the rise of Alexander the Great (286; following Abu Ma'shar). It is important to note Bacon's phrase "nor can there be more"; in his presentation, there are never more or less than six sects. The reason for this, unsurprisingly, lies within natural philosophy and, more deeply, within mathematics itself.[36] In explaining the shape of the world and how it can be measured, Bacon explains that there are "three lines" that divide it into parts: one going east to west, the equator; one going north to south, transecting the poles; and a third, in Bacon's words, "forward and backward, that is, from the point in the middle of the heavens above us to the opposite point in the heavens below the earth." He concludes, "Thus Aristotle teaches us to imagine six differences of position in the heavens in the second book of the Heavens and the World" (309). These six sectors of the world conform to a range of phenomena occurring in nature, including the six-sided form of the prism, the six colors that Bacon identifies in the rainbow, and so on. More pertinently, however, they conform to the celestial bodies that exert control on the regions of the world and on the individuals that inhabit them.

For Bacon, following Islamic astronomers such as Abu Ma'shar, the planets not only influence the individual destinies of human beings, but also determine the national characteristics of groups of peoples. Bacon specifies that "a sect is changed more quickly or slowly according to the properties of the

---

35. The phrase Bacon uses, "Jesus, son of Mary," is characteristically Islamic, and may be drawn from Bacon's source in the astrology of Abu Ma'shar. See the edition of the Arabic and Latin texts of Abu Ma'shar, *Kitab al-milal wa-al-duwal.*

36. An additional context for Bacon's six-fold schema is Joachim of Fiore's apocalyptic model of history, divided into six ages plus a final, "sabbath" age. On Joachim and his influence, see Reeves, *Influence of Prophecy;* also Reeves, *Joachim of Fiore.*

planets bearing sway over different regions," so that "Saturn controls India; Jupiter, Babylonia," and so on (287). This six-fold structure is also dominant in the unfolding of history, as the changing conjunctions of Jupiter with now one planet, now another, results in the rise of various religious laws. Bacon cites "the philosophers" (that is, Islamic astronomers) on these conjunctions: "Since there are six planets with which [Jupiter] can be united and in conjunction, they therefore assert that there must be six principal sects in the world" (278). When Jupiter is in conjunction with Saturn, he elaborates, Judaism arose; when in conjunction with Mars, the Chaldeans worshipped fire; when in conjunction with the sun, the Egyptians devoted themselves to the sun god.[37] Bacon, unsurprisingly, is obliged to deviate from his source, Abu Ma'shar, in describing the astrological conjunction that facilitated the rise of Islam: "If [Jupiter] is in conjunction with Venus, his reference is said to be to the law of the Saracens, which is wholly voluptuous and lascivious" (278). The Qur'an, in Bacon's account, is simply a written codification of the so-called "lascivious sect" described by "Ovid the poet" (278) long before: "This law [that is, Ovid's 'lascivious sect'] more than six hundred years later Muhammad reduced to writing in a book called the Qur'an" (279). Here, Bacon conforms his presentation of Muslim belief to that dominant strand in Western views of Islam that saw the "law of Muhammad" as characterized by sexual license and excess, even while he draws his exposition of astrology's role in religious history from the writings of the Muslim writer Abu Ma'shar. Moreover, by identifying the Qur'an as merely a codification of the deviant practices of Ovid's "lascivious sect," Bacon produces a retrogressive view of Islam, comparable to those which identify the "law of Muhammad" as a return to the "law of Moses" rather than a theological innovation that builds upon the foundations of both Judaism and Christianity.

As we have seen, in book 4 of the *Opus Maius*, on mathematics, Bacon provides his exposition of the six sects that have existed over the ages. This is an appropriate place for such an exposition, for it occurs within the context of Bacon's explanation of how a knowledge of mathematics is essential to the construction of accurate chronologies, and consequently a reliable prediction of when to expect the advent of Antichrist. He returns to a similar six-fold exposition of religious sects in the last book of the *Opus Maius*, on moral philosophy; here, however, the six-fold division covers not the six dominant

---

37. The astrological sequence is as follows: Saturn—Jews; Mars—Chaldeans (fire-worshippers); Sun—Egyptians (polytheistic, with both natural and man-made objects of worship); Venus—Saracens; Mercury—"Church of Christ"; Moon—"sect of Antichrist" (necromancers) (*Opus Maius* book 4; 276–78).

sects over the span of the past ages, but rather the six-fold division currently existing in the world. This exposition is based not on categories of religious difference, as the one in book 4 did, but rather on categories of geographical difference, defined in terms of "nation." Bacon writes, "I shall now state the principal nations in which the various sects are found that are now existing throughout the world, namely, Saracens, Tartars, Pagans, Idolaters, Jews, Christians. For the principal sects do not exceed this number nor can they do so until the sect of Antichrist appears" (788).[38] Clearly, this six-fold division is not historically structured, like that found in book 4; instead, the detailed exposition that follows makes it clear that Bacon here groups the Saracens together with other "nations" excluded from the covenant made by God with the Jews, and subsequently fulfilled in the Christian "new law." These "nations" include "Saracens," "Tartars," "Pagans" (among whom Bacon specifies "the Praceni [Prussians] and the nations bordering on them" [789]), and "Idolaters" (whom he characterizes as the 'virtuous pagans' of India). He then couples the Jews, who rightly "hoped for blessings both temporal and eternal," but failed by "interpreting their law in its literal sense" (789). These errors were rectified by the Christians, who "secure spiritual blessings by spiritual means" (790).

Bacon next reviews the "principal sects" found in the "various nations" once again, but this time in a different order.[39] Here, he ranges them from least sophisticated to most sophisticated, beginning with the simple "Pagans" who worship things of nature. These are followed by the "Idolaters," who construct images, and the "Tartars," who worship fire (790). Fourth among these "principal sects" come the Jews, who (Bacon writes) "should have had a better knowledge of God in accordance with their law, and should have truly desired the Messiah, who is Christ" (790–91). Fifth come the Christians, "who accept the law of the Jews spiritually and complete it by adding the faith of Christ. Last of all," he concludes, "will come the law of Antichrist" (791). It is immediately apparent that this sequence of "six laws" differs from the preceding ones in two important ways: first, in its different ordering of the "principal sects"; second, in its conspicuous omission of Islam. A reader prepared to view Islam very negatively might choose to identify the "law of Muhammad" with the "law of Antichrist" named by Bacon in the final

---

38. The sequence of "principal nations in which the various sects are found" is as follows: Saracens; Tartars; Pagans; Idolaters; Jews; Christians (*Opus Maius* book 7; 788).

39. The sequence of "principal sects" is as follows: Pagans (natural objects of worship); Idolaters (man-made objects of worship); Tartars (fire-worship); Jews; Christians; "Law of Antichrist" (*Opus Maius,* book 7; 790–91).

position of the six sects. Bacon himself does not state this explicitly, and in fact in book 4 of the *Opus Maius* specifies that the "law of Muhammad" is *not* to be identified with the "law of Antichrist": he writes, "after the law of Mahomet we do not believe that any other law will come except the law of Antichrist" (289).

I would suggest that the inconsistency, in this last sequence, arises in part from the difficulty of inserting Islam within the logic of Christian supersession, in which the "old law" of Judaism is fulfilled (and supplanted) by the "new law" of Christianity. Within the logic of supersession, where to place Islam? As dangerous innovation, a *new* "new law" that sees itself as a fulfillment of the promise of Christian belief? Or as a retrogressive return to a literal understanding of the law, closely aligned with Judaism? In medieval Christian views of Islam, we find both of these perspectives; for Bacon, the former view, with Islam as a novel development beyond Christian doctrine, would surely have been dangerously close to his presentation of the "succession" of great thinkers within the history of philosophy. He was already on dangerous ground in lauding the moral philosophy of Avicenna and Averroës; it would be still more dangerous to allow any equation to be drawn between his presentation of Islamic theology and his presentation of philosophical ascent. Perhaps for this very reason, in book 7 Bacon emphasizes the close relationship between Judaism and Islam: he writes that, although the Saracens "follow in the main the law of Venus, yet [they] derive much from the Jewish law." He cannot avoid, nonetheless, pointing out the proximity of Islamic doctrine to Christianity: "They say, moreover, that Christ is the Son of the Virgin and the greatest of the prophets, and they retain many words of the Evangelists in their law" (791–92). In the end, however, a debate among the three rival "sects" of Judaism, Islam, and Christianity can result only in the conclusion that "Christ alone is the lawgiver whom we are seeking" (810–11).

In the geographical section of book 4, on mathematics, Bacon writes, "He who is ignorant of the places of the world lacks a knowledge not only of his destination, but of the course to pursue" (321). This passage both provides a rationale for the inclusion of his detailed geography and sheds light on a broader theme in Bacon's work: that is, the role of place in his system of knowledge.[40] Specifying relative positions within the many six-fold structures to be found in nature, in chronologies, and in history enables Bacon to

---

40. Bacon's inclusion of his geography, like his account of the need for fuller language study, must be interpreted in the light of the imperatives of missionary work to convert Islamic and other nations, especially those views expressed within Bacon's own Franciscan community (*Opus Maius,*

order the world in space and time, generating a "theory of everything" that, he hoped, would provide sound guidance for the future of Christendom. This rigid framework, however, fit very awkwardly with the model of "succession" outlined by Bacon in the history of philosophy he presents in the first books of the *Opus Maius*. The "perfection" and "completion" of philosophy is, potentially, an open-ended process, an ascent that has the promise of generating new insights, new observations, new knowledge. Because this completion is, however, simply a recuperation of the "complete philosophy" bestowed by God on man at the beginning of time and subsequently lost, the bounty of philosophy is inevitably limited. It is a love of wisdom that can only generate what it already *knows* to be there: that is, the revelation of Christian truth, the Trinity, the Incarnation of Christ, and the redemption of mankind. For Bacon, Islamic philosophy was both tantalizing and dangerous, essential to his great work and yet its point of greatest vulnerability. In order to integrate the work of Muslim philosophers such as Avicenna within his own work, Bacon had to separate philosophy from theology, stripping away the taint of Islam from the pure exercise of reason. But in order to keep philosophy properly subordinate to Christian revealed truth, however, he had to identify philosophy as the very basis of Christian belief, articulated through theology. This contradiction is never resolved in the *Opus Maius*.

The famous *Dialogue of a Philosopher with a Jew and a Christian* by Peter Abelard is, in a sense, a twelfth-century prefiguration of the confluence of the three "sects" of Judaism, Christianity, and Islam elaborated by Roger Bacon a century later.[41] For Abelard, the Saracen is, precisely, the "philosopher": this means both that philosophy is understood as emanating from the realms where Islamic rule holds sway, and that a learned Saracen is necessarily a "philosopher." For Bacon, this alignment of philosophy and theological orientation was precisely what had to be split apart; therefore, like other medieval writers of the period, he insisted on the fundamental irrationality of Islam, epitomized in the sensuous, fleshly paradise depicted in the Qur'an. Even Avicenna himself, in Bacon's view, rejected this plainly irrational supposition.

The Islamic paradise was thus a focal point for a whole range of Western perspectives on Islam. It was the very heart of the irrationality of Islam, for philosophers such as Bacon; and it epitomized the essential emptiness of the "law of Muhammad," its dedication to the pleasures of the flesh and the

---

book 3, chap. 13; 110). On Franciscan missions of conversion and their modes of representing Islam, see Tolan, *Saracens,* 214–32; see also Tolan, *Saint Francis and the Sultan.*
   41. Abelard, *Dialogus inter philosophum, iudaeum et christianum.*

superficiality of the letter. The luxurious pleasures of Islam, expressed not only in the vision of paradise but in the lascivious behaviors associated with and supposedly encouraged by Muhammad, were seen as a seductive trap for the curious westerner. More important, however, they were also seen as a symptom, a visible manifestation of the defect lying at the center of Islamic theology. Medieval Christians thought that Muslims, like Jews, privileged the letter over the spirit and that they therefore had only a very imperfect understanding of matters pertaining to the welfare of the soul. At the same time, however, they recognized the appeal of the luxurious pleasures of the Islamic paradise, and consequently assimilated some aspects of it in popular texts, such as the poems devoted to the land of Cockaigne. Moreover, descriptions of the afterlife found in major works of the Western tradition, including Dante's *Commedia,* drew upon the depiction of the mi'raj, or night-time journey to the afterworld made by the Prophet Muhammad, found in the *Book of the Ladder.* In the Western assimilation of the idea of the Islamic paradise—negatively, in anti-Islamic polemics; positively, in Dante's appropriation of the layered heavens of the mi'raj—it is possible to observe the fundamental ambivalence at the heart of European Christian views of Islam and the Orient. They were at once attracted and repelled, fascinated and disturbed.

Conclusion

A Glance at Early Modern Orientalism

The preceding chapters of *Idols in the East* have surveyed a wide range of texts—literary, historical, scientific, and cartographic. Instead of focusing narrowly on medieval representations of "Saracens," I have tried to sketch out the wider contours of the discourse within which medieval Muslims were described. This has required me to explore two distinct vectors within premodern Orientalism: alterity defined in terms of religious difference, and alterity defined in terms of geographical diversity. Far more than in modern Orientalism—which, as suggested in the introduction, can be said to have its origins in the eighteenth-century colonial period—these two vectors were complexly intertwined, so that religious difference and geographical diversity were simultaneously invoked. When the Orient was described, Islam was also in the picture; and where Islam was described, the Orient was continually in the background.

Yet more was at stake, for medieval Western Christians: defining Islam and the Orient was for, the most part, simply a way to indirectly define the self. This was particularly the case in the later Middle Ages, as engagement with the Islamic world became gradually less intense both on the military front (with the repeated failure of the Crusades) and on the intellectual front (with the growing independence of Western philosophy from figures such as Avicenna and Averroës). Even at the height of Islamic military power and intellectual accomplishments, however, self-definition was also an integral

part of Orientalism. During the twelfth century, Islamic science and philosophy were exerting an ever-increasing influence on Western thought, and
political engagement with Muslim forces (both on the Iberian peninsula and
in the Levant) was in full force. Nonetheless, as Dominique Iogna-Prat has
eloquently shown, the detailed and articulate account of Islamic theology
provided by Peter the Venerable had as its goal not conversion of Muslims to
Christianity, but rather the fuller elaboration of the role of the Church and,
more specifically, of the Cluniac order. As Iogna-Prat signals in the original
French title of his study, *Ordonner et exclure,* to create order—that is, to define
that which is interior, pure, and sacred—is to exclude, identifying that which
is exterior, filthy, and abominable. Through defining Islam, then, medieval
Christians were able to define themselves. This was a process, as we have
seen especially in chapters 3 and 5, that was constructed on the foundation of
Jewish identity: Christians understood themselves to be the "true Israel," and
the Church as the fulfillment and replacement of the community of the faithful that had existed prior to the Incarnation. Islam had to be inserted within
this hermeneutics of supersession, sometimes as a third "new" law upon the
foundations of the other two, sometimes as a retrogressive "old" law that returned obstinately to the literalist teachings of Moses. This ambiguity regarding Islam's place within the hermeneutics of supersession is an expression of
a broader ambivalence expressed in medieval Orientalism, where admiration
vies with contempt, as we saw in chapter 6.

Significantly, it is not the case that Jewish identity served as a foundation
for the articulation of Christian and Muslim identity only in terms of the
vector of religious alterity. On the contrary, Jewish identity was conceived as
foundational in corporeal terms as well, as we saw in chapters 3 and 4, which
explored the role of climate in determining bodily diversity based on geographical distribution. The Jewish body was at once a test case for the role
of climate in determining bodily diversity and a disturbing anomaly, owing
to the wandering nature of the Jews, who were thought to be no longer
stably fixed within a climate "proper" to their physiological makeup. In medieval texts depicting Jewish bodies, it is possible to observe the interaction
of two vectors of alterity, religious and geographical. This discursive formation, in which the two vectors mutually reinforce one another, makes up the
background of medieval Christian efforts at self-definition and concomitant
definition of the "Saracen" other.

In the discourse of medieval Orientalism, along both vectors of alterity,
space is the key mode through which difference and identity is expressed.
From the interior space of the Sultan's chamber in the *Book of John Mandeville*
to the chamber of Candace frequented by Alexander in the *Roman de toute*

chevalerie, the Orient is shown to contain private, secret realms in which the Western self can come into contact with its Other. As we have seen, however, what one finds in those spaces is, precisely, a mirror of the self: Mandeville's narrator hears the Sultan tell him about the current state of Western Christendom, while Alexander gazes, bemused, at a statue of himself made at the behest of the Oriental queen. These spaces are individual manifestations of the "regio solis," the place of the sun described in apocalyptic texts such as that of pseudo-Methodius. Paradoxically, this apparently singular "region of the sun" proves to be multiple, appearing on maps as the several lands of India and Ethiopia, together making up the torrid region of the Orient. Because it is presently inhabited by a heterogeneous range of peoples, many of them under the sway of the pernicious "law of Muhammad," the Orient is multiple and fragmented. Insofar as the Orient is characterized as a harbinger of the rule of Christ, however, epitomized in the anticipated advance of the armies of Prester John's Land, it is singular and redemptive. This is the exquisitely pure Orient lauded by Dante as he opens his eyes and looks up after leaving behind in the pit of Hell the suspended body of Satan below: "Dolce color d'orïental zaffiro...a li occhi miei ricominciò diletto" (Sweet hue of oriental sapphire...to my eyes restored delight [Pg. 1:13–15]).

In the preceding chapters, I have not hesitated to signal moments where modern attitudes toward Muslims and Islam are foreshadowed in medieval texts: these include the fantasy of the luxurious Islamic paradise evoked in the *Doonesbury* cartoon mentioned at the opening of chapter 6, and General Boykin's infamous condemnation of the Islamic "idol" in Somalia noted in chapter 5. It is striking that the closest correspondences between premodern and contemporary Orientalism center on religious alterity, that is, on the ways in which Islam is supposedly a false, deceptive religion of sensuous surfaces, lacking substantial truth. The complementary vector of geographical diversity, in which bodily differences of anatomy, physiology, and behavior were thought to be dictated by variations of climate, does not seem to have persisted past the early modern period. In part, this is due to the development of notions of race based on "blood" (later, genetics) rather than on climate, as discussed in chapter 3: while bodily diversity, in the medieval past as in the present, is thought to separate "them" from "us," that diversity is thought to be a function of genealogical descent rather than of environment. Nonetheless, some of the qualities ascribed to Saracens under the old discourse of bodily diversity, such as irascibility and a propensity to violence, persist in modern depictions of Muslims. The fierce, warlike nature of Fierabras, like the "wood" rages of his father, the "Sowdone of Babylone," bore witness to the fundamental irrationality of Islam.

The intellectual limitations of Muslims were also signaled in medieval Western texts, though these, significantly, centered specifically on the irrationality of
Islam rather than the irrationality of the Arabs and Persians who followed the
"law of Muhammad." This is especially evident, as we saw in the last chapter,
in Roger Bacon's heroic effort to disentangle the brilliant philosophical mind
of Avicenna from the "error" of Muhammad and his "lascivious sect." A
similar emphasis on the intellectual impoverishment thought to be character-
istic of Islam can be seen in the *Roman de Mahomet*'s contemptuous dismissal
of the "foolish people" who believe the false miracles shown to them by the
Prophet. Here, a crucial disjunction between premodern and present-day
views of Muslims is clearly in evidence. In the great age of Islamic learning,
when Western scientists looked admiringly on Avicenna and Abu Ma'shar,
and Western philosophers referred to Averroës simply as "the Commentator," irrationality could not be imputed to Muslims at large, but only (at best)
to the supposed irrationality of their religion. The modern West, however,
after its eras of religious reform and social revolution, Enlightenment and
colonial expansion, could have no difficulty in seeing the Islamic world as
backward, uneducated—and, worst of all, "medieval."

Perhaps the single most striking distinction between medieval and modern views of Muslims centers on the imputation of sexual licentiousness
to Islam and, in particular, to Muhammad. As we saw in chapters 5 and 6,
Western biographies of the Prophet describe him as a polygamist motivated
by sexual desire, advocating sexual liberties to his followers and promising
a Paradise to the believers replete with every form of physical satisfaction.
This view of Islam persisted, in a sense, into the modern period of colonialism, but with some significant differences. While medieval Orientalism had
associated Islam with sexual license, and even specifically with heterosexual
sodomy, literature of the modern colonial period came increasingly to associate the Orient with same-sex relations. More recent perspectives on Islam,
however, especially those engendered since the Islamic Revolution in Iran
in 1979, have invariably depicted Islam as a rather puritanical, abstemious
religion, characterized by excessive modesty and even "unnatural" sexual
restraint. On one level, this is an inversion of the medieval stereotype of Muslim licentiousness; on another level, however, it pathologizes Islamic practice
as fully as the medieval stereotype had done. When sexual restraint is a virtue in the West, the Muslim is licentious; when sexual liberty is a virtue, the
Muslim is a prude.

Idols in the East can only sketch out one phase in the long, complex history
of Orientalism, beginning with the profound rupture of the years around
1100, with the First Crusade and its apocalyptic mission to Jerusalem, and

ending with the manifold disjunctions introduced by the fall of Constantinople in 1453. The last pages of the book, therefore, will offer just a glance at some of the factors involved in the emergence of what we might identify as the early modern phase of Orientalism. The mid-fifteenth century was a time marked by religious reform, the rise of early modern nationalism, and—perhaps most important for this study—a redrawing of the political boundaries of the Islamic frontier with the West. With the conquest of Constantinople, the territory disputed by Muslims and Christians shifted from Jerusalem to the eastern frontiers of Europe, and Orientalism accordingly underwent a dramatic paradigm shift that was both literal and symbolic. It was literal in that the effort to conquer Jerusalem through military means had largely been abandoned, while efforts to deflect Ottoman incursions into eastern Europe were intensified. The shift was symbolic in that the bodily pilgrimage to Jerusalem had come to be supplanted by the spiritual pilgrimage of the soul, a trend in late medieval piety that became increasingly prominent with the dawn of the Reformation. Medieval world maps, with their conventional placement of Jerusalem at their symbolic center and eastward orientation, would soon become quaint relics of a period when geography reflected pious belief in a particularly transparent way.

Early modern Orientalism exhibits a number of distinct features, as scholars including Nabil Matar, Daniel Vitkus, Nancy Bisaha, and Margaret Meserve have eloquently shown. While it is always true that discursive formations (Orientalist or otherwise) must be seen in the context of other constitutive discourses, early modern Orientalism is expressed in conjunction with other discourses of alterity with greater frequency and consistency than during the Middle Ages. Gender and sexuality come to function as constitutive elements of Oriental alterity in two respects. First, we find a fully developed notion of a feminized Orient, a notion that had already been manifested in a much simpler form within medieval rhetorical descriptions of the Holy Land as a vulnerable female; the opening passage of *The Book of John Mandeville* provides a good illustration of this. Second, we find depictions of the Oriental male as essentially "effeminate," a notion that developed only in the sixteenth century in the wake of European interactions with the Ottoman empire. Both of these examples illustrate the extent to which, within early modern Orientalism, gender and sexuality served as vectors within the discourse of Eastern alterity. Comparable intersections of discursive categories can be identified with regard to nationalism (which is implicated in early modern Orientalism far more dynamically than during the medieval period) and class, which came to be a marker of Oriental alterity during the early modern period in ways quite foreign to medieval texts.

A far more explicit marker of the distinguishing features of early modern Orientalism can be found in the name used to identify the object of these discourses of alterity. While modern constructions of Orientalism center on the idea of the "Arab" or the "Muslim," focusing alternatively on ethnic and religious identities, medieval constructions conflated categories of ethnicity and religion within a single term that served as a marker of both: that is, "Saracen." This term identified its object as religiously different (not a follower of Christ, but of Muhammad), and ethnically or racially different (from Oriental regions). As we have seen, the word "Saracen" is not used to identify Christian Arabs, demonstrating that the term was generally understood as defining alterity in both dimensions; that is, in terms of both religion and race. During the early modern period, however, the term "Saracen" was largely replaced by two much more common terms: "Turk" and "Moor." It is certainly the case that each of these terms can be found in medieval texts, though not with much frequency: "Turk," in the medieval context, refers to one subgroup within the larger "Saracen" enemy, while "Moor" (a term even less common than "Turk") refers specifically to north African Saracens. By the late fifteenth century, however, these terms had come to be far more prominent, both of them more frequently used than the old term "Saracen." This change in terminology signals a paradigm shift in the discourse of Orientalism, where the distinct social character and political role of Ottoman Turkey, on the one hand, and North Africa, on the other, were directly relevant to European national networks of alliance and rivalries. As separate players in European and Mediterranean politics, they could no longer be conflated into a single "Saracen" Other. Moreover, the predominance of terms that denote ethnic or racial alterity ("Turk" and "Moor") in place of a term that had denoted both racial and religious alterity ("Saracen") signals a fundamental distinction between medieval and early modern Orientalism. Religion ceases to be the primary factor in Orientalist discourse and becomes a secondary quality, a defect of knowledge that can be readily improved through education. Religion is replaced in Orientalist discourse by a more complex and sophisticated set of categories of nation, ethnicity, and race.

In order to draw together the strands that have been methodically unraveled in the previous chapters, it is useful to look back at the role of the city in anchoring Orientalist discourse. This is most evident, of course, in the place of Jerusalem as figurative linchpin of medieval cosmography, being the spiritual and geographical center of the world. That center, which the author of *The Book of John Mandeville* more specifically identifies as the little circle sketched on the floor where Christ's body was laid, marks the spatial and temporal point of reference in sacred history. Like the empty tomb, the drawn circle designates spiritual gravity without itself being a physical object of worship. It gestures toward the divine without claiming to embody it. In this respect, its parodic opposite is, of course, the foot of Muhammad, whether in the form of the footprint that (for Fulcher of Chartres) transforms the stone at the base of the Dome of the Rock into a "filthy idol," or the "suspended" foot of the maimed schismatic tormented in Dante's *Inferno.*

Yet Jerusalem also had other parodic opposites in medieval Orientalism: the degenerate site of Mecca, identified by the author of the *Roman de Mahomet* as the seat of all perversion and iniquity, and the ancient city of Babylon, ruled over by "Sultans" who figure as important characters in *Fierabras,* the *King of Tars,* and *The Book of John Mandeville.* Unlike its parodic companion, Mecca, Babylon was viewed as ambivalent, as can be seen in the openness to conversion that is repeatedly associated with the Sultan in all of his various manifestations. While the Sultan of Babylon in *Fierabras* ultimately refuses to convert when brought to the font, the Sultan in the *King of Tars* not only converts but also undergoes a physical metamorphosis, while the Sultan of Babylon in Mandeville's text expresses detailed knowledge of Christianity and testifies to its inevitable triumph at the end of time. This ambiguity is derived from the legacy of Babylon's role in the transmission of imperial power, not only in the expression of *translatio imperii* as formulated by Orosius (where imperial power was passed from Babylon to Macedonia, to Carthage, to Rome) but also as reenacted in the many versions of the Alexander romance, where the Macedonian king appears not so much as the conqueror of Darius, Persian king and ruler of Babylon, but as his heir. The opposition of Babylon and Jerusalem in the eschatological vision of Revelation necessarily led to a view of Babylon as "the great whore," symbol of religious deviance and perversion. The originary role of Babylon in *translatio imperii,* however, led to a more positive view of Babylon, as a source of enormous wealth and the repository of imperial potency.

The framework of *translatio imperii* laid still more of the groundwork for medieval Orientalism and, more particularly, for the paradigm shift that marked the emergence of early modern Orientalism in the mid-fifteenth century. Over the later Middle Ages, the story of the fall of Troy and the subsequent rise of Rome came to be integrated within the Orosian history of imperial power. This development was made easy by the fact that the trajectory of empire both in the *Aeneid* and in Orosius' universal history passes from the eastern regions to Rome by way of Carthage. In spite of the tendency of modern readers to emphasize the disjunction between Virgilian and Augustinian modes of historiography, medieval readers eagerly integrated the two, adding Trojan genealogies and even entire narratives of the fall of Troy into late medieval adaptations of Orosius: in one extreme case, a fourteenth-century adaptation of the thirteenth-century *Histoire ancienne jusqu'á César* actually pops the whole of the *Roman de Troie* into the sequence of Orosian *translatio imperii*. Troy thus took its place alongside other imperial precursors of Rome.

Yet there was another dimension to the role of Troy in imperial history, centering on the outward stream of migrants from the doomed city who went on to populate not only Rome (as recounted in the *Aeneid*) but also a host of other nations including France, Germany, and Britain. This dispersal of peoples was modeled on earlier templates of scattered populations, including the sons of Noah after the Flood, the confused peoples at the Tower of Babel, and the Apostles at Pentecost. The most apposite template, however, was centered on the unwilling dispersal of peoples from a great city: Jerusalem. The outward flow of refugees from Troy was understood in terms of the diaspora recounted by Josephus and echoed (as we have seen) in the *Siege of Jerusalem* and a host of related texts. Medieval readers familiar with the Latin version of Josephus attributed to Hegesippus read accounts of the forced dispersal of the inhabitants of Troy with a strong sense of the repetitious, cyclical nature of history, in which urban destruction is followed by the scattering of peoples to the four corners of the earth. It is therefore unsurprising that a whole series of medieval chronicles integrate the history of diaspora within the history of *translatio imperii*. This is evident not only in the many medieval redactions and continuations of Orosius' universal history, in which the account of the exile of Jews from Jerusalem in the first century serves as a model for all dispersals of peoples from cities after siege (most especially, Troy), but also in other histories of national origin. The implicit comparison of Troy and Jerusalem is heightened through each city's supersessionist relationship to Rome: Troy gives rise to Rome in the national narrative first recounted in the *Aeneid,* just as Jerusalem gives rise to Christian Rome in the ecclesiastical narrative recounted in the many redactions and adaptations of Josephus' *Bellum Iudaicum*. The alignment of the fall of Troy with the fall of Jerusalem, and their common participation in the larger trajectory of Orosian *translatio imperii,* is perhaps most fully expressed in the *Flores historiarum* of Matthew Paris, in which the chronologies of Jewish and Trojan history are alternately recounted until both give way to the linear sequence of successive imperial powers as they devolve from Babylon, to Persia, to Greece, to Rome.

The fall of Constantinople to the Ottoman Turks threw a wrench into this vision of history. If the conquest of its eastern capital spelled the end of the old Roman Empire, there was a certain appropriateness, at least, in the fact that these conquerors were—of all people—Trojans. As Nancy Bisaha has shown in detail, Western writers were quick to recall medieval texts that identified the Turks with Trojans, a connection that made the conquest of Constantinople intelligible in historical terms. The conquest of the Byzantine "Greeks" by the Ottoman Turks could be read as a modern, inverted re-enactment of the conquest of the Trojans by the ancient Greeks. In this case, just as in past iterations of diaspora, refugees would flow outward from the doomed city, their arms as heavy with learned books as were those of the Jews who fled from Josephus' Jerusalem. They too would find their way to Rome, this time to engender a rebirth of classical learning, bearing the treasures of Greek learning that would soon become the only intellectual patrimony acknowledged by the West. We might think of this "imaginative historiography" as the next generation of the "imaginative geography" sketched out in *Idols in the East*.

⤺ WORKS CITED

Abbreviations

CCCM: *Corpus Christianorum Continuatio Medievalis*
EETS: *Early English Text Society*
MGH: *Monumenta Germania Historica*
PG: *Patrologia Graeca*
PL: *Patrologia Latina*
PPTS: *Palestine Pilgrims' Text Society*
RHC: *Recueil des historiens des croisades*
SATF: *Société des anciens textes français*

Primary Sources

Abelard, Peter. *Dialogus inter philosophum, iudaeum et christianum*. Trans. Pierre J. Payer as *A Dialogue of a Philosopher with a Jew, and a Christian*. Toronto: Pontifical Institute of Mediaeval Studies, 1979.

Abu Ma'shar. *Kitab al-milal wa-al-duwal*. In *On Historical Astrology: The Book of Religions and Dynasties (On the Great Conjunctions)*, ed. and trans. Keiji Yamamoto and Charles Burnett. Islamic Philosophy, Theology, and Science 33–34. 2 vols. Leiden: Brill, 2000.

Aethicus Ister. *Cosmographia. Die Kosmographie des Aethicus*. Ed. Otto Prinz. MGH, Quellen zur Geistesgeschichte des Mittelalters 14. Munich: Monumenta Germaniae Historica, 1993.

Albertus Magnus. "De natura loci." In *Opera Omnia*, volume 5, part 2, ed. Paul Hossfeld. Aschendorff: Monasterii Westfalorum, 1980.

———. *Quaestiones super De animalibus*. In *Opera Omnia*, volume 12, ed. Ephrem Filthaut. Münster: Aschendorff, 1955. 77–309.

Alexander Neckam. *De naturis rerum*. Ed. Thomas Wright. London: Longman, Green, Longman, Roberts, and Green, 1863.

Alexandre de Bernay. *The Medieval French* Roman d'Alexandre. Vol. VI: *The Version of Alexandre de Paris*. Ed. Edward C. Armstrong. Princeton: Princeton University Press, 1976.

Alexandre du Pont. *Le Roman de Mahomet de Alexandre du Pont (1258) avec le texte des Otia de Machomete de Gautier de Compiègne (XIIe siècle), établi par R. B. C. Huygens*. Ed. Yvan G. Lepage. Paris: Klincksieck, 1977.

Andreas Capellanus. *The Art of Courtly Love.* Trans. John Jay Parry. New York: Columbia University Press, 1990.

Aquinas, Thomas. *Nicomachean Ethics.* In *In decem libros Ethicorum Aristotelis ad Nicomachum expositio,* ed. Raimondo M. Spiazzi. 3rd ed. Turin: Marietti, 1964.

———. *Summa Theologica.* In *Opera Omnia,* vols. 1–4. 1852–73. Reprint, New York: Musurgia, 1948–50.

Aristotle. *De animalibus: Michael Scot's Arabic-Latin translation.* Ed. Aafke M. I. van Oppenraaij. Aristoteles Semitico-latinus 5. 3 vols. Leiden: Brill, 1992–98.

Ashenden, John. *Summa judicialis de accidentibus mundi.* In Johannes Eschuid, *Summa astrologiae judicialis.* Venice: Franciscus Bolanus, J. Sanctiter, 1489.

Avicenna. *Liber canonis.* Venice, 1507. Reprint, Hildesheim: Olms, 1964.

Bacon, Roger. [*Opus Maius*] *Opus Majus.* Ed. John H. Bridges. 3 vols. London, 1897–1900. Reprint, Frankfurt am Main: Minerva, 1964.

———. [*Opus Maius*] *Opus Majus.* Trans. Robert B. Burke. 2 vols. Philadelphia: University of Pennsylvania Press, 1928.

———. *Roger Bacon and the Origins of Perspectiva in the Middle Ages: A Critical Edition and English Translation of Bacon's* Perspectiva *with Introduction and Notes.* Ed. David C. Lindberg. Oxford: Clarendon Press, 1996.

———. *Roger Bacon's Philosophy of Nature: A Critical Edition, with English Translation, Introduction, and Notes of* De multiplicatione specierum *and* De speculis comburentibus. Ed. David C. Lindberg. Oxford: Clarendon Press, 1983.

Bagnyon, Jehan. *Histoire de Charlemagne (parfois dite Roman de Fierabras).* Ed. Hans-Erich Keller. Textes littéraires français 413. Geneva: Droz, 1992. Trans. William Caxton as *The Hystory and Lyf of the Noble and Chrysten Prynce Charles the Grete.* Westminster, 1485. Ed. Sidney J. H. Herrtage. EETS e.s. 36 and 37. Oxford: Oxford University Press, 1880–81. Reprinted in one vol. 1967.

Bartholomaeus Anglicus. *De proprietatibus rerum.* Frankfurt, 1601. Reprint, Frankfurt: Minerva, 1964.

———. *De proprietatibus rerum.* Ed. B. van den Abeele. Turnhout: Brepols, 2007–.

———. *The Parts of the World: The Geography of Bartholomaeus Anglicus,* De proprietatibus rerum. Ed. and trans. Winston Black and Suzanne Conklin Akbari with Emily Reiner. Toronto: Pontifical Institute for Mediaeval Studies Press, forthcoming.

Boccaccio, Giovanni. *Decameron.* Ed. Vittore Branca. Tutte le opere di Giovanni Boccaccio 4. Milan: Mondadori, 1976.

———. *Decameron.* Trans. G. H. MacWilliam. 1972. Reprint, Harmondsworth: Penguin, 1995.

Bodel, Jehan. *Le Jeu de saint Nicolas.* Ed. Albert Henry. Textes littéraires français 290. Geneva: Droz, 1981.

———. *Jeu de saint Nicolas.* In *Medieval French Plays.* Trans. Richard Axton and John Stevens. New York: Barnes and Noble, 1971.

Book of the Ladder. See Liber Scale; Livre de l'Eschiele; Prophet of Islam.

Brunetto Latini. *Li Livres dou Tresor.* Ed. Francis J. Carmody. Berkeley: University of California Press, 1948.

Caesarius of Heisterbach. *Dialogus Miraculorum.* Ed. Joseph Strange. 2 vols. Cologne: H. Lempertz, 1851.

La Chanson d'Antioche. Ed. Suzanne Duparc-Quoic. 2 vols. Paris: Librairie Orientaliste Paul Geuthner, 1976–78.

La Chanson de Roland / The Song of Roland: The French Corpus. Gen. ed. Joseph J. Duggan. 3 vols. Turnhout: Brepols, 2005.

La Chanson de Roland: Edition établie d'après le manuscrit d'Oxford. Ed. Luis Cortés and Paulette Gabaudan. Mayenne: Nizet, 1994.

[*La Chanson de Roland.*] *The Song of Roland: An Analytical Edition.* Ed. and trans. Gerald J. Brault. 2 vols. University Park: Penn State University Press, 1978.

[*Collatio Alexandri et Dindimi*]. *Die "Collatio Alexandri et Dindimi": lateinisch-deutsch.* Ed. and trans. Marc Steinmann. Göttingen: Duehrkohp und Radicke, 2000.

Constantinus Africanus. *Pantegni.* In *Omnia opera Ysaac cum quibusdam aliis opusculis.* Lugduni: Bartholomeus Trot in officina Johannis de Platea, 1515.

d'Ailly, Pierre. *Imago Mundi: Texte latin et traduction française des quatre traités cosmographiques de d'Ailly et les notes marginales de Christophe Colomb.* Ed. and trans. Edmond Buron. 3 vols. Paris: Maisonneuve frères, 1930.

Dante Alighieri. *Il Convivio.* Ed. Maria Simonelli. Bologna: Riccardo Pàtron, 1966.

———. *The Banquet.* Trans. Christopher Ryan. Stanford French and Italian Studies 61. Saratoga: Anma Libri, 1989.

———. *La Commedia secondo l'antica vulgata.* Ed. Georgio Petrocchi. 4 vols. Societá Dantesca Italiana. Milan: Mondadori, 1966–68.

———. *The Divine Comedy.* Trans. Charles S. Singleton. 3 vols. Bollinger Series 80. Princeton: Princeton University Press, 1970–75.

De ortu et tempore Antichristi: necnon et tractatus qui ab eo dependunt. Ed. Daniel Verhelst. CCCM 45. Turnhout: Brepols, 1976.

Digby Mary Magdalen. In *The Late Medieval Religious Plays of Bodleian MSS Digby 133 and E Museo 160,* ed. Donald C. Baker, John L. Murphy, and Louis B. Hall, Jr. EETS o.s. 283. Oxford: Oxford University Press, 1982.

Embricon de Mayence. *La vie de Mahomet.* Ed. Guy Cambier. Collection Latomus 20. Brussels: Latomus, 1961.

Les Enfances Guillaume, chanson de geste du XIIIe siècle. Ed. Patrice Henry. Paris: SATF, 1935.

Epistola Alexandri ad Aristotelem ad Codicum Fidem Editit et Commentario Critico Instruxit. Ed. W. Walther Boer. Beiträge zur klassischen Philologie 50. Meisenheim am Glan: Anton Hain, 1973.

[*Epistola*] *Alexander's Letter to Aristotle about India.* Trans. Lloyd L. Gunderson. Beiträge zur klassischen Philologie 110. Meisenheim am Glan: Anton Hain, 1980.

Fierabras. Ed. A. Kroeber and G. Servois. Les Anciens Poètes de la France 4, gen. ed. M. F. Guessard. Paris: F. Vieweg, 1860.

Fierabras [Anglo-Norman text]. In Louis Brandin, "*La Destruction de Rome* et *Fierabras.*" *Romania* 64 (1938): 18–100.

Fierabras: Chanson de geste du XIIe siècle. Ed. Marc Le Person. Paris: Champion, 2003.

Fierabras: Roman en prose de la fin du XIVe siècle. Ed. Jean Miquet. Ottawa: University of Ottawa Press, 1983.

Fulcher of Chartres. *Historia Hierosolymitana (1095–1127).* Ed. Heinrich Hagenmeyer. Heidelberg: Carl Winter, 1913. Trans. A. C. Krey in *The First Crusade: The Chronicle of Fulcher of Chartres and Other Source Materials,* ed. Edward Peters. 2nd ed. Philadelphia: University of Pennsylvania Press, 1998.

Gaufrey. Ed. F. Guessard and P. Chabaille. Les Anciens Poètes de la France 3, gen. ed. M. F. Guessard. Paris: n.p., 1859.

Gerald of Wales. *Topographia Hiberniae. The History and Topography of Ireland.* Trans. John J. O'Meara. Harmondsworth: Penguin, 1982.

Gesta Francorum et aliorum Hierosolymitanorum. In *The Deeds of the Franks and the Other Pilgrims to Jerusalem,* Ed. and trans. Rosalind Hill. 1962. Oxford: Clarendon Press, 1979.

Godeffroy of Boloyne or The Siege and Conqueste of Jerusalem. Ed. Mary Noyes Colvin. 1893. EETS e.s. 64. Reprint, Oxford: Oxford University Press, 1926.

Gower, John. *The Complete Works of John Gower.* Ed. G. C. Macaulay. 4 vols. Oxford: Clarendon Press, 1901.

Guibert de Nogent. *The Deeds of God through the Franks.* Trans. Robert Levine. Woodbridge: Boydell, 1997.

——. *Dei gesta per Francos.* Ed. R. B. C. Huygens. Corpus Christianorum Continuatio Mediaevalis 127A. Turnhout: Brepols, 1996.

Guillaume d'Orange: Four Twelfth-Century Epics. Trans. Joan M. Ferrante. Records of Civilization 92. New York: Columbia University Press, 1974.

Higden, Ranulf. *Polychronicon Ranulphi Higden monachi Cestrensis.* Ed. Churchill Babington (vols. 1–2) and Joseph Rawson Lumby (vols. 3–9). 9 vols. Rerum Britannicarum medii aevi scriptores 41. London: Longman, Green, Longman, Roberts, and Green, 1865–1886.

Historia Alexandri Magni (Historia de Preliis). Rezension J2 (Orosius-Rezension). Vol. 1, ed. Alfons Hilka and H. J. Bergmeister; vol. 2, ed. Alfons Hilka and R. Grossmann. Meisenheim am Glan: Anton Hain, 1976–77.

Hrabanus Maurus. *Commentariorum in Genesim.* PL 107, cols. 439–670.

——. *De universo.* PL 111, cols. 9–614.

Hugh of Fouilloy. *The Medieval Book of Birds: Hugh of Fouilloy's Aviarium.* Ed., trans., and commented upon by Willene B. Clark. Binghamton, NY: Medieval and Renaissance Texts and Studies, 1992.

Hugh of Saint Victor. *Adnotationes elucidatoriae in Pentateuchon.* PL 175, cols. 29–86.

——. "De Arca Noe Mystice." PL 176, cols. 682–704.

——. *Hugonis de Sancto Victore De Archa Noe.* Ed. Patrice Sicard. CCCM 176. Turnhout: Brepols, 2001.

——. *La Descriptio mappe mundi de Hugues de Saint-Victor.* Ed. Patrick Gautier Dalché. Paris: Etudes Augustiniennes, 1988.

Isidore of Seville. *Etymologies. Isidori Hispalensis Episcopi Etymologiarum sive Originum Libri XX.* Ed. William Lindsay. 2 vols. 1911. Reprint, Oxford: Oxford University Press, 1989.

Jacopo Alighieri. *Chiose all'Inferno.* Ed. Saverio Bellomo. Padua: Antenore, 1990.

Jacques de Vitry. *Historia Hierosolymitana.* PPTS XI-2. London, 1896. See also *Godeffroy of Boloyne.*

Jerome. *Commentariorum in Ezechielem.* PL 25, cols. 15–490.

——. *Liber de nominibus hebraicis.* PL 23, cols. 815–904.

John of Damascus. *De haeresibus.* In *Jean Damascène. Ecrits sur l'Islam,* Ed. and trans. Raymond Le Coz. Sources chrétiennes 383. Paris: Éditions du Cerf, 1992.

Josephus, Flavius. *Antiquitates Judaicae.* Loeb Classical Library 489–90. 9 vols. Cambridge: Harvard University Press, 1998. Vol. 4 [books IX–XI] with English translation by Ralph Marcus.

The King of Tars. Ed. Judith Perryman. Middle English Texts 12. Heidelberg: Carl Winter, 1980.

Kyng Alisaunder. Ed. G. V. Smithers. 2 vols. EETS o.s. 227 and 237. Oxford: Oxford University Press, 1952–57.

Lambert of St. Omer. *Liber Floridus* [facsimile of Ghent University Library ms.]. *Lamberti S. Audomari Canonici Liber Floridus: codex autographus bibliothecae universitatis Gandavensis: avspiciis eiusdem universitatis in commemorationem diei natalis.* Ed. Albert Derolez. Ghent: Story-Scientia, 1968.

"The Land of Cockaygne." In *Early Middle English Verse and Prose,* ed. J. A. W. Bennett and G. V. Smithers, 138–44. 2nd ed. Oxford: Clarendon Press, 1968.

Liber Scale Machometi: Die lateinische Fassung des Kitab al mi'radj. Studia humaniora. Ed. Edeltraud Werner. Düsseldorf: Droste, 1986.

Le Livre de l'Eschiele Mahomet: Die Französische Fassung einer alfonsinischen Übersetzung. Ed. Peter Wunderli. Bern: Francke, 1968.

[Mandeville, John.] *Jean de Mandeville: Le Livre des merveilles du monde.* Ed. Christiane Deluz. Sources d'histoire médiévale 31. Paris: CNRS, 2000.

Nicetas of Byzantium. *Refutatio Mohamedis.* PG 105, cols. 669–842.

Odoric of Pordenone. "Relatio." *Sinica Franciscana.* Vol. 1, *Itinera et relationes fratrum minorum saeculi XIII et XIV,* ed. Anastasius van den Wyngaert. Florence: Collegium S. Bonaventura, 1929.

Omnes Homines. In *Problemata Varia Anatomica: MS 1165 The University of Bologna,* ed. L. R. Lind. Lawrence: University of Kansas Publications, 1968.

Orderic Vitalis. *Ecclesiastical History.* PL 188, cols. 15–984.

Orosius, Paulus. *Historiarum adversum paganos libri vii.* In *Orose: Histoires (Contre les Païens),* Ed. and trans. Marie-Pierre Arnaud-Lindet. 3 vols. Paris: Les Belles Lettres, 1990.

——. *The Seven Books of History against the Pagans.* Trans. Roy J. Deferrari. Washington, DC: Catholic University of America Press, 1964.

L'Ottimo commento della Divina Commedia: *Testo inedito d'un contemporaneo di Dante citato dagli Accademici della Crusca.* Ed. A. Torri. 3 vols. Pisa: Niccolò Capurro, 1827–29. Reprint, with preface by F. Mazzoni, Bologna: Forni, 1995.

Otto of Freising. *Ottonis Episcopi Frisingensis Chronica sive Historia de duabus civitatibus.* Ed. Adolf Hofmeister. Revised edition, MGH Scriptores 45. Hanover and Leipzig, Impensis Bibliopolii Hahniani, 1912.

——. *The Two Cities: A Chronicle of Universal History to the Year 1146 AD by Otto, Bishop of Freising.* Trans. Charles Mierow. New York: Columbia University Press, 1928.

Paris, Matthew. *Chronica majora.* Ed. H. R. Luard. 7 vols. London: Longman, 1872–83.

Paschasius Radbertus. *Expositio in Lamentatione Hieremiae.* Ed. B. Paulus. Corpus Christianorum Series Mediaevalis 85. Turnhout: Brepols, 1988.

Passion of St. Bartholomew. In *Acta Apostolorum apocrypha,* vol. 3, ed. R. A. Lipsius and M. Bonnet. Leipzig, 1898.

Peter Comestor. *Historia Scholastica.* PL 198, cols. 1053–1722.

——. *Scolastica historia. Liber Genesis.* Ed. Agneta Sylwan. CCCM 191. Turnhout: Brepols, 2005.

Piemonte, Nicolas de. *Hystoria del Emperador Carlo Magno y de los doze pares de Francia: e de la cruda batalla que ovo Oliveros con Fierabras Rey de Alexandria hijo del grande almirante Balan.* Seville, 1521.

Plato. *Timaeus a Calcidio Translatus commentarioque instructutus.* Ed. J. H. Waszink. Plato Latinus 4. London: Brill, 1975.

——. *Timaeus.* Trans. R. G. Bury. Loeb Classical Library. 1929. Reprint, Cambridge: Harvard University Press, 1966.

Pliny. *Historia naturalia. Natural History.* Ed. and trans. H. Rackham. 10 vols. Loeb Classical Library 352. 1942. Reprint, Cambridge: Harvard University Press, 1989.

The Prophet of Islam in Old French: The Romance of Muhammad (1258) and the Book of Muhammad's Ladder (1264). Trans. Reginald Hyatte. Leiden: Brill, 1997.

Pseudo-Albertus Magnus. *Women's Secrets: A Translation of Pseudo-Albertus Magnus's de Secretis Mulierum with Commentaries.* Trans. Helen R. Lemay. Albany: State University of New York Press, 1992.

Pseudo-Methodius. *Die Apokalypse des Pseudo-Methodius die ältesten griechischen und lateinischen Übersetzungen.* Ed. W. J. Aerts and G. A. A. Kortekaas. 2 vols. Corpus Scriptorum Christianorum Orientalium 569–70, subsidia 97–98. Louvain: Peeters, 1998.

——. "The Bygynnyng of the World and the Ende of Worldes." In *Dialogus inter Militem et Clericum.* EETS o.s. 167, ed. Aaron Jenkins Perry, 94–112. 1925. Reprint, Oxford: EETS, 1971.

Pseudo-Tudebodus. *Tudebodus imitatus et continuatus Historia peregrinorum.* RHC Occ. 3: 165–229.

Ralph of Coggeshall. *Radulphi de Coggeshall: Chronicon Anglicanum: De Expugnatione Terrae Sanctae.* Ed. Joseph Stevenson. Rerum Britannicarum medii aevi scriptores 66. 1875. Wiesbaden: Kraus Reprint, 1965.

Raoul de Caen. *Gesta Tancredi.* RHC Occ. 3: 493–590.

Raymond of Aguilers. RHC Occ. 3: 235–309.

[*Richard Coer de Lion*]. *Der mittelenglische Versroman über Richard Löwenherz.* Ed. Karl Brunner. Weiner Beiträge zur englischen Philologie 42. Vienna: Wilhelm Braumüller, 1913.

Robert of Reims (Robert the Monk). RHC Occ. 3: 717–882.

Rudolph von Schlettstadt. *Historiae Memorabiles: Zur Dominikanerliteratur und Kulturgeschichte des 13. Jahrhunderts.* Ed. Erich Kleinschmidt. Cologne: Böhlau, 1974.

Sacrobosco, Johannes de. *The Sphere of Sacrobosco and Its Commentators.* Ed. and trans. Lynn Thorndyke. Chicago: University of Chicago Press, 1949.

The Siege of Jerusalem. Ed. Ralph Hanna and David Lawton. EETS o.s. 320. Oxford: Oxford University Press, 2003.

The Siege of Melayne. In *Six Middle English Romances,* ed. Maldwyn Mills. 2nd ed. London: Dent, 1992.

The Sowdone of Babylone. In *Three Middle English Charlemagne Romances,* ed. Alan Lupack. Kalamazoo: Medieval Institute Publications, 1990.

Thomas of Kent. *The Anglo-Norman "Alexander (Le Roman de toute chevalerie)" by Thomas of Kent.* Ed. Brian Foster and Ian Short. 2 vols. Anglo-Norman Text Society 29–33. London: Anglo-Norman Text Society, 1976–77.

——. *Le Roman d'Alexandre ou Le roman de toute chevalerie.* Trans. Catherine Gaullier-Bougassas and Laurence Harf-Lancner. Paris: Champion, 2003.

Trevisa, John. *On the Properties of Things: John Trevisa's Translation of "Bartholomaeus Anglicus, De proprietatibus rerum." A Critical Text*. Ed. M. C. Seymour et al. 3 vols. Oxford: Clarendon Press, 1975–78.

Vincent of Beauvais. *Speculum quadruplex sive Speculum maius*. Vol. 4, *Speculum historiale*. 1624. Reprint, Graz: Akademische Druck—und Verlagsanstalt, 1964.

"The Vintners Playe." In *The Chester Mystery Cycle*, ed. R. M. Lumiansky and David Mills, 156–74. EETS s.s. 3. Oxford: Oxford University Press, 1974.

Walter of Châtillon. *Galteri de castellione Alexandreis*. Ed. Marvin Colker. Padua: Antenore, 1978.

———. *The Alexandreis of Walter of Châtillon: A Twelfth-Century Epic*. Trans. David Townsend. Philadelphia: University of Pennsylvania Press, 1996.

William of Conches. *Dragmaticon philosophiae*. Ed. Italo Ronca. CCCM 152. Turnhout: Brepols, 1997.

———. *A Dialogue on Natural Philosophy: Dragmaticon Philosophiae*. Trans. Italo Ronca and Matthew Curr. Notre Dame: University of Notre Dame Press, 1997.

William Wey. *The Itineraries of William Wey, Fellow of Eton, to Jerusalem, AD. 1458 and A.D. 1462*. Ed. George Williams. London: J. B. Nichols, 1857.

Wolfram von Eschenbach. *Parzival*. Ed. Karl Lachmann, Peter Knecht, and Bernd Schirok. 6th ed. Berlin: Walter de Gruyter, 1998.

———. *Parzival with Titurel and the Love-Lyrics*. Trans. Cyril Edwards. Cambridge: D. S. Brewer, 2004.

Secondary Sources

Abulafia, Anna Sapir. "Bodies in the Jewish-Christian Debate." In *Framing Medieval Bodies*, ed. Sarah Kay and Miri Rubin, 124–37. Manchester: Manchester University Press, 1994.

Ahmad, Aijaz. *In Theory: Classes, Nations, Literature*. New York: Verso, 1992.

Ailes, Marianne J. "A Comparative Study of the Medieval French and Middle English Verse Texts of the *Fierabras* Legend." PhD diss., University of Reading, 1989.

Ailes, Marianne J. "Faith in *Fierabras*." In *Charlemagne in the North: Proceedings of the Twelfth International Conference of the Société Rencesvals*, ed. Philip E. Bennett, Anne Elizabeth Cobby, and Graham A. Runnals, 125–33. Edinburgh: Société Rencesvals British Branch, 1993.

Akbari, Suzanne Conklin. "Alexander in the Orient: Bodies and Boundaries in the *Roman de toute chevalerie*." In *Postcolonial Approaches to the European Middle Ages: Translating Cultures*, ed. Ananya Jahanara Kabir and Deanne Williams, 105–26. Cambridge: Cambridge University Press, 2005.

———. "Between Diaspora and Conquest: Norman Assimilation in Petrus Alfonsi's *Disciplina Clericalis* and Marie de France's *Fables*." In *Cultural Diversity in the British Middle Ages: Archipelago, Island, England*, ed. Jeffrey Jerome Cohen, 17–37. New Middle Ages. New York: Palgrave Macmillan, 2008.

———. "Currents and Currency in Marco Polo's *Devisement dou monde* and *The Book of John Mandeville*." In *Marco Polo and the Encounter of East and West*, ed. Suzanne Conklin Akbari and Amilcare A. Iannucci, 110–30. Toronto: University of Toronto Press, 2008.

——. "The Diversity of Mankind in *The Book of John Mandeville*." In *Eastward Bound: Medieval Travel and Travellers, 1050–1500,* ed. Rosamund Allen, 156–76. Manchester: Manchester University Press, 2004.

——. "East, West, and In-between." In *Marco Polo and the Encounter of East and West,* ed. Suzanne Conklin Akbari and Amilcare A. Iannucci, 2–20. Toronto: University of Toronto Press, 2008.

——. "From Due East to True North: Orientalism and Orientation." In *The Postcolonial Middle Ages,* ed. Jeffrey Jerome Cohen, 19–34. New York: St. Martin's, 2000.

——. "The Hunger for National Identity in *Richard Coer de Lion*." In *Reading Medieval Culture,* ed. Robert M. Stein and Sandra Pierson Prior, 198–227. Notre Dame: University of Notre Dame Press, 2005.

——. "Incorporation in the *Siege of Melayne*." In *Pulp Fictions of Medieval England,* ed. Nicola F. McDonald, 22–44. Manchester: Manchester University Press, 2004.

——. "Orientation and Nation in Chaucer's *Canterbury Tales*." In *Chaucer's Cultural Geography,* ed. Kathryn L. Lynch, 102–34. New York: Routledge, 2002.

——. "The Rhetoric of Antichrist in Western Lives of Muhammad." *Islam and Christian-Muslim Relations* 8 (1997): 297–307.

——. *Seeing through the Veil: Optical Theory and Medieval Allegory.* Toronto: University of Toronto Press, 2004.

Akbari, Suzanne Conklin, and Karla Mallette, eds. *A Sea of Languages: Literature and Culture in the Medieval Mediterranean.* Toronto: University of Toronto Press, forthcoming.

Albert, Bat-Sheva. "*Adversos Iudaeos* in the Carolingian Empire." In *Contra Iudaeos: Ancient and Medieval Polemics between Christians and Jews,* ed. Ora Limor and Guy G. Stroumsa, 119–42. Tübingen: J. C. B. Mohr, 1996.

Amer, Sahar. *Esope au féminin: Marie de France et la politique de l'interculturalité.* Amsterdam: Rodopi, 1999.

Anderson, Andrew Runni. *Alexander's Gate, Gog and Magog and the Inclosed Nations.* Cambridge: Medieval Academy of America, 1932.

Ashcroft, Bill, Gareth Griffiths, and Helen Tiffin, eds. *The Empire Writes Back: Theory and Practice in Post-colonial Literatures.* London: Routledge, 1989.

Bancourt, Paul. *Les Musulmans dans les chansons de geste du cycle du roi.* 2 vols. Aix-en-Provence: Université de Provence, 1982.

Bannach, Klaus. *Die Lehre von der doppelten Macht Gottes bei Wilhelm von Ockham.* Wiesbaden: Franz Steiner, 1975.

Baron, S. W. *A Social and Religious History of the Jews.* Vol. 11. New York: Columbia University Press, 1967.

Beckett, Katherine Scarfe. *Anglo-Saxon Perceptions of the Islamic World.* Cambridge: Cambridge University Press, 2003.

Beckwith, Sarah. *Christ's Body: Identity, Culture, and Society in Late Medieval Writings.* London: Routledge, 1993.

Bedard, Walter Maurice. *The Symbolism of the Baptismal Font in Early Christian Thought.* Washington, DC: Catholic University of America Press, 1951.

Bekker, Immanuel. "Der Roman vom Fierabras provenzalisch." *Preussisches Akademie der Wissenschaften zu Berlin, Abhandlungen aus dem Jahre, Philologische-Historische Klasse* 10 (1826): 133–278.

Bell, Albert A. "An Historical Analysis of the *De excidio hierosolymitano* of Pseudo-Hegesippus." Phd diss., University of North Carolina, Chapel Hill, 1977.

Bennett, Philip E. "The Storming of the Other World, the Enamoured Muslim Princess and the Evolution of the Legend of Guillaume d'Orange." In *Guillaume d'Orange and the Chanson de geste: Essays Presented to Duncan McMillan,* ed. Wolfgang van Emden and Philip E. Bennett, 1–14. Reading: Société Rencesvals, 1984.

Berry, Virginia. "Peter the Venerable and the Crusades." In *Petrus Venerabilis, 1156–1956: Studies and Texts Commemorating the Eighth Centenary of his Death,* ed. Giles Constable and James Kritzeck, 141–62. Anselmiana 40. Rome: Orbis Catholicus / Herder, 1956.

Biddick, Kathleen. *The Typological Imaginary: Circumcision, Technology, History.* Philadelphia: University of Pennsylvania Press, 2003.

Biller, Peter. "Black Women in Medieval Scientific Thought." In *La pelle umana / The Human Skin,* ed. Agostino Paravicini Bagliani, 477–92. Micrologus 13. Florence: SISMEL edizioni del Galluzzo, 2005.

——. "A 'Scientific' View of Jews from Paris around 1300." *Micrologus* 9 (2001): 137–68.

——. "Views of Jews from Paris around 1300: Christian or 'Scientific'?" In *Christianity and Judaism,* ed. Diana Wood, 187–207. Studies in Church History 29. Oxford: Blackwell, 1992.

Bisaha, Nancy. *Creating East and West: Renaissance Humanists and the Ottoman Turks.* Philadelphia: University of Pennsylvania Press, 2004.

Blanks, David R. "Western Views of Islam in the Premodern Period: A Brief History of Past Approaches." In *Western Views of Islam in Medieval and Early Modern Europe: Perception of Other,* ed. David R. Blanks and Michael Frassetto, 11–53. New York: St. Martin's, 1999.

Bober, H. "Structure and Content of the Imagery of the *Liber Floridus.*" *Liber Floridus Colloquium* 19. Ghent: E. Story-Scientia, 1973.

Bosley, Richard N., and Martin Tweedale, eds. "Determination, Free Will, and Divine Foreknowledge." In *Basic Issues in Medieval Philosophy: Selected Readings Presenting the Interactive Discourses among the Major Figures,* 245–307. Peterborough, ON: Broadview Press, 1997.

Boyarin, Daniel. *Carnal Israel: Reading Sex in Talmudic Culture.* Berkeley: University of California Press, 1993.

——. *A Radical Jew: Paul and the Politics of Identity.* Berkeley: University of California Press, 1997.

——. "'This We Know to be the Carnal Israel': Circumcision and the Erotic Life of God and Israel." *Critical Inquiry* 18 (1992): 474–505.

Braude, Benjamin. "Mandeville's Jews among Others." In *Pilgrims and Travellers to the Holy Land, Proceedings of the Seventh Annual Symposium of the Philip M. and Ethel Klutznick Chair in Jewish Civilization, October 2–3, 1994,* ed. Bryan F. LeBeau and Menahem Mor, 133–58. Omaha: Creighton University Press, 1996.

——. "The Sons of Noah and the Construction of Ethnic and Geographical Identities in the Medieval and Early Modern Periods." *William and Mary Quarterly* 54 (1997): 103–42.

Brennan, Timothy. "The Illusion of a Future: Orientalism as Traveling Theory." *Critical Inquiry* 26 (2000): 558–83.

Buber, Salomon, ed. *Midrasch Echa rabbati: Sammlung agadischer Auslegungen der Klagelieder.* Vilna, 1899. Reprint, Hildesheim: Georg Olms, 1967.

Bunt, Gerrit H. V. *Alexander the Great in the Literature of Medieval Britain.* Groningen: Egbert Forsten, 1994.

Burger, Glenn. "Cilician Armenian Métissage and Hetoum's *La Fleur des histoires de la terre d'Orient.*" In *The Postcolonial Middle Ages,* ed. Jeffrey Jerome Cohen, 67–83. New York: St. Martin's, 2000.

Burman, Thomas E. "Cambridge University Library MS Mm.v.26 and the History of the Study of the Qur'an in Medieval and Early Modern Europe." In *Religion, Text and Society in Medieval Spain and Northern Europe: Essays in Honor of J. N. Hillgarth,* ed. Thomas E. Burman, Mark D. Meyerson, and Leah Shopkow, 335–63. Toronto: Pontifical Institute of Mediaeval Studies, 2002.

——. *Reading the Qur'an in Latin Christendom, 1140–1560.* Philadelphia: University of Pennsylvania Press, 2007.

——. *Religious Polemic and the Intellectual History of the Mozarabs.* Leiden: Brill, 1994.

——. "*Tafsir* and Translation: Traditional Arabic Qur'an Exegesis and the Latin Qur'ans of Robert of Ketton and Mark of Toledo." *Speculum* 73 (1998): 703–32.

Burns, E. Jane. *Courtly Love Undressed: Reading through Clothes in Medieval French Culture.* Philadelphia: University of Pennsylvania Press, 2002.

Butler, Judith. *Bodies That Matter: On the Discursive Limits of "Sex."* New York and London: Routledge, 1993.

Bynum, Caroline Walker. "The Body of Christ in the Later Middle Ages: A Reply to Leo Steinberg." In *Fragmentation and Redemption: Essays on Gender and the Human Body in Medieval Religion,* 79–117. New York: Zone, 1991.

——. *Holy Feast, Holy Fast.* Berkeley: University of California Press, 1987.

——. *The Resurrection of the Body in Western Christianity, 200–1336.* New York: Columbia University Press, 1995.

Cahn, Walter. "The Expulsion of the Jews as History and Allegory in Painting and Sculpture of the Twelfth and Thirteenth Centuries." In *Jews and Christians in Twelfth-Century Europe,* ed. Michael A. Signer and John Van Engen, 94–109. Notre Dame: University of Notre Dame Press, 2001.

Calkin, Siobhain Bly. "Marking Religion on the Body: Saracens, Categorization and *The King of Tars.*" *Journal of English and Germanic Philology* 104 (2005): 219–38.

Camille, Michael. *The Gothic Idol: Ideology and Image-Making in Medieval Art.* Cambridge: Cambridge University Press, 1982.

——. *Image on the Edge.* London: Reaktion Books, 1992.

Campbell, Mary B. *The Witness and the Other World: Exotic European Travel Writing, 400–1600.* Ithaca: Cornell University Press, 1988.

Campbell, Tony. "Portolan Charts from the Late Thirteenth Century to 1500." In *The History of Cartography,* vol. 1, *Cartography in Prehistoric, Ancient, and Medieval Europe and the Mediterranean,* ed. J. B. Harley and David Woodward, 371–463. Chicago: University of Chicago Press, 1987.

Cantarino, Vicente. "Dante and Islam: History and Analysis of a Controversy." In *A Dante Symposium in Commemoration of the 700th Anniversary of the Poet's Birth*

(1265–1965), ed. William de Sua and Gino Rizzo, 172–92. Chapel Hill: University of North Carolina Press, 1965.

——. "Dante and Islam: Theory of Light in the *Paradiso.*" *Kentucky Romance Quarterly* 15 (1968): 3–35.

Cary, George, and D. J. A. Ross. *The Medieval Alexander.* Cambridge: Cambridge University Press, 1956.

Castro, Americo. "The Presence of the Sultan Saladin in the Romance Literatures." In *An Idea of History: Selected Essays of Americo Castro,* trans. Stephen Gilman and Edmund L. King, 241–69. Columbus: Ohio State University Press, 1977.

Cerulli, Enrico. *Il "Libro della Scala" e la questione delle fonti arabo-spagnole della "Divina Commedia."* Studi e Testi 150. Città del Vaticano: Biblioteca Apostolica Vaticana, 1949.

——. *Nuove ricerche sul "Libro della Scala" e la conoscenza dell'Islam in Occidente.* Città del Vaticano: Biblioteca Apostolica Vaticana, 1972.

Chaplin, Joyce E. "Natural Philosophy and an Early Racial Idiom in North America: Comparing English and Indian Bodies." *William and Mary Quarterly* 54 (1997): 229–52.

Chatterjee, Partha. *Nationalist Thought and the Colonial World: A Derivative Discourse?* London: Zed Books for the United Nations University, 1986.

Chism, Christine. "*The Siege of Jerusalem:* Liquidating Assets." *Journal of Medieval and Early Modern Studies* 28 (1998): 309–40.

——. "Too Close for Comfort: Dis-Orienting Chivalry in the *Wars of Alexander.*" In *Text and Territory: Geographical Imagination in the European Middle Ages,* ed. Sylvia Tomasch and Sealy Gilles, 116–39. Philadelphia: University of Pennsylvania Press, 1998.

Clifford, James. "On *Orientalism.*" In *The Predicament of Culture: Twentieth-Century Ethnography, Literature, and Art,* 255–76. Cambridge: Harvard University Press, 1988.

Cohen, Jeffrey Jerome. *Of Giants: Sex, Monsters, and the Middle Ages.* Minneapolis: University of Minnesota Press, 1999.

——. "On Saracen Enjoyment: Some Fantasies of Race in Late Medieval France and England." *Journal of Medieval and Early Modern Studies* 30 (2001): 113–46.

——, ed. *The Postcolonial Middle Ages.* New York: St. Martin's, 2000.

Cohen, Jeremy. *Living Letters of the Law: Ideas of the Jew in Medieval Christianity.* Berkeley: University of California Press, 1999.

——. "The Muslim Connection; or, On the Changing Role of the Jew in High Medieval Theology." In *From Witness to Witchcraft: Jews and Judaism in Medieval Christian Thought,* ed. Jeremy Cohen, 141–62. Wolfenbütteler Mittelalter-Studien 11. Wiesbaden: Harrassowitz, 1996.

Cole, Penny J. "'O God, the heathen have come into your inheritance' (Ps. 78.1): The Theme of Religious Pollution in Crusade Documents, 1095–1188." In *Crusaders and Muslims in Twelfth-Century Syria,* ed. Maya Shatzmiller, 84–111. The Medieval Mediterranean: Peoples, Economies, and Cultures 400–1453 1. Leiden: Brill, 1993.

Colish, Marcia L. "The Virtuous Pagan: Dante and the Christian Tradition." In *The Unbounded Community: Papers in Christian Ecumenism in Honor of Jaroslav Pelikan,* ed. William Caferro and Duncan G. Fisher, 43–77. New York: Garland, 1996.

Combs-Schilling, M. E. *Sacred Performances: Islam, Sexuality, and Sacrifice.* New York: Columbia University Press, 1989.

Constable, Giles. "Petri venerabilis sermones tres." *Revue benedictine* 64 (1954): 232–54.

Corrigan, Kathleen. *Visual Polemics in the Ninth-Century Byzantine Psalters.* Cambridge: Cambridge University Press, 1992.

Corti, Maria. "La 'Commedia' di Dante e l'oltretomba islamico." *Belfagor* 50 (1995): 301–14.

Cousins, Mark, and Athar Hussain. *Michel Foucault.* Basingstroke: Macmillan, 1984.

Crang, Mike, and Nigel Thrift, eds. *Thinking Space.* London: Routledge, 2000.

Curtius, Ernst Robert. *European Literature and the Latin Middle Ages.* Trans. Willard R. Trask. Bollingen Series 36. New York: Pantheon, 1953.

Cutler, Allan, and Helen Cutler. *The Jew as the Ally of the Muslim: The Medieval Roots of Anti-Semitism.* Notre Dame: University of Notre Dame Press, 1986.

Dahan, Gilbert. *Les intellectuels chrétiens et les juifs au moyen âge.* Paris: Cerf, 1999.

——. "Juifs et judaïsme dans la littérature quodlibétique." In *From Witness to Witchcraft: Jews and Judaism in Medieval Christian Thought,* ed. Jeremy Cohen, 221–45. Wolfenbütteler Studien 11. Wiesbaden: Harrassowitz, 1996.

d'Alverny, Marie-Thérèse. *La connaissance de l'Islam dans l'Occident medieval.* Aldershot: Variorum, 1994.

d'Ancona, Alessandro. "La leggenda di Maometto in Occidente." *Giornale storica della letteratura Italiana* 13 (1889): 199–281. Reprinted as *La leggenda di Maometto in Occidente.* Ed. Andrea Borruso. Rome: Salerno, 1994.

Daniel, Norman. *The Arabs and Mediaeval Europe.* London: Longman, 1975.

——. *Heroes and Saracens: An Interpretation of the Chansons de geste.* Edinburgh: Edinburgh University Press, 1984.

——. *Islam and the West: The Making of an Image.* 1960. Rev. ed. Oxford: Oneworld, 1993.

Daston, Lorraine, and Katherine Park. *Wonders and the Order of Nature, 1150–1750.* New York: Zone, 1998.

Davidson, Arnold. "Archeology, Genealogy, Ethics." In *Foucault: A Critical Reader,* ed. David Couzens Hoy, 221–34. Cambridge: Basil Blackwell, 1986.

Delany, Sheila. "Chaucer's Prioress, the Jews, and the Muslims." *Medieval Encounters* 5 (1999): 198–213. Reprinted in *Chaucer and the Jews,* ed. Sheila Delany, 43–57. New York: Routledge, 2002.

——. "Geographies of Desire: Orientalism in Chaucer's *Legend of Good Women.*" *Chaucer Yearbook* 1 (1992): 1–32.

——. *The Naked Text: Chaucer's "Legend of Good Women."* Berkeley: University of California Press, 1994.

Delaporte, François. "The History of Medicine According to Foucault." In *Foucault and the Writing of History,* ed. Ian Goldstein, 137–49. Oxford: Blackwell, 1994.

Delisle, Léopold. "Notice sur les manuscrits du *Liber Floridus* de Lambert, chanoine de Saint-Omer." *Notices et extraits des manuscrits de la Bibliothèque nationale et autres bibliothèques* 38 (1906): 577–791.

de Mandach, André. *La Geste de Fierabras: Le jeu du réel et de l'invraisemblable.* Geneva: Droz, 1987.

Denby, David. *Great Books: My Adventures with Homer, Rousseau, Woolf, and Other Inde-structable Writers of the Western World.* New York: Simon and Schuster, 1996.

Derolez, Albert. *The Autograph Manuscript of the "Liber Floridus": A Key to the Ency-clopedia of Lambert of Saint-Omer.* Corpus Christianorum Autographa Medii Aevi 4. Turnhout: Brepols, 1998.

——, ed. *Lamberti S. Audomari Canonici Liber Floridus: codex autographus bibliothecae universitatis Gandavensis: avspiciis eiusdem universitatis in commemorationem diei natalis.* Ed. Albert Derolez. Ghent: Story-Scientia, 1968.

Despres, Denise L. "Mary of the Eucharist: Cultic Anti-Judaism in Some Fourteenth-Century English Devotional Manuscripts." In *From Witness to Witchcraft: Jews and Judaism in Medieval Christian Thought,* ed. Jeremy Cohen, 375–401. Wolfen-bütteler Mittelalter-Studien 11. Wiesbaden: Harrassowitz, 1996.

D'Evelyn, Charlotte. "The Middle-English Metrical Version of the *Revelations* of Methodius, with a Study of the Influence of Methodius in Middle-English Writings." *PMLA* 33 (1918): 135–203.

De Weever, Jacqueline. *Sheba's Daughters: Whitening and Demonizing the Saracen Woman in Medieval French Epic.* New York: Garland, 1998.

Douglas, Mary. "The Forbidden Animals in Leviticus." *Journal for the Study of the Old Testament* 59 (1993): 3–23.

——. *Purity and Danger: An Analysis of Concepts of Pollution and Taboo.* 1966. London: Routledge, 2002.

d'Ovidio, Francesco. "Sette chiose alla *Commedia.*" *Studi danteschi* 7 (1923): 5–82.

Eckhardt, Alexandre. "Le cercueil flottant de Mahomet." In *Mélanges de philologie ro-mane et de littérature médiévale offerts à Ernest Hoepffner,* 77–88. Publications de la faculté des lettres de l'Université de Strasbourg 113. Paris: Belles Lettres, 1949.

Eco, Umberto. *Serendipities: Language and Lunacy.* New York: Harcourt, Brace, 1998.

Edson, Evelyn. *Mapping Time and Space: How Medieval Mapmakers Viewed Their World.* London: British Library, 1997.

Elden, Stuart. *Mapping the Present: Heidegger, Foucault and the Project of a Spatial History.* London: Continuum, 2001.

Ferrante, Joan M. *To the Glory of Her Sex: Women's Roles in the Composition of Medieval Texts.* Bloomington: Indiana University Press, 1997.

——. *Woman as Image from the Twelfth Century to Dante.* New York: Columbia Uni-versity Press, 1975.

Ferreiro, Alberto. *Simon Magus in Patristic, Medieval, and Early Modern Traditions.* Le-iden: Brill, 2005.

Fleck, Andrew. "Here, There, and In Between: Representing Difference in the *Travels* of Sir John Mandeville." *Studies in Philology* 97 (2000): 379–401.

Flint, Valerie I. J. "Monsters and the Antipodes in the Early Middle Ages and the Enlightenment." *Viator* 15 (1984): 65–80.

Foucault, Michel. *Archéologie du savoir.* Trans. Alan Sheridan as *Archeology of Knowl-edge.* New York: Pantheon, 1972.

——. *Histoire de la folie.* Paris: Gallimard, 1972. Trans. Richard Howard as *Madness in Culture.* New York: Pantheon, 1954.

——. *Les mots et les choses: Une archéologie des sciences humaines.* Paris: Gallimard, 1966. Trans. Alan Sheridan as *The Order of Things: An Archeology of the Human Sciences.* New York: Vintage, 1970.

Frakes, Jerold C. "Race, Representation, and Metamorphosis in Middle High German Literature." *North-Western European Language Evolution (NOWELE)* 31–32 (1997): 119–33.

Friedman, John B. "Cultural Conflicts in Medieval World Maps." In *Implicit Understandings: Observing, Reporting, and Reflecting on the Encounters Between Europeans and Other Peoples in the Early Modern Era,* ed. Stuart B. Schwartz, 64–95. Cambridge: Cambridge University Press, 1997.

Garcia-Arenal, Mercedes. *Messianism and Puritanical Reform: Mahdis of the Muslim West.* The Medieval and Early Modern Iberian World 29. Leiden: Brill, 2006.

Gardet, Louis. *Dieu et la destinée de l'homme.* Paris: J. Vrin, 1967.

Gautier Dalché, Patrick. "Pour une histoire du regard géographique: Conception et usage de la carte au XVe siècle." *Micrologus* 4 (1996): 77–103.

——, ed. *La "Descriptio mappe mundi" de Hugues de Saint-Victor.* Paris: Etudes Augustiniennes, 1988.

Geary, Patrick J. *Furta Sacra: Thefts of Relics in the Central Middle Ages.* Princeton: Princeton University Press, 1978.

——. "Humiliation of Saints." In *Saints and Their Cults: Studies in Religious Sociology, Folklore, and History,* ed. Stephen Wilson, 123–40. Cambridge: Cambridge University Press, 1983.

Gilbert, Jane. "Putting the Pulp into Fiction: The Lump-Child and Its Parents in *The King of Tars.*" In *Pulp Fictions of Medieval England,* ed. Nicola McDonald, 102–23. Manchester: Manchester University Press, 2004.

Glikson, Y. "Wandering Jew." *Encyclopedia Judaica* 16: cols. 259–63. Jerusalem: Encyclopedia Judaica, 1972.

Goodich, Michael. *Miracles and Wonders: The Development of the Concept of Miracle, 1150–1350.* Aldershot: Ashgate, 2007.

Gosman, Martin. *La légende d'Alexandre le Grand dans la littérature française du 12e siècle: une réécriture permanente.* Amsterdam: Rodopi, 1997.

——. *La lettre du prêtre Jean: les versions en ancien français et en ancien Occitan.* Groningen: Bouma, 1982.

Gourlay, Kristina E. "'Faire Maide' or 'Venomouse Serpente': The Cultural Significance of the Saracen Princess Floripas in France and England, 1200–1500." PhD diss., University of Toronto, 2002.

Gow, Andrew. "Gog and Magog on *Mappaemundi* and Early Printed World Maps: Orientalizing Ethnography in the Apocalyptic Tradition." *Journal of Early Modern History* 2 (1998): 61–88.

——. *The Red Jews: Antisemitism in an Apocalyptic Age, 1200–1600.* Studies in Medieval and Reformation Thought 55. Leiden: Brill, 1995.

Grady, Frank. *Representing Righteous Heathens in Late Medieval England.* New York: Palgrave Macmillan, 2005.

Gravestock, Pamela. "Did Imaginary Animals Exist?" In *The Mark of the Beast: The Medieval Bestiary in Art, Life, and Literature,* ed. Debra Hassig [Strickland], 119–39. New York: Garland, 1999.

Grayzel, Solomon. *The Church and the Jews in the Thirteenth Century.* Vol. 2. Detroit: Wayne State University Press, 1989.

Greenblatt, Stephen. *Marvelous Possessions: The Wonder of the New World.* Chicago: University of Chicago Press, 1991.

Greetham, David. "The Fabulous Geography of John Trevisa's Translation of Bartholomaeus Anglicus' *De proprietatibus rerum*." PhD diss., City University of
New York, 1974.

Greetham, D[avid] C. "The Concept of Nature in Bartholomaeus Anglicus." *Journal
of the History of Ideas* 41 (1980): 663–77.

Gregory, Derek. "Edward Said's Imaginative Geographies." In *Thinking Space*, ed.
Mike Crang and Nigel Thrift, 302–48. London: Routledge, 2000.

Groos, Arthur. "Orientalizing the Medieval Orient: The East in Wolfram von Eschenbach's *Parzival*." In *Kulturen des Manuskriptzeitalters: Ergebnisse der amerikanisch-
deutschen Arbeitstagung an der Georg-August-Universität Göttingen vom 17. bis 20.
Oktober 2002*, ed. Arthur Groos and Hans-Jochen Schiewer, 61–86. Göttingen: V&R unipress, 2004.

Gruber, Christiane. "The Prophet Muhammad's Ascension (Mi'raj) in Islamic Art
and Literature, ca. 1300–1600." PhD diss., University of Pennsylvania, 2005.

Hamel, Mary. "*The Siege of Jerusalem* as a Crusading Poem." In *Journeys Toward God:
Pilgrimage and Crusade*, ed. Barbara N. Sargent-Baur, 177–94. Kalamazoo, MI:
Medieval Institute Publications, 1992.

Hamilton, G. L. "Quelques notes sur l'histoire de la légende d'Alexandre le Grand
en Angleterre au moyen âge." In *Mélanges Paul Thomas*, 195–202. Bruges: Im-
primerie Sainte Catherine, 1930.

Hanawalt, Barbara A., and Michal Kobialka, eds. *Medieval Practices of Space*. Minneapolis: University of Minnesota Press, 2000.

Harvey, David. *Justice, Nature, and the Geography of Difference*. Oxford: Blackwell, 1996.

Helleiner, Karl F. "Prester John's Letter: A Medieval Utopia." *Phoenix* 13 (1959):
47–57.

Heng, Geraldine. *Empire of Magic: Medieval Romance and the Politics of Cultural Fantasy*.
New York: Columbia University Press, 2003.

Heyse, Elisabeth. "*De rerum naturis*." *Untersuchungen zu den Quellen und zur Meth-
ode der Kompilation*. Münchener Beiträge zur Mediävistik—und Renaissance
Forschung 4. München: Arbeo-Gesellschaft, 1969.

Higgins, Iain Macleod. "Defining the Earth's Center in a Medieval 'Multi-Text':
Jerusalem in *The Book of John Mandeville*." In *Text and Territory: Geographical
Imagination in the European Middle Ages*, ed. Sylvia Tomasch and Sealy Gilles,
29–53. Philadelphia: University of Pennsylvania Press, 1997.

———. "Shades of the East: Orientalism, Religion, and Nation in Late-Medieval Scot-
tish Literature." *Journal of Medieval and Early Modern Studies* 38.2: 197–228.

———. *Writing East: The "Travels" of Sir John Mandeville*. Philadelphia: University of
Pennsylvania Press, 1997.

Hillis, Ken. "The Power of Disembodied Imagination: Perspective's Role in Cartography." *Cartographica* 31 (1994): 1–17.

Holland, Meridel. "An Edition of Three Unpublished Translations by Robert
Grosseteste of Three Short Works of John of Damascus." PhD diss., Harvard
University, 1980.

———. "Robert Grosseteste's Translations of John of Damascus." *Bodleian Library Record* 11 (1983): 138–54.

Holsinger, Bruce W. "Medieval Studies, Postcolonial Studies, and the Genealogies of
Critique." *Speculum* 77 (2002): 1195–1227.

Honigmann, Ernst. *Die sieben Klimata und die Poleis episemoi: Eine Untersuchung zur Geschichte der Geographie und Astrologie im Altertum und Mittelalter.* Heidelberg: Carl Winter, 1929.

Howard, Donald R. *Writers and Pilgrims: Medieval Pilgrimage Narratives and Their Posterity.* Berkeley: University of California Press, 1980.

Hsia, R. Po-chia. *The Myth of Ritual Murder: Jews and Magic in Reformation Germany.* New Haven: Yale University Press, 1988.

Hutcheon, Linda. "*Orientalism* as Post-Imperial Witnessing." In *Edward Said and the Post-Colonial,* ed. Bill Ashcroft and Hussein Kadhim, 91–106. Huntington, NY: Nova Science, 2001.

——. *A Theory of Parody: The Teachings of Twentieth-Century Art Forms.* New York: Methuen, 1985.

Iannucci, Amilcare A. "Limbo: The Emptiness of Time." *Studi danteschi* 52 (1979–80): 69–128.

Ingham, Patricia Clare, and Michelle R. Warren, eds. *Postcolonial Moves: Medieval through Modern.* New York: Palgrave Macmillan, 2003.

Iogna-Prat, Dominique. *Order and Exclusion: Cluny and Christendom Face Heresy, Judaism, and Islam.* 1998. Trans. Graham Robert Edwards. Ithaca: Cornell University Press, 2001.

James, Mervyn. "Ritual, Drama and Social Body in the Late Medieval English Town." *Past and Present* 98 (1983): 3–29.

Johnson, Willis. "The Myth of Jewish Male Menses." *Journal of Medieval History* 24 (1998): 273–95.

Kabir, Ananya Jahanara, and Deanne Williams, eds. *Postcolonial Approaches to the European Middle Ages: Translating Cultures.* Cambridge: Cambridge University Press, 2005.

Kahf, Mohja. *Western Representations of the Muslim Woman: From Termagant to Odalisque.* Austin: University of Texas Press, 1999.

Kampers, Franz. *Alexander der Grosse und die Idee des Weltimperiums in Prophetie und Sage.* Freiburg: Herder, 1901.

Kay, Sarah. *The Chansons de geste in the Age of Romance.* Oxford: Clarendon Press, 1995.

——. "La représentation de la fémininité dans les chansons de geste." In *Charlemagne in the North,* ed. Philip E. Bennett, Anne Elizabeth Cobby, and Graham A. Runnalls, 223–40. Edinburgh: Société Rencesvals, 1993.

Keller, Hans-Erich. "La belle Sarrasine dans *Fierabras* et ses derives." In *Charlemagne in the North,* ed. Philip E. Bennett, Anne Elizabeth Cobby, and Graham A. Runnalls, 299–307. Edinburgh: Société Rencesvals, 1993.

Kennedy, Valerie. *Edward Said: A Critical Introduction.* Cambridge: Polity, 2000.

Khoury, Adel-Théodore. *Polémique Byzantine contre l'Islam (VIIIe–XIIIe s).* 2nd ed. Leiden: Brill, 1972.

King, David A. "Islamische Weltkarten mit Mekka als Mittelpunkt." In *Der Weg der Wahrheit: Aufsätze zur Einheit der Wissenschaftgeschichte. Festgabe zum 60. Geburtstag von Walter G. Saltzer,* ed. Peter Eisenhardt, Frank Linhard, and Kaisar Petanides, 93–107. Hildesheim: Olms, 1999.

——. "Two Iranian World Maps for Finding the Direction and Distance to Mecca." *Imago Mundi* 49 (1997): 1–20.

──. "Weltkarten zur Ermittlung der Richtung nach Mekka." In *Focus Behaim-Globus,* 2 vols., ed. Gerhard Bott, 1: 167–71, 689–91. Nuremberg: Germanisches National-Museum, 1992.

──. *World Maps for Finding the Direction to Mecca: Innovation and Tradition in Islamic Science.* Leiden: E. J. Brill; London: al-Furqan Islamic Heritage Foundation, 1999.

King, David A., and Richard Lorch. "Qibla Charts, Qibla Maps, and Related Instruments." In *The History of Cartography,* vol. 2, book 1, *Cartography in the Traditional Islamic and South Asian Societies,* ed. J. B. Harley and David Woodward, 189–205. Chicago: University of Chicago Press, 1992.

Kinoshita, Sharon. "Almería Silk and the French Feudal Imaginary: Toward a 'Material' History of the Medieval Mediterranean." In *Medieval Fabrications: Dress, Textiles, Clothwork, and Other Cultural Imaginings,* ed. E. Jane Burns, 165–76. New York: Palgrave Macmillan, 2004.

──. *Medieval Boundaries: Rethinking Difference in Old French Literature.* Philadelphia: University of Pennsylvania Press, 2006.

──. "'Pagans Are Wrong and Christians Are Right': Alterity, Gender, and Nation in the *Chanson de Roland.*" *Journal of Medieval and Early Modern Studies* 31 (2001): 79–111.

──. "The Politics of Courtly Love: *La Prise d'Orange* and the Conversion of the Saracen Queen." *Romanic Review* 86 (1995): 265–87.

Kirkham, Victoria, and Maria-Rosa Menocal. "Reflections on the 'Arabic' World: Boccaccio's Ninth Stories." *Stanford Italian Review* 7 (1987): 95–110.

Klawans, Jonathan. *Impurity and Sin in Ancient Judaism.* Oxford: Oxford University Press, 2000.

──. "Ritual Purity, Moral Purity, and Sacrifice in Jacob Milgrom's *Leviticus.*" *Religious Studies Review* 29 (2003): 19–28.

Kritzeck, Peter. *Peter the Venerable and Islam.* Princeton: Princeton University Press, 1964.

Krueger, Roberta. *Woman Readers and the Ideology of Gender in Old French Verse Romance.* Cambridge: Cambridge University Press, 1993.

Kruger, Steven F. "The Bodies of Jews in the Late Middle Ages." In *The Idea of Medieval Literature: Essays on Chaucer and Medieval Culture in Honor of Donald R. Howard,* ed. James M. Dean and Christian K. Zacher, 301–23. Newark: University of Delaware Press, 1992.

──. "Medieval Christian (Dis)identifications: Muslims and Jews in Guibert of Nogent." *New Literary History* 28 (1997): 185–203.

Kuhn, Thomas S. *The Structure of Scientific Revolutions.* 1962. 3rd rev. ed. Chicago: University of Chicago Press, 1996.

Kusch, Martin. *Foucault's Strata and Fields: An Investigation into Archeological and Genealogical Science Studies.* Synthese Library Studies in Epistemology, Logic, Methodology, and Philosophy of Science 218. Dordrecht: Kluwer, 1991.

Lampert, Lisa. *Gender and Jewish Difference from Paul to Shakespeare.* Philadelphia: University of Pennsylvania Press, 2004.

──. "Race, Periodicity, and the (Neo-) Middle Ages." *Modern Language Quarterly* 65 (2004): 391–421.

Langmuir, Gavin. *History, Religion, and Antisemitism.* Berkeley: University of California Press, 1990.

——. *Toward a Definition of Antisemitism.* Berkeley: University of California Press, 1990.

Larner, John. "Plucking Hairs from the Great Cham's Beard: Marco Polo, Jan de Langhe, and Sir John Mandeville." In *Marco Polo and the Encounter of East and West,* ed. Suzanne Conklin Akbari and Amilcare A. Iannucci, 135–55. Toronto: University of Toronto Press, 2008.

Laureys, Marc, and Daniel Verhelst, "Pseudo-Methodius, *Revelationes:* Textgeschichte und kritische Edition. Ein Leuven-Groninger Forschungsprojekt." In *Use and Abuse of Eschatology in the Middle Ages,* ed. Werner Verbeke, Daniel Verhelst, and Andries Welkenhuysen, 112–36. Leuven: University Press, 1988.

Lawton, David. "Sacrilege and Theatricality: The Croxton *Play of the Sacrament.*" *Journal of Medieval and Early Modern Studies* 33 (2003): 281–309.

——. "Titus Goes Hunting and Hawking: The Poetics of Recreation and Revenge in *The Siege of Jerusalem.*" In *Individuality and Achievement in Middle English Poetry,* ed. O. S. Pickering, 105–17. Woodbridge: D. S. Brewer, 1997.

Leclercq, Jean. "L'Encyclique de Saint Bernard en faveur de la croisade." *Revue benedictine* 81 (1971): 282–308.

Lecoq, Danielle. "La Mappemonde du *Liber Floridus* ou La Vision du Monde de Lambert de Saint-Omer." *Imago Mundi* 39 (1987): 9–49.

Lefèvre, Yves. "Le *Liber Floridus* et la littérature encyclopédique au moyen âge." In *Liber Floridus Colloquium: Papers Read at the International Meeting held in the University Library, Ghent, on 3–5 September 1967,* ed. Albert Derolez, 1–9. Ghent: E. Story-Scientia, 1973.

Le Goff, Jacques. *The Birth of Purgatory.* 1981. Trans. Arthur Goldhammer. Chicago: University of Chicago Press, 1984.

Lemay, Richard Joseph. *Abu Ma'shar and Latin Aristotelianism in the Twelfth Century: The Recovery of Aristotle's Natural Philosophy through Arabic Astrology.* Beirut: American University of Beirut, 1962.

Lewis, Martin W., and Kären E. Wigen. *The Myth of Continents: A Critique of Metageography.* Berkeley: University of California Press, 1997.

Lida de Malkiel, Maria-Rosa. "Alejandro en Jerusalén." *Romance Philology* 10 (1956–57): 185–96.

Limor, Ora. "Christian Sacred Space and the Jew." In *From Witness to Witchcraft: Jews and Judaism in Medieval Christian Thought,* ed. Jeremy Cohen, 55–77. Wolfenbütteler Mittelalter-Studien 11. Wiesbaden: Harrassowitz, 1996.

Lipton, Sara. *Images of Intolerance: The Representation of Jews and Judaism in the "Bible moralisée."* Berkeley: University of California Press, 1999.

——. "The Temple is My Body: Gender, Carnality, and Synagoga in the *Bible Moralisée.*" In *Imagining the Self, Imagining the Other: Visual Representation and Jewish-Christian Dynamics in the Middle Ages and Early Modern Period,* ed. Eva Frojmovic, 129–64. Leiden: Brill, 2002.

Lynch, Kathryn L. "East Meets West in Chaucer's Squire's and Franklin's Tales." *Speculum* 70 (1995): 530–51.

Malik, Kenan. *The Meaning of Race: Race, History, and Culture in Western Society.* Basingstroke: Macmillan, 1996.

Mallette, Karla. "Dante e l'Islam: Sul canto III del *Purgatorio.*" *Rivista di storia e letteratura religiosa* 41 (2005): 39–62.

———. *The Kingdom of Sicily, 1100–1250: A Literary History.* Philadelphia: University of Pennsylvania Press, 2005.

———. "Reading Backward: The *Thousand and One Nights* and Philological Practice." In *A Sea of Languages: Literature and Culture in the Medieval Mediterranean,* ed. Suzanne Conklin Akbari and Karla Mallette. Toronto: University of Toronto Press, forthcoming.

Manzalaoui, Mahmoud. "English Analogues to the *Liber Scalae.*" *Medium Aevum* 34 (1965): 21–35.

Marchello-Nizia, Christiane. "Entre l'Histoire et la poétique, le Songe politique." *Moyen Age flamboyant, XIVe–XVe siècles,* special issue of *Revue des Sciences humaines* 183 (1981): 39–53.

———. "L'historien et son prologue: forme littéraire et stratégies discursives." In *La Chronique et l'Histoire au Moyen Age,* ed. Daniel Poirion, 13–25. Paris: Presses de l'Université de Paris—Sorbonne, 1986.

Marcus, Ivan G. "Images of the Jews in the *Exempla* of Caesarius of Heisterbach." In *From Witness to Witchcraft: Jews and Judaism in Medieval Christian Thought,* ed. Jeremy Cohen, 247–56. Wolfenbütteler Mittelalter-Studien 11. Wiesbaden: Harrassowitz, 1996.

Matar, Nabil. *Turks, Moors, and Englishmen in the Age of Discovery.* New York: Columbia University Press, 1999.

Mayo, Penelope C. "The Crusaders Under the Palm: Allegorical Plants and Cosmic Kingship in the *Liber Floridus.*" *Dumbarton Oaks Papers* 27 (1973): 29–67.

McCash, June Hall, ed. *The Cultural Patronage of Medieval Women.* Athens: University of Georgia Press, 1996.

McCracken, Peggy. *The Romance of Adultery: Queenship and Sexual Transgression in Old French Literature.* Philadelphia: University of Pennsylvania Press, 1998.

McDonald, Nicola F. "Eating People and the Alimentary Logic of *Richard Coeur de Lion.*" In *Pulp Fictions of Medieval England,* ed. Nicola F. McDonald, 124–50. Manchester: Manchester University Press, 2004.

McGinn, Bernard. *Visions of the End: Apocalyptic Traditions in the Middle Ages.* New York: Columbia University Press, 1979.

Mellinkoff, Ruth. *Outcasts: Signs of Otherness in Northern European Art of the Late Middle Ages.* 2 vols. Berkeley: University of California Press, 1993.

Menocal, María Rosa. "An Andalusianist's Last Sigh." *La corónica* 24.2 (1996): 179–89.

———. *The Arabic Role in Medieval Literary History: A Forgotten Heritage.* 1987. 2nd ed. Philadelphia: University of Pennsylvania Press, 1990.

Meserve, Margaret. *Empires of Islam in Renaissance Historical Thought.* Cambridge: Harvard University Press, 2008.

Metlitzki, Dorothee. *The Matter of Araby in Medieval England.* New Haven: Yale University Press, 1979.

Meyvaert, Paul. "'Rainaldus est malus scriptor Francigenus': Voicing National Antipathy in the Middle Ages." *Speculum* 66 (1991): 743–63.

Millar, Bonnie. *The "Siege of Jerusalem" in Its Physical, Literary, and Historical Contexts.* Dublin: Four Courts, 2000.

Minnis, Alastair J. *Chaucer and Pagan Antiquity.* Cambridge: D. S. Brewer; Totowa, NJ: Rowman and Littlefield, 1982.

Morgan, Alison. *Dante and the Medieval Other World*. Cambridge: Cambridge University Press, 1990.

Muñoz, Fernando Gonzalez. *"Liber nycholay:* La leyenda de Mahoma y el cardenal Nicolás." *Al-Qantara* 25 (2004): 5–43.

Muratova, Xenia. "Western Chronicles of the First Crusade as Sources for the History of Art in the Holy Land." In *Crusader Art in the Twelfth Century,* ed. Jaroslav Folda, 47–69. B.A.R. International Series 152. Oxford: British School of Archeology in Jerusalem, 1982.

Neunheuser, Burkhard. *Baptism and Confirmation*. Trans. J. J. Hughes. Freiburg: Herder, 1964.

Nirenberg, David. *Communities of Violence: Persecution of Minorities in the Middle Ages*. Princeton: Princeton University Press, 1996.

Noltze, Holger. *Gahmurets Orientfahrt: Kommentar zum ersten Buch von Wolframs "Parzival" (4,27–58,26)*. Würzburg: Königshausen und Neumann, 1995.

Obrist, Barbara. "Wind Diagrams and Medieval Cosmology." *Speculum* 72 (1997): 33–84.

Olsen, Birger Munk. *L'étude des auteurs classiques latins aux XIe et XIIe siècles*. 3 vols. Paris: Editions du Centre national de la recherche scientifique, 1982–89.

Oltrogge, Doris. *Die Illustrationszyklen zur "Histoire ancienne jusqu'à César" (1250–1400)*. Frankfurt am Main: Peter Lang, 1989.

Palacios, Miguel Asín. *La escatología musulmana en la "Divina Comedia."* 1919. Madrid: Libros Hiperión, 1984. Trans. Harold Sutherland as *Islam and the Divine Comedy*. London: John Murray, 1926.

Papadopoulo, Alexandre, ed. *Le Mihrab dans l'architecture et la religion musulmanes: Actes du colloque international tenu à Paris en mai 1980*. Leiden: E. J. Brill, 1988.

Paris, Gaston. "La Légende de Saladin." *Journal des savants* (May-Aug. 1893): 284–99, 354–64, 428–38, 486–98.

Paster, Gail Kern. *Humoring the Body: Emotions and the Shakespearean Stage*. Chicago: University of Chicago Press, 2004.

——. "The Unbearable Coldness of Female Being: Woman's Imperfection in the Humoral Economy." *English Literary Renaissance* 28 (1998): 416–40.

Patterson, Lee. "Chaucer's Pardoner on the Couch: Psyche and Clio in Medieval Literary Studies." *Speculum* 76 (2001): 638–80.

Patton, Pamela A. "'Ex partu fontis exceptum': The Typology of Birth and Baptism in an Unusual Spanish Image of Jesus Baptized in a Font." *Gesta* 33 (1994): 79–92.

Pfister, Friedrich. "Alexander der Grosse in der Sage." In *Kleine Schriften zum Alexanderroman,* 1–35. Meisenheim am Glan: Anton Hain, 1976.

Platti, Emilio. "Bagdad-Beauvais-Bruges." In *Les relations culturelles entre chrétiens et musulmans au moyen âge: Quelle leçons en tirer de nos jours,* ed. Max Lejbowicz, 31–44. Rencontres médiévales européennes 5. Turnhout: Brepols, 2005.

Pleij, Herman. *Dreaming of Cockaigne: Medieval Fantasies of the Perfect Life*. 1997. Trans. Diane Webb. New York: Columbia University Press, 2001.

Pryor, John H. "The *Eracles* and William of Tyre: An Interim Report." In *The Horns of Hattin: Proceedings of the Second Conference of the Society for the Study of the Crusades and the Latin East (Jerusalem and Haifa, 2–6 July 1987),* ed. Benjamin Z. Kedar, 270–93. Jerusalem: Yad Izhak Ben-Zvi; Hampshire: Variorum, 1992.

Rajiva, Lila. *The Language of Empire: Abu Ghraib and the American Media.* New York: Monthly Review Press, 2005.

Ramey, Lynn Tarte. *Christian, Saracen, and Genre in Medieval French Literature.* New York: Routledge, 2001.

Reed, Annette Yoshiko. *Fallen Angels and the History of Judaism and Christianity: The Reception of Enochic Literature.* Cambridge: Cambridge University Press, 2005.

Reeves, Marjorie. *The Influence of Prophecy in the Later Middle Ages: A Study in Joachimism.* 1969. Rev. ed. Notre Dame: University of Notre Dame Press, 1993.

———. *Joachim of Fiore and the Prophetic Future: A Medieval Study in Historical Thinking.* 1976. Rev. ed. Stroud: Sutton, 1999.

Reiner, Emily. "The Ambiguous Greek in Old French and Middle English Literature," PhD diss., University of Toronto, 2008.

Resnick, Irven M. "On Roots of the Myth of Jewish Male Menses in Jacques de Vitry's *History of Jerusalem.*" *Bar-Ilan University International Rennert Guest Lecture Series* 3 (1998): 1–27.

Rey-Flaud, Henri. *Pour une dramaturgie du Moyen Age.* Paris: Presses universitaires de France, 1980.

———. "Le sentiment religieux dans *Le Jeu de saint Nicolas.*" In *Mélanges de langue et littérature françaises du moyen âge offerts à Pierre Jonin,* 571–77. Aix-en-Provence: Publications du CUERMA, Université de Provence; Paris: Champion, 1979.

Riant, Paul Edouard Didier. *Catalogue des Manuscrits de* L'Eracles. Archives de L'Orient Latin 1. Paris, 1881.

Rivière, J. "Jugement." In *Dictionnaire de Théologie Catholique.* Gen. ed. A. Vacant and E. Mangenot. Paris: Letouzey et Ané, 1899–1950. 15 vols. (in 23). Volume 8, part 2: col. 1721–1828.

Rotter, Ekkehart. *Abendland und Sarazenen: Das okzidentale Araberbild und seine Entstehung im Frühmittelalter.* Berlin: Walter de Gruyter, 1986.

Rubin, Miri. *Corpus Christi: The Eucharist in Late Medieval Culture.* Cambridge: Cambridge University Press, 1991.

———. *Gentile Tales: The Narrative Assault on Late Medieval Jews.* New Haven: Yale University Press, 1999.

———. "Small Groups: Identity and Solidarity in the Late Middle Ages." In *Enterprise and the Individual in Fifteenth-Century England,* ed. Jennifer Kermode, 132–50. Stroud: Alan Sutton, 1991.

Sahas, Daniel. "'Holosphyros'? A Byzantine Perception of 'The God of Muhammad.'" In *Christian-Muslim Encounters,* ed. Yvonne Yasbeck Haddad and Wadi Zaidan Haddad, 109–27. Gainesville: University Press of Florida, 1995.

———. *John of Damascus on Islam: The "Heresy of the Ishmaelites."* Leiden: Brill, 1972.

Said, Edward. *Culture and Imperialism.* 1993. New York: Vintage, 1994.

———. "Foucault and the Imagination of Power." In *Foucault: A Critical Reader,* ed. David Couzens Hoy, 149–55. Oxford: Basil Blackwell, 1986.

———. "Invention, Memory, Place." *Critical Inquiry* 26 (2000): 175–92.

———. *Orientalism.* 1978. 2nd ed. New York: Vintage, 1994.

Schibanoff, Susan. "Worlds Apart: Orientalism, Antifeminism, and Heresy in Chaucer's Man of Law's Tale." *Exemplaria* 8 (1996): 59–96

Schildgen, Brenda Deen. "Dante and the Indus." *Dante Studies* 111 (1993): 177–93.

———. *Dante and the Orient.* Urbana: University of Illinois Press, 2002.

——. "Wonders on the Border: Precious Stones in the *Comedy.*" *Dante Studies* 113 (1995): 131–50.

Schiller, Gertrude. *Iconography of Christian Art.* Trans. Janet Seligman. 2 vols. Greenwich, CT: New York Graphic Society, 1971–72.

Schlauch, Margaret. "The Allegory of Church and Synagogue." *Speculum* 14 (1939): 448–64.

Schreckenberg, Heinz. *Die Flavius-Josephus-Tradition in Antike und Mittelalter.* Leiden: Brill, 1972.

Seiferth, Wolfgang S. *Synagogue and Church in the Middle Ages: Two Symbols in Art and Literature.* Trans. Lee Chadeayne and Paul Gottwald. New York: Frederick Unger, 1970.

Seymour, M. C. *Sir John Mandeville.* Aldershot: Variorum, 1993.

Simonsohn, Schlomo. *The Apostolic See and the Jews, Documents: 492–1404.* Studies and Texts 94. Toronto: Pontifical Institute of Mediaeval Studies, 1988.

Smith, Jane, and Yvonne Haddad. *The Islamic Understanding of Death and Resurrection.* Albany: State University of New York Press, 1981.

Smith, Julian. "Precursors to Peregrinus: The Early History of Magnetism and the Mariner's Compass." *Journal of Medieval History* 18 (1992): 21–74.

Snedegar, Keith Voltaire. "John Ashenden and the Scientia Astrorum Mertonensis, with an Edition of Ashenden's *Prognosticationes,*" PhD diss., University of Oxford, 1988.

Southern, Richard W. *Western Views of Islam in the Middle Ages.* Cambridge: Harvard University Press, 1962.

Speed, Diane. "The Saracens of *King Horn.*" *Speculum* 65 (1990): 564–95.

Stacey, Robert C. "History, Religion, and Medieval Antisemitism: A Response to Gavin Langmuir." *Religious Studies Review* 20 (1994): 95–101.

——. "Jews and Christians in Twelfth-Century England: Some Dynamics of a Changing Relationship." In *Jews and Christians in Twelfth-Century Europe,* ed. Michael A. Signer and John Van Engen, 340–54. Notre Dame: University of Notre Dame Press, 2001.

Stecher, Gudrun Theresia. *Magnetismus im Mittelalter: Von den Fähigkeiten und der Verwendung des Magneten in Dichtung, Alltag, und Wissenschaft.* Göppingen: Kümmerle, 1995.

Stock, Markus. "Alexander in der Echokammer: Intertextualität in Ulrichs von Etzenbach Montagewerk." In *Dialoge: Sprachliche Kommunikation in und zwischen Texten im deutschen Mittelalter,* ed. Nikolaus Henkel, Martin H. Jones, and Nigel F. Palmer, 113–33. Tübingen: Max Niemeyer, 2003.

——. "Vielfache Erinnerung: Universaler Stoff und partikulare Bindung in Ulrichs von Etzenbach *Alexander.*" In *Alexanderdichtungen im Mittelalter: Kulturelle Selbstbestimmung im Kontext literarischer Beziehungen,* ed. Jan Cölln, Susanne Friede, and Hartmut Wulfram, 407–48. Göttingen: Wallstein, 2000.

Strickland, Debra Higgs. *Saracens, Demons, and Jews: Making Monsters in Medieval Art.* Princeton: Princeton University Press, 2003.

Strohm, Paul. *Theory and the Premodern Text.* Medieval Cultures 26. Minneapolis: University of Minnesota Press, 2000.

Stroumsa, Guy G. "From Anti-Judaism to Antisemitism in Early Christianity?" In *Contra Iudaeos: Ancient and Medieval Polemics between Christians and Jews,* ed. Ora Limor and Guy G. Stroumsa, 1–26. Tübingen: J. C. B. Mohr, 1996.

Subtelny, Maria. "'Holy, Holy, Holy': *The Book of Muhammad's Ladder* as Missionary Text among Christians of Muslim Spain." Medieval Academy of America, Toronto, April 12–14, 2007.

Sumption, Jonathan. *Pilgrimage: An Image of Mediaeval Religion.* London: Faber and Faber, 1975.

Takács, Sarolta. "Divine and Human Feet: Records of Pilgrims Honouring Isis." In *Pilgrimage in Graeco-Roman and Early Christian Antiquity: Seeing the Gods,* ed. Jas Elsner and Ian Rutherford, 353–69. Oxford: Oxford University Press, 2005.

Thomson, Samuel. *The Writings of Robert Grosseteste, Bishop of Lincoln, 1235–1253.* Cambridge: Cambridge University Press, 1940.

Thorndike, Lynn. "Four British Manuscripts of Scientific Works by Pierre d'Ailly." *Imago Mundi* 16 (1962): 157–60.

Tolan, John V. "Anti-Hagiography: Embrico of Mainz's *Vita Mahumeti.*" *Journal of Medieval History* 22 (1996): 25–41.

——, ed. *Medieval Christian Perceptions of Islam: A Book of Essays.* New York: Garland, 1996.

——. "Muslims as Pagan Idolaters in Chronicles of the First Crusade." In *Western Views of Islam in Medieval and Early Modern Europe: Perception of Other,* ed. David R. Blanks and Michael Frassetto, 97–117. New York: St. Martin's, 1999.

——. *Petrus Alfonsi and His Medieval Readers.* Gainesville: University Press of Florida, 1993.

——. *Saint Francis and the Sultan: The Curious History of a Christian-Muslim Encouneter.* Oxford: Oxford University Press, 2009.

——. "Saracen Philosophers Secretly Deride Islam." *Medieval Encounters* 8 (2002): 184–208.

——. *Saracens: Islam in the Medieval European Imagination.* New York: Columbia University Press, 2002.

——. "Un cadavre mutilé: Le déchirement polémique de Mahomet." *Le Moyen Âge* 104 (1998): 53–72.

Tomasch, Sylvia. "Judecca, Dante's Satan, and the Dis-placed Jew." In *Text and Territory,* ed. Sylvia Tomasch and Sealy Gilles, 247–67. Philadelphia: University of Pennsylvania Press, 1998.

Tooley, Marian J. "Bodin and the Medieval Theory of Climate." *Speculum* 28 (1953): 64–83.

Toorawa, Shawkat. "Muhammad, Muslims, and Islamophiles in Dante's *Commedia.*" *Muslim World* 82.1–2 (2004): 133–43.

Townsend, David, and Uppinder Mehan. "'Nation' and the Gaze at the Other in Eighth-Century Northumbria." *Comparative Literature* 53 (2001): 1–26.

Tuttle, V. G. "An Analysis of the Structure of the *Liber Floridus.*" PhD diss., Ohio State University, 1979.

Uebel, Michael. "The Pathogenesis of Medieval History." *Texas Studies in Literature and Language* 44 (2002): 47–65.

Väänänen, Veikko. "Le 'fabliau' de Cocagne." *Neuphilologische Mitteilungen* 48 (1947): 3–36.

Van Caenegem, Raoul C. "The Sources of Flemish History in the *Liber Floridus.*" In *Liber Floridus Colloquium: Papers Read at the International Meeting held in the University Library, Ghent on 3–5 September 1967,* ed. Albert Derolez, 71–85. Ghent: Story-Scientia, 1973.

Van Court, Elisa Narin. "The Hermeneutics of Supersession: The Revision of the Jews from the B to the C text of Piers Plowman." *Yearbook of Langland Studies* 10 (1996): 43–87.

———. *"The Siege of Jerusalem* and Augustinian Historians: Writing about Jews in Fourteenth-century England." *Chaucer Review* 29 (1995): 227–48. Reprinted in *Chaucer and the Jews,* ed. Sheila Delany, 165–84. New York: Routledge, 2002.

———. "Socially Marginal, Culturally Central: Representing Jews in Late Medieval English Literature." *Exemplaria* 12 (2000): 293–326.

van der Lugt, Maaike. "La peau noire dans la science médiévale." In *La pelle umana / The Human Skin,* ed. Agostino Paravicini Bagliani, 439–75. Micrologus 13. Florence: SISMEL edizioni del Galluzzo, 2005.

Verhelst, Daniel. "Les textes eschatologiques dans le *Liber Floridus.*" In *Use and Abuse of Eschatology in the Middle Ages,* ed. Werner Verbeke, Daniel Verhelst, and Andries Welkenhuysen, 299–305. Leuven: University Press, 1988.

Visker, Rudi. *Michel Foucault: Genealogy as Critique.* German ed., 1991. Trans. Chris Turner. London: Verso, 1995.

von den Brincken, Anna-Dorothee. *Fines Terrae: Die Enden der Erde und der vierte Kontinent auf mittelalterlichen Weltkarten.* MGH Schriften 36. Hannover: Hannsche, 1992.

———. "Oceani Angustior Latitudo: Die Ökumene auf der Klimatenkarte des Pierre d'Ailly." In *Studien zum 15. Jahrhundert: Festschrift Erich Meuther,* 2 vols., ed. Johannes Helmrath and Heribert Müller, 2: 565–81. München: R. Oldenbourg, 1994.

Walther, Hans. "Scherz und Ernst in der Völker—und Stämme-Charakteristik mittellateinischer Verse." *Archiv für Kulturgeschichte* 41 (1959): 263–301.

Watson, Nicholas, and Jocelyn Wogan-Browne. "The French of England: Ancrene Wisse, the *Compileison* and the Idea of Anglo-Norman." *Journal of Romance Studies* 4 (2004): 31–58.

Westrem, Scott D. "Against Gog and Magog." In *Text and Territory: Geographical Imagination in the European Middle Ages,* ed. Sylvia Tomasch and Sealy Gilles, 54–75. Philadelphia: University of Pennsylvania Press, 1998.

Weynand, Johanna. *Der "Roman de toute chevalerie" des Thomas von Kent in seinem Verhältnis zu seinen Quellen.* Bonn: Carl Georgi, 1911.

Williams, John. "Isidore, Orosius and the Beatus Map." *Imago Mundi* 49 (1997): 7–32.

Wogan-Browne, Jocelyn. "'Our Steward, St Jerome': Theology and the Anglo-Norman Household." In *Household, Women and Christianities,* ed. Anneke B. Mulder-Bakker and Jocelyn Wogan-Browne, 133–66. Turnhout: Brepols, 2005.

Woodward, David. "Medieval *Mappaemundi.*" In *The History of Cartography,* vol. 1, *Cartography in Prehistoric, Ancient, and Medieval Europe and the Mediterranean,* ed. J. B. Harley and David Woodward, 286–370. Chicago: University of Chicago Press, 1987.

Yeager, Suzanne. *Jerusalem in Medieval Narrative.* Cambridge: Cambridge University Press, 2008.

———. "Remembering the Passion: Spiritual and Practical Aspects of Medieval Pilgrimage." In *Medieval Travel Writing, 1096–1492,* ed. Joan Curbet. Frankfurt: Peter Lang, forthcoming.

Zacher, Christian K. *Curiosity and Pilgrimage: The Literature of Discovery in Fourteenth-Century England.* Baltimore: Johns Hopkins University Press, 1976.

Zafran, Eric. "The Iconography of Antisemitism: A Study of the Representation of the Jews in the Visual Arts of Europe, 1400–1600." Phd diss., New York University, Institute of Fine Arts, 1973.

Zink, Michel. "Apollin." In *La Chanson de geste et le mythe carolingien: Mélanges René Louis,* 2 vols., 1: 503–9. Saint-Père-sous-Vézelay: Musée Archéologique Régional; Comité de publication des Mélanges René Louis, 1982.

← Index